Obenaus / Weidacher

•

This is the Manager Speaking

This is the Manager Speaking

Erfolgreich kommunizieren im Alltags- und Geschäftsleben

3., aktualisierte Auflage

Wolfgang Obenaus
Josef Weidacher

Linde
international

Bibliografische Information der Deutschen Bibliothek

Die Deutsche Bibliothek verzeichnet diese Publikation in der Deutschen Nationalbibliografie; detaillierte bibliografische Daten sind im Internet über http://dnb.ddb.de abrufbar.

ISBN 978-3-7143-0143-4

1210 Wien, Scheydgasse 24, Tel.: 0043 / 1 / 24 630

www.lindeverlag.at

Druck: Hans Jentzsch & Co. GmbH.

1210 Wien, Scheydgasse 31

VORWORT

Das vorliegende Buch, das sich hauptsächlich an den internationalen Manager und alle, die es noch werden wollen, wendet, ist das dritte Werk im Rahmen unserer Publikationsreihe „Wirtschaftsenglisch“. Während sich die beiden ersten mit den grammatikalischen Aspekten von Wirtschaftstexten bzw. mit der Wirtschaftsterminologie und -phraseologie befassen, ist **This is the Manager Speaking** der mündlichen Kommunikation in Alltags- und Wirtschaftssituationen gewidmet. Es erübrigt sich wohl, lange zu erklären, warum mündliche Kommunikation im Zeitalter der zunehmenden Verflechtung der Nationalwirtschaften und der zunehmenden Dominanz des Englischen als Lingua franca des internationalen Geschäftslebens für den Manager von zentraler Bedeutung ist. Auf eine Kurzformel gebracht: „Ohne Englisch – und besonders ohne mündliches Englisch – geht im Management nichts mehr.“

Auch der Aufbau des Buches erfordert keine langatmigen Erklärungen. Die wesentlichen kommunikativen Situationen werden in Form von Einzelsätzen und Kurzdialogen abgedeckt. Zu jedem der Sätze bzw. Dialoge werden ausreichend Übersetzungshilfen geboten, so dass das Buch auch für den Interessenten mit relativ bescheidenen Englischkenntnissen nutzbar sein sollte. Dabei ist zu beachten, dass die deutschen Entsprechungen nur für den jeweiligen sprachlichen oder situativen Zusammenhang gelten und nicht notwendigerweise auf andere Kontexte übertragbar sind. Um die Benutzerfreundlichkeit des Buches zu erhöhen, wurde die Anzahl der Abkürzungen auf ein Minimum beschränkt. Eine Liste findet sich im Anschluss an dieses Vorwort.

Wien, im September 2008 Wolfgang Obenaus Sepp Weidacher

ABKÜRZUNGEN

sbdy. – somebody
sthg – something
U.S. – United States / amerikanisch

jmdm. – jemandem
jmdn. – jemanden

INHALTSVERZEICHNIS

Contents

MEETING PEOPLE

Vorstellung

INTRODUCING YOURSELF

Sich selbst vorstellen

* A: **May I introduce myself: My name is Fred Artner and I'm Head of Marketing here.**
(introduce – vorstellen / Head of Marketing – Leiter der Marketingabteilung; Marketingleiter)
B: **How do you do. My name is Mary Bell.**
(Im britischen Englisch wird mit 'How do you do' nicht nach dem Befinden der angesprochenen Person gefragt. Es ist eine mehr oder minder inhaltslose Grußformel, die im Deutschen je nach Kontext etwa mit „Sehr erfreut" oder „Guten Tag" wiedergegeben werden kann.)

* **Hello, let me introduce myself. I'm Norbert Teufelberger from Deuter AG, Augsburg. I'm in charge of Controlling.**
(be in charge of – Leiter sein von)

* **Good morning. Allow me to introduce myself. Hannes Dopsch from Bonn. Here's my business card.**
(business card – Visitenkarte)

* **I'd like to introduce myself: Hans-Jörg Ertl, Raiffeisen-Zentralbank, Vienna.**

* A: **How do you do. I'm Thomas Auer.**
B: **How do you do. My name is Brown, Neil Brown.**

* A: **How do you do. My name is Philipp Aigner, Advertising Manager for General Motors Austria.**
(advertising – Werbung)

B: Pleased to meet you, Mr. Aigner. I'm Gary Baker, Assistant Marketing Manager of Electrovans PLC, London.
(Freut mich, Sie kennenzulernen, … . / Assistant Marketing Manager – stellvertretender Marketingleiter)
A: I'm sorry. I didn't catch your name.
(catch – verstehen)
B: Baker, Gary Baker.

* **A: Excuse me. I don't think we've met before. My name is Tom Abbey. I work with Mr. Smith.**
(meet – sich begegnen; sich kennenlernen)
B: How do you do, Mr. Abbey. I'm Karl Bender from Austrian Industries.
A: How do you do, Mr. Bender. How long are you going to be here?

* **A: Good morning. My name's Adams.**
B: Good morning, Mr. Adams, I'm Fritz Baumann. May I introduce our Sales Manager for Eastern Europe, Mr. Wagner?
(Sales Manager – Verkaufsleiter)

* **A: Hello, my name's Adrian.**
B: Mine's Barbara. Nice to meet you.
A: You're German, aren't you?
(aren't you? – nicht wahr?)
B: Yes, that's right. I come from Frankfurt.

* **Hi! I'm Paul. I'm a friend of John's.**

* **A: Excuse me. Are you Mr. Brown, by any chance?**
(by any chance – zufällig)
B: Yes, that's me.
A: It's nice to meet you. Anger's my name.
B: Nice to meet you too.

* **You're not Miss Kelly by any chance, are you?**
(are you? – oder?)

* **A: Mr. Brand, isn't it?**
(isn't it? – nicht wahr?)
B: Yes, that's right. Walter Brand.
A: How do you do. I'm Tony Adams.
B: How do you do, Mr. Adams. I hope I'm not putting you to any trouble.
(… . Ich hoffe, dass ich Ihnen keine Umstände mache.)
A: Not at all.
(Nein, überhaupt nicht.)

* **A: Miss Brannigan?**
B: Yes, that's right, I'm Donna Brannigan.
A: Hello, I'm Robert Achatz. Welcome to Voest Alpine AG. It's great to have you with us.
B: Pleased to meet you Mr. Achatz.
A: How long are you planning to stay?
(stay – bleiben)

* **A: Hello! You must be Charles Bolder.**
B: Yes, that's right.
A: I'm Werner Aumann. Pleased to meet you.
B: Pleased to meet you too.

* **A: Hello. You're the new export clerk, aren't you? My name is Sarah Adlington. I do most of the secretarial work in the office.**
(export clerk – Exportsachbearbeiter / aren't you? – nicht wahr? / office – Büro)
B: It's very nice to meet you, Miss Adlington. I'm Peter Baumer.
A: Please call me Sarah.
(Dies entspricht etwa dem Anbieten des Du-Wortes. Beachten Sie, dass in England diese Art des Du-Wortes oft schon bei der ersten Begegnung angeboten wird.)
B: And I'm Peter.

INTRODUCING OTHER PEOPLE
Jemand anderen vorstellen

* **A: Let me introduce you to my wife. Brigitte, this is Chris Carter.**
(introduce – vorstellen)
B: Hello, Chris. Nice to meet you.
C: How do you do, Mrs. Auer.
B: Oh, do call me Brigitte.
C: Oh, right.

* **A: I'd like to introduce you to Mrs. Chlepac. She's from Austria.**
B: Nice to meet you, Mrs. Chlepac. My name's Boyd, James Boyd.
C: Very nice to meet you too.

* **A: Dr. Beer, may I introduce you to Dr. Crimson? Dr. Crimson, Dr. Beer.**
B: How do you do.
C: How do you do.
B: I'm pleased to meet you at long last. I've heard so much about you from Dr. Aliber.
(at long last – endlich)

* **A: Mr. Bond, allow me to introduce one of our consultants, Jane Colby from New York.**
(consultant – Konsulent)
B: Pleased to meet you, Miss Colby.
C: The pleasure's all mine. And please call me Jane.
(Ganz meinerseits. … .)

* **A: Mr. Bacher, I'd like you to meet Linda Clemence. She's our new Advertising Manager.**
(… , ich möchte Sie gerne mit … bekannt machen. … .)
B: How do you do.
C: How do you do. I'm very pleased to meet you, Mr. Bacher.

* A: **Barbara, I want you to meet a business colleague of mine, Carol Simpson. Carol, this is Barbara Baxter. I don't think you've met.**
(business colleague – Kollegin aus der Firma)
B: **Hello, Carol.**
C: **Hello.**

* A: **Bruno, I'd like you to meet Miss Taylor. She has just arrived from London and is going to work as a management trainee.**
(just – gerade / arrive – ankommen / trainee – Praktikantin, Trainee)
B: **How do you do. I'm delighted to meet you, Miss Taylor. I hope you had a good flight.**
(be delighted – sich sehr freuen)

* A: **Bob, have you met Peter Cromwell, my new assistant, yet?**
(yet – schon)
B: **No, I don't think I have. How do you do, Mr. Cromwell.**
C: **How do you do.**

* A: **I don't think you've met Dr. Randolph yet, have you?**
(have you? – oder?)
B: **No, I haven't yet had the pleasure.**
(Nein, ich hatte noch nicht das Vergnügen.)

* A: **Have you two already met?**
B: **Yes, I think we have, haven't we?**
(haven't we? – oder?)

* A: **By the way, do you know Mr. Redford?**
(Übrigens, … ?)
B: **No, I don't think so. Pleased to meet you.**

* **No, I don't actually. But I've heard a lot about you. How do you do, Mr. Redford. I'm delighted to meet you.**
(a lot – viel)

* A: **I don't think you know Mr. Crane, our Production Manager, do you?**
(do you? – oder?)
B: **No, we haven't met. How do you do, Mr. Crane.**
C: **How do you do. I'm very pleased to meet you, Mr. Benson.**

* A: **Do you two know each other?**
B: **I don't believe we do. Nice to meet you.**
(believe – glauben)

* A: **Mrs. Böhm, this is Brian Clough. He's visiting us from England.**
B: **How do you do, Mr. Clough.**
C: **How do you do.**
B: **Which part of England are you from?**

* A: **Brian, this is Wolfgang Cech from Austria. He's over here on business. Wolfgang, Brian Baxter, our Export Manager.**
(on business – geschäftlich)
B: **Nice to have you with us.**
C: **How do you do, Mr. Baxter.**
B: **Have you been to London before, Mr. Cech?**
C: **No, this is my first time. I went to Brighton a year ago, but I didn't come here.**

* **George, this is Mary. Mary, this is George. He's a friend of mine.**

GREETING PEOPLE

Begrüßung

* **A: Good morning, Mr. Brown!**
  B: Morning, Ann.

* **A: Hi, Betty.**
  B: Hello, Adrian.

* **Hello you two.**

* **Hi there, Trevor!**

* **A: Morning, Barbara. How did you enjoy your holiday?**
  (… . Wie war's im Urlaub?)
  B: Oh, hello, Andy. It was wonderful. Just what I needed.
  (just – genau)

* **A: Hi, Bill.**
  B: Hello, Alex. You're back?
  A: Yes, I got back this afternoon.
  B: Did you have a good crossing?
  (crossing – Überfahrt)
  A: The sea was a bit choppy, but otherwise it was fine.
  (sea – Meer / choppy – unruhig / otherwise – sonst)

* **Hello, Tony. How was your trip to Brazil?**

* **Hello, Jane. I'm afraid I'm rather late. Have you been waiting long?**
  (… . Tut mir leid, ich bin ziemlich spät dran. Wartest du schon lange?)

* **A: Morning, Bill. Nice to see you!**
  B: Hello Ann. You're looking very well.

* A: **Hello, Brian. How nice to see you again!**
B: **Hello Arnold. Haven't seen you for ages. Where've you been?**
(for ages – ewig; seit einer Ewigkeit)
A: **I've been back in Austria as a matter of fact.**

* A: **Good evening, Mrs. Bracknell.**
B: **Good evening. It's good to see you again.**
A: **It's good to see you too.**

* A: **Hello, Bill.**
B: **Hello. This is a pleasant surprise.**
(pleasant surprise – freudige Überraschung)
A: **It's very nice to see you again, Bill. It's been a long time.**
(… . Es ist lange her, seit wir uns das letzte Mal gesehen haben.)

* A: **Good morning, Mr. Beeston. Come along in. Do sit down.**
B: **Thank you.**
A: **Well, now. I'm pleased to see you again. You don't smoke, do you?**
(do you? – oder?)
B: **No, I don't.**

* A: **Hello, Mr. Bauer, I don't know if you remember me. David Allen, we met at …**
(remember sbdy. – sich an jemanden erinnern)
B: **Of course! It's nice to meet you again, Mr. Allen.**

* **I'm very pleased to meet you again, Mr. Allen.**

* A: **Hello, Miss Brenner. I'm delighted to meet you again. Did you have a good journey?**
(be delighted – sich sehr freuen / journey – Reise)
B: **Yes, it was fine, thanks.**
A: **So, what are you doing in London?**
B: **Well, I'm here on business for a few days. I've got quite a few meetings here.**
(on business – geschäftlich / quite a few – ziemlich viele / meeting – Sitzung)
A: **And when are you going back to Vienna?**
B: **Well, I'm staying till the end of the week. My flight's on Friday morning.**

——— ❖ ———

* A: **Good evening, Mr. Bloch. How are you?**
(… . Wie geht es Ihnen?)
B: **Very well, thank you. And how are you?**
A: **I'm very well, too, thank you.**

* A: **Nice to see you again, Mrs. Bear. How are you?**
B: **Very well, thank you, Mr. Auer. I hope you are well too.**

* A: **Hello, Mr. Berger. How are you?**
B: **I'm fine, thank you. And you?**
(I'm fine – mir geht es gut)
A: **All right, thank you.**

* A: **Good afternoon, Miss Brophy.**
B: **Good afternoon. How are you today, Mr. Alber?**
A: **Not too well, I'm afraid. Must've caught a bit of a cold I think.**
(Leider nicht allzu gut. Ich muss wohl eine leichte Verkühlung erwischt haben.)
B: **Oh, I'm sorry to hear that.**

* **A: Bill! Good to see you again! How are you?**
B: I'm fine, thanks. How are you?
A: I'm okay, thanks. Nice of you to come.

* **A: Hi, Ben, how are things?**
(… , wie läuft's denn so?)
B: Great, thanks. I've got a really interesting new job. What about you?
(great – super)
A: I'm all right, thanks.

* **A: Hello, Betty! How are you doing?**
B: Fine, thanks. And you?
A: Oh, not so bad.

* **A: Good morning, Berta. How're you getting on?**
(… . Wie geht's dir denn so?)
B: Fine, thanks.
A: And how's the family?
B: Oh, the usual problems. But they're all well, thanks.
(well – gesund)

* **A: Morning. How are things with you, Brigitte?**
B: Oh, not too bad, thanks.
A: How are you enjoying your stay in London?
(Wie gefällt es dir in London?)
B: Very much. I love it here.

* **A: Barbara! It's great to see you again. So – how's life?**
(great – schön / how's life – wie geht's denn so)
B: Oh, pretty good, thanks.
(pretty – ganz)

* **A: Hi, Brian! How's it going?**
(… . Wie läuft's denn so?)
B: Oh, mustn't grumble.
(Kann mich nicht beklagen.)

* A: **How's life treating you?**
(Wie geht's dir denn so?)
B: **Can't complain, thanks.**
(Kann mich nicht beklagen, … .)

* A: **Hello, Bettina, I haven't seen you for a while. How's everything going?**
(… . Wie läuft's denn so bei dir?)
B: **Quite well, thanks. And yourself? I heard you got a new job. How are you enjoying it?**
(quite – ganz)
A: **Okay, so far. Everything's going very smoothly and I'm enjoying the challenge.**
(go very smoothly – wie geschmiert laufen / challenge – Herausforderung)

SAYING GOODBYE

Verabschiedung

* **A: Goodbye, Dr. Benson.**
  (Auf Wiedersehen, … !)
  B: Goodbye.

* **A: I'll see you then, Bill. Bye!**
  (Bis dann, Bill. Grüß dich!)
  B: See you, Ann.
  (Servus, Ann!)

* **A: See you on Friday!**
  (Bis Freitag!)
  B: OK. Bye for now!
  (… . Bis dann also. Servus!)

* **A: See you later, bye!**
  (Bis später. | Bis nachher. … !)
  B: Take care. Bye now!
  (take care – mach's gut)

* **A: I'll be seeing you!**
  (Bis dann!)
  B: Look after yourself. Bye-bye!
  (Pass gut auf dich auf! … !)

———— ❖ ————

* **A: Goodbye. It's been nice meeting you.**
  (… . Es war nett, Sie kennenzulernen.)
  B: Goodbye, and thank you very much for coming!

* **Goodbye. I have enjoyed talking to you.**
  (… . War nett, mit Ihnen zu plaudern.)

* **A: Bye, Berta, and thanks for the lift.**
(… , und danke fürs Mitnehmen.)
B: Goodbye, Mr. Abraham. Best of luck!
(… . Viel Glück!)

* **A: Goodbye, Barbara. Have a good holiday and I'll see you when you get back.**
B: Yes, bye, and I hope your meeting goes well this afternoon.
(meeting – Sitzung)

* **A: Cheerio, Bob. Have a good trip!**
(Servus, Bob! Gute Reise!)
B: Thanks, and you!
(Danke, dir auch!)

* **A: Goodbye, Dr. Brown, I trust you have a pleasant journey.**
(trust – hoffen / pleasant journey – angenehme Reise)
B: Thank you, and have a good weekend!

* **A: Goodbye and all the best. It's been a pleasure meeting you.**
(… . Es war mir ein Vergnügen, Ihre Bekanntschaft zu machen.)
B: Yes, I've thoroughly enjoyed my stay. I hope to see you again soon. Goodbye.
(Ganz meinerseits, mir hat es hier wirklich sehr gut gefallen. … .)

* **A: Good night, Elisabeth. Have a good evening. I'll see you tomorrow, before you go back to England, won't I?**
(won't I – ohnehin noch)
B: Yes, indeed. See you tomorrow!
(indeed – sicher)
A: Good night.

* A: **I'll see you again tonight, Brian.**
(tonight – heute abend)
B: **Yes, I'm looking forward to the party. Bye.**
(look forward to – sich freuen auf)
A: **Bye!**

* A: **Well, thanks very much, Bill. Very pleased to have met you.**
(be pleased – sich freuen)
B: **It's been most enjoyable. I'll look forward to seeing you next week. Goodbye for now.**
(War wirklich sehr nett. … .)
A: **Bye, Bill.**

* A: **You're going back to Austria tomorrow, aren't you?**
(aren't you? – nicht wahr?)
B: **That's right. We won't be seeing each other for a while.**
(won't – will not)
A: **Well, take care of yourself and do keep in touch.**
(Pass gut auf dich auf und bleib auf alle Fälle in Kontakt!)
B: **Right, bye.**

* A: **I've come to say goodbye.**
B: **When are you off?**
(be off – abreisen)
A: **Tomorrow morning, first thing.**
(Gleich morgen in der Früh.)
B: **Goodbye then, and all the very best.**

* A: **I'd like to say goodbye to you all.**
B: **Oh, are you off now? Have a good journey!**
A: **Thanks. Goodbye and remember to look me up if ever you're in Vienna.**
(remember – nicht vergessen / look sbdy. up – jemanden aufsuchen; bei jemandem vorbeischauen)

* **A: I think that's everything, Mr. Bene. We've covered all the points we need to discuss for the moment.**
(cover – sich befassen mit / need – müssen)
B: Fine, I'll say goodbye for now then, and thank you. It's been a useful meeting.

* **A: Well, I must go. Goodbye then, Betty.**
B: Bye then. Come again soon!

* **I think I'd better be going or I'll be late. Goodbye.**
(Ich glaube, ich sollte lieber gehen, sonst komme ich zu spät. … .)

* **Must dash – I'm meeting Paul at eight thirty.**
(dash – rennen, sausen / meet – treffen)

* **Sorry, I must be off now.**
(Tut mir leid, ich muss nun weg.)

* **I think I really ought to be going.**
(Ich glaube, ich sollte jetzt wirklich gehen.)

* **I really should be getting back to my hotel. It's getting very late and I've got an early morning flight.**

* **A: I hope you don't mind but I really have to go now.**
(Ich hoffe, dass es Ihnen nichts ausmacht, aber … .)
B: That's OK, see you again soon.

* **It's been very nice talking to you, but I'm afraid I can't stay any longer.**
(I'm afraid – leider)

——— ❖ ———

* **A: Goodbye then, and remember me to your parents.**
(… , und schöne Grüße an Ihre Eltern!)
B: Thank you, I certainly will. Goodbye. See you next year!
(certainly – sicher)

* **A: Give my best wishes to John Carter.**
(wishes – Grüße)
B: Thank you, I will.

* **Please give my kind regards to your wife.**
(kind regards – schöne Grüße)

* **Give my love to Doris. Hope to see her here next year.**
(Grüß Doris von mir! … .)

* **Say hello to Simon for me.**

REQUESTS AND REPLIES

Bitten/Aufforderungen und wie man darauf reagiert

* A: **Could you send a price-list, please?**
B: **I'll send one straight away.**
(straight away – gleich)

* A: **Could you possibly lend me your dictating machine for a couple of hours? I've got a report to dictate.**
(possibly – vielleicht / lend – leihen, borgen / dictating machine – Diktiergerät / a couple of – ein paar / report – Bericht)
B: **I'm sorry but I'll be needing it myself this afternoon. You can have it as soon as I've finished, though.**
(I'm sorry – tut mir leid / need – brauchen / have finished – fertig sein / though – aber)

* A: **Do you think you could come back later, Mr. Bretschneider?**
(come back – nochmals kommen)
B: **OK, no problem.**

* A: **I wonder if you could have a look at this letter and check it for grammatical errors and spelling mistakes, please.**
(Könnten Sie bitte … / check for – überprüfen auf … hin / error – Fehler / spelling mistake – Rechtschreibfehler)
B: **With pleasure.**
(Aber gern.)

* A: **You couldn't just help me for a minute, could you?**
(could you? – oder?)
B: **All right.**

* A: **I'd be very grateful if you could get me a spare key.**
(grateful – dankbar / get – besorgen / spare key – Ersatzschlüssel)
B: **Of course, no problem.**

* **A: Could you do me a favour and post this letter, please?**
  (do favour – Gefallen tun / post letter – Brief aufgeben)
  B: Yes, OK. I don't mind.
  (… . Mach' ich schon.)

* **A: I wonder if I could possibly ask you to let us use your meeting room to discuss the details of our negotiations in confidence.**
  (meeting room – Sitzungszimmer / negotiation – Verhandlung / in confidence – vertraulich)
  B: I'm terribly sorry, Mr. Andrews, but it's not convenient at the moment.
  (terrible – schrecklich, fürchterlich / …, aber das geht im Moment nicht gut.)

* **A: Excuse me, do you think I could have a look at your newspaper?**
  B: Yes, here you are.
  (Ja gern, hier bitte!)

* **Could I borrow your lighter a minute, please?**
  (borrow – ausborgen / lighter – Feuerzeug)

* **Could I have a light, please?**
  (light – Feuer)

* **Do you have a light, by any chance?**
  (Haben Sie zufällig Feuer?)

* **You haven't got a cigarette by any chance, have you?**
  (have you? – oder?)

* **A: Excuse me, can you give me a hand, please?**
  (give sbdy. a hand – jemandem helfen)
  B: Yes, of course.

* **A: Would you put me through to Daphne, please?**
  (put through – verbinden)
  B: I'm sorry that's not possible, she's on holiday today.

* A: **Mr. Brennan, would you kindly move your car? Our delivery van can't get past.**
(... , würden Sie bitte mit Ihrem Auto wegfahren? Unser Lieferwagen kommt nicht vorbei.)
B: **I'll do it right away.**
(right away – sofort)

* A: **Would you mind lending me your calculator for a minute?**
(Würde es Ihnen etwas ausmachen, mir kurz Ihren Rechner zu borgen?)
B: **Not at all, here you are.**
(Aber nein, hier bitte!)

* A: **Would you mind showing a group of representatives from Midwest Ltd. around tomorrow afternoon?**
(show around – herumführen / representatives – Firmenangehörige / Ltd. – private limited company | [brit.] etwa: Gesellschaft mit beschränkter Haftung)
B: **No, not at all. I'd be delighted to.**
(... . Sehr gerne.)

* A: **Mind if I join you?**
(Etwas dagegen, wenn ich mitkomme?)
B: **No, of course not.**

* A: **Would you be so kind as to send a telex to confirm that?**
(kind – freundlich / confirm – bestätigen)
B: **No problem at all.**
(Überhaupt kein Problem.)

* A: **I hope you don't mind me asking, but I wonder if it might be possible for you to get me a car for the weekend?**
(... , aber wäre es Ihnen vielleicht möglich, mir für das Wochenende ein Auto zu besorgen?)
B: **I'll see what I can do.**

* **A: Sorry, but would it be possible for you to shut the window? I'm in a draught here.**
(shut – schließen / draught – Luftzug)
B: I'm afraid I can't. It's stuck.
(Tut mir leid, das geht nicht. Es klemmt.)

* **A: I'd like you to inspect the machinery you delivered last Tuesday.**
(inspect sthg. – sich etwas anschauen / deliver – liefern)
B: I'll send someone round at once.
(at once – sofort)

* **A: Any chance of borrowing your car tonight, Ben? Mine's being serviced.**
(borrow – ausborgen / tonight – heute abend / … . Meines ist beim Service.)
B: I'm afraid not. Cath needs it tonight.
(Geht leider nicht. … .)

HOW TO SAY "BITTE" AND "DANKE" IN ENGLISH

* **Please sit down.**

* **I'd like a double room for two nights, please.**
  (double room – Doppelzimmer)

* **A: What would you like?**
  B: A gin and tonic, please.

* **Sign here, please.**
  (sign – unterschreiben)

* **A: Would you like tea or coffee, Barbara?**
  B: Oh, I'll have tea, please.

* **A: Could I speak to Mr. Wright, please?**
  B: Just a moment, please.

* **Could you please send me a quotation?**
  (quotation – Angebot)

* **Could you show me how to work the photocopier, please?**
  (work – bedienen)

* **Would you please come this way?**
  (Würden Sie mir bitte hier folgen?)

* **Can you help me, please?**

* **May I leave at 4 o'clock, please, Mr. Telford? I've got to be at the dentist's at a quarter past.**
  (leave – weggehen)

——— ❖ ———

- ✳ **Thank you for your attention.**
  (attention – Aufmerksamkeit)

- ✳ **A: Is your office all right?**
  B: Yes, it’s fine, thanks.

- ✳ **A: Have you had any lunch, Ben?**
  B: Yes, thanks.

- ✳ **A: Have a good weekend!**
  B: Thanks a lot. You too!

- ✳ **A: Merry Christmas!**
  B: Thanks very much. Same to you!

——— ❖ ———

- ✳ **A: Thank you for all your help.**
  B: That’s quite all right.
  (Bitte sehr! | Nichts zu danken! | Gern geschehen!)

- ✳ **A: Thank you very much for standing by me in this difficult situation.**
  (stand by – beistehen)
  B: Don’t mention it.
  (Das war doch selbstverständlich!)

- ✳ **A: Thanks very much for letting me use your office.**
  B: That’s okay.
  (Gern geschehen!)

- ✳ **A: Thanks a lot for the information.**
  B: You’re welcome.
  (Bitte!)

* **A: It was a good party, thanks for inviting me.**
  (invite – einladen)
  B: My pleasure.
  (Es war mir ein Vergnügen!)

* **A: Thanks for everything.**
  B: That's all right.

* **A: Thank you very much for showing me around.**
  (show sbdy. around – jemanden herumführen)
  B: It was a pleasure. Hope to see you again next year.

* **A: Thank you very much for finding out about the theatre.**
  B: That's okay. It was no trouble.
  (trouble – Problem)

* **A: I really can't thank you enough for all you've done.**
  B: Not at all, it was a pleasure.
  (not at all – nichts zu danken)

* **A: Well, many thanks for lunch, Bill. It really was very good.**
  B: Good, glad you enjoyed it.
  (Freut mich, dass es dir geschmeckt hat.)

* **A: Thank you very much for the lift.**
  (Vielen Dank fürs Mitnehmen.)
  B: Delighted I was able to help.
  (be delighted – erfreut sein; sehr froh sein)

* **A: Thank you very much indeed for the delicious meal.**
  (delicious meal – ausgezeichnetes Essen)
  B: Thank <u>you</u> for coming.

* **A: Could I have a light, please?**
(light – Feuer)
B: Yes, here you are.
(Hier, bitte!)
A: Thanks.
B: That's all right.

* **A: Where is the information desk, please?**
(information desk – Informationsschalter)
B: It's just round that corner over there.
(Er ist gleich um die Ecke dort drüben.)
A: Thank you very much.
B: It's a pleasure.

* **A: The cab will be here in about ten minutes.**
(cab – Taxi)
B: Oh, thank you so much, Ann.
A: Not at all.

* **A: There is a telegram for you, Mr. Baxter. Here you are.**
(… . Hier, bitte! | Da haben Sie es! | Hier ist es!)
B: Thank you very much indeed.
A: That's quite all right.

* **A: Here's my car. Let me give you a lift.**
B: Thank you. That's very kind of you.
(kind – freundlich)
A: Not at all.

* **A: Here's a copy of "Time". I thought you might like to have a look at it on the plane.**
(copy – Ausgabe, Nummer / plane – Flugzeug)
B: Thanks very much. That's very kind of you.
A: You're welcome.

✻ A: **Oh, I'll take your suitcase.**
(suitcase – Koffer)
B: **Many thanks. That is really nice of you.**
(nice – nett, freundlich)
A: **Not at all.**

——— ❖ ———

✻ A: **The success of my trip was in large part due to your efforts, and I am most grateful to you.**
(Der Erfolg meiner Reise war großteils auf Ihre Bemühungen zurückzuführen, und ich bin Ihnen sehr dankbar dafür.)
B: **It was a pleasure to help you.**

✻ **Oh, that's excellent. I'm really very grateful.**

✻ **Tony, I'm extremely grateful to you for all your help.**
(extremely grateful – wirklich dankbar)

——— ❖ ———

✻ A: **May I help you?**
B: **Yes, please.**

✻ A: **Would you like a cup of tea?**
B: **Yes, please. I'd love one.**
(Ja bitte, gerne!)

✻ A: **Would you like us to deliver the flowers to your home?**
(Wollen Sie, dass wir die Blumen zu Ihnen nach Hause schicken?)
B: **Oh yes, please. That would be lovely.**
(lovely – nett; sehr freundlich)

✻ A: **Do you want me to photocopy this for you?**
B: **Yes, that's very kind of you.**

* **A: Could you come to a party at my place next Wednesday?**
(at my place – bei mir zu Hause)
B: Yes, with pleasure.

* **A: Could I tempt you with another piece of cake?**
(tempt – verführen / piece – Stück)
B: Thank you, yes. I'd very much like to have another one. The cake's delicious.
(delicious – köstlich, ausgezeichnet)

* **A: Would you like to come and watch a game of cricket with me?**
(watch – anschauen)
B: Thank you, I'd like to very much.
(Danke, sehr gerne!)

* **A: Would you like to come to a concert with me tonight?**
B: I'd love to. Thanks very much.
(Sehr gerne, danke!)

* **A: Cigarette?**
B: No, thank you. I've given up, you know.
(give up – aufgeben, aufhören)

* **A: Brian, can I get you another coffee?**
(get – holen, bringen)
B: No, thank you very much. Not at the moment.

* **A: Would you like anything else?**
B: No, thanks. That'll be all.

* **A: Would you like some more soup?**
B: Thank you, no. I'd rather not.
(I'd rather not – eher nicht)

* **A: Would you like to sit down?**
B: No, I'm all right, thanks.
(Nein danke, es geht schon!)

* **A: Are you sure you won't have a scotch?**
(won't – will not)
B: Thanks very much, but I'm driving.
(drive – mit dem Auto fahren)

* **A: Will you have a cigar?**
(Möchten Sie eine Zigarre haben?)
B: That's very kind, but I won't, thank you.

* **A: Would you like to leave a message, or can I ask him to call you back?**
(leave message – Nachricht hinterlassen / call back – zurückrufen)
B: No, it's all right, I'll call back.
(Nein danke, ich werde nochmals anrufen.)

—— ❖ ——

* **A: These fast trains are very noi … .**
B: Pardon?
(Wie bitte?)

* **A: The paper says the price of petrol is going up.**
(paper – Zeitung / petrol – Benzin)
B: I beg your pardon?
(Wie bitte?)

—— ❖ ——

* **A: Oh, I'm so sorry Mr. Brewer.**
(Es tut mir wirklich leid, … .)
B: That's quite all right.
(Aber bitte, macht doch nichts!)

* **A: I'm terribly sorry.**
(Es tut mir schrecklich leid!)
B: It's all right.
(Aber bitte, schon gut!)

* **A: Sorry to trouble you.**
(trouble – belästigen, stören)
B: That's all right.

* **A: Oh! I'm sorry to disturb you.**
(disturb – stören)
B: That's okay, Ann.

APOLOGIES AND REACTIONS

Entschuldigungen und wie man darauf reagiert

* **A: Sorry!**
(Verzeihung! | Entschuldigung! | Tut mir leid!)
B: That's all right.
(Schon gut! | Nichts passiert!)

* **A: I'm awfully sorry for being late.**
(Es tut mir schrecklich leid, dass ich zu spät komme.)
B: That doesn't matter.
(Das macht doch nichts!)

* **A: Sorry if I'm disturbing you.**
(Tut mir leid, wenn ich Sie störe.)
B: Not at all. I'm not doing anything that can't wait until later.
(Sie stören überhaupt nicht. … .)

* **A: Sorry to bother you.**
(bother – belästigen, stören)
B: It's all right, it's no trouble at all.
(Aber bitte, überhaupt kein Problem!)

* **A: I really am very sorry to have kept you waiting. I got stuck in the traffic on the way down here.**
(keep sbdy. waiting – jemanden warten lassen / get stuck – steckenbleiben / traffic – Verkehr)
B: Oh, that's quite all right.
(Aber bitte, macht doch nichts!)

* **I'm sorry but I didn't quite catch what you were saying.**
(Es tut mir leid, aber ich habe Sie nicht ganz verstanden.)

* **A: I can't tell you how sorry I am for not preparing the report in time.**
(prepare report – Bericht erstellen / in time – rechtzeitig)
B: Well, that kind of thing really shouldn't happen, you know. But let's forget it this once.
(that kind of thing – so etwas / happen – passieren / this once – dieses eine Mal)

* **A: I didn't mean to do it. Sorry.**
(Ich habe das nicht absichtlich gemacht. Tut mir leid.)
B: It's not your fault. I'm entirely to blame.
(… . Es ist einzig und allein meine Schuld.)

* **Joanna has asked me to say she's sorry she can't be with us but she's tied up elsewhere all day.**
(be tied up elsewhere – unabkömmlich sein / all day – den ganzen Tag)

* **A: I'm so sorry about this afternoon. I'm afraid it was my fault.**
(Es tut mir wirklich leid … . / Tut mir leid, es war meine Schuld.)
B: Never mind.
(Ist schon in Ordnung!)

* **A: I'm afraid I'm rather late.**
(Tut mir leid, dass ich so spät komme.)
B: Don't worry, we haven't started yet anyway.
(Kein Grund zur Aufregung, wir haben ohnehin noch nicht begonnen.)

* **A: I'm afraid I can't make it on Sunday.**
(Ich kann leider am Sonntag nicht.)
B: Oh dear, that's a pity!
(Das ist aber schade!)

* **I'm afraid I've forgotten your name, sorry.**
(Ich habe leider Ihren Namen vergessen.)

* A: **Could you give me a hand with a few things tomorrow afternoon, please?**
  (give sbdy. a hand – jemandem helfen)
  B: **I'm afraid not. I'm away on business for the rest of this week.**
  (Geht leider nicht. / on business – geschäftlich)

* A: **I'd like to apologise for being late.**
  (apologise – sich entschuldigen)
  B: **That's O.K.**

* A: **I really must apologise to you for what happened.**
  B: **There's no need to apologise, it's just one of those things.**
  (Sie brauchen sich nicht zu entschuldigen, so etwas kann schon einmal passieren.)

* A: **Please accept my apologies.**
  (apology – Entschuldigung)
  B: **I quite understand. Please don't worry.**
  (So etwas kann schon einmal passieren. Bitte machen Sie sich keine Sorgen.)

* A: **I've got an apology to make. I seem to have lost that umbrella you lent me.**
  (... . Ich dürfte den Schirm, den Sie mir geborgt haben, verloren haben.)
  B: **Not to worry. It was only an old one anyway.**
  (not to worry – macht nichts; lassen Sie sich darüber keine grauen Haare wachsen / anyway – ohnehin)

* **Excuse me, but I must go and find Bill.**
  (Entschuldigen Sie mich, ...)

* **Excuse me for interrupting, but this is very urgent.**
  (Verzeihen Sie mir, dass ich Sie unterbreche, aber es ist sehr dringend.)

* A: **I hope you will excuse me for not calling in earlier.**
(call in – vorbeikommen)
B: **It really doesn't matter at all.**
(Das macht überhaupt nichts.)

* A: **Please forgive me for having caused you any inconvenience.**
(Ich möchte mich für etwaige Unannehmlichkeiten, die ich Ihnen bereitet habe, entschuldigen.)
B: **Don't give it another thought.**
(Verschwenden Sie keinen weiteren Gedanken mehr daran.)

* **Forgive me for asking again, but where did you say you came from?**

* **I do beg your pardon. I've found out that what you said was in fact absolutely correct.**
(Ich muss mich wirklich entschuldigen. ... .)

* A: **Oh dear, my mistake!**
(mistake – Fehler)
B: **Well, these things happen.**
(So etwas kann schon einmal passieren.)

CONGRATULATIONS AND GOOD WISHES

Gratulationen, Genesungs- und sonstige Wünsche

* **A: I'd like to congratulate you on your promotion. And the best of luck in your new position.**
(congratulate on – gratulieren zu / promotion – Beförderung / best of luck – alles Gute / position – Position, Stellung)
B: Thank you. That's very kind of you.
(kind – freundlich)

* **A: May I congratulate you on being nominated salesman of the year.**
(salesman – Verkäufer)
B: Thanks.

* **A: I didn't get a chance to congratulate you on being appointed Marketing Manager. Your board made a very wise decision I must say.**
(appoint – ernennen, bestellen / board – Verwaltungsrat; Führungsgremium einer britischen / amerikanischen Kapitalgesellschaft)
B: Thank you. That's very kind of you to say so.

* **By the way, I must congratulate you on your new job.**
(by the way – übrigens)

* **Congratulations on winning the IBM contract.**
(win contract – Auftrag erhalten)

* **A: That was a super performance. Congratulations!**
(performance – Leistung)
B: Thank you.

* **A: I passed my driving test.**
  (Ich habe meine Fahrprüfung bestanden.)
  B: That's great. Congratulations!
  (great – super, toll)
  A: Thank you.

* **That's really good news. Well done!**
  (Das ist wirklich eine gute Nachricht. Gratuliere! | Gut gemacht! | Bravo! | Sehr gut! | Super!)

* **A: Well done, Betty!**
  B: Thanks.

* **A: I haven't had time to congratulate you yet. Well done!**
  B: Thanks. Although I was quite lucky.
  A: Well, fortune favours the brave.
  (Glück hat nur der Tüchtige.)

❖

* **A: Happy birthday!**
  (Alles Gute zum Geburtstag.)
  B: Thanks.

* **A: Many happy returns of the day!**
  (Alles Gute zum Geburtstag.)
  B: Thank you.

* **A: I'd like to wish you many happy returns of the day, Barbara.**
  B: Oh, thank you very much.

* **A: I'd like to wish you a happy birthday.**
  B: Thank you. That's very kind of you.

* **A: Hello Bill. Many happy returns!**
B: Oh, thank you. How did you know?
A: Ah, a little bird told me.
(Jemand hat es mir geflüstert.)

——— ❖ ———

* **I hope you get better soon.**
(Ich hoffe, dass es Ihnen bald besser geht. | Ich wünsche Ihnen baldige Besserung.)

* **I do hope you get well soon.**
(Ich hoffe sehr, dass Sie bald gesund werden. | Ich wünsche Ihnen baldige Genesung.)

* **Have fun!**
(Viel Vergnügen!)

* **A: Enjoy yourself!**
(Viel Spaß!)
B: Thanks. I'm sure I will.

* **A: Have a good time!**
(Viel Vergnügen!)
B: Thanks, Andrew. You too!

* **A: Have a good weekend!**
(Schönes Wochenende!)
B: Thank you. The same to you!

* **A: Have a nice day!**
B: Thanks. You too!

* **Have a good trip, Peter! I hope everything goes well.**
(Gute Reise, Peter! … .)

* **I hope you have a nice holiday.**

* **A: Well, I do hope you have a nice journey.**
  B: Thank you very much.

* **I wish you a pleasant journey.**
  (Ich wünsche Ihnen eine angenehme Reise.)

* **A: All the best, Mr. Bail!**
  B: Thank you. I'll see you next year sometime.
  (sometime – irgendwann einmal)

* **A: All the very best!**
  B: Thank you.

* **All the best, Keith! And give my best wishes to your mother.**

* **I wish you all the best for the future.**
  (future – Zukunft)

* **A: Good luck!**
  (Viel Glück!)
  B: Thanks.

* **A: Best of luck with the IBM deal!**
  (deal – Geschäft)
  B: Thank you very much.

* **A: I'd like to wish you every success in your new company.**
  (success – Erfolg / company – Firma)
  B: Thank you very much. It'll be a challenge, anyway.
  (challenge – Herausforderung / anyway – ohnehin)

SEASON'S GREETINGS

Weihnachts- und Neujahrswünsche

* A: Merry Christmas!
  B: Merry Christmas!

* A: A merry Christmas to you, Mr. Brown!
  B: A merry Christmas to you too!

* A: Merry Christmas to you, Miss Bell!
  B: And to you too!

* A: Have a good Christmas!
  B: Thank you. Same to you!

* A: Happy Christmas!
  B: Thanks, the same to you!

* A: A merry Christmas and a happy New Year!
  B: Thank you. And the same to you!

* A: A happy New Year to you!
  B: Thank you. And a happy New Year to you too!

* A: Happy New Year!
  B: Thank you very much. You too!

* A: A very happy New Year!
  B: Thanks. And you, too!

SYMPATHY, REGRETS AND CONSOLATION, CONDOLENCES

Mitgefühl, Bedauern und Beileid

* **A: What's wrong?**
  (Ist etwas nicht in Ordnung? | Fehlt Ihnen etwas?)
  B: Oh, it's nothing really.

* **A: What's the matter?**
  (Was ist los mit dir?)
  B: I'm just not feeling too well.
  (Nichts Besonderes, ich fühl' mich nur nicht ganz gut.)

* **You don't look too well. What's the matter?**
  (look well – gesund aussehen)

* **A: I can't stay long I'm afraid.**
  (Ich kann leider nicht lange bleiben.)
  B: Oh, what a pity!
  (Das ist aber schade!)

* **A: I have to leave tomorrow.**
  (leave – wegfahren)
  B: Oh, what a shame!
  (Das ist aber wirklich schade!)

* **A: My wife and I would like to invite you for a meal on Saturday. Can you come?**
  (invite sbdy. for a meal – jemanden zum Essen einladen)
  B: What a pity! I don't think I can. We've got some friends staying all weekend.
  (all weekend – das ganze Wochenende)

* **A: I'm going back to Canada on Sunday.**
B: Sunday? Oh, that's a shame.
(that's a shame – das ist schade)

* **It really is a shame that you didn't get the job.**

* **It's a great pity that you can only stay two days.**
(Es ist sehr schade, dass … .)

* **A: I missed the bus, so I was late for the interview.**
(miss – versäumen)
B: How annoying! That was too bad, wasn't it?
(how annoying – wie ärgerlich)

* **A: John's mother died in that air crash last week.**
(air crash – Flugzeugabsturz)
B: How terrible!
(Furchtbar!)

* **Craig, I was so sorry to hear about your wife. How is she?**
(how is she – wie geht es ihr)

* **A: I'm afraid she's broken both her legs.**
(I'm afraid – leider)
B: Oh no, how awful! I am sorry. Is there anything you'd like me to do?
(awful – furchtbar, schrecklich)

* **A: I've lost my wallet somewhere. It's got over £300 in it.**
(wallet – Brieftasche / somewhere – irgendwo)
B: Oh, I'm very sorry to hear that. Do you remember when you had it last?
(last – zuletzt; das letzte Mal)

* **A: The bad news is I lost my job.**
B: Oh dear, I'm sorry to hear that. What a terrible situation for you.

* **I feel sorry for you, Paul. That's a terrible blow.**
(blow – Schlag)

* **That's really a shame. They shouldn't have done that to you.**
(shame – Schande)

* **No, this can't be true! They can't have fired you after 20 years.**
(fire – feuern, hinauswerfen, entlassen)

* **I'm awfully sorry to hear that your wife is in hospital. Is there anything I can do?**

* A: **We've broken off our engagement.**
(break off engagement – Verlobung lösen)
B: **Oh dear, I am sorry. That's too bad.**

* **I really sympathise with you.**
(Ich kann mir gut vorstellen, wie Sie sich fühlen.)

——— ❖ ———

* A: **I need the draft contract, but I can't find it.**
(draft contract – Vertragsentwurf)
B: **Don't worry. I'll find it for you.**
(don't worry – reg dich nicht auf)

* A: **I'm sure I'm going to fail my exam.**
(Ich bin sicher, daß ich bei der Prüfung durchfallen werde.)
B: **There's nothing to worry about. Your German seems very good to me.**
(Du brauchst dich doch nicht zu ängstigen. … . / seem – scheinen)

* **Don't worry, there's plenty of time.**
(Keine Angst, es ist noch genug Zeit.)

* **A: I'm afraid I've made a mess of your desk.**
(Tut mir leid, ich habe Ihren Schreibtisch in Unordnung gebracht.)
B: Oh, that doesn't matter.
(Das macht doch nichts!)

* **A: Oh dear, I've forgotten my umbrella.**
(umbrella – Regenschirm)
B: Well, never mind. I don't suppose it will rain.
(never mind – das macht nichts / suppose – annehmen)

* **A: I didn't manage to get a ticket.**
(manage – es schaffen)
B: Oh, bad luck!
(So ein Pech! | Pech gehabt!)

* **A: There was so much traffic that we didn't get back till after midnight.**
(Der Verkehr war so stark, dass wir erst nach Mitternacht heimgekommen sind.)
B: Well, it could have been worse. At least you got home safely.
(Nun, es hätte schlimmer sein können. Wenigstens sind Sie sicher nach Hause gekommen.)

* **Hard luck, Tom!**
(So ein Pech, Tom!)

* **How silly of me to leave my brief-case on the bus!**
(leave – liegenlassen / brief-case – Aktenkoffer)

——— ❖ ———

* **Sorry to hear that your father has died, Mr. Redford. I'd like to express my heartfelt sympathy.**
(… . Ich möchte Ihnen mein aufrichtiges Beileid ausdrücken.)

* **My heartfelt sympathy, Mr. Ryan.**

* **I really don't know what to say, but I know how you must feel.**

EXCLAMATIONS

Ausrufe

* **What a nuisance! I've lost a button off my coat.**
(Wie ärgerlich! Ich habe einen Knopf von meinem Mantel verloren.)

* A: **What's the name of that pub where we're supposed to be meeting Joseph?**
(… , wo wir Joseph treffen sollen?)
B: **For heaven's sake, I've told you three times already. It's the Red Lion.**
(for heaven's sake – du meine Güte; das darf doch nicht wahr sein)

* **Oh my god, you don't mean to say they're not going to be able to pay, do you?**
(… , du willst doch damit nicht sagen, dass sie nicht zahlen können, oder?)

* **Oh my goodness, it's two o'clock already! It'll be a tough job meeting the deadline.**
(oh my goodness – du meine Güte / Es wird sehr schwer werden, den Termin einzuhalten.)

* **For Christ's sake, Tom, can't you just stop talking for one minute? I can't hear a word Nigel's saying.**
(for Christ's sake – verdammt noch mal)

* **ATG is up for sale again. Just imagine! They were taken over by STF just two months ago.**
(ATG wird schon wieder zum Verkauf angeboten. Stellen Sie sich das nur vor! Die Gesellschaft wurde erst vor zwei Monaten von STF übernommen.)

* **Goodness me, what's happening out there? There's a hell of a noise!**
  (Du meine Güte, was ist da draußen los? Das ist aber ein fürchterlicher Lärm.)

* **A: Steven's been promoted to department head.**
  (Steven ist zum Abteilungsleiter befördert worden.)
  B: Well I never! I thought that position was reserved for Rachel.
  (Nein, so was! … .)

* **Fancy meeting you here of all people. I thought you'd gone to live in Sweden.**
  (Na so was, dass ich gerade dich hier treffe! … .)

* **Fancy meeting you here of all places. I didn't know you liked jazz.**
  (Na so was, dass ich dich gerade hier treffe! … .)

* **A: Ronnie said AFK were going to place another order with us.**
  (place another order with sbdy. – jemandem einen weiteren Auftrag erteilen)
  B: My foot! They went bust last week!
  (Quatsch! … . / go bust – pleite gehen)

* **Good heavens! Have you seen the latest news? Interest rates are going up by another 1/2%.**
  (Du lieber Himmel! Hast du die letzten Nachrichten gesehen? / interest rate – Zinssatz)

* **Damn! I can't find that customer file anywhere!**
  (Verflixt! Ich kann diesen Kundenordner nirgends finden.)

* **What the hell did he think he was doing? He's ruined everything now.**
  (Was zum Teufel hat er sich denn dabei gedacht? … .)

* **A: We lost another order to Finland last week.**
  B: Oh dear! That's the second in three weeks, isn't it?
  (Du meine Güte! / isn't it? – nicht?)

* **A: Did you know Jack Trilby's having a retirement party next Thursday?**
(retirement – Pensionierung)

B: Good gracious! Is he 65 already?
(Na so was! … ?)

LANGUAGE PROBLEMS

Sprachliche Probleme

* **Excuse me, how do you pronounce this word?**
  (pronounce – aussprechen)

* **[...] – is that the right pronunciation?**
  (pronunciation – Aussprache)

* **That's very difficult to pronounce.**

* **That's a real tongue-twister.**
  (tongue-twister – Zungenbrecher)

* **Will you correct me if I pronounce something wrongly, please?**
  (Würden Sie mich bitte korrigieren, wenn … .)

——— ❖ ———

* **How do you spell 'accommodation'?**
  (spell – buchstabieren, schreiben / accommodation – Unterkunft, Unterbringung)

* **How do you spell it, please?**

* **Could you spell that word, please?**

* **I'm not sure if I've spelt this name correctly. Can you check it for me, please?**
  (check – überprüfen)

* **Do you spell 'transferred' with one or two r's?**
  (transfer – übertragen, überweisen)

* **Do the Americans spell this word in the same way as the British?**

* **Is this the right spelling of 'separate'?**
(spelling – Schreibweise, Rechtschreibung / separate – separat, getrennt)

—— ❖ ——

* **Can I use 'Hello' when I meet someone for the first time?**
(meet – treffen, begegnen)

* **What should I say if I want to attract someone's attention?**
(attract attention – Aufmerksamkeit erregen)

* **In German, when friends drink together, we say 'Prost!'. How would you say that in English?**

* **What would you say for this in English?**

* **What is that in English?**

* **What do you call that in English?**
(Wie heißt das auf englisch?)

—— ❖ ——

* **Is it correct to say, 'I have been waiting for one hour'?**
(… , ‚Ich warte schon seit einer Stunde'?)

* **Is this sentence correct?**

* **Is that the right word?**

* **I'm trying to find the right word, perhaps you can help me?**

* **What is the plural of 'crisis'?**
(plural – Mehrzahl)

* **What is the singular of 'media'?**
(singular – Einzahl / media – Medien)

* **Which is correct: 'at a low price' or 'on a low price'?**

* **Can I say, 'The current account is in the red'?**
(current account – Leistungsbilanz / in the red – in den roten Zahlen; in der Verlustzone; passiv)

* **Will you tell me if I make a mistake, please?**
(Würden Sie mir bitte sagen, wenn … .)

* **When do you use 'economical'? Can you give me an example?**
(economical – wirtschaftlich, sparsam / example – Beispiel)

❖

* **Could you speak a bit more slowly?**
(a bit – ein bisschen; ein wenig)

* **Could you possibly speak a little more slowly?**
(a little – ein bisschen; ein wenig)

* **Could you speak a little louder, please?**

* **I wonder if you could speak up a little?**
(Könnten Sie etwas lauter sprechen?)

* **Please don't speak so fast, I can't follow you.**
(fast – schnell / follow – folgen)

❖

* **If we don't meet these deadlines, our customers will lose faith in us. Do you see what I mean?**
(meet deadline – Termin einhalten / customer – Kunde / faith – Vertrauen / see – verstehen)

* **Do you know what I mean?**

* **If there's anything you haven't understood, please say so.**

——— ❖ ———

* **I'm not sure I understand. Does that mean you've lost your job?**
(mean – heißen, bedeuten)

* **Does that mean 'no'?**

* **Do you mean you can't come tomorrow evening?**

* **If I understand you correctly, you think we need to do a market survey first.**
(market survey – Marktstudie, Markterhebung, Marktuntersuchung)

——— ❖ ———

* **Sorry, but I didn't catch the last word.**
(catch – verstehen)

* **I'm sorry, I didn't hear what you said.**

* **I'm sorry, I'm not with you.**
(… , ich kann Ihnen nicht folgen.)

* **A: I'm sorry, what did you say?**
B: I said, could – you – turn – the – music – down.
(turn down – leiser stellen)

* **What was his name again please?**
(Wie war noch eben sein Name, bitte?)

* **What was that again? I didn't quite catch what you said.**
(Was war das eben? Ich habe nicht ganz verstanden, was Sie gesagt haben.)

* **Could you repeat what you just said, please?**
(repeat – wiederholen / just – gerade)

* **Would you please repeat that last remark?**
(remark – Bemerkung)

* **Sorry, can you say that again, please?**

* **Would you mind repeating your last point, please?**
(Würden Sie bitte so freundlich sein und den letzten Punkt wiederholen.)

* **A: Strictly speaking, you can't say that.**
(Strenggenommen … .)
B: Pardon?
(Wie bitte?)

——— ❖ ———

* **Could you explain it in simple terms?**
(explain – erklären / in simple terms – mit einfachen Worten)

* **Excuse me, could you explain that in more detail?**
(in more detail – detaillierter)

* **Would you please elaborate on that?**
(Würden Sie das bitte näher ausführen?)

——— ❖ ———

* **A: What exactly do you mean by 'turnover' in this context?**
(mean by – meinen mit / turnover – Fluktuation / context – Zusammenhang)
B: Well, it refers to the employees of our firm. It's a ratio which shows the percentage of people leaving the firm.
(refer to – sich beziehen auf / employee – Arbeitnehmer, Mitarbeiter / ratio – Verhältniszahl, Kennzahl / percentage – Prozentsatz / leave – ausscheiden aus)

* **I'm sorry ... I don't quite understand what you mean by irresponsible.**
(irresponsible – unverantwortlich, verantwortungslos)

* **What does 'factoring' mean?**
(mean – bedeuten)

* **A: What is the exact meaning of this word?**
(exact meaning – genaue Bedeutung)
B: Sorry, I don't know that word.

* **What's the meaning of 'clean floating'?**
(clean floating – sauberes Floaten der Wechselkurse)

* **I don't understand this expression. Can you help me?**
(expression – Ausdruck)

* **What is thc opposite of 'polite'?**
(opposite – Gegenteil / polite – höflich)

* **What is another word for 'exposure'?**
(exposure – Risikoposition)

* **What other words are there for 'depreciation-prone'?**
(depreciation-prone – abwertungsanfällig, abwertungsverdächtig, abwertungsbedroht)

* **What is another way of saying 'prices sky-rocket'?**
  (way – Möglichkeit, Art, Weise / sky-rocket – stark in die Höhe schnellen)

* **Do 'drop' and 'decline' mean the same thing?**
  (drop – fallen, zurückgehen / decline – fallen, zurückgehen)

* **What's the difference between 'franchising' and 'licensing'?**
  (difference – Unterschied / licensing – Lizenzvergabe)

* **Is there a difference in meaning between 'force majeure' and 'act of god'?**
  (force majeure – höhere Gewalt / act of god – Naturereignis)

* **A: What is the word for people who always think that they are ill?**
  B: Oh, it's on the tip of my tongue – hypochondriacs, that's it.
  (it's on the tip of my tongue – es liegt mir auf der Zunge / hypochondriac – Hypochonder)

* **Is there an English word to describe the fact that unit costs come down the more you produce?**
  (describe – bezeichnen / unit costs – Stückkosten / come down – zurückgehen, abnehmen)

* **What do you call someone who makes out a bill of exchange?**
  (Wie bezeichnet man jemanden, der einen Wechsel ausstellt?)

* **A: What do you call a cheque which cannot be cashed over the bank counter, but must be paid into an account?**
  (cash cheque – Scheck einlösen / bank counter – Bankschalter / account – Konto)
  B: Um, let me think – it's called a crossed cheque.
  (crossed cheque – gekreuzter Scheck; Verrechnungsscheck)

* **When would you use the word 'underwriting'?**
  (underwriting – Emissionsgarantie)

* **When would you use the expression 'once bitten, twice shy'?**
(once bitten, twice shy – ein gebranntes Kind scheut das Feuer)

* **Does 'turnover' have more than one meaning?**
(turnover – Umschlagshäufigkeit, Umsatz, Fluktuation)

* **A: I'm sorry, but I don't quite see what you mean.**
(see – verstehen)
B: What I mean is, we can't offer you more than our normal 10% discount on the list price.
(offer – anbieten / discount – Rabatt / list price – Listenpreis)

* **What does this abbreviation stand for?**
(abbreviation – Abkürzung)

* **Could you translate that word into German?**
(translate – übersetzen)

❖

* **Could you put it in a different way?**
(Könnten Sie es anders ausdrücken?)

* **Would you mind putting that in different words?**
(Würde es Ihnen etwas ausmachen, das mit anderen Worten auszudrücken?)

* **To put it another way: it's too expensive.**
(expensive – teuer)

❖

* **Your German is very good. Where did you learn it?**

* **That goes without saying.**
(Das versteht sich von selbst. | Das ist doch selbstverständlich.)

* **I can't make head or tail of it.**
(Ich werde daraus überhaupt nicht klug.)

* **You're telling me.**
(Wem sagen Sie das.)

* **You must be joking!**
(Das können Sie doch wohl nicht ernst meinen.)

JOKES

Witze

* **Have you heard any good jokes recently?**
  (joke – Witz / recently – in der letzten Zeit)

* **Do you know any good jokes?**

* **A: Have you heard the one about … ?**
  B: No, go on.
  (Nein, erzähl weiter! | erzähl schon!)

* **While we're on the subject of animals, do you know the one about the little monkey?**
  (Da wir gerade über Tiere sprechen, kennen Sie den über den kleinen Affen schon?)

* **Let me tell you a good joke I heard the other day.**
  (the other day – neulich)

* **In Austria we make fun of the people from Burgenland in the east of Austria – a bit like you with the Irish!**
  (make fun of sbdy. – sich über jemanden lustig machen)

* **I know a good one. There was this man … .**

* **I like that one.**

* **I know a similar joke, but it's actually a dirty one.**
  (dirty – unanständig)

* **I can never remember the best jokes.**

* **I'm sorry, I didn't catch the punch line.**
  (… , ich habe die Pointe nicht verstanden.)

MY FAMILY

Meine Familie

* A: **Do you have a family?**
B: **Yes, I'm married and have two boys and one girl.**

* **Have you got a family?**

* A: **Do you come from a big family?**
B: **Yes, as a matter of fact, I've got two elder brothers and two younger sisters.**

* A: **Have you any brothers and sisters?**
B: **No, I'm an only child.**
(only child – Einzelkind)

* A: **Are your parents still alive?**
(Leben Ihre Eltern noch?)
B: **My mother is, but unfortunately my father died three years ago.**
(unfortunately – leider)

* A: **Both my parents have been dead for a long time.**
(Meine Eltern sind beide schon seit langem tot.)
B: **Oh, I'm sorry to hear that.**

* A: **So I see you're married.**
B: **Yes, I've been married for ten years now.**
(Ja, ich bin nun schon seit zehn Jahren verheiratet.)

* A: **Are you married?**
B: **No, but I'll be getting married next year – I'm engaged.**
(get married – heiraten / engaged – verlobt)

* **I'm still single.**
(Ich bin noch immer ledig.)

* **I used to be married, but now I'm divorced.**
  (Ich war früher einmal verheiratet, aber nun bin ich geschieden.)

* **I got married two years ago.**

* **A: What does your wife do, Brian?**
  (do – [beruflich] machen)
  B: She's a journalist.

* **She's a teacher.**

* **She's a full-time mother.**

* **A: What does your husband do, Betty?**
  B: He works for IBM.

* **A: Do you have any children?**
  B: No, but we would like to have some.

* **A: How old are your children?**
  B: My eldest is 21 and my youngest is 12.

* **A: Do your children still live at home?**
  B: Oh yes, they are still at school.

* **My daughter has just started university.**

* **A: Are your children still living at home?**
  B: No, not any more – my son is doing his military service and my daughters are married and have their own families.
  (do military service – Militärdienst ableisten)

* **Did you bring any of your family over with you?**
  (Haben Sie jemanden von Ihrer Familie mitgebracht?)

- **A: Have you got any pets, Bill?**
  (pet – Haustier)
  B: Yes, I've got a dog.

- **We used to have a dog, but it was too much of a bind when we wanted to go away.**
  (it was too much of a bind – wir waren zu sehr gebunden)

- **We've got a couple of cats.**
  (Wir haben ein paar Katzen.)

- **My sons have got a hamster, a guinea-pig and a rabbit.**
  (guinea-pig – Meerschweinchen)

- **My daughter has a pony.**

- **I keep tropical fish actually.**

- **Is it right that most people have a dog over here?**

WEATHER

Wetter

* **A: What's the weather like today?**
  (Wie ist das Wetter heute?)
  B: The sun is shining.

* **It's raining.**

* **It looks like rain.**
  (Es sieht nach Regen aus.)

* **It's cold, wet and very stormy.**
  (wet – nass / stormy – stürmisch)

* **It's drizzling.**
  (drizzle – nieseln)

* **It's coming down in buckets.**
  (Es gießt in Strömen.)

* **It's pouring.**
  (Es gießt in Strömen.)

* **It's snowing heavily.**
  (Es schneit stark.)

* **It's freezing.**
  (freeze – eiskalt sein)

* **The sky is overcast, and it is very sultry.**
  (overcast – bedeckt / sultry – schwül)

* **It's very close. I think there's going to be a thunderstorm this afternoon.**
(close – schwül / there's going to be – es wird geben / thunderstorm – Gewitter)

* **The sky is clear, not a cloud in sight.**
(cloud – Wolke / in sight – in Sicht; zu sehen)

* **It is snowing, but I'm sure it'll stop soon.**

* **It seems to be clearing up.**
(seem – scheinen / clear up – aufhellen, aufklaren)

* **It's a miserable day today.**

* **The sun is scorching. It's too hot to walk.**
(scorch – herunterbrennen)

* **It's bitterly cold.**

* **It's not as cold as I imagined it'd be.**
(imagine – sich etwas vorstellen)

* **Do you think the weather will stay like this?**
(stay like this – so bleiben)

* **A: What is the temperature today?**
B: It is 20 degrees centigrade.
(20 degrees centigrade – 20° Celsius)

* **It is minus twenty.**
(Wir haben 20° unter Null.)

* **A: What's the weather going to be like today?**
(Wie wird das Wetter heute?)
B: I think it's going to be fine.
(Ich glaube, es wird schön.)

* **What's the weather forecast for today?**
  (weather forecast – Wetterprognose, Wettervorhersage)

* **It's going to stay fine.**
  (Es bleibt schön.)

* **It's going to get colder.**
  (Es wird kälter.)

* **I think we're going to have a fine day.**

* **It's going to be mainly cloudy with rainy spells.**
  (mainly cloudy with rainy spells – vorwiegend bewölkt mit vereinzelten Regenschauern)

* **There will be heavy showers in the afternoon.**
  (heavy showers – starke Schauer)

* **D'you think it'll rain?**

* **Is the fog going to lift?**
  (Wird sich der Nebel lichten?)

* **I don't think the weather is going to be very good.**

* **A: What is the weather forecast for tomorrow?**
  B: Very hazy and humid with scattered showers.
  (hazy – dunstig, diesig / humid – feucht / scattered showers – vereinzelte Regenschauer)

* **Mainly cloudy with sunny spells in the afternoon.**
  (sunny spells – einige sonnige Aufhellungen)

* **Light rain showers during the night, mostly cloudy sky in the early morning hours but sunny in the afternoon.**

* **The weathermen think that it is going to be bright and sunny tomorrow.**
(weatherman – Wetterprophet, Meteorologe / bright – heiter)

* **Have you heard the weather forecast yet?**
(yet – schon)

* **According to the weather forecast, it's going to get even hotter.**
(according to – laut / get even hotter – noch heißer werden)

* **A: What does the weather report say?**
(weather report – Wetterbericht)
B: It doesn't look very promising.
(promising – vielversprechend)

* **There is going to be a change in the weather.**
(change in the weather – Wetterveränderung, Wetterumschwung)

* **We are in for changeable weather.**
(Es ist unbeständiges Wetter zu erwarten.)

* **We are in for a spell of fine weather.**
(spell of fine weather – Schönwetterperiode)

* **There'll be a heatwave.**
(heatwave – Hitzewelle)

* **Drive slowly; the weather forecast says there will be patches of fog on the M4.**
(drive – fahren / patches of fog – Nebelschwaden / M4 – Autobahnbezeichnung)

* **A: Do you think the weather will remain stable?**
(remain – bleiben / stable – beständig)
B: No, it looks very unsettled.
(unsettled – unbeständig)

* **A: Looks a bit like rain, don't you think?**
B: I think it may hold off.
(hold off – aushalten)

* **What are the road conditions like?**
(Wie ist der Straßenzustand?)

* **The roads are icy.**
(icy – vereist)

* **A: What was the weather like when you were on holiday?**
(holiday – Urlaub)
B: We had a week of brilliant sunshine and yet not too hot.
(brilliant sunshine – strahlender Sonnenschein / yet – trotzdem)

* **We had terrible weather every day.**
(terrible – schrecklich, furchtbar, fürchterlich)

* **It rained all the time we were in Paris.**

* **The weather in California was splendid, just fantastic.**
(splendid – prachtvoll, prächtig, herrlich)

* **A: How was the weather in Spain?**
B: Well, not too good actually, we had quite a lot of rain.
(quite a lot of – ziemlich viel)

* **It's raining all the time. I'll have to buy an umbrella or a raincoat.**
(umbrella – Schirm / raincoat – Regenmantel)

* **It's not unusual for the temperature to remain below zero for weeks on end.**
(unusual – ungewöhnlich / on end – ohne Unterbrechung)

* **I think the rain's over.**
(over – vorbei, vorüber)

* **The wind has changed.**
(Der Wind hat gedreht.)

* **The wind has dropped.**
(Der Wind hat sich gelegt.)

* **The barometer's rising.**

* **I wish the weather was better.**

* **The weather can only get better.**

* **The weather is bound to get better soon.**
(Das Wetter muss einfach bald besser werden.)

* **It's too wet to go on foot.**

* **We can't go out in this weather.**
(Wir können bei diesem Wetter nicht hinausgehen.)

* **We'll go out in all weathers.**
(in all weathers – bei jeder Witterung)

* **It's too chilly to sit outside.**
(chilly – kühl, frostig)

* **I hope the weather will stay fine over the weekend. I want to go for a hike on the moors.**
(… . Ich will eine Wanderung auf dem Hochmoor machen.)

* **The weather looks pretty awful, John. Bet we have some rain before long.**
(pretty awful – ziemlich schlecht / bet – wetten / before long – bald)

* **Just look at that rain! The weather's terrible. I wish I was in Greece now.**
(Greece – Griechenland)

* **A: When does the tide come in?**
  (Wann kommt die Flut? | Wann ist Flut?)
  B: It is in at ten in the morning and at eight in the evening.

* **A: Does it rain a lot here at this time of year?**
  B: No, not really. But we have had an exceptionally wet summer so far.
  (exceptional – ungewöhnlich, außergewöhnlich / so far – bisher)

* **A: Is it always this windy here?**
  B: Yes, there is usually a wind from the west.

* **There is always a breeze here. So it never gets really hot and sweltering.**
  (breeze – Brise / sweltering – schwül)

* **A: Do you get any snow here in winter?**
  B: Not down here in the valley. But there is snow up in the mountains. Not enough for skiing though.
  (valley – Tal / though – aber)

* **You should go to Austria. We usually have plenty of snow there.**
  (plenty of snow – sehr viel Schnee)

* **A: What kind of climate does your country have?**
  B: Fairly mild, on the whole.
  (fairly – ziemlich / on the whole – im Großen und Ganzen)

* **In Austria we have got what I suppose is called 'continental climate'. Fairly hot summers and quite cold winters with lots of snow.**
  (suppose – vermuten / climate – Klima / quite – ziemlich)

* **It's pretty cold in your country in the winter, I suppose.**

* **We haven't had much luck with the weather so far.**

* **That hailstorm is said to have destroyed most of the crops.**
(Dieses Hagelgewitter soll angeblich den Großteil der Ernte zerstört haben.)

* **I wouldn't shelter under the tree. You might get struck by lightning.**
(shelter – sich unterstellen; Schutz suchen / get struck by lightning – von einem Blitz getroffen werden)

* **The snow seems to be turning into sleet.**
(Der Schnee scheint in Eisregen überzugehen.)

* **Don't drive so fast, the road looks pretty slippery.**
(slippery – rutschig)

* **The weather's driving me up the wall.**
(Das Wetter macht mich ganz verrückt.)

* **What awful weather!**
(awful – scheußlich)

* **What a lovely breeze!**
(lovely – angenehm, herrlich)

* **Nice and bright this morning, isn't it?**
(isn't it? – nicht wahr?)

* **It's a real scorcher today, isn't it?**
(scorcher – sehr heißer Tag)

* **It was pretty cold this morning, wasn't it?**
(wasn't it? – nicht wahr?)

* **What a dreadful day, isn't it?**
(Schrecklicher Tag heute, nicht wahr?)

* **It's getting cold, isn't it?**

* **A: Isn't it a lovely day?**
B: Yes, we're having beautiful weather.

* **A: Fairly mild for the time of year, isn't it?**
B: Yes. Quite different from the forecast.

* **A: Looks as if it's going to rain, doesn't it?**
(Es sieht so aus, als wollte es regnen, nicht wahr?)
B: Yes, I'm afraid so.
(Ja, ich fürchte schon.)

* **A: What d'you think of this weather?**
B: It's very nice, isn't it?

POLITICS

Politik

(see also "Talking about the Economy")

POLITICAL SYSTEMS

Politische Systeme

* **A: Austria is certainly less centralised than Britain. We have a number of federal states, called "Bundesländer".**
  (certainly – sicher / number – Anzahl / federal state – Bundesland)
  B: That's similar to the German system, isn't it?
  (similar – ähnlich / isn't it? – nicht wahr?)
  A: Yes, only that in Germany the "Länder" are even more independent.
  (even – noch / independent – unabhängig, selbständig)

* **In Austria and Germany, the president is not the country's chief executive. That role is reserved for the "Bundeskanzler", or "Federal Chancellor".**
  (chief executive – Regierungschef)

* **In theory, the president's powers are quite far-reaching. In practice, he is a mere figurehead, in fact not unlike your Queen.**
  (power – Befugnis / quite – ziemlich / mere – bloß / be a figurehead – eine repräsentative Rolle spielen / unlike – unähnlich)

* **No, he is not elected for life. His term of office is six years.**
  (elect – wählen / for life – auf Lebenszeit / term of office – Amtszeit)

* **No, in Germany and Austria the Kanzler, or Chancellor, is not the Minister of Finance but the Prime Minister. The terminology is a bit confusing – also for German-speaking people.**
  (confusing – verwirrend)

* **There is an interesting difference, however: the Austrian president is elected by popular vote. In Germany it is the so-called "Bundesversammlung" that elects the head of state.**
(however – jedoch / by popular vote – direkt vom Volk / head of state – Staatsoberhaupt)

* A: **How are the candidates for the presidential election selected? Do you have anything like the American primary system?**
(primary – Vorwahl)
B: **No, the candidates are usually nominated by the parties, which also finance the election campaign.**

* **The most important difference is that our electoral system is more or less based on proportional representation. That is also true of Germany.**
(electoral system – Wahlsystem / be based on – basieren auf / proportional representation – Verhältniswahlrecht / be true of – gelten für)

* A: **You seem to have a completely different system here in Britain, some kind of all-or-nothing principle.**
(seem – scheinen / different – anders, verschieden)
B: **Yes, the candidate who obtains the highest number of votes in a constituency takes the seat and all the other votes are lost.**
(obtain – erhalten / vote – Stimme / constituency – Wahlkreis / seat – [Parlaments-]Sitz)

* **The British system may not be fair but at least it delivers working majorities.**
(at least – zumindest / deliver – liefern, ermöglichen / working majority – funktionsfähige Mehrheit)

* **Under the Austrian and German systems, absolute majorities are much more difficult to achieve than in Britain. That's probably why coalitions between parties are much more common.**
(under – im Rahmen von / achieve – erreichen / probably – wahrscheinlich / common – üblich)

* **Yes, we do have a second chamber, called "Bundesrat" or "Federal Council". It represents the federal element in our constitution, a bit like the US Senate. But it's less powerful, and the members are not elected by popular vote. The German system is very similar.**
(chamber – Kammer / constitution – Verfassung / be powerful – Macht haben)

* **A: Apart from government and parliament, the so-called "social partners" have to be reckoned with.**
(apart from – abgesehen von / reckon – rechnen)
B: I've heard of this system. Sounds a bit strange. How does it work?
(sound – klingen / strange – seltsam / work – funktionieren)
A: Well, it's all rather complicated. But what it basically means is that a lot of the political decisions are not really taken by the government in power but by various bodies representing employers, employees and farmers.
(rather – ziemlich / basically – im Wesentlichen / a lot of – eine Menge / decision –Entscheidung / body – Gremium / employer – Arbeitgeber / employee – Arbeitnehmer)

* **Is it true that you have no written constitution?**
(constitution – Verfassung)

* **Don't you think that the Crown is a bit of an anachronism?**
(Crown – Krone, Monarchie)

POLITICAL CULTURE

Politische Kultur

* **Our political culture in Austria is perhaps less adversarial than yours. Most people seem to prefer some form of co-operation between the two main parties. Although we had government by one party between 1970 and 1983.**
(adversarial – konfliktträchtig / seem – scheinen / prefer – vorziehen / main – wichtigst / although – obwohl)

* **There is a tendency to avoid hard choices and just to muddle through.**
(avoid – vermeiden / hard choice – harte Entscheidung / just – nur / muddle through – durchwursteln)

* **The Austrians are probably more likely to fight shy of tough decisions than we are here in Germany, although we have our fair share of unsolved problems.**
(be more likely to do – eher tun / fight shy of – zurückschrecken vor / tough – hart / fair share – gerüttelt Maß / unsolved – ungelöst)

* **Although the two countries have a lot in common, there is a certain amount of distrust. We regard the Germans as bossy know-alls, while they probably think that we are shifty and unreliable.**
(have in common – gemein haben / certain – gewiss / amount – Ausmaß / distrust – Misstrauen / regard – betrachten / bossy – herrisch, rechthaberisch / know-all – Besserwisser / while – während / shifty verschlagen / unreliable – unzuverlässig)

POLITICAL PARTIES

Politische Parteien

* A: **Currently, we have five parliamentary parties here in Austria. The biggest three (in terms of the number of votes achieved at the last election) are the Social Democrats (the *Reds* as they are popularly called), the Conservatives (nicknamed the *Blacks*) and the Greens.**
(currently – zurzeit / in terms of – gemessen an / number of votes – Stimmenanzahl / achieve – erreichen / election – Wahl / nicknamed – mit Spitznamen)

B: **Haven't you got any right-wing parties?**
(right-wing – rechtsgerichtet)

A: **Yes, of course. There are two worth mentioning. The Freedom Party and the Alliance for the Future of Austria (BZÖ), which broke away from the Freedom Party over a squabble about strategy.**
(worth mentioning – erwähnenswert / break away – sich loslösen von / squabble – Streiterei)

* A: **Right-wing parties seem to depend on charismatic leaders.**
(depend on – abhängen von)

B: **Yes, but don't forget that they often focus on important social issues.**
(issue – Problem, Anliegen)

* A: **Right-wing parties are often criticised for not offering any practical solutions and for relying too much on populist slogans.**
(offer – anbieten / solution – Lösung / rely on – sich stützen auf)

B: **This may be true, but they often thrive because the current government is doing a poor job.**
(thrive – florieren / current – gegenwärtig / poor – schlecht)

* **It is important not to mix up the German Free Democrats and Austria's Freedom Party. It is further to the right than its German namesake.**
(mix up – verwechseln / further – weiter / namesake – Namensvetter)

* **No, the Greens are no longer represented in Parliament. One reason is certainly that voters did not like the constant squabbles between realists and fundamentalists.**
(represent – vertreten / reason – Grund / constant – ständig / squabble – Streiterei)

* **A: Some people are still frightened by the anti-business stance of some radical Greens.**
(still – noch immer / frightened – verschreckt / anti-business – wirtschaftsfeindlich / stance – Haltung)
B: But that's silly! The modern Greens are prepared to co-operate and make compromises.

* **The irony is that a lot of the original green issues have been taken up by the mainstream parties.**
(irony – Witz / issue – Anliegen / take up – übernehmen / mainstream – traditionell)

* **One must not forget that the Greens are only the political wing of a much wider and deeper environmental and alternative movement.**
(must not – nicht dürfen / wing – Flügel / environmental movement – Umweltbewegung)

* **Do you think that the party is ready to switch sides again, as it did in 1982?**
(switch sides – die Fronten wechseln)

* **A: How long has the party been in opposition?**
B: Since the Conservatives formed a government with one of the small parties.

* **Parties are often criticised, and a lot of the criticism is certainly justified. But ultimately I think they are necessary to focus political opinions.**
(justified – gerechtfertigt / ultimately – letzten Endes / focus – bündeln / opinion – Meinung)

* **In Italy, the present electoral system encourages the formation of small parties; in Germany and Austria, small parties do not have much of a chance because of the 5% hurdle.**
  (encourage – begünstigen / formation – Entstehen / hurdle – Hürde)

* **How are parties financed in your country? Government grants, political donations, or both?**
  (government grant – staatliche Zuwendung / donation – Schenkung, Spende)

* **Austria is again governed by a "Grand Coalition" between the Social Democrats and the Conservatives.**
  (govern – regieren / grand – groß)

BILLS, LAWS AND VOTES

Gesetzesvorlagen, Gesetze und Abstimmungen

* **Of course, before a law is drafted there is considerable consultation with various groupings.**
  (Bevor es zu einem Gesetzesentwurf kommt, gibt es natürlich umfangreiche Beratungen mit verschiedenen Gruppierungen.)

* **I'm sure government will introduce a bill to deal with this problem before the middle of next year.**
  (introduce bill – [formelle] Gesetzesvorlage einbringen / deal with – behandeln)

* **I hope that the new incentives will be on the law books before the year is out.**
  (incentive – Förderungsmaßnahme / be on the law books – gesetzlich verankert sein / out – vorüber)

* **The Government has published another White Paper on the issue. This means that it will take years before there is a vote in Parliament.**
  (publish – herausbringen / White Paper – Weißbuch / issue – Thema, Problem / take – brauchen / vote – Abstimmung)

* **The new law is basically sound. It's the implementation that's going to be a problem.**
(basically – im Grunde genommen / sound – vernünftig, solide / implementation – Vollzug, Durchführung)

* **The new act provides just a loose framework. It needs to be fleshed out by detailed regulations.**
(act – Gesetz / provide – bieten, bereitstellen / framework – Rahmen / flesh out – konkretisieren / regulation – [etwa] Verordnung)

* **I hope that Parliament will pass the law before it goes into its summer recess.**
(pass law – Gesetz verabschieden / recess – [Parlaments-]Ferien)

* **A: There was a three-line whip and government offered generous bribes to the most important backbenchers. But would you believe it, it nearly lost the vote.**
(three-line whip – strenger Fraktionszwang / bribe – Bestechungsgeschenk / backbencher – Hinterbänkler / would you believe it – kaum zu glauben / nearly – fast / lose – verlieren / vote – Abstimmung)
B: Its majority was reduced to three, wasn't it?
(majority – Mehrheit / wasn't it? – oder?)
A: Yes, that's true because quite a few MPs abstained.
(quite a few – eine ganze Menge / MP – Member of Parliament | Abgeordneter / abstain – sich der Stimme enthalten)

* **If the PM risks a vote of confidence, I'm sure the backbenchers will cave in. They don't want to bring the government down. It would cost a lot of them their jobs.**
(PM – Prime Minister | Bundeskanzler, Regierungschef / vote of confidence – Vertrauensabstimmung / cave in – klein beigeben / bring down – stürzen)

ELECTIONS AND REFERENDA
Wahlen und Volksabstimmungen

✳ A: **When is your next election?**
(election – Wahl)
B: **I really don't know. The PM can call an election at any time before next spring, when the five-year term of the present Parliament runs out.**
(call an election – wählen lassen / spring – Frühling / term – Legislaturperiode / run out – auslaufen)

✳ A: **What are the odds of the Libs winning the next election?**
(odds – Chancen / Libs – Liberals; the Liberal Party)
B: **If you can believe the polls, their lead has fallen to three per cent.**
(believe – glauben / poll – Meinungsumfrage / lead – Vorsprung)
A: **That's not much, considering that there's always a margin of error.**
(considering – wenn man bedenkt / margin of error – Fehlerquote)

✳ **The latest opinion poll gives the party an eight per cent lead.**
(latest – neuest / opinion poll – Meinungsumfrage)

✳ A: **What are the main issues in the forthcoming election?**
(main issue – Hauptanliegen / forthcoming – bevorstehend)
B: **Social security, the EU, the environment, crime, if not necessarily in that order.**
(environment – Umwelt / order – Reihenfolge)

✳ **It's probably inevitable in a parliamentary democracy. As usual, the candidates promised too much in the run-up to the election.**
(probable – wahrscheinlich / inevitable – unvermeidlich / promise – versprechen / run-up to the election – Vorwahlzeit)

✳ **Who do you normally vote for?**
(vote for – wählen)

* **A: Who do you think will be the next Prime Minister? Kettler?**
B: No, not Kettler! He hasn't got a chance.
A: Do you really think so?

* **I think the present government have done quite a good job, considering the difficult circumstances. So I'm going to vote for them again.**
(do a good job – es gut machen / considering – wenn man bedenkt / difficult circumstances – schwierige Umstände)

* **Personally I think it's time for a change. The present lot have been in office for too long. I'm all for giving the opposition a chance.**
(change – Wechsel, Änderung / present – jetzig / lot – Gruppe, Crew / office – Amt / all – sehr)

* **I think the number of floating voters is bound to increase.**
(Ich glaube, die Zahl der Wechselwähler wird sich zwangsläufig erhöhen.)

* **A: The votes are still being counted. The final results won't be in before the end of next week.**
(vote – Stimme / still – noch / count – zählen / won't be in – werden nicht vorliegen)
B: What do the computer projections say?
(computer projection – [Computer-]Hochrechnung)
A: According to the exit polls, the present government might manage to hang on.
(according to – laut / exit poll – Nachwahlbefragung / hang on – sich halten)

* **A: It has been a very close race all along and none of the five candidates can hope to win an absolute majority in the first round.**
(close race – knappes Rennen / all along – die ganze Zeit / none – keiner / majority – Mehrheit)
B: Does this mean there will be a run-off?
(run-off – Stichwahl)

* **At the last election the party took only 35 per cent of the vote and lost three seats. It's not expected to do much better this year.**
(vote – abgegebene Stimmen / seat – Sitz [z.B. im Parlament] / expect – erwarten / do better – besser abschneiden)

* **On the whole we have a higher turnout than most other European countries. But the percentage of people willing to go to the polls has been declining steadily.**
(on the whole – insgesamt gesehen / turnout – Wahlbeteiligung / percentage – Prozentsatz / go to the polls – wählen gehen / decline – fallen / steadily – ständig, stetig)

* A: **Do you think it was a good idea to postpone the vote?**
(postpone – verschieben / vote – Abstimmung)
B: **Well, I think the PM did not have much choice.**
(PM – Prime Minister / choice – Wahl)

* **The coalition won the referendum by a very small margin.**
(referendum – Referendum, Volksabstimmung / by a small margin – mit geringem Vorsprung)

GOVERNMENT AND DEPARTMENTS

Regierung und Ministerien

* A: **It's difficult to keep track of what the various government departments are doing.**
(keep track of – Übersicht behalten / department – Ministerium)
B: **Yes, their responsibilities are constantly being reshuffled, aren't they?**
(responsibility – Zuständigkeit / reshuffle – neu verteilen)
A: **Another way to confuse the ordinary citizen is to change their names or use abbreviations.**
(confuse – verwirren / citizen – Bürger / abbreviation – Abkürzung)

* **A: What does *Defra* stand for?**
(stand for – stehen für; bedeuten)
B: *Defra* is an abbreviation for Department for Environment, Food and Rural Affairs. It's the department responsible for the environment, the production of food and all agricultural matters.
(environment – Umwelt / food – Lebensmittel / rural – ländlich / agricultural – landwirtschaftlich)

* **A: Who is responsible for old monuments in Austria?**
B: Basically, it's the Department for Education. By the way, the secretary in charge is an ex-banker. But, in practice, the Federal Monuments Office looks after things like this.
(basically – grundsätzlich, eigentlich / education – Bildung / by the way – übrigens / secretary – Minister / be in charge – am Ruder sein; verantwortlich sein / Federal Monuments Office – Bundesdenkmalamt / look after – sich kümmern um)
A: What is the situation in Germany?
B: I'm not quite sure, but I think protecting cultural heritage is not a federal responsibility there.
(protect – schützen / heritage – Erbe)
A: Does this mean it is part of the powers reserved to the Bundesländer?
(powers – Zuständigkeit)

* **In the latest Cabinet reshuffle the Minister of Agriculture and the Minister of Education switched jobs. I'm not sure whether this makes sense.**
(cabinet reshuffle – Kabinettsumbildung / agriculture – Landwirtschaft / education –Bildung[-swesen] / switch jobs – Posten tauschen / whether – ob / make sense – sinnvoll sein)

* **The Home Secretary was forced to resign over a sex scandal.**
(home secretary – Innenminister / force – zwingen / resign – zurücktreten)

* **The Foreign Secretary offered to resign, but the Prime Minister refused to accept his resignation.**
(foreign secretary – Außenminister / offer – anbieten / refuse – sich weigern)

* **By Christmas, the President-elect had appointed most members of his Administration. It included a number of women.**
(by – [bis] zu / president-elect – der gewählte [aber noch nicht in sein Amt eingesetzte] Präsident; Präsidentschaftsanwärter / appoint – ernennen / administration – Regierung, Kabinett)

* **The Liberals have staked out a claim for the Economics Ministry.**
(stake out a claim for – Anspruch anmelden auf / economics ministry – Wirtschaftsministerium)

* A: **The present Prime Minister has been in office for over eight years now.**
(be in office – im Amt sein)
B: **Yes, and I personally feel that it's time for him to step down and give younger people a chance.**
(feel – der Meinung sein / step down – abtreten, zurücktreten)

* **As far as I know, their president was removed in a coup d'état.**
(remove – beseitigen / coup d'état – Staatsstreich)

CIVIL SOCIETY AND NON-GOVERNMENTAL ORGANISATIONS

Zivilgesellschaft und Nichtregierungsorganisationen

* A: **It's interesting to see how important NGOs have become in recent years.**
(in recent years – in den letzten Jahren)
B: **Yes, it's difficult to imagine the world without them. There is hardly a day when they are not at least mentioned in the media.**
(imagine sthg. – sich etwas vorstellen / hardly – kaum / at least – zumindest / mention – erwähnen)

* **A: I have read somewhere that they prefer to be called *civil society organisations* now.**
(prefer – es vorziehen)
B: Not a bad idea! *Non-governmental* does not sound very constructive, does it? Moreover, it is a misnomer. After all, Shell and BP are "non-governmental" too in their own way, aren't they?
(sound – klingen / does it? – oder? / moreover – außerdem / misnomer – Fehlbezeichnung / after all – schließlich / in their own way – auf ihre Art / aren't they? – nicht wahr?)

* **A: NGOs are no longer what they used to be. Just compare Greenpeace 20 years ago and now.**
(what they used to be – was sie früher einmal waren / compare – vergleichen)
B: Yes, instead of chaining themselves to factory gates and climbing up smokestacks, they have started hobnobbing with Shell executives.
(chain – anketten / factory gate – Fabrikstor / smokestack – Fabriksschlot / hobnob – freundschaftlich verkehren / executive – Führungskraft)

FOREIGN POLICY
Außenpolitik

* **Who is in charge of foreign policy in your country at the moment?**
(be in charge of – Verantwortung haben für)

* **Yes, Austria's foreign policy has changed since Kreisky stepped down in 1986. The changes did not amount to a U-turn, but they were quite marked.**
(step down – abtreten / amount to – sich belaufen auf / U-turn – komplette Kehrtwende; Schwenk um 180 Grad / quite marked – ziemlich deutlich)

* **Is it true that one of your ministers resigned in protest over your government's policy on the war in Bosnia?**

* A: **Does your country participate in international peace-keeping and peace-making missions?**
(peace-keeping – friedenserhaltend / peace-making – friedensstiftend)
B: **Yes, it does. But it's a controversial issue. How do you square sending soldiers abroad with being a neutral country? After all, the concept of our "ever-lasting neutrality" is part of our constitution.**
(issue – Problem / square – in Einklang bringen / abroad – ins Ausland / ever-lasting – immer während / constitution – Verfassung)

* A: **There still seems to be a strong pacifist element in German politics.**
B: **You are right! But that's not really surprising if you consider our role in World War II.**
(surprising – überraschend / consider – bedenken)

WAR AND PEACE
Krieg und Frieden

* **Of course CNN was there when the war broke out and fighting started in earnest.**
(of course – natürlich / break out – ausbrechen / fighting – Kampfhandlungen)

* **Would you believe it? The hostilities commenced without either country having declared war on the other.**
(believe – glauben / hostilities – Feindseligkeiten, Kampfhandlungen / commence – beginnen / either country – eines der beiden Länder / declare – erklären)

* **I don't think it was a good idea to break off the peace talks.**
(peace talks – Friedensgespräche)

* **I have a feeling that we can no longer avoid military intervention.**
(avoid – vermeiden)

* **A: It is amazing how quickly the joint forces crushed the enemy.**
(amazing – erstaunlich / joint forces – vereinigte Streitkräfte / crush – zermalmen / enemy – Feind)
B: Yes, the invasion was beaten back in three weeks. Incredible, isn't it?
(beat back – zurückschlagen / incredible – unglaublich / isn't it? – oder?)

* **A: Are the two countries still at war?**
(Sind die zwei Länder noch immer im Kriegszustand?)
B: I don't think they ever signed a peace treaty, although hostilities stopped years ago.
(sign – unterzeichnen / peace treaty – Friedensvertrag / although – obwohl)

* **A: Terrible what's happening in Sudan, isn't it?**
(terrible – schrecklich / happen – passieren, geschehen)
B: Yes, and nobody seems to be able to do much to stop the fighting there.
(seem – scheinen)

* **Since the outbreak of the war more than 100,000 people have been killed.**
(kill – töten)

* **I don't know how many ceasefires have been agreed and broken. I've simply lost count.**
(ceasefire – Waffenstillstand / agree – vereinbaren / simple – einfach / lose count – Überblick verlieren)

* **What could be done, though, is knock out artillery positions and air bases from the air.**
(though – aber / knock out – ausschalten / air base – Luftwaffenstützpunkt)

* **A: The naval blockade does not seem to be very effective.**
(naval blockade – Seeblockade)
B: Not surprising really, considering that the target is basically a land-locked country.
(surprising – überraschend / considering – wenn man bedenkt / target – Blockadeziel / basically – im Grunde / land-locked country – Binnenland)

* **It's not just the war and the fact that soldiers are being killed. Even more shocking are the atrocities to which the civilian population and especially children are subjected.**
(even – noch / atrocity – Gräueltat / population – Bevölkerung / be subjected to – ausgesetzt sein)

* **Don't you agree that it was a bit naive to declare the country a no-fly zone without deciding what to do if the ban on military flights was violated?**
(agree – zustimmen / no-fly zone – Flugverbotszone / decide – beschließen / ban – Verbot / violate – verletzen, übertreten)

* **Everybody thought that the end of the cold war would mean the end of war in general. How wrong we were!**
(be wrong – unrecht haben; sich irren)

MILITARY SERVICE
Militärdienst

* **Unlike you, we don't have a professional army. Our defence system is based on general conscription.**
(unlike – im Gegensatz zu / defence – Verteidigung / general conscription – allgemeine Wehrpflicht)

* **Yes, basically all young men have to do a stint in the army. It's six months at the moment and a bit longer in Germany. Personally I was lucky, I didn't have to do military service.**
(basically – im Prinzip / do stint – Zeit abdienen / be lucky – Glück haben)

* **There is an alternative for conscientious objectors though. They may do community service in hospitals and so on instead.**
(conscientious objector – Wehrdienstverweigerer aus Gewissensgründen / though – jedoch / community service – Zivildienst / hospital – Krankenhaus / instead – stattdessen)

INTERNATIONAL NEGOTIATIONS, AGREEMENTS AND INSTITUTIONS

Internationale Verhandlungen, Abkommen und Institutionen

* **The foreign ministers are expected to meet in July to deal with the problem. The talks will be held in Geneva, I think.**
(foreign minister – Außenminister / expect – erwarten / meet – sich treffen / deal with – sich befassen mit / talk – Gespräch)

* **The moment he was in the chair he called a summit of all heads of government.**
(Sobald er den Vorsitz übernommen hatte, berief er ein Gipfeltreffen aller Regierungschefs ein.)

* **There is a distinct danger that the trade talks might fail; and that won't be good for the economy. Nor will it be good for my company.**
(distinct – eindeutig / danger – Gefahr / trade – Handel / fail – scheitern / won't – will not / economy – Wirtschaft / nor – auch nicht / company – Firma, Gesellschaft)

* **I hope that a compromise can be reached in the forthcoming negotiations. Otherwise there is a danger that the conflict will escalate.**
(forthcoming – bevorstehend / negotiation – Verhandlung / otherwise – sonst / escalate – eskalieren; sich aufschaukeln)

* **When their key negotiator demanded further concessions, our team decided to walk out.**
(key negotiator – Chefverhandler, Delegationsleiter / demand – verlangen / further – weiter / decide – sich entschließen / walk out – Sitzung verlassen)

* **The deal should not be struck at the expense of the weakest members. That would be really unfair.**
(deal – Abmachung / strike – treffen, vereinbaren / at the expense of – auf Kosten von / weak – schwach / member – Mitglied)

* **A number of countries seem to be dragging their heels in the peace talks.**
(number – Anzahl, Reihe / drag heels – Verschleppungstaktik anwenden / peace – Frieden)

* **There is not much time left to reach an agreement.**
(left – übrig)

* **It was another one of those pointless summits. Everybody talked a lot but avoided hard decisions.**
(pointless – sinnlos / avoid – vermeiden / decision – Entscheidung)

* **It won't be easy to find a solution to the problem in the round of talks scheduled for next month.**
(solution to – Lösung für / schedule – [terminlich] planen)

* **I think it's time that our negotiators called the Americans' bluff.**
(call sbdy.'s bluff – jemanden zwingen, die Karten auf den Tisch zu legen)

* **He came to Washington in the middle of a domestic crisis to sign the first bilateral treaty between the two countries.**
(domestic crisis – Krise im Inland / sign – unterzeichnen / treaty – [internationaler] Vertrag)

* A: **I think the ministers initialled the agreement last week.**
(initial – paraphieren)
B: **That's right. But don't forget that it has to be ratified by parliament and that the outcome is by no means certain.**
(outcome – Ergebnis / by no means – keinesfalls / certain – sicher)

* **The meeting of the ministers of agriculture was adjourned. They said they needed further consultation with their respective governments.**
(agriculture – Landwirtschaft / adjourn – vertagen / further – weiter / respective – jeweilig)

* A: **I am wholeheartedly for the UN taking on a bigger role.**
(wholeheartedly – ohne Vorbehalte / UN – United Nations / take on – übernehmen)
B: **Well, I can't see the UN becoming a "world cop".**
(cop – Polizist)

* A: **The UN is slowly but steadily nibbling away at the principle of national sovereignty, and I'm not sure whether this is a good thing.**
(slowly but steadily – langsam aber sicher / nibble away at – anknabbern / whether – ob)
B: **Well, I don't agree. I think that the UN should intervene more often and more forcefully.**
(agree – zustimmen / forceful – energisch)

* A: **The members of the WTO are preparing for another Ministerial Meeting as part of the Doha Round.**
(WTO – World Trade Organization | Welthandelsorganisation / prepare – sich vorbereiten)
B: **Good luck to them! They did not achieve much at the previous ones.**
(luck – Glück / achieve – erreichen / previous – vorherig)

EUROPEAN UNION

Europäische Union

* **One of the main motives for a united Europe was to end the frequent and bloody wars between neighbours.**
  (main – Haupt- / united – vereinigt / frequent – häufig)

* **At the time, the pros and cons of Austria joining the EU were hotly debated, with the two main parties in favour and the small opposition parties highlighting the potential disadvantages.**
  (at the time – zum damaligen Zeitpunkt / pros and cons – das Für und Wider / join – beitreten / in favour – dafür / highlight – herausstreichen / disadvantage – Nachteil)

* **There was a referendum on the issue, just as there was in your country, wasn't there?**
  (referendum – Volksabstimmung / issue – Problem, Frage / just as – genauso wie / wasn't there? – oder?)

* A: **Many leaders in the EU are keen on close political union. But they may have been moving too fast for the average citizen.**
  (keen on – erpicht auf / close – eng / move – vorgehen / fast – schnell / average – durchschnittlich / citizen – Bürger)
  B: **Yes, there is widespread skepticism among people. After all, full political union would involve a loss of sovereignty.**
  (widespread – weit verbreitet / after all – schließlich / involve – mit sich bringen / loss – Verlust)

* **It's understandable that people are wary of too much centralization. They don't want to give too much power to faceless bureaucrats in Brussels.**
  (wary of – misstrauisch gegenüber / power – Macht / faceless – gesichtslos)

* **A: Correct me if I'm wrong, but disillusion with the EU seems to be growing.**
(be wrong – Unrecht haben; falsch liegen / seem – scheinen / grow – wachsen)
B: No, you are absolutely right. One contributing factor is that the EU meddles in relatively unimportant affairs, but leaves the really big issues unregulated.
(contribute – beitragen / meddle – sich einmischen / leave – lassen / issue – Sache, Problem)
A: You mean such things as atomic energy and external affairs?
(affair – Angelegenheit)

* **If recent polls are to be believed, around 25 per cent of Austrians are in favour of exiting the EU.**
(poll – Umfrage / believe – glauben / exit – austreten)

* **A: There seem to be many people that feel uneasy about the recent enlargement of the EU.**
(uneasy – unbehaglich / recent – jüngst / enlargement – Erweiterung)
B: Yes, and I think most are against letting Turkey in.

* **A: According to the latest statistics, the number of people skeptical of the whole EU-project has been increasing.**
(according to – nach, laut / increase – steigen, zunehmen)
B: Beats me! Just look at the economic benefits that membership has brought.
(beats me – kann ich nicht verstehen / benefit – Vorteil / membership – Mitgliedschaft)

* **A: Suddenly "subsidiarity" is all the rage. Ten years ago, the word did not even exist in English.**
(suddenly – plötzlich / subsidiarity – Subsidiarität / be all the rage – in aller Munde sein / not even – nicht einmal)
B: What exactly does it mean anyway?
(mean – bedeuten / anyway – eigentlich)
A: Well, the main idea is that decisions should be taken as close to the people as possible.
(decision – Entscheidung / close to – nahe an)

* **I think that the role of the European Parliament should be strengthened. That would defuse a lot of issues.**
(strengthen – stärken / defuse – entschärfen / a lot of – viele / issue – Problem, Sachfrage)

* **A: What about Austria's neutrality and membership of the EU?**
B: Yes, that's still an important issue. You must not forget that originally most Austrians regarded giving up political and economic sovereignty as incompatible with neutrality.
(still – noch immer / issue – Problem, Frage / must not – nicht dürfen / regard – ansehen / incompatible – unvereinbar)

* **I can understand that some people are worried about a more powerful Germany. After all, it has become bigger as a result of reunification and usually has close ties with France.**
(worried – besorgt / powerful – mächtig / reunification – Wiedervereinigung / close ties – enge Bindung)

* **Another important issue is transit. Our geographical position means that a lot of trade between Italy and the northern members of the EU passes through Austria.**
(trade – Handel / member – Mitglied / pass through – gehen über)

TERRORISM

Terrorismus

* **A: International terrorism has become a major problem in recent years.**
(major – wichtig, Haupt- / in recent years – in den letzten Jahren)
B: Yes, and people are wondering why. Some blame fundamentalist muslims. Others point to the gap between rich and poor nations. Not a few see America's international arrogance as a major factor.
(wonder – sich fragen / blame – beschuldigen / point to – hinweisen auf / gap – Lücke, Abstand / not a few – nicht wenige; viele)
A: Yes, I know, probably it's a mixture of all these things.

∗ **A: A group of terrorists have threatened to kill all hostages if our government does not fulfil their demands.**
(threaten – drohen / hostage – Geisel / demand – Forderung)
B: I think we should stand up to this kind of blackmail. Don't you agree?
(stand up to – die Stirn bieten / blackmail – Erpressung / agree – zustimmen)
A: Well, whatever government does, it's a dreadful dilemma. Would you like to be responsible for the death of a group of your own countrymen?
(dreadful – schrecklich / responsible – verantwortlich / death – Tod / countrymen – Landsleute)

∗ **The newspaper says that this time the kidnappers have not demanded the release of prisoners. Instead they have asked for a high ransom.**
(this time – dieses Mal / demand – fordern / release – Freilassung / ransom – Lösegeld)

∗ **A: Isn't it terrible? A fundamentalist group has kidnapped another businessman in Pakistan.**
(terrible – schrecklich)
B: Buh! I hope my company won't send me there.
(company – Firma, Gesellschaft / won't – will not)

∗ **A: The chances of becoming a victim of international terrorism are still very slim.**
(victim – Opfer / still – noch immer / slim – gering)
B: Yes, I agree up to a point. But it was right to tighten security measures, especially at airports.
(tighten – verschärfen / security measures – Sicherheitsvorkehrungen / airport – Flughafen)
A: But some governments have definitely gone too far since September 11. The fight against terrorism is undermining basic civil liberties.
(civil liberties – Bürgerrechte)

* **A: Is it really true that Britain has the world's biggest network of surveillance cameras?**
  (surveillance – Überwachung)
  B: Unfortunately, yes. Big Brother is watching us. And our record of protecting privacy in other areas is not much to write home about either.
  (unfortunately – leider / record – Bilanz / protect – schützen / not much to write home about – nichts, worauf wir stolz sein können)

* **Luckily the bomb on the train was discovered in time and defused by a team of experts.**
  (luckily – glücklicherweise / discover – entdecken / in time – rechtzeitig / defuse – entschärfen)

* **I had a close shave. A terrorist group blew up the train I was supposed to be travelling on.**
  (have a close shave – knapp davonkommen / blow up – in die Luft jagen / train – Zug / be supposed to – sollen)

* **I would give the country a wide berth. There is always the chance of a terrorist attack.**
  (give sthg. a wide berth – um etwas einen weiten Bogen machen / attack – Überfall)

* **Suicide bombers are the greatest problem. If somebody doesn't mind being killed, how can you stop him, or her for that matter?**
  (suicide bomber – Selbstmordattentäter / mind – ausmachen / for that matter – in diesem Zusammenhang auch)

REFUGEES AND IMMIGRATION

Flüchtlinge und Zuwanderung

* A: **All European countries are tightening their immigration laws and procedures, mostly to check the inflow of people from the former Eastern-bloc countries.**
  (tighten – verschärfen / law – Gesetz / procedure – Verfahren, Vorgangsweise / mostly – größtenteils / check – bremsen, verlangsamen / former – ehemalig)
  B: **Yes, isn't it ironic that the countries that hailed the lifting of the Iron Curtain are busy replacing it with administrative barriers?**
  (hail – begrüßen / lift – aufheben / Iron Curtain – Eiserner Vorhang / be busy – eifrig dabei sein / replace – ersetzen / barrier – Schranke, Hindernis)

* **It is often very difficult to distinguish between political and economic refugees.**
  (distinguish – unterscheiden / refugee – Flüchtling)

* **I don't think you should be so critical of the way we are handling the refugee problem in Germany. What would you do if 60,000 people knocked on your door every month?**
  (way – Art und Weise / handle – umgehen mit / knock – klopfen / door – Tür)

* **Don't forget that we have probably the world's most liberal asylum law.**
  (probably – wahrscheinlich)

* **We'll have to sort out the wider immigration issues. Should we have quotas like the Americans, let in only skilled workers, or take pity on the poor? I don't know myself, but we certainly cannot continue as if nothing had happened.**
  (sort out – lösen, regeln / issue – Frage, Problem / quota – Kontingent; mengenmäßige Beschränkung / skilled worker – Facharbeiter / take pity on – Mitleid haben mit / certainly – sicherlich)

* **Government and opposition are trying to find a compromise. This will probably involve limiting the constitutional right of asylum.**
(involve – beinhalten / limit – beschränken / constitutional – verfassungsmäßig)

* **People don't seem to realise how much foreign workers contribute to our gross national product.**
(realise – verstehen, einsehen / foreign worker – Fremdarbeiter / contribute – beitragen / gross national product – Bruttosozialprodukt)

* **The irony is that we'll need immigrants if we want to maintain economic growth and to finance our old-age pensions.**
(irony – Witz / need – brauchen / maintain – aufrechterhalten / economic growth – Wirtschaftswachstum)

* **The region has a low birth rate and is short of children. Its lab our force will soon start to shrink, if it is not supplemented by immigration.**
(region – geographische Großregion / birth rate – Geburtenrate / be short of sthg. – von etwas zu wenig haben / labour force – [etwa] Erwerbsbevölkerung / shrink – schrumpfen / supplement – aufstocken, ergänzen)

* **What annoys a lot of people is that the other countries are reluctant even to talk about sharing the burden created by the influx of refugees.**
(annoy – ärgern / a lot of – viele / be reluctant – sich weigern / even – sogar / share burden – Last aufteilen / influx – Zustrom)

NATIONALISM / XENOPHOBIA / ISOLATIONISM

Nationalismus / Fremdenhass / Isolationismus

* **The extremist violence and the revival of Naziism have shocked many people. Are they really just the result of an uncontrolled influx of refugees and asylum-seekers?**
(violence – Gewalttätigkeit / revival – Wiederaufleben / asylum-seeker – Asylwerber)

* **There seems to be a consensus that government has waited too long before speaking out. It should have cracked down on extreme right-wing organisations much earlier.**
(consensus – übereinstimmende Meinung / speak out – Stimme erheben / crack down on – scharf vorgehen gegen; durchgreifen bei / right-wing – rechtsgerichtet)

* **But there are also positive signs. For instance, the national students' union organised a week of protests against anti-foreigner sentiment and tighter immigration laws. A number of companies have issued statements against racial violence.**
(sign – Zeichen / for instance – zum Beispiel / students' union – Hochschülerschaft / sentiment – Stimmung / tight – scharf, rigoros / issue – abgeben / statement – Erklärung / racial violence – rassistisch motivierte Gewalttätigkeit)

* **A: The surge in nationalism in the territory of the former Soviet Union is frightening, isn't it?**
(surge – Aufflackern, Woge / former – ehemalig / frightening – furchterregend, beängstigend / isn't it? – nicht wahr?)
B: Yes, it's amazing how quickly the old animosities surfaced when the lid screwed on by the Communists came off.
(amazing – erstaunlich / animosity – Feindseligkeit / surface – auftauchen / lid – Deckel / screw on – festschrauben / come off – entfernt werden)

* **One unpleasant side-effect of the refugee problem is that it is working into the hands of right-wing groupings.**
(unpleasant – unangenehm / side-effect – Nebenwirkung / refugee – Flüchtling / right-wing – dem rechten Flügel zuzurechnen; rechtsgerichtet)

* **A: Is there really a danger that the country will become more isolationist under the new prime minister?**
B: I don't think so, if the names of his shadow cabinet are anything to go by.
(… , wenn die Namen in seinem Schattenkabinett auch nur ein einigermaßen verlässlicher Indikator dafür sind.)

PERSONAL ATTITUDES
Persönliche Einstellung

* **I'm not interested in politics. Wouldn't dream of joining a political party.**
(dream – im Traume daran denken / join – beitreten)

* **Well, I find politics very exciting. I might even put my name down as a candidate for the next election.**
(exciting – aufregend / even – sogar / put name down as candidate – sich als Kandidat aufstellen lassen / election – Wahl)

* **All politicians try to con the public, and it is a shame that they get away with it most of the time.**
(con – hineinlegen / public – die Öffentlichkeit / shame – Schande / get away with sthg. – etwas ungestraft tun)

* **If you ask me, politics is a dirty business and most politicians are crooks.**
(dirty – schmutzig / business – Geschäft / crook – Gauner)

* **A: There always seems to be some scandal or other brewing: it's somebody bribing government officials, or diverting funds to numbered accounts in Switzerland, or turning a blind eye to illegal arms exports, or just plainly lying to the public.**
(brew – am Kochen sein / bribe – bestechen / government official – Regierungsbeamter / divert funds – Gelder abzweigen / numbered account – Nummernkonto / turn a blind eye to – geflissentlich übersehen / arms – Waffen / plain – einfach / lie to – belügen)
B: Yes, you're right. And once the facts have been leaked to the press there is the usual cover-up by the politicians involved. Nobody has noticed anything. Everything is denied.
(once – wenn einmal / leak to the press – der Presse zuspielen / cover-up – Verschleierungsaktion / involved – involviert / notice – bemerken / deny – dementieren, leugnen)

* **Little wonder that a lot of people are fed up with politics.**
(little wonder – kein Wunder / be fed up with sthg. – von etwas genug haben)

* **Politics at the local level is different. There is closer contact between those governing and the governed.**
(level – Ebene / close – eng / govern – regieren)

* **It's a fact proven by dozens of opinion polls. Politicians are held in low esteem by most people. They just don't trust them anymore.**
(prove – beweisen / dozen – Dutzend / opinion poll – Meinungsumfrage / hold in low esteem – geringschätzen / trust – vertrauen)

* **It's easy to grumble about politicians, but somebody's got to do their job.**
(grumble – meckern)

* **In my line you need to maintain close contacts with politicians. No, no, this does not mean you have to bribe them. But it's good to be on friendly terms with the key people in the administration. It's called lobbying.**
(line – Branche, Sparte / need – müssen / maintain – pflegen / close – eng / be on friendly terms with – gut auskommen mit / key people – die wichtigen Leute / administration – Regierung)

* **No, we don't have a professional lobbyist in Brussels, but our CEO goes there twice a year to discuss things with a top-level official.**
(CEO – Chief Executive Officer | Generaldirektor, Vorstandsvorsitzender / twice – zweimal / top-level – hochrangig)

POLITICAL PAST
Politische Vergangenheit

* **No, you are wrong there. Austria and Germany were not just allies in World War II. As a matter of fact, Austria was part of the Third Reich. Hitler annexed it in 1938.**
(ally – Verbündeter / annex – annektieren)

* **The post-war period was very tough. I still remember when we had food-rationing and not enough to eat.**
(post-war period – Nachkriegszeit / tough – hart / still – noch / remember – sich erinnern / food – Lebensmittel)

* **Yes, you're right. Austria was divided into four "Zones". The British Zone, for instance, covered Carinthia and parts of Styria in the south of Austria.**
(divide – teilen / for instance – zum Beispiel / cover – umfassen)

* **A: Do you remember the signing of the State Treaty?**
(sign – unterzeichnen / State Treaty – Staatsvertrag)
B: Not really. I was too young then.

* **The most dramatic events in our recent history were certainly the Third Reich, the Holocaust, the erection of the Berlin Wall and finally, on the positive side, the reunification of the two parts of Germany.**
(event – Ereignis / recent history – jüngere Geschichte / certainly – sicherlich / erection – Errichtung / reunification – Wiedervereinigung)

* **I'm not sure whether we have really come to terms with our recent political past.**
(whether – ob / come to terms with – zu Rande kommen mit; bewältigen / recent – jüngst / past – Vergangenheit)

* **Of course we have some skeletons in our cupboard. For instance, the way we treated Jewish people in the 1930s and during World War II is nothing to write home about.**
(skeleton in cupboard – unbewältigtes Vergangenheitsproblem; Leiche im Keller / way – Art und Weise / treat – behandeln / Jewish – jüdisch / nothing to write home about – kein Ruhmesblatt)

* **It's true, quite a few Austrians welcomed Hitler when he occupied our country in 1938.**
(quite a few – ziemlich viele / occupy – besetzen)

* **In spite of this we always pretended that we were just victims of Hitler's aggression and conveniently forgot that he was an Austrian.**
(in spite of – trotz / pretend – vorgeben / victim – Opfer / conveniently – bequemerweise)

* **The Germans seem to have been a bit more honest in this respect. After all it was they that coined the term "Trauerarbeit". It means the painful process of coming to terms with the negative aspects of one's past.**
(seem – scheinen / honest – ehrlich / respect – Hinsicht / after all – schließlich / coin – prägen / term – Ausdruck / painful – schmerzlich)

HEALTH

Befinden und Gesundheit

GENERAL; MINOR ILLNESSES

Allgemeines Befinden; kleinere Wehwehchen

* A: **How are you?**
(Wie geht es Ihnen?)
B: **I'm fine, thanks.**
(Mir geht es gut, danke.)

* **Very well, thanks.**
(Sehr gut, danke.)

* **I'm on top of the world.**
(Mir geht es ausgezeichnet. Ich könnte Bäume ausreißen.)

* A: **Hi, how are you feeling today?**
B: **I feel a bit under the weather.**
(Ich fühl' mich nicht ganz auf der Höhe.)

* A: **You don't look yourself, is anything the matter?**
(Du siehst heute aber gar nicht gut aus, … ?)
B: **As a matter of fact, I've got a splitting headache.**
(splitting headache – rasende | stechende Kopfschmerzen)

* A: **How are things?**
(Wie geht's?)
B: **I'm feeling completely run down.**
(Ich fühl' mich völlig ausgebrannt.)

* **I'm under so much stress at work, I feel pretty lousy.**
(pretty lousy – ziemlich elend)

* **A: What's the matter, Barbara?**
(Was ist los mit dir, … ?)
B: I'm not feeling very well to be honest.
(Ich fühl' mich nicht sehr wohl, um ehrlich zu sein.)

* **I'm feeling stressed.**

* **A: I'm not feeling myself at all. Do you mind if I call it a day?**
(Ich bin gesundheitlich überhaupt nicht auf der Höhe. Macht es Ihnen etwas aus, wenn ich für heute Schluss mache?)
B: Not at all, you go and get a rest.
(not at all – überhaupt nicht)

* **I think I've got a bad cold coming on.**
(Ich glaube, bei mir ist eine starke Verkühlung im Anzug.)

* **I've got a temperature. I think I must be going down with the flu.**
(Ich habe Fieber. Ich glaube, ich habe die Grippe erwischt.)

* **I'm aching all over. I think I must have caught the flu.**
(Mir tut alles weh. Ich glaube, mich hat die Grippe erwischt.)

* **I've got a cough.**
(cough – Husten)

* **A: What's the trouble?**
(Was fehlt Ihnen?)
B: My back is playing me up again. It aches terribly.
(Mein Rücken fängt schon wieder an. Er tut fürchterlich weh.)

* **I'm suffering from hay fever.**
(Ich leide an Heuschnupfen.)

* **My eyes are inflamed.**
(inflamed – entzündet)

* **I'm allergic to pollen – my eyes and throat are very itchy.**
(Ich bin allergisch gegen Blütenstaub – meine Augen und mein Hals jucken sehr.)

* **My feet are killing me.**
(kill – umbringen)

* **I'm fit to drop.**
(Ich krieche bereits auf dem Zahnfleisch daher.)

* **A: I'm absolutely exhausted.**
(Ich bin völlig erschöpft.)
B: You need to put your feet up for a while.
(Sie müssen sich eine Weile ausrasten.)

* **A: What's up, Bill?**
(Was hast du denn, … ?)
B: Oh nothing much, I've just got pins and needles in my leg.
(… , mir ist nur mein Fuß eingeschlafen.)

* **I'm feeling rather faint.**
(Ich fühle mich ziemlich schwach | matt.)

* **I feel dizzy.**
(dizzy – schwindlig)

* **I've got a sore throat.**
(Ich habe Halsschmerzen.)

* **I've got terrible toothache.**

* **I think I must have picked up that virus that's going round.**
(pick up virus – Virus erwischen)

* **A: I'm having trouble sleeping. I think I'll have to get some sleeping tablets.**
(Ich schlafe zur Zeit schlecht. Ich glaube, ich muss mir irgendwelche Schlaftabletten besorgen.)
B: Why don't you try an alternative remedy. Drink a cup of hot milk with some honey in it.
(remedy – Mittel)

* **I had terrible indigestion all night and I couldn't sleep a wink.**
(Ich hatte die ganze Nacht fürchterliche Verdauungsstörungen und konnte kein Auge zutun.)

* **I've got an upset stomach – that Chinese food didn't agree with me at all.**
(Ich habe mir den Magen verdorben – dieses chinesische Essen ist mir überhaupt nicht bekommen.)

* **I feel sick.**
(Mir ist schlecht.)

* **I've just been sick. I think I'd better go home.**
(Ich habe gerade erbrochen. Ich glaube, ich sollte lieber nach Hause gehen.)

* **I've hurt my leg.**
(hurt – verletzen)

* **I've got stitch.**
(Ich habe Seitenstechen.)

* **My eyes are hurting.**
(Meine Augen tun mir weh.)

* **I've lost my appetite.**
(Ich habe keinen Appetit.)

AT THE CHEMIST'S

In der Apotheke

* **Could you help me, please? I'm trying to find my way to the nearest chemist's.**
(chemist's – Apotheke)

* **Have you got something for a sunburn, please?**
(something for – etwas gegen; ein Mittel gegen / sunburn – Sonnenbrand)

* **Can you give me something for a common cold, please?**
(common cold – Erkältung, Schnupfen)

* **Have you got anything for indigestion?**
(Haben Sie irgend etwas gegen Verdauungsstörungen?)

* **What have you got for headaches?**

* **Do you have anything for the flu?**

* **I'd like something for insect bites, please.**
(insect bite – Insektenstich)

* **Could you recommend something for diarrhoea?**
(recommend – empfehlen / diarrhoea – Durchfall)

* **Could you give me some headache pills, please?**

* **I'd like some pain-killers, please.**
(pain-killer – schmerzstillende Tablette)

* **Do you have homoeopathic medicines here?**
(homoeopathic medicines – homöopathische Mittel)

* **A: What could you give me for a sore throat?**
  B: Here, suck one of these lozenges after each meal.
  (suck – lutschen / lozenge – Lutschtablette)

* **I need some laxatives, please.**
  (laxative – Abführmittel)

* **I've been stung. Do you have any ointment for wasp stings?**
  (Mich hat eine Wespe gestochen, haben Sie irgendeine Salbe dagegen?)

* **Do I need a prescription for the medicine?**
  (prescription – Rezept)

* **When can I pick it up, please?**
  (pick up – abholen)

* **A: How many times a day do I have to take these tablets?**
  (how many times – wie oft)
  B: Take two three times a day and dissolve them in water.
  (dissolve – auflösen)

AT THE DOCTOR'S

Beim Arzt

* **A: I would like to make an appointment, please.**
  (make appointment – Termin vereinbaren)
  B: Would this afternoon suit you?
  (suit – passen)
  A: Yes, that would be fine, thank you.

* **I've got acute pains in my chest.**
  (Ich habe akute Schmerzen in meiner Brust.)

* **I've got earache.**
  (Ich habe Ohrenschmerzen.)

* **I've got an irritating cough.**
(Ich habe einen Reizhusten.)

* **I'm suffering from catarrh.**

* **I'm having difficulty breathing.**
(Ich habe Atembeschwerden.)

* **My glands are swollen.**
(Meine Drüsen sind geschwollen.)

* **I've had this rash all over my body for two days now.**
(Ich habe diesen Hautausschlag am ganzen Körper nun schon seit zwei Tagen.)

* **It hurts when I breathe in deeply.**

* **Would you please examine my throat?**
(examine – ansehen)

* **Should I get undressed?**
(Soll ich mich ausziehen?)

* A: **Are you being treated at home?**
(treat – behandeln)
B: **No, I've never had any treatment for it.**

* **Do you think it's anything serious?**
(anything serious – etwas Ernstes)

AT THE DENTIST'S

Beim Zahnarzt

* **I've had terrible toothache for the past three days.**
  (Ich habe schon seit drei Tagen fürchterliche Zahnschmerzen.)

* **It hurts here.**

* **This filling fell out during a meal.**
  (filling – Füllung, Plombe)

* **My crown broke off while I was eating.**
  (crown – Krone / break off – ausbrechen)

* **Will I have to pay for the treatment?**

* **Could you just do a temporary job?**
  (do a temporary job – den Zahn provisorisch behandeln)

* **Before you fill it, could I have an injection, please?**
  (fill – plombieren)

* **May I rinse my mouth out now?**
  (rinse out – ausspülen)

* **A: I'll have to extract it.**
  (extract – ziehen)
  B: Does it really have to come out?

* **How long should I go without eating?**
  (Wie lange darf ich nichts essen?)

* **Do you want to see me again?**
  (Muss ich nochmals kommen?)

EMERGENCIES

Notfälle

LOST PROPERTY

Verlust von Sachen

* A: **Excuse me, I wonder if you could help me. I've lost my wallet.**
(… , vielleicht können Sie mir helfen. Ich habe meine Brieftasche verloren.)
B: **You'll have to inquire at the lost-property office.**
(Sie müssen sich im Fundbüro erkundigen.)

* **I've lost my passport, can you tell me what to do about it?**

* **Have any car keys been handed in by any chance?**
(Sind zufällig irgendwelche Autoschlüssel abgegeben worden?)

* **All my personal effects have been stolen. Could you call the Austrian Embassy, please?**
(personal effects – persönliche Habe / embassy – Botschaft)

* A: **I seem to have mislaid my passport. What can I do?**
(seem – scheinen / mislay – verlegen)
B: **You'll have to report it to the Austrian Consulate.**
(report – melden)

* **I'll need a receipt for my insurance company.**
(receipt – Bestätigung / insurance company – Versicherung, Versicherungsgesellschaft)

* **I'd like to inform you that my credit cards have gone missing.**
(go missing – verlorengehen)

IN HOSPITAL

Im Krankenhaus

* **Nurse, would you get in touch with my family, please. Here's my phone number.**
  (Schwester, verständigen Sie bitte meine Familie. … .)

* **Could you please inform my boss that I'm in hospital.**

* **I'm allergic to plaster and penicillin.**
  (plaster – Gips)

* **Does it have to be X-rayed?**
  (X-ray – röntgen)

* **Do you think a local anaesthetic is sufficient?**
  (Glauben Sie, dass eine örtliche Betäubung ausreicht?)

* **How long will I have to stay here?**
  (stay – bleiben)

* **I'll need a certificate confirming how long I stayed in hospital together with a complete diagnosis.**
  (certificate – Bescheinigung / confirm – bestätigen)

ACCIDENTS

Unfälle

* **Please get a doctor quickly!**
  (get – holen)

* **Where is the nearest hospital?**

* **Can you give the kiss of life?**
  (kiss of life – Mund-zu-Mund-Beatmung)

* **Do you have a first-aid kit?**
  (Haben Sie einen Erste-Hilfe-Koffer?)

* **Call an ambulance!**
  (ambulance – Krankenwagen)

* **We need some bandages.**
  (bandages – Verbandszeug)

CAR ACCIDENTS
Autounfälle

* **Is anybody hurt?**
  (Ist irgend jemand verletzt?)

* **Where's the damage?**
  (damage – Schaden)

* A: **Is there any serious damage?**
  (serious – ernst)
  B: **No, it seems to be only slightly damaged.**
  (Nein, es scheint nur leicht beschädigt zu sein.)

* **You've dented the wing.**
  (dent – verbeulen / wing – Kotflügel)

* **It's a write-off.**
  (write-off – Wrack)

* **You went through a red light.**

* **You were driving too fast! You were doing 50 in a 30 miles-per-hour limit.**
(limit – Geschwindigkeitsbeschränkung)

* **It was your fault. You didn't observe the right of way.**
(Es war Ihre Schuld. Sie haben den Vorrang nicht beachtet.)

* **It was my right of way.**
(Ich hatte Vorrang.)

* **Could I see your driving-licence?**
(driving-licence – Führerschein)

* **I need particulars of your insurance.**
(particulars – Einzelheiten)

* **We'll have to call the police so that I can claim on my insurance.**
(claim on insurance – einen Anspruch bei einer Versicherung geltend machen)

* **Would you act as a witness, please?**
(witness – Zeuge)

TIME

Zeit und Zeitangaben

APPOINTMENTS

Terminvereinbarungen und Verabredungen

* **A: Hello. Can I make an appointment to see Sandra Henderson, please?**
(make appointment – Termin vereinbaren / see sbdy. – jemanden sprechen)
B: What day would you like to come?
A: Thursday, if possible. Do you think she would be free in the afternoon?

* **I'd like to fix an appointment.**
(fix – vereinbaren)

* **A: I'd need to talk to Mr. Clemence, your Materials Manager. Could you arrange an appointment for me?**
(Ich müsste mit Herrn Clemence, dem Leiter der Materialwirtschaft, sprechen. Könnten Sie einen Termin für mich fixieren?)
B: Yes, would tomorrow three o'clock suit you?
(suit – passen; recht sein)
A: Yes, three o'clock would be perfect. I have another appointment at two just round the corner.
(just round the corner – gleich um die Ecke)

* **Yes, three o'clock would suit me very well.**

* **Couldn't you make it half past three? I've got another appointment at two and I'm not sure how long it will take.**
(take – dauern)

* **A: When would it be convenient for you?**
(be convenient – passen)
B: Well, next Tuesday afternoon would be all right.

* **A: What time does it suit you?**
B: Can we make it quarter past five?
(quarter past five – Viertel nach fünf)
A: Yes, that would be fine by me.

* **A: Would twelve thirty be any good?**
(Würde 12.30 Uhr passen?)
B: No, that wouldn't do because I have to chair a meeting at our branch at twelve.
(Nein, das würde nicht gehen, weil ich um zwölf eine Sitzung in unserer Zweiganstalt leiten muss.)

* **A: How about Tuesday evening?**
(Wie wär's mit Dienstag abend?)
B: Would it be possible on Friday instead?
(instead – stattdessen)

* **A: Could you manage Tuesday, at about six? Or would you prefer to come a bit later?**
(Geht es Ihnen am Dienstag aus, so um sechs herum? / prefer to come – lieber kommen)
B: No, six o'clock suits me fine.
(suit fine – ausgezeichnet passen)

* **A: I think I could fit you in at around five.**
(fit in – einschieben)
B: I'll just check my diary. Sorry, I've got something scheduled then.
(Ich sehe nur rasch in meinem Terminkalender nach. Leider habe ich zu dieser Zeit schon etwas.)

* A: **Do you think Mr. Thompson would be able to see me this morning?**
B: **You'd better see his secretary about an appointment.**
(Wegen eines Termins sollten Sie lieber zu seiner Sekretärin gehen.)

* A: **Could you suggest a time for an appointment? Early next week, say?**
(suggest – vorschlagen / … . Wie wär's mit Anfang nächster Woche?)
B: **Sorry, but Dr. Evans is fully booked until Wednesday, the earliest possible time he could see you is Wednesday afternoon.**

* **What time should I come?**

* A: **Could I come and see you on Wednesday?**
(Kann ich Sie am Mittwoch sprechen? | Kann ich am Mittwoch zu Ihnen kommen?)
B: **Check with my secretary whether Wednesday at nine is O.K.. She's got a list of all my appointments.**
(whether – ob)

* **Could you spare me a minute, please?**
(Hätten Sie bitte einen Augenblick für mich Zeit?)

* A: **Good morning. We have an appointment with Mr. Dobson. It's Mr. Schmidt and Mr. Weber of IBM Austria.**
(appointment – Termin, Verabredung)
B: **Yes, he's expecting you, go straight in.**
(expect – erwarten / straight – gleich)

* A: **Good morning, my name is Frank Holzer. I have an appointment to see Mr. Glover, the Sales Manager, at eleven forty-five. My secretary rang you last week about it.**
(Sales Manager – Verkaufsleiter / ring about – anrufen wegen)
B: **Yes, he'll be here shortly.**
(shortly – gleich)

* **Sorry to be late! How long have you been waiting for me?**
(… . Wie lange warten Sie schon auf mich?)

* **Sorry to have kept you waiting, Mr. Thorpe, but somebody from Headquarters was on the phone and I just couldn't ring off.**
(keep waiting – warten lassen / Headquarters – Konzernzentrale / ring off – auflegen)

* **A: There is a Mr. Martin here in the office. He says he has an appointment with you. But I can't find anything in the appointment book.**
(appointment book – Terminkalender)
B: Sorry, I forgot to tell you that I had promised to see him at four. It's all right. Show him in.
(promise – versprechen / show in – hereinführen)

* **I'm just ringing to inform you that the meeting is now scheduled for tomorrow, at the same time.**
(meeting – Sitzung / schedule – ansetzen)

* **A: What time is the board meeting?**
(board – Verwaltungsrat; Führungsgremium einer britischen / amerikanischen Kapitalgesellschaft)
B: Well, we've arranged it for four o'clock this afternoon.
(arrange – festsetzen)

* **A: When am I to see the Managing Director?**
(Wann soll ich mich beim Generaldirektor melden?)
B: He suggests a meeting on Friday at eight o'clock or at the weekend. Please phone him as soon as possible.
(meeting – Treffen)

* **Would it suit you if we met at quarter to one at the Ship Restaurant? Then we could discuss things over a meal.**
(meet – sich treffen / at quarter to one – um Viertel vor eins / over a meal – bei einem Essen)

* **A: Let's meet about two o'clock, shall we?**
  (Treffen wir uns also um ca. 2 Uhr.)
  B: Right then, two o'clock on Monday the twenty-third. Goodbye.

* **A: Can we meet Thursday night or Friday morning?**
  B: I'm tied up all week I'm afraid.
  (Ich bin leider die ganze Woche voll.)

* **I'm afraid I'm not free this week. Perhaps another time.**
  (... . Vielleicht ein andermal.)

* **I'm meeting Jane for lunch in an hour's time.**
  (meet sbdy. – jemanden treffen / in an hour's time – in einer Stunde)

* **I'll meet you in about ten minutes under the station clock, O.K.?**
  (about – etwa / station clock – Bahnhofsuhr)

* **I'll pick you up at the hotel at around seven, then.**
  (pick up – abholen / at around seven – gegen sieben)

* **I'll call for you at three tomorrow.**
  (call for – abholen)

* **I'm afraid I'll be late.**
  (Tut mir leid, ich werde zu spät kommen.)

* **I'll look forward to meeting you in London this evening.**
  (look forward to – sich freuen auf)

—— ❖ ——

* **I'd just like to ask if we can meet an hour earlier next week.**

* **Could you possibly bring our appointment forward by one and a half hours?**
  (bring forward – vorverlegen)

* **Would it be possible to postpone the meeting?**
(postpone – verschieben, aufschieben)

* **It seems I won't be able to attend the meeting tomorrow.**
(Es sieht eher danach aus, dass ich an der morgigen Sitzung nicht teilnehmen kann.)

* **It looks as if I won't be able to keep my appointment on Friday.**
(won't – will not / keep – einhalten)

* **I'm calling about my appointment tomorrow morning with Mr. Bennet, your Marketing Manager. I'm afraid I won't be able to come because I've gone down with the flu.**
(call about – anrufen wegen / go down with the flu – die Grippe erwischen)

* **I'm ringing from the airport. Unfortunately, I have to cancel my appointment with Mr. Charlton, your Product Manager.**
(unfortunately – leider / cancel – stornieren, absagen)

* **A: I'm afraid I can't manage tomorrow evening.**
(Ich kann leider morgen abend nicht.)
B: Let's fix another date, then.
(date – Termin)

* **I'm afraid I can't make it on Sunday. I hope it won't mess up your arrangements.**
(make – schaffen / mess up arrangements – alles durcheinanderbringen)

DEADLINES

Termine und Fristen

- **We must finish this by four o'clock at the latest.**
  (Wir müssen das bis spätestens vier Uhr fertig haben.)

- **They need to know by the end of the week.**

- **I don't think we can promise to do it by the thirty-first. It'll be two weeks at least.**
  (promise – versprechen / … . Es wird mindestens zwei Wochen dauern.)

- **I'm afraid it won't be ready till tomorrow.**
  (won't – will not / ready – fertig)

- **The suits will certainly be ready in March.**
  (suit – Anzug / certainly – sicher)

- **It won't be ready in time.**
  (in time – rechtzeitig)

- **They've always delivered on time.**
  (Sie haben immer pünktlich geliefert.)

- **Make sure you're on time.**
  (Sei ja pünktlich!)

- **I'd like you to have them ready on Friday so that I can look at them over the weekend.**

- **The ticket must be collected not later than eleven fifteen.**
  (collect – abholen)

* **We would like to receive your proposals within the next two months.**
(Würden Sie uns bitte Ihre Vorschläge innerhalb der nächsten zwei Monate unterbreiten.)

* **Could you have a quick look at this questionnaire before tomorrow morning?**
(questionnaire – Fragebogen)

* **They'll let us know before the end of the month.**

* **A: Have you finished that report for me yet?**
(report – Bericht / yet – schon)
B: Yes, but I haven't had time to prepare the sales figures yet, I'm afraid.
(not … yet – noch nicht / prepare – zusammenstellen / sales figures – Umsatzzahlen)

* **Oh damn! We missed the deadline again.**
(miss deadline – Termin verpassen)

* **They've set us the deadline for next Monday, but to be honest I don't think we'll meet it.**
(set – setzen / honest – ehrlich / meet – einhalten)

PRESSED FOR TIME

Unter Zeitdruck

* **A: Can I see you for a minute, please?**
(Kann ich Sie kurz sprechen?)
B: I'm afraid I haven't got time just now. Would you mind waiting for a few minutes?
(Leider habe ich jetzt gerade keine Zeit. Würde es Ihnen etwas ausmachen, ein paar Minuten zu warten?)

* **I'm terribly sorry, but I'm pressed for time at the moment.**
(terrible – schrecklich / be pressed for time – unter Zeitdruck sein)

* **I've only got ten minutes to spare. Is it urgent?**
(Ich habe nur zehn Minuten Zeit. Ist es dringend?)

* **He's no time to spare.**
(Er hat im Augenblick keine Zeit.)

* **Listen, I'm a bit busy at the moment. Could you call back later? Say, in half an hour?**
(Du, ich bin im Augenblick etwas unter Zeitdruck. … . / call back – nochmals anrufen)

* **We're very busy at the moment. Can you come back again on the twenty-fourth?**
(busy – beschäftigt)

* **We can't do this before tomorrow, I'm afraid. We've got a lot of work on at the moment.**

* **I have to hurry up. I'm leaving for Brussels in a few minutes.**
(hurry up – sich beeilen / leave for Brussels – nach Brüssel fahren)

* **Sorry, I can't stay. I must dash – I'm meeting someone at nine.**
(dash – sausen)

* **I really should be going, David. I've got an appointment at two thirty.**

* **I'm afraid I must be going soon.**

* **It's high time we went home.**
(Es ist höchste Zeit, dass wir nach Hause gehen.)

* **Oh! It's five to twelve! You'd better leave now!**
(Es ist fünf vor zwölf. Sie sollten jetzt lieber gehen.)

* A: **Come on! Let's get going now!**
B: **Just a moment. I haven't finished yet. I won't be long.**
(Einen Augenblick noch! Ich bin noch nicht fertig. Ich bin gleich soweit.)

* **Just look at the time! Twenty past three! The banks shut at half past.**
(shut – schließen)

* A: **How about another cup of tea?**
(Wollen Sie nicht noch eine Tasse Tee?)
B: **Oh, do you think we have time?**

TIME OF DAY

Tageszeitangaben

(see also "Time: Appointments")

* A: **Could you tell me the time, please?**
B: **I make it about ten to eight.**
(Bei mir ist es ca. zehn vor acht.)

* A: **What time is it?**
B: **I still make it ten o'clock – my watch must have stopped.**
(still – noch immer / watch – Uhr)

* A: **Excuse me, my watch has stopped. Can you tell me the time?**
B: **By my watch it's just gone half past three, but it's a bit fast.**
(Auf meiner Uhr ist es knapp nach halb vier, aber sie geht etwas vor.)

* **My watch is five minutes slow.**
(Meine Uhr geht fünf Minuten nach.)

* A: **What time is it by your watch?**
B: **It's exactly twenty minutes past eleven.**

* **A: What's the time, please?**
  B: It's five thirty on the dot.
  (on the dot – genau)

* **Good heavens, it's three o'clock in the morning.**
  (good heavens – oh du meine Güte)

* **I wonder if you could tell me what time the shops close here?**
  (Könnten Sie mir bitte sagen, um welche Zeit hier die Geschäfte schließen?)

* **What time does it start?**

* **Is this clock right? It says twenty-five to five.**

* **My watch keeps good time.**
  (Meine Uhr geht genau.)

* **The first bus leaves at nine a.m. and the second at three p.m..**
  (Der erste Bus fährt um 9 und der zweite um 15 Uhr. / a.m. – ante meridiem | before noon | vor Mittag / p.m. – post meridiem | after noon | nach Mittag)

* **We have flexi-time, actually, so I can start work any time between seven and nine o'clock.**
  (flexi-time – Gleitzeit)

* **A: When do you think he'll be back?**
  B: He'll be home by sixish.
  (by sixish – so um sechs)

* **I'll be there at six sharp.**
  (sharp – genau)

* **I'll see him at twelve noon.**
  (noon – Mittag)

* **My plane leaves at eighteen hundred hours.**
  (Meine Maschine geht um 18 Uhr.)

* **What were you doing at ten o'clock at night yesterday?**

OTHER EXPRESSIONS INDICATING TIME

Sonstige Zeitangaben

* **A: What's the date today, please?**
  (date – Datum)
  B: It's October the third.

* **Have you got any plans for the day after tomorrow?**

* **Where were you the day before yesterday?**

* **That was a good party last night, wasn't it?**
  (wasn't it? – nicht wahr?)

* **I was there last month, so I'm not going this time.**

* **I'm going to Toronto tonight.**
  (tonight – heute abend)

* **I talked to him the other day and he said that I should arrange things with you.**
  (the other day – neulich)

* **He came back the next morning.**

* **We are not planning to launch a modified version in the near future, not before 2010.**
  (launch – auf den Markt bringen / future – Zukunft)

✳ **It must have been shortly after seven.**
(shortly – kurz)

✳ **What are you doing at Easter?**

✳ **You can call me at any time during the day.**

✳ **Mrs. Vernon called just a couple of minutes ago.**
(Frau Vernon hat gerade vor ein paar Minuten angerufen.)

✳ **Some years ago I did a six-month training course.**

✳ **I was Marketing Manager for Casinos Austria until about three years ago.**

✳ **I've been working as export manager since the beginning of last year.**
(Ich bin seit Beginn letzten Jahres als Exportleiter tätig.)

✳ **I've been here since the first of May 1990. How time flies!**
(Ich bin nun schon seit dem 1. Mai 1990 hier. Wie die Zeit vergeht!)

✳ **I've known her for more than two years.**
(Ich kenne sie schon seit mehr als zwei Jahren.)

✳ **We haven't heard from him for some time.**
(Er lässt schon seit einiger Zeit nichts mehr von sich hören.)

✳ **A: How long did the interview take?**
(take – dauern)
B: It took about three quarters of an hour.

✳ **A: How long is this going to take?**
B: It won't take more than fifty minutes.
(won't – will not)

* **A: How long is it going to take you to obtain the necessary data?**
(Wie lange werden Sie brauchen | benötigen, um die notwendigen Daten zu beschaffen?)
B: A week, I suppose.
(suppose – annehmen)

* **The meeting started late in the afternoon and lasted five and a half hours.**
(last – dauern)

* **Some banks are open on Saturdays from nine to twelve.**

* **From October 1971 until March 1976 I studied at the University of Economics and Business Administration in Vienna.**
(… Wirtschaftsuniversität Wien.)

* **A fortnight today we'll be in Sydney.**
(Heute in 14 Tagen … .)

* **A: How long will you be staying?**
B: I'll be in London for several days, until the end of next week. My flight's on Saturday morning.
(several – einige)

* **A: What's Scotland like in summer?**
B: Well, I went there in the summer of 1979 and it was unusually hot.

* **Our sales are usually higher in the winter months.**
(sales – Umsatz)

* **I have a dental appointment in three days' time.**
(dental appointment – Termin beim Zahnarzt)

* **He did it in no time.**
(in no time – sehr schnell)

* **Have you been to Manchester recently?**
(recently – in der letzten Zeit)

* **Have you done anything special lately?**
(lately – in der letzten Zeit)

* **Have you ever been to London?**

* **Have you been to Vienna yet?**
(yet – schon einmal)

* **Have you been to Berlin before?**

* **There's a train every hour, on the hour.**
(Es geht ein Zug zu jeder vollen Stunde.)

* **I catch the seven fifty-eight train every day.**
(catch – nehmen)

* **I play squash every second day.**

* **There's a bus every twenty minutes.**
(every – alle)

* **We get together annually.**
(Wir treffen uns jedes Jahr.)

* **We see each other twice a month.**
(twice – zweimal)

* **Could you wait a moment, please?**

* **I play golf from time to time.**

* **I have to work in this building temporarily while my office is being renovated.**
(building – Gebäude / temporarily – vorübergehend)

* **Have we had any complaints so far?**
  (complaint – Beschwerde, Reklamation / so far – bis jetzt)

* **I hear you've just been to Jamaica. Is it worth a visit?**
  (just – gerade / worth – wert)

* **In the past few months, we have received a large number of inquiries concerning our new telephone answering machine.**
  (in the past few months – in den letzten Monaten / receive – erhalten / inquiry – Anfrage / concerning – betreffend)

* **During the past five years, we have been able to increase our exports constantly.**
  (Wir waren in der Lage, in den letzten 5 Jahren unseren Export ständig zu steigern.)

* **Sales fell during the first half of 2007. They then increased steadily over the next twelve months until the middle of 2008.**
  (during – während / increase steadily – ständig steigen / over – während)

* **In Europe as a whole, our market share has increased over the past two and a half years from four per cent at the beginning of 2006 to twelve per cent in mid-2008.**
  (market share – Marktanteil)

AGE

Altersangaben

* **A: May I ask you how old you are actually?**
  B: I'll be thirty next year.

* **I turned twenty-eight last month.**
  (turn – werden)

* **A: How old are you?**
  B: I'm on the wrong side of forty.
  (… leider schon über 40.)

* **I was born on the eleventh of August nineteen sixty-two.**

* **I was born in Vienna in 1959.**

* **My birthday's on the thirtieth of January.**

* **You don't look your age.**
  (Sie sehen jünger aus, als Sie sind.)

* **You look much younger.**

* **At the age of nineteen I went to live in New York.**
  (age – Alter)

* **All our executives are under forty.**
  (executive – Manager)

* **They say you shouldn't rush around at my age!**
  (… , man sollte in meinem Alter etwas leisertreten.)

* **A: What's your star sign?**
  (star sign – Sternzeichen)
  B: I'm Sagittarius.
  (Sagittarius – Schütze)

* **A: What sign of the zodiac are you?**
  (sign of the zodiac – Sternzeichen)
  B: I'm Capricorn. What about you?
  (Capricorn – Steinbock)

MISCELLANEOUS
Sonstiges

* **We have plenty of time.**
  (Wir haben viel Zeit.)

* **It's getting late.**
  (Es wird schon spät.)

* **You can save so much time by using a computer.**

* **We're going through hard times in our company.**
  (company – Firma, Gesellschaft)

* **A: I'll be going back to Austria on Friday.**
  B: Really? Time's flying, isn't it?
  (… . Na, wie die Zeit vergeht!)

* **Take your time.**
  (Lassen Sie sich Zeit!)

* **Time's up.**
  (Die Zeit ist um!)

* **Better late than never.**
  (Besser spät als nie.)

* **It's a race against time.**
  (… ein Wettlauf mit der Zeit.)

ASKING THE WAY AND PUBLIC TRANSPORT

Erkundigung nach dem Weg und öffentliche Transportmittel

ASKING THE WAY – GENERAL

Erkundigung nach dem Weg – allgemein

* **A: Where is the International Trading Centre, please?**
B: You see that high building there? That's the International Trading Centre.
(building – Gebäude)

* **A: Excuse me, could you tell me where the police station is?**
B: Walk along this street and it's on the left next to the cinema.
(Gehen Sie diese Straße entlang, und es ist auf der linken Seite neben dem Kino.)

* **A: Excuse me. Can you tell me where Perth Road is, please?**
B: Carry on up this road, and it's the third road on the right, I think.
(Gehen Sie weiter diese Straße entlang, … .)

* **A: Could you tell me where the Palladium Theatre is, please?**
B: Yes, go straight on and turn left at the traffic lights, and you'll see it a little way along, on the right-hand side of the road.
(straight on – geradeaus / turn left – nach links abbiegen | gehen / traffic lights – Verkehrsampel)

* **A: Excuse me. Can you tell me where the Conference Centre is?**
B: You're going in the wrong direction. It's the other way. Cross the bridge and it's just on the other side of the river.
(direction – Richtung / cross bridge – über Brücke gehen / just – direkt / river – Fluss)

* **A: Excuse me, please. Could you tell me the way to the ABC cinema?**
B: Yes, certainly. Go along this street until you come to a set of traffic lights. Then turn right into Shaftesbury Avenue. Then take the first turning on the left and it's at the end of that road.
(first turning on the left – erste Straße | Abzweigung links)

* **A: Excuse me, could you tell me the way to the station? It should be somewhere around here.**
(somewhere around here – irgendwo hier in der Nähe)
B: Yes, it's not far from here. Go straight down there, and take the first turning to your right.

* **A: Excuse me, but could you tell me the way to the British Museum, please?**
B: Actually, you have been walking away from it. Turn round, walk back up the road as far as the traffic lights. It's just around the corner.
(turn round – umdrehen, kehrtmachen / as far as – bis zu / just around the corner – gleich um die Ecke)

* **A: Excuse me. Can you tell me the way to Victoria Street?**
B: Let me see. Go straight along this road until you come to a zebra crossing. Then turn to the left and keep straight on as far as the bus stop. Then take the next turning to the right, cross the square and you'll be on Victoria Street.
(zebra crossing – Zebrastreifen / bus stop – Bushaltestelle / square – Platz)

* **A: Could you tell me how to get to Leicester Square, please?**
(Könnten Sie mir bitte sagen, wie ich zum Leicester Square komme?)
B: I'm afraid I can't help you.
(Tut mir leid, ich kann Ihnen nicht helfen.)

* **A: Excuse me, please. Could you tell me how to get to the Bank of England?**
  B: First right, second left. You can't miss it.
  (miss – verfehlen)

* **A: Excuse me, is there a bank near here?**
  B: Yes, there is one on the opposite side of the road, only about five minutes from here.
  (opposite – gegenüberliegend)

* **A: Excuse me please, I'm a stranger here. Is this the right way to Trafalgar Square?**
  (I'm a stranger here – ich bin hier fremd)
  B: Sorry, I don't know, I am a stranger here myself.

* **A: Which is the shortest way to Paddington Station, please?**
  B: Let me show you on your map.
  (map – Stadtplan)

* **A: Could I get there by bus?**
  B: Yes, but in that case you'll have to go back a little way. Keep on this side of the road until you come to the bus stop. All the buses from there pass the station.
  (pass the station – zum Bahnhof fahren)

* **A: Can you tell me which way Soho is, please?**
  B: It's rather complicated. You'd better ask again when you get to the Telecom Tower.
  (Das ist ziemlich kompliziert. Sie sollten lieber nochmals fragen, sobald Sie beim Telecom Tower sind.)

* **A: Excuse me. The National Gallery – it's near Trafalgar Square, isn't it?**
  (isn't it? – oder?)
  B: Yes, that's right, it's actually in Trafalgar Square.

* **A: Where can I get a taxi, please?**
  B: There's a taxi rank just round the corner.
  (taxi rank – Taxistand)

* **A: Excuse me. Can you show me where the Apollo Theatre is?**
  B: Well, that's quite easy. You are right in front of it.
  (… . Sie stehen direkt davor.)

* **A: Excuse me, how far away is Radford Street?**
  B: Not very far. It's the first turning on the right.

* **A: Is it very far from here?**
  B: No, not really. It's about a ten-minute walk I'd say.

* **A: Is it too far to walk?**
  B: No, it's only about five minutes from here.

* **A: Should I take a taxi?**
  B: No, it's not very far. You can walk it in less than ten minutes.

* **A: Excuse me. Where is room 405, please?**
  B: Come out of the lift on the fourth floor and take the corridor on the right. Room 405 is on the left.
  (floor – Stock)

* **Sorry, I'm new here.**

* **A: Excuse me. Where is the canteen, please?**
  B: It's downstairs in the basement.
  (basement – Kellergeschoß)

UNDERGROUND

U-Bahn

* **A: Can you tell me the best way to get to Wimbledon, please?**
B: Well, you can go by tube, by bus or by mainline train. I reckon the tube's best.
(tube – U-Bahn / mainline train – Eisenbahn / reckon – schätzen)

* **A: I wonder if you could tell me where the nearest tube station is?**
(Könnten Sie mir bitte sagen, wo die nächste U-Bahn-Station ist?)
B: Sorry, I've no idea.

* **A: Excuse me, could you tell me how to get to Gatwick Airport from here?**
B: You can take the underground. The station ist just round the corner. Take the District Line as far as Victoria, and from there take a train to Gatwick. There's one every 20 minutes.
(underground – U-Bahn / station – U-Bahn-Station)

* **A: Excuse me. Do you know how I can get to Victoria from here?**
B: I think the best way is to take the Piccadilly Line to Green Park, and then change to the Victoria Line.
(change – umsteigen)

* **A: How do I get to Bank station, please?**
B: Take the Northern Line to Tottenham Court Road, then catch the Central Line eastbound.
(catch – nehmen / eastbound – Richtung Osten)

* **A: Which underground line goes to Wimbledon, please?**
B: I don't know, let's have a look at the underground map.
(underground map – U-Bahn-Plan)

* **A: Excuse me, where can I get tickets for the underground?**
  B: If you've got some change you can get them from the ticket-machines, otherwise you'll have to queue at the ticket-office over there.
  (change – Kleingeld / ticket-machine – Fahrkartenautomat / queue – sich anstellen / ticket-office – Fahrkartenschalter / over there – dort drüben)

* **How much is the fare to Tottenham Court Road, please?**
  (fare – Fahrpreis)

* **Two to Marble Arch, please.**

* **A: Where's the Northern Line, please?**
  B: Go down that escalator over there and then if you're going north follow the signs to Platform 3, southbound you need Platform 6.
  (escalator – Rolltreppe / follow signs – Schildern folgen / platform – Bahnsteig / southbound – Richtung Süden)

* **A: Which direction do I have to go?**
  (direction – Richtung)
  B: You need the eastbound train.

* **Where do I have to change for Elephant & Castle, please?**

* **Knightsbridge is four stops from here, isn't it?**
  (stop – Haltestelle / isn't it? – nicht wahr?)

* **Mind the gap!**
  (Vorsicht beim Ein- und Aussteigen!)

* **Where's the way out, please?**
  (Wo ist der Ausgang, bitte?)

BUS / COACH

Bus / Überlandbus

* **A: Excuse me, where's the nearest bus stop, please?**
  B: It's just down this road opposite the police station.
  (opposite – gegenüber)

* **A: How do I get to the air terminal from here, please?**
  B: Well, actually the best way is by bus.
  (by bus – mit dem Bus)
  A: I see. How long does it take?
  (… . Wie lange braucht man?)
  B: About twenty minutes – maybe more in the rush hour.
  (rush hour – Stoßzeit)

* **A: Excuse me, how far is it to the airport from here?**
  B: It's rather a long way. I'd take the bus to Merton Road and then ask again.
  (rather – ziemlich)

* **A: Is there a bus or underground to the Royal Exhibition Centre?**
  B: Yes, you should take a Greenline bus – a number three, I think – and get off at the third stop.
  (get off – aussteigen)

* **A: Does the number 52 go down Shooters Hill Road?**
  B: Yes, it goes past the Sun in the Sands, then round the roundabout and then it turns left down Shooters Hill Road to the station.
  (go past – vorbeifahren an / roundabout – Kreisverkehr)

* **A: I have to go for an interview. I wonder if you could tell me how to get there? The address is 23 Ridgeway Avenue.**
B: Oh, yes, that's not very far from here. You can take a number 12 bus and ask the conductor to put you off at Ridgeway Cemetery. It's a ten-minute ride I'd say.
(conductor – Schaffner / put sbdy. off – jemanden aussteigen lassen / cemetery – Friedhof / ride – Fahrt)

* **A: Excuse me, I'd like to go to Heathrow Airport. Can I take a bus?**
B: You can take the bus from Victoria to Heathrow. But I'd take the underground if I were you. The Piccadilly Line takes you right to the airport.

* **Shall I find out when the coaches leave for Stratford?**
(coach – Bus, Überlandbus / leave for – abfahren nach)

* **Where does the airport coach leave from, please?**

* **A: These coaches are very comfortable and almost as fast as a train.**
(almost – fast, beinahe)
B: I'm not so sure.

* **How often do the buses run to Brighton Beach?**
(run – fahren)

* **Do you happen to know if there are any night buses to Croydon?**
(Wissen Sie zufällig, ob … .)

* **Does this bus go to the Royal Exchange, please?**
(Royal Exchange – Börse in London)

* **A: Excuse me, is this the right bus for Marylebone?**
B: No, you're going the wrong way. You want the 134 from Victoria.
(want – brauchen)

* **A: Excuse me, how long does it take to get to Hyde Park Corner by bus?**
  B: It won't take you long to get there, it's not far from here at all.
  (won't – will not / at all – überhaupt)

* **Do you want to sit upstairs on the top deck or shall we stay down here?**
  (top deck – Oberdeck)

* **A: Excuse me, how many stops is it to the Royal Pavillion?**
  B: Six, I think, but I'm not quite sure. You'd better ask the driver.
  (… . Sie sollten lieber den Fahrer fragen.)

* **Would you mind telling me when we get there?**
  (Könnten Sie mich bitte aufmerksam machen, wenn wir dort sind?)

* **Could you tell me where to get off for the Royal Festival Hall, please?**

* **A: Well, this is where I get off.**
  (Ich steige hier aus.)
  B: Let me give you a hand with your suitcase.
  (give sbdy. a hand – jemandem helfen / suitcase – Koffer)

* **Could you put me down at the Olympia Fair Building, please?**
  (put sbdy. down – jemanden aussteigen lassen)

* **I've left my umbrella on the bus.**
  (leave – liegenlassen / umbrella – Schirm)

TRAM

Straßenbahn

* **A: How do I get to the soccer stadium, please?**
  (soccer stadium – Fußballstadion)
  B: Go straight ahead, cross the road at the traffic lights and take a number four tram.
  (straight ahead – geradeaus / tram – Straßenbahn)

* **A: Excuse me, do you happen to know where the number one tram stop is, please?**
  (do you happen to know – wissen Sie zufällig)
  B: Sorry, I haven't a clue. Ask the policeman over there.
  (clue – Ahnung)

* **I'm sorry, I haven't the slightest idea.**
  (slightest idea – geringste Ahnung)

* **What number tram should I take?**

* **Is this the stop for the World Trade Centre, please?**

AIR TRAVEL

Mit dem Flugzeug

BOOKINGS AND OTHER ARRANGEMENTS

Buchungen und alles, was dazugehört

* **Could you tell me how much a first-class ticket to Edinburgh costs?**

* **What is the fare for a return flight to Sydney, please?**
(fare – Flugpreis / return flight – Hin- und Rückflug)

* **When is the next plane to Boston, please?**
(plane – Maschine, Flugzeug)

* **What's the flying time, please?**
(flying time – Flugzeit)

* A: **What time does the last flight to Düsseldorf leave?**
(Wann geht der letzte Flug nach Düsseldorf?)
B: **There's a flight leaving London Heathrow at 18.10 and arriving in Düsseldorf at 20.45 local time.**
(arrive – ankommen)

* A: **Could you please tell me the time of the first morning plane to Frankfurt?**
B: **Yes. The first plane leaves at 8.15.**
A: **Thanks. And can you tell me when it arrives so that I can let my secretary know?**

* **What are the times of the flights after the 12.45?**

* **A: Do you happen to know the time of the last plane this evening?**
(Wissen Sie zufällig … ?)
B: Well, there is one at 11.15 but it's fully booked I'm afraid.
(I'm afraid – leider)
A: Oh. Well, I wonder if you'd let me know at my hotel if there's any cancellation on that flight. I'd be very grateful.
(cancellation – Stornierung / grateful – dankbar)

* **I wonder if you'd let me know if there is a seat available on the 9.30 flight?**
(Könnten Sie mir bitte sagen, ob in der Maschine um 9.30 Uhr noch ein Platz frei ist?)

* **Are there any seats left on the early morning flight to Vienna?**
(left – frei)

* **A: Is there a connecting flight to Vienna?**
(Gibt es einen Anschlussflug nach Wien?)
B: Of course, and you can transfer to a connecting flight without reclaiming your luggage.
(Selbstverständlich, und Sie können umsteigen, ohne das Gepäck neu einchecken zu müssen.)

* **Is it a scheduled or a charter flight?**
(scheduled flight – Linienflug)

* **Is there a direct flight from Brussels? I'd have to be in Dublin by Friday afternoon.**

* **Is there a stopover in Singapore?**
(stopover – Zwischenaufenthalt)

* **A: Do you make reservations for Lauda Air flights?**
B: Yes, we do.
A: Well, I'd like to book a return flight to Vienna, please.

* A: **I'd like to book an open return to New York on flight PA 104 leaving this Thursday, please.**
(open return – Hinflug mit offenem Rückflug)
B: **First class or economy?**
A: **Oh, first class, please.**
B: **There are no first-class seats available on that flight, I'm afraid. Would you mind travelling economy class?**
(would you mind – würde es Ihnen etwas ausmachen)

* **I want to get to Glasgow on Tuesday afternoon. Could I book a one-way flight?**
(one-way flight – Einfachflug)

* **I wonder if you'd tell me which airport the plane leaves from?**
(Könnten Sie mir bitte sagen, von welchem Flughafen die Maschine abfliegt?)

* **I'd like to book a seat on flight number BA 706 to London on Monday.**

* A: **I'd like two reservations from London to Alicante, if possible this evening, please.**
B: **I'm afraid there are no direct flights. You'll have to fly to Madrid and then take a domestic flight to Alicante.**
(I'm afraid – tut mir leid / domestic flight – Inlandsflug)

* **I see you don't have a service from Paris to Munich on Mondays. Could you book me on a direct flight on a different airline, preferably a late evening flight, on the 19th?**
(service – Flug, Flugverbindung / preferably – am liebsten wäre mir)

* **Please make sure you book me on a non-stop flight.**
(Bitte buchen Sie mich aber ja sicher auf einen Nonstopflug.)

* **Can you get me on the afternoon flight from Gatwick to Dublin?**
(get on – unterbringen auf)

* **A: The tickets should be collected from our reservations desk at the airport at least forty-five minutes before departure this evening, madam.**
(collect – abholen / reservations desk – Buchungsschalter / departure – Abflug)
B: All right. Thank you very much.

* **How long will it take to confirm my booking?**
(take – brauchen / confirm booking – Buchung bestätigen)

* **I'm flying to Washington, D.C. tomorrow. Could you tell me if I have to change at J.F.K.?**
(change – umsteigen / J.F.K. – John F. Kennedy Airport in New York)

* **My conference is ending sooner than I expected and I'd like to take an earlier flight back, would that be possible?**
(expect – erwarten)

* **I'm booked on flight number 567 to Vienna this Thursday at 13.40 and I'd like to change my booking.**

* **A: Could we change our flight booking here?**
B: Certainly. May I have your tickets, please? Thank you.
(certainly – selbstverständlich)
A: Can we make it two weeks earlier?

* **A: I need to change my flight back to San Francisco. I won't be able to catch the plane at 6.30. Do you think you could arrange that for me?**
(need – müssen / won't – will not / catch – erwischen)
B: Certainly, I'll see what I can do.

* **A: I have a reservation on flight BE 344 to Paris, leaving London tonight at eight ten. I'm afraid it'll be difficult for me to make it at that time. Is there a later flight this evening?**
  (make – schaffen)
  B: There's another flight at ten to twelve tonight.
  A: Can you change the reservation, then, please?

* **Thank you for changing the flights. I'm sorry it was so complicated.**

* **Unfortunately, I have to cancel my flight. What is the cancellation fee, please?**
  (unfortunately – leider / cancellation fee – Stornogebühr)

* **What time do I have to check in?**

* **A: Check-in time is about an hour before departure, is that right?**
  (check-in – Abfertigung)
  B: Yes, you should go to the Austrian Airlines check-in desk at the airport at least 60 minutes before departure.
  (desk – Schalter)

* **What is the free-luggage allowance?**
  (Wieviel Freigepäck darf man mitnehmen?)

* **What is the charge for excess baggage?**
  (charge – Zuschlag / excess baggage – Übergepäck)

* **Could you arrange for someone to meet me at the airport? I'm due to arrive at Shannon Airport at 17.15 on flight BA 121.**
  (arrange for – veranlassen / meet – abholen / I'm due to arrive – laut Flugplan komme ich an)

* **A: What time are you arriving?**
  B: Well, my flight leaves just after two. I should be in around 3.30 your time.
  (just – knapp / be in – ankommen)

CHECK-IN
Einchecken

* **I think I'd better check in right away. I don't want to have to rush.**
(Ich glaube, ich sollte lieber sofort einchecken. … . / rush – sich beeilen; hasten)

* **A: Where is the information desk, please?**
B: It's just over there on the other side of the hall, sir.
(just over there – gleich dort drüben)

* **Where is the Lufthansa counter, please?**
(counter – Schalter)

* **Are there any luggage trolleys around here?**
(luggage trolley – Gepäckswagen)

* **Is this the queue for flight OS 456 to Vienna?**
(Stellen Sie sich hier für … an?)

* **Is this where I have to check in for the Austrian Airlines flight to Salzburg?**

* **Put your luggage on the scales, please.**
(scales – Waage)

* **A: I'm afraid there'll be an excess baggage charge on this.**
(excess baggage charge – Übergepäckszuschlag)
B: Are you sure it's overweight?

* **A: Your luggage doesn't seem to be labelled, sir. Could you pop one of those sticky labels on it for now?**
(seem – scheinen / label – beschriften / pop – kleben / sticky label – „Pickerl", Aufkleber / for now – vorläufig einmal)
B: No problem, but could you lend me something to write with, please?
(lend – borgen)

* **Can I take this as hand luggage?**

* **A: Can you give me a window-seat?**
B: Smoking or non-smoking?
A: Non-smoking, please.

* **I'd like a seat next to the window.**

* **Is the plane going to be late?**
(Hat die Maschine Verspätung?)

* **Is the plane going to be delayed because of the fog?**
(delayed – verspätet/fog – Nebel)

* **A: Can I have my boarding card?**
(boarding card – Einsteigkarte)
B: Here it is. Go to Gate 23 at least half an hour before the expected departure.
(gate – Flugsteig, Ausgang)

BETWEEN CHECK-IN AND DEPARTURE

Zwischen Einchecken und Abflug

* **I hope you have a pleasant flight back.**
(pleasant – angenehm)

* **Have a good flight!**

* **Could you tell me where the duty-free shop is, please?**

* **I'll go to the duty-free until my flight is called.**
(call – aufrufen)

* **What is the duty-free allowance for non-EU countries?**
(duty-free allowance – Zollfreigrenze)

* **I seem to have mislaid my boarding card.**
(mislay – verlegen)

* **Could you page a Ms. Sue Trim for me?**
(page sbdy. – jemanden durch den Lautsprecher ausrufen lassen)

* **Sorry, I didn't quite catch the announcement over the public-address system. Did they say that Austrian Airlines flight 342 had to be diverted to Manchester because of the fog?**
(quite – ganz / catch announcement – Durchsage verstehen / public-address system – Lautsprecheranlage / divert – umleiten)

* **A: Excuse me, do you know if flight ST 109 will be leaving on time?**
(on time – pünktlich)
B: No, I'm afraid it's going to be twenty minutes late.

* **Sorry to trouble you, but is flight BH 105 on schedule?**
(trouble – belästigen / on schedule – pünktlich)

* **A: Can you tell me why there's a delay on the flight to Chicago?**
(delay – Verspätung)
B: Due to unforeseen circumstances, we have had to change the aircraft. It'll leave at quarter past five.
(Infolge unvorhergesehener Umstände mussten wir das Flugzeug wechseln. … .)

* **A: Can you tell me where gate 58 is, please?**
B: Straight ahead, then it's on your left.
(straight ahead – geradeaus)

* **Did they say the 11.40 flight to Vienna is now boarding?**
(… , dass die Passagiere für den 11.40-Uhr-Flug nach Wien jetzt an Bord gehen können?)

* **I really must be going. They're calling my flight.**

* **Was that the last call for flight LH 890 to Frankfurt?**
(call – Aufruf)

ON BOARD THE AIRCRAFT

Im Flugzeug

* **A: Is it O.K. to put this piece of hand luggage in the overhead locker, or is it too heavy?**
(piece – Stück / overhead locker – Handgepäcksfach / heavy – schwer)
B: It's rather bulky, sir, you'll have to put it under the seat in front of you.
(rather bulky – ziemlich groß / in front of – vor)

* **I think you must be in the wrong seat. I have row 15, seat B. Look, it says it on the boarding card.**
(row – Reihe)

* **When are we due to take off?**
(Wann starten wir laut Flugplan?)

* **What time do we arrive?**

* **When are we due in London?**

* **A: I don't feel well.**
B: Would you like a travel-sickness pill?
(travel-sickness – Reisekrankheit)
A: Yes, please.

* **I feel sick.**
(Mir ist schlecht.)

* **A: The seats are a bit narrow, aren't they?**
(narrow – eng / aren't they? – nicht wahr?)
B: Next time I'll book a seat in the business class.

* **A: Do you have to pay extra for drinks?**
B: Only for spirits. Beer, wine and soft drinks are free of charge.
(Nur für Spirituosen. Bier, Wein und alkoholfreie Getränke sind gratis.)

* **Can I pay in euros?**

* **I ordered a vegetarian dish – I don't eat meat.**
(order – bestellen / dish – Essen)

* **Could I have a towlette, please?**
(towlette – Erfrischungstuch)

* **Excuse me, I don't seem to have a pillow or a blanket. Could you get me them, please?**
(pillow – Polster / blanket – Decke)

* **Can we get duty-frees on this flight, do you know?**

* **A: Excuse me, these headphones don't work. Could you get me another pair?**
(headphones – Kopfhörer)
B: Certainly, I'll exchange them straight away.
(exchange – austauschen / straight away – sofort)

* **If the weather is fine, one gets such a marvellous view from up here, cruising at 30,000 feet.**
(marvellous view – herrliche Aussicht / cruise – fliegen)

* **Did he say we would be passing through some turbulence?**
(pass through – durchfliegen / turbulence – Turbulenzen)

* **It's getting rather bumpy, I think I'll fasten my seat-belt again.**
(bumpy – unruhig / fasten one's seat-belt – sich anschnallen)

* **A: Have we already started our descent into London?**
(descent – Landeanflug)
B: Yes, we will be landing in 15 minutes from now.

POST FLIGHT

Nach dem Flug

* **Where can I claim my luggage?**
(claim – abholen, bekommen)

* **Where does the luggage arrive?**

* **Could you tell me where I can find a baggage trolley?**

* **A: Shall I get a porter?**
(porter – Gepäckströger)
B: No thanks. I've only got this hand luggage.

* **My suitcase is damaged.**
(Mein Koffer ist beschädigt.)

* **My luggage has been lost. Where can I report it?**
(report – melden)

* **A: I'm afraid my luggage has not arrived, what can I do?**
B: We will do our best to trace it for you.
(trace – ausfindig machen)
A: Here, the number of the baggage check is UI 45621.
(baggage check – Gepäckschein)

* **Which way do I go if I have goods to declare?**
(declare – verzollen)

* **How much is the duty on this?**
(duty – Zoll)

* **A: Where did Dr. Grey say he would meet us?**
(meet sbdy. – auf jemanden warten)
B: Just outside the baggage reclaim.
(just – gleich / baggage reclaim – Gepäcksausgabe)

* **Where does the air terminal bus leave?**
(leave – abfahren)

* **A: What is the best way to get to Victoria Station? I've booked a room in a hotel near there.**
B: Take a train. They go every 20 minutes.

* **Has the plane from Vienna landed yet?**
(yet – schon)

* **I hope you had a good flight.**

* **Did you have a good flight?**

* **A: How was your flight?**
  B: The flight was quite good, a bit bumpy on the way down, but not too bad.

* **There was fog at the airport, but our plane landed safely.**
  (safe – sicher)

* **We had to make an emergency landing in Frankfurt. – It was pretty hair-raising!**
  (emergency landing – Notlandung / … . Das hat mir einen ganz schönen Schrecken eingejagt.)

* **A: How did you get from London to Vienna?**
  B: I flew from Gatwick.

* **Did the plane leave on time?**

* **Did the plane arrive on time?**

* **I'm suffering from jet lag. Do you have any good remedies?**
  (suffer from – leiden an / remedy – Mittel)

RAIL TRAVEL

Mit der Eisenbahn

INQUIRIES AND TICKETS

Auskünfte und Fahrkarten

* **Can I get to Wimbledon on British Rail or do I have to go by tube?**
(tube – U-Bahn)

* **Which station do trains to Manchester go from?**

* A: **I'm going to Brighton. Let me see – the right station for Brighton's Waterloo, isn't it?**
(isn't it? – nicht wahr?)
B: **No, it isn't, actually. You'll have to go to Victoria.**

* A: **Good morning. Do you sell rail tickets here?**
(rail ticket – Bahnfahrkarte)
B: **No, I'm afraid not. You'll have to get them at the British Rail desk or at the ticket-office at the station.**
(I'm afraid not – leider nicht / desk – Schalter / ticket-office – Fahrkartenschalter)

* **Sorry to bother you, but could you tell me the way to the station?**
(bother – belästigen)

* **Where is the timetable?**
(timetable – Fahrplan)

* **Can you give me details of the trains to Edinburgh, please?**

* A: **Do I have to change?**
(Muss ich umsteigen?)
B: **Yes, at Birmingham New Street.**

* **Is there a good connection at Birmingham New Street?**
  (connection – Anschluss)

* **What time is there a connecting train to Burnley?**
  (Wann habe ich Anschluss nach Burnley?)

* **A: Excuse me, what time does the next train to Coventry leave, please?**
  (leave – abfahren)
  B: At six fifty-one. Platform 5.
  (platform – Gleis)

* **A: When's the last train back to Victoria?**
  B: It leaves here at 23.35.
  A: And when does it get in?
  (get in – ankommen)
  B: At two minutes to midnight.

* **Is there an express to Brighton before ten o'clock?**
  (express – Schnellzug)

* **Is there a fast train that gets me into Watford Junction by 9.00?**
  (fast train – Eilzug)

* **A: When does the 9.45 get to Milton Keynes Central?**
  (get to – ankommen in)
  B: It's duc in at 10.44.
  (Laut Fahrplan kommt er um 10.44 Uhr an.)

* **How long does it take to get from Euston to Manchester Piccadilly?**
  (Wie lange braucht man von … ?)

* **Is there a motorail service to Inverness?**
  (motorail service – Autoreisezug)

* **Are there any sleepers on the 22.40?**
  (sleeper – Schlafwagen)

* **Where's the ticket-office, please?**

* **A: I'd like to reserve a seat on the 8 o'clock train to Glasgow, please.**
  B: A window-seat?
  A: Yes, facing the engine please in a non-smoking compartment.
  (Ja, bitte in Fahrtrichtung in einem Nichtraucherabteil.)

* **Do I have to buy a supplementary ticket for the Intercity?**
  (supplementary ticket – Zusatzkarte)

* **A: How much is the fare?**
  (fare – Fahrpreis)
  B: It depends if you go during peak hours or off-peak after 9.30.
  (Es hängt davon ab, ob Sie während der Verkehrsspitze oder später nach 9.30 Uhr fahren.)

* **A: Two first class returns to Brighton, please.**
  (Zweimal 1. Klasse retour nach Brighton, bitte.)
  B: That'll be £48.90, please.

* **A: Does the train stop anywhere?**
  B: No, it goes to Brighton non-stop.

* **How long is the ticket valid?**
  (valid – gültig)

* **One day return to Oxford, please.**
  (day return – Tagesrückfahrkarte)

* **A second class single to Liverpool, please.**
  (Einmal 2. Klasse einfach nach … .)

* **A: I'd like a ticket to Milton Keynes Central, please. Is it cheaper to get two singles or a return?**
(single – einfache Fahrkarte / return – Rückfahrkarte)
B: When are you coming back?
A: In a week's time – next Friday.
B: In that case there's no difference.

* **Can I break my journey with this ticket?**
(break journey – Fahrt unterbrechen)

* **Could I check my luggage through to Vienna, please?**
(Kann ich bitte mein Gepäck als Reisegepäck nach Wien aufgeben?)

AT THE STATION
Auf dem Bahnhof

* **Could you tell me where the left-luggage office is, please?**
(left-luggage office – Gepäcksaufbewahrung)

* **I'd like to leave these two cases here until this evening, please.**
(leave – lassen / case – Koffer)

* **Are there any luggage lockers at this station?**
(luggage locker – Gepäckschließfach)

* **I really must be going or I won't catch my train.**
(won't – will not / catch – erwischen)

* **I don't want to miss my train.**
(miss – versäumen)

* **Where's platform 6, please?**

* **Which platform is it for the Watford Junction train?**
(Von welchem Gleis fährt der Zug nach Watford Junction ab?)

* **Which platform does the night train to Aberdeen leave from?**

* **Does this train go to Dover?**

* **A: Has the train to Bath left yet?**
  (yet – bereits)
  B: No, it's still standing at platform 11, if you hurry you'll catch it.

* **I was told I could put my bike in the guard's carriage, is that right?**
  (bike – Fahrrad / guard's carriage – Zugsbegleiterwagen)

* **What platform does the train from Canterbury arrive at?**
  (arrive – ankommen)

* **A: Is the train from Bristol running late?**
  (run late – Verspätung haben)
  B: Yes, I'm afraid it is 20 minutes late.
  (I'm afraid – leider)

* **A: Excuse me, has the 8.15 from Cambridge arrived yet?**
  B: Yes, madam. It came in five minutes ago. Platform 11, over there.
  (come in – einfahren / over there – dort drüben)

* **A platform ticket, please.**
  (Eine Bahnsteigkarte, bitte!)

* **A: Let me get you a porter.**
  (porter – Gepäckträger)
  B: No, that's all right I can manage, thanks.
  (manage – zurechtkommen)

IN THE TRAIN

Im Zug

* **A: Excuse me, is this seat free?**
  B: No, I'm afraid it's taken.

* **Excuse me, that's my seat. I have a reservation.**

* **Excuse me, but is this a smoker?**
  (smoker – Raucherabteil)

* **Could you give me a hand with this suitcase, please? I can't reach the rack.**
  (give sbdy. a hand – jemandem helfen / suitcase – Koffer / rack – Gepäcksnetz)

* **Do you want to sit by the window?**

* **Could we change places? I don't like travelling with my back to the engine.**
  (Könnten wir Platz tauschen? Ich sitze nicht gerne gegen die Fahrtrichtung.)

* **A: Do you mind if I shut the window? It's a bit draughty.**
  (Haben Sie etwas dagegen, wenn ich das Fenster schließe? Es zieht ein wenig.)
  B: Not at all.
  (Überhaupt nicht.)

* **Mind if I read your paper?**
  (paper – Zeitung)

* **Is this the through carriage to Plymouth?**
  (through carriage – Kurswagen)

- **Does this train stop in Norwich?**

- **A: Is there a dining car on this train?**
  (dining car – Speisewagen)
  B: Yes, it's at the rear.
  (Ja, am Ende des Zuges.)

- **Do you happen to know when dinner is being served?**
  (Wissen Sie zufällig, wann das Abendessen serviert wird?)

- **Would you mind watching my bag for a moment? I'll be back in a minute.**
  (watch – aufpassen auf)

- **When do we arrive in Exeter?**

- **How long are we stopping in York?**

- **A: Will we be arriving on time, do you know?**
  (on time – pünktlich)
  B: No, I'm afraid we'll be ten minutes late.

- **Doesn't a ticket collector come round and check the tickets?**
  (ticket collector – Schaffner / check – kontrollieren)

- **I'm sorry, I seem to have mislaid my ticket.**
  (seem – scheinen / mislay – verlegen)

- **Where do I have to get off for the National Exhibition Centre, please?**
  (get off – aussteigen / exhibition – Ausstellung)

- **The attendant said he would wake us up 20 minutes before our stop.**
  (attendant – Schlafwagenschaffner)

GENERAL
Allgemeines

* A: **Shall we take the train, then?**
B: **It's much more convenient going by train. If you count getting to and from the airport, it's actually faster than going by plane.**
(convenient – bequem / count – einrechnen / plane – Flugzeug)

* **Throughout Europe they are trying to make the railways more efficient. The TGV in France is already a definite alternative to travelling by air.**

* **From an environmental point of view, trains are much better than either cars or planes.**
(environmental point of view – Umweltstandpunkt)

MOTORING

Mit dem Auto unterwegs

CAR RENTAL

Autovermietung

* A: **I'd like to hire a car, please.**
  (hire – mieten)
  B: **Would you like a small, medium or large car? We have several different models to choose from.**
  (medium – mittelgroß / several – einige / choose – auswählen, wählen)

* **May I see your price-list, please?**

* **How much does it cost to rent a car?**
  (rent – mieten)

* A: **I need a large car for three days. What's the rate for an Audi 100?**
  (rate – Miete, Tarif)
  B: **The daily rate is £58.50 including insurance and with 100 miles free mileage per day. If you exceed the 100 miles it'll cost 15 pence per mile extra.**
  (insurance – Versicherung / exceed – mehr fahren als)

* **Could you tell me, is there an additional mileage charge? It does say in the leaflet that on some models there is unlimited mileage.**
  (additional mileage charge – Mehrkilometergebühr / leaflet – Prospekt / unlimited mileage – unbegrenzte Kilometer)

* A: **Could you tell me the weekly rate for a compact car including insurance, please?**
  (compact car – Kompaktwagen)
  B: **For a Vauxhall Astra it's £310 a week including liability insurance, Collision Damage Waiver, and tax.**
  (liability insurance – Haftpflichtversicherung / Collision Damage Waiver – Haftungsausschluss für Unfallschäden am Mietwagen / tax – Steuer)

* **I'd like to rent an estate car for a week. What makes do you have?**
  (estate car – Kombi / make – Marke)

* **I'd like a car with a large boot because I've got quite a lot of luggage.**
  (boot – Kofferraum / quite a lot of luggage – ziemlich viel Gepäck)

* **What convertibles do you have?**
  (convertible – Kabrio)

* **I'd like a car with manual transmission.**
  (manual transmission – Handschaltung)

* **Do you have any cars with automatic transmission?**
  (automatic transmission – Automatik)

* **Have you got any cars with telephones?**

* **Can you show me how to operate the telephone, please?**
  (operate – bedienen)

* A: **Do I have to bring the car back here or can I leave it in Dover?**
  (leave – lassen)
  B: **You can take it back to any of our offices throughout the UK, but we do charge a drop-off fee of £100 for this.**
  (charge – verrechnen / drop-off fee – Rückholgebühr)

* **Do I have to pay a deposit?**
  (pay deposit – Kaution hinterlegen)

* **Do you accept credit cards?**

* **I have a few questions because I haven't driven a Ford Escort before.**
  (drive – fahren mit)

* **What happens if the car breaks down?**
  (break down – Panne haben)

* **Do we have to wear the safety-belts?**
  (Müssen wir uns anschnallen?)

* **A: Is there any petrol left in the tank?**
  (Ist noch Benzin im Tank?)
  B: It's full up but you'll have to return it with a full tank of petrol, otherwise we'll charge you for filling it up.
  (return – zurückbringen / otherwise – sonst)

* **Will there be somebody there when I return the car? It might be rather late.**
  (rather – ziemlich)

* **A: Now I need to see your driving licence … Thank you. Will there be an additional driver?**
  (need – müssen / driving licence – Führerschein / additional driver – zusätzlicher Fahrer)
  B: No, just me.
  (just – nur)

* **Could you bring the car round to my hotel, please?**

ASKING THE WAY

Erkundigung nach dem Weg

* A: **We seem to have been going round in circles for ages. Where on earth are we?**
(Es scheint, dass wir schon seit einer Ewigkeit im Kreis fahren. Wo um Himmels willen sind wir denn?)
B: **Don't ask me! I haven't the foggiest.**
(… . Ich habe nicht den blassesten Schimmer.)
A: **I really think we'd better ask or we're going to be terribly late.**
(Ich glaube wirklich, wir sollten lieber fragen, oder wir werden viel zu spät kommen.)

* **Excuse me, where does this road go?**
(road – Straße)

* A: **How long will it take me to get to Bath?**
(Wie lange brauche ich nach Bath?)
B: **I've no idea, I'm afraid. I've never driven there myself.**
(I'm afraid – leider / drive – fahren)

* **I wonder if you could tell me how many miles it is to the nearest town?**
(Könnten Sie mir bitte sagen, … ?)

* A: **Excuse me, is this the road to Swindon?**
B: **No, I'm afraid you're on the wrong road. Let me think, you'll have to turn round here, go back down to the crossroads and turn right. Just after the zebra crossing there's a mini-roundabout. Go straight over it and then you're on the Swindon road.**
(turn round – umdrehen / back down to the crossroads – bis zur Kreuzung zurück / turn right – nach rechts abbiegen | fahren / just – gleich / zebra crossing – Zebrastreifen / roundabout – Kreisverkehr / go straight over it – fahren Sie gerade weiter)

* **A: How do I get to Junction 12 of the M1 from here, please?**
(get – kommen / junction – Autobahnauffahrt / M1 – Autobahnbezeichnung)
B: I'll show you on the map.
(map – Karte)

* **A: Excuse me, how do I get to the sea front, please?**
(sea front – „Meer"; ans Meer angrenzender Stadtteil)
B: Just go straight up to the T-junction and turn left. Follow that road right round, go over the level crossing and then you'll see it straight ahead.
(straight – gerade / up to the T-junction – bis dorthin, wo die Straße einmündet / … . Fahren Sie nur immer auf dieser Straße weiter, überqueren Sie den Bahnübergang und dann sehen Sie es direkt vor sich.)

* **A: Excuse me, I've lost my way, I must have taken a wrong turning. Can you tell me how to get to the conference centre, please?**
(lose one's way – sich verfahren / turning – Abzweigung)
B: Yes, certainly. Go straight over the first set of lights to the roundabout, then take the second exit. Then take the first left, drive down there for about 500 yards and then you'll see a sign to the right for the conference centre.
(certainly – gern / set of lights – Ampel / exit – Ausfahrt / first left – erste Straße links / down – entlang / yard – 0,914 Meter / sign – Schild, Tafel)

* **A: Excuse me, how do I get to that factory over there? That's a one-way street.**
(factory – Fabrik / over there – dort drüben / one-way street – Einbahnstraße)
B: Ah yes, you'll have to go round the block.

AT THE PETROL STATION

An der Tankstelle

* **Where's the nearest petrol station, please?**
(petrol station – Tankstelle)

* **I've rented this car. Do I need regular or super?**
(rent – mieten / regular – Normalbenzin)

* **A: How much is diesel, please?**
B: It's 52 pence a litre.

* **A: Four gallons of super, please.**
(gallon – Gallone | U.K.: 4,54 l | U.S.: 3,78 l)
B: Leaded or unleaded?
(unleaded – bleifrei, unverbleit)
A: Unleaded, please.

* **How much is that?**

* **Twenty-five pounds worth of super, please.**
(Um 25 Pfund Super, bitte!)

* **Fill it up, please.**
(Volltanken, bitte!)

* **Would you clean the windscreen and the windows, please?**
(clean – putzen / windscreen – Windschutzscheibe)

* **Please check the oil, the water and the tyre pressure.**
(check – kontrollieren / water – Kühlwasser / tyre pressure – Reifendruck)

* **A pint of oil, please.**
(pint – U.K.: 0,568 l | U.S.: 0,473 l)

* **Top up the oil, please.**
  (top up – nachfüllen)

* **Will you check the brake fluid, please?**
  (Bitte kontrollieren Sie die Bremsflüssigkeit.)

* **A: Shall I check the tyres?**
  B: No thanks, I'm in a bit of a hurry.
  (… , ich bin etwas in Eile.)

* **Do you have a car wash here?**
  (car wash – Autowaschanlage)

* **I'd like a road map of this area, please.**
  (road map – Straßenkarte / area – Gegend)

* **Where is the toilet, please?**

BREAKDOWNS AND MINOR REPAIRS

Pannen und kleinere Reparaturen

* **We've run out of petrol and there's no petrol can.**
  (Uns ist das Benzin ausgegangen, und wir haben keinen Benzinkanister mit.)

* **My car won't start. Could you give me a push, please?**
  (Mein Auto springt nicht an. Könnten Sie mich bitte anschieben?)

* **Where is there a service garage, please?**
  (service garage – Reparaturwerkstatt)

* **A: My car has broken down. Could I use your phone to call the breakdown service, please?**
(call – anrufen / breakdown service – Pannendienst)
B: Do you want the AA or the RAC?
(AA – Automobile Association / RAC – Royal Automobile Club)
A: Well, actually I don't belong to either so it doesn't matter.
(I don't belong to either – ich bin von keinem dieser beiden Mitglied / it doesn't matter – es ist egal)

* **I'm on the M1 and my car has just boiled over, the fan belt doesn't seem to be working properly. Could you come and fetch me, please?**
(Ich bin auf der M1, und der Kühler kocht; der Keilriemen scheint nicht in Ordnung zu sein. Könnten Sie mich bitte holen?)

* **I've got a flat tyre. I can't change it myself as there's no jack in the boot. Could you send a breakdown truck, please? My car is a red Mercedes and I'm on the A5 just outside Milton Keynes, my registration number is G456 RCP.**
(flat tyre – Patschen, Reifendefekt / change tyre – Reifen wechseln / jack – Wagenheber / boot – Kofferraum / breakdown truck – Pannenwagen / just – knapp / registration number – Autonummer)

* **Excuse me, can you help me? My car's broken down and I need to push it off the road.**
(push off – wegschieben von)

* **It might be the engine. Would you be so kind as to tow me to the nearest garage?**
(engine – Motor / kind – freundlich / tow – abschleppen / garage – Werkstatt)

* **Could I speak to one of your mechanics, please?**
(mechanic – Mechaniker)

* **Should I open up the bonnet?**
(bonnet – Motorhaube)

* **Have you got any spare parts for Ford cars, please?**
(spare part – Ersatzteil)

* **I need a new wing mirror, please.**
(wing mirror – Außenspiegel)

* **I've lost a hub-cap.**
(hub-cap – Radkappe)

* **The battery is flat. Can you recharge it, please?**
(flat – leer / recharge – aufladen)

* **There's something wrong with the clutch. Could you have a look, please?**
(Mit der Kupplung stimmt etwas nicht. Könnten Sie bitte mal nachsehen?)

* **The exhaust seems to be making a really loud noise.**
(exhaust – Auspuff / noise – Lärm)

* **Something keeps rattling every time I accelerate.**
(keep rattling – andauernd klappern / accelerate – beschleunigen)

* **It's very difficult to change gear.**
(change gear – schalten)

* **I can't get into second gear.**
(Ich bringe den zweiten Gang nicht hinein.)

* **The windscreen wipers and the indicators don't work.**
(Die Scheibenwischer und Blinker funktionieren nicht.)

* **I think the spark-plugs need changing.**
(Ich glaube, die Zündkerzen müssen ausgewechselt werden.)

* **Would you check the brakes and the shock absorbers, please?**
  (check – kontrollieren / brake – Bremse / shock absorber – Stoßdämpfer)

* **My windscreen's shattered. Could you replace it immediately, please?**
  (windscreen – Windschutzscheibe / shatter – zerbrechen / replace – auswechseln / immediately – gleich)

* **Would you repair the left headlight and the bumper, please?**
  (left headlight – linker Scheinwerfer / bumper – Stoßstange)

* **How long will it take?**
  (take – dauern)

* **When will the car be ready?**
  (ready – fertig)

* **Could you have it ready tomorrow at ten?**

* **Could you give me a rough estimate of the cost?**
  (rough estimate – ungefähre Schätzung; ungefährer Kostenvoranschlag)

* **Here is my key.**
  (key – Schlüssel)

PARKING

Parken

* **A: Can I park my car here?**
B: No, you can't park here, there are double yellow lines.
(… , hier ist Parkverbot.)

* **You can't park here, you'll get clamped.**
(… , sonst hängt man Ihnen Sperrklammern auf das Auto.)

* **It says No Parking on that sign over there.**
(sign – Schild, Tafel / over there – dort drüben)

* **I've got my car in front of the hotel, do you have a car-park?**
(in front of – vor / car-park – Parkplatz, Parkgarage)

* **A: Can you tell me where the nearest car-park is, please?**
B: There's a multi-storey just around the corner on the left-hand side.
(multi-storey – Parkhaus / just around the corner – gleich um die Ecke)

* **Is it open all night?**

* **Excuse me, my car's parked in a No Parking area. How do I get to the hotel car-park, please?**
(… , mein Auto steht im Parkverbot. … .)

* **A: It looks like I may have got a parking-ticket.**
(parking-ticket – Strafzettel wegen Falschparkens)
B: It's OK, it's only an advert.
(advert – Reklame)

* **Do you think you could move your car, please? I can't get mine out.**
(move car – mit dem Auto etwas wegfahren)

* **Could you push back a little, please?**
(push back – zurückschieben)

* **Where can I pay for the car-park, please?**
(car-park – Parkplatz, Parkgarage, Parkhaus)

* **Could I have a receipt, please?**
(receipt – Quittung)

* **I seem to have mislaid my car-park ticket.**
(seem – scheinen / mislay – verlegen / car-park ticket – Parkschein)

* **I parked my car on the fifth floor.**
(floor – Etage)

* **Sorry I'm late. I couldn't find a parking-space.**
(parking-space – Parkplatz, Einzelparkplatz)

* **When is the next lay-by?**
(lay-by – Rastplatz)

CAR FERRY
Autofähre

* **How often does the car ferry to Cork run, please?**
(car ferry – Autofähre / run – verkehren)

* **When does the next ferry leave for Calais, please?**
(leave for – abfahren nach)

* **What time is the next sailing, please?**
(sailing – Abfahrt)

* A: **How long does the crossing take, please?**
  (crossing – Überfahrt)
  B: **It's 75 minutes by ferry, but only 30 minutes on the hovercraft.**
  (hovercraft – Luftkissenboot)

* **Where does the ferry to Dunkirk dock, please?**
  (dock – anlegen)

* **Do I have to apply the hand-brake?**
  (apply hand-brake – Handbremse anziehen)

* **Could you tell me the way down to the car deck, please?**

* **Do you ever get seasick, Maggy?**
  (seasick – seekrank)

MISCELLANEOUS

Sonstiges

* **Finally I'm getting used to driving on the left!**
  (finally – endlich / get used to – sich gewöhnen an)

* **I've never driven a right-hand drive before.**
  (right-hand drive – rechtsgelenktes Fahrzeug)

* **What are the speed limits in Britain?**
  (speed limit – Geschwindigkeitsbegrenzung)

* **I got stopped for speeding on the way over.**
  (speeding – Schnellfahren / on the way over – auf der Fahrt hierher)

* **I was just overtaking a tractor and suddenly it was so slippery that I came off the road.**
(Ich überholte gerade einen Traktor, und plötzlich war es so rutschig, dass ich von der Straße abkam.)

* **A: Was the traffic bad this morning?**
(traffic – Verkehr)
B: It was really heavy. There were serious congestions on the motorway.
(heavy – sehr stark / serious – beträchtlich / congestion – Stau / motorway – Autobahn)

* **The traffic wasn't moving at all and I sat in a traffic jam for over half an hour.**
(Der Verkehr kam völlig zum Erliegen, und ich saß mehr als eine halbe Stunde in einem Stau fest.)

* **There are so many road-works on the M25, the tail-backs are worse than ever.**
(road-works – Baustellen / tail-back – Rückstau / worse than ever – schlimmer als je zuvor)

* **They said on the radio that there are long hold-ups on the M45.**
(hold-up – Stau)

* **Here's my car. Let me give you a lift.**
(give sbdy. a lift – jemanden mit dem Auto mitnehmen)

* **A: Where can I drop you off?**
(Wo kann ich Sie aussteigen lassen?)
B: You can drop me right here, that'll do fine.
(… , das passt schon.)

* **A: Any chance of a lift?**
B: I'd like to, but I'm not going that way today, sorry.

* **Can I give you a lift to the station? It's on my way home.**

* **If I can just ask you to wait here, I'll bring the car round. I won't be a minute.**
  (… . Ich bin gleich wieder hier.)

* **Would you like to go for a drive this evening? I could show you a bit of the countryside around here and then we could go to a country pub.**
  (go for a drive – eine Spazierfahrt machen / countryside – Gegend)

* **I can pick you up at the office.**
  (pick up – abholen)

TAXI

Taxi

* **We'd better take a taxi. The train leaves in twenty minutes.**
  (Wir sollten lieber ein Taxi nehmen. … . / leave – abfahren)

* **A: Would you like me to call you a taxi?**
  B: Thank you, but really don't bother. It's not far and I'd like to stretch my legs a bit anyway.
  (Danke, aber das ist wirklich nicht notwendig. Es ist nicht weit, und ich würde mir ohnehin gerne die Füße etwas vertreten.)

* **How are you getting back to town? Shall I get you a taxi?**
  (get back – zurückkommen / get – besorgen)

* **Good evening, I'd like a taxi for 125 London Road, please.**

* **Where's the nearest taxi rank, please?**
  (taxi rank – Taxistand)

* **Would you hail a taxi, please?**
  (hail – anhalten, rufen)

* **To the station, please.**
  (Zum Bahnhof, bitte!)

* **Will you take me to the airport, please?**
  (Bringen Sie mich bitte zum Flughafen.)

* **Do you think you can get me to Victoria Station by 3.30?**
  (get – bringen)

* **Do you think we'll make it?**
  (make – schaffen)

* **Would you stop here for a minute, please?**

* **What's the fare?**
  (fare – Fahrpreis)

* **That's for you.**

HOTEL

Hotel

INQUIRIES, RESERVATIONS, ETC.

Anfragen, Zimmerreservierungen usw.

* A: **I need your advice. Which hotel in Oxford would you recommend?**
(advice – Rat / recommend – empfehlen)
B: **I'd recommend the Punting Lodge Hotel.**
A: **Is it central?**
(central – zentral gelegen)

* A: **Listen, do you know a decent hotel in Cardiff?**
(Du, kennst du ein anständiges Hotel … ?)
B: **What about the "Western View"?**
(Wie wär's mit … ?)
A: **What's it like?**
(Wie ist es?)

* **What are the prices like?**
(Wie sind die Preise dort?)

* **I've heard the Central Hotel is five minutes from the centre of town, next to the railway station, and is therefore very convenient for people arriving or leaving by train.**
(railway station – Bahnhof / convenient – praktisch / arrive – ankommen / leave – abfahren)

* **Do you think that the Hilton is very full just at present?**
(just at present – zur Zeit; im Augenblick)

* **A: Shall we make a hotel reservation for you?**
B: Yes, that would be a good idea. It would be rather a nuisance for me to do this from London.
(be rather a nuisance – ziemlich umständlich sein)

* **Book me into my usual hotel, would you?**
(would you? – bitte)

* **Could you book me a single room for tonight, please. At the Grand Hotel if possible.**
(single room – Einzelzimmer / for tonight – für die Nacht von heute auf morgen)

* **Cath, would you reserve me a hotel room for Tuesday night?**

* **Sally, have you booked a room for me?**

* **If you can't get me into a hotel in Bristol you could try to find some private accommodation.**
(get into – unterbringen in / accommodation – Unterkunft)

* **I'll be arriving on a late flight from Vienna, so could you book me into a hotel near the airport and arrange dinner?**
(arrange dinner – Essen vorbestellen)

* **I wish to make a reservation. Would you put me through to the reception dcsk, please.**
(put through to – verbinden mit / reception desk – Rezeption)

* **I'd like to book a single room with bathroom for three nights from the night of Wednesday, February the twenty-second. The reservation is for our Managing Director, Mr. Sepp Volter.**
(Managing Director – Generaldirektor)

* **Could you let me have written confirmation that the reservation has been made.**
(confirmation – Bestätigung)

* **Is that Advance Reservations? I'd like to reserve a single room with shower for four nights, half board, please. I'll be arriving Tuesday afternoon.**
  (Advance Reservations – Zimmerreservierung / shower – Dusche / half board – Halbpension)

* **I'd like to reserve a double room with full board for five nights, starting next Saturday.**
  (double room – Doppelzimmer / full board – Vollpension)

* **Could you let me have your accommodation charges so that I can prepare an estimate of expenses.**
  (accommodation charges – Zimmerpreise / prepare – erstellen / estimate of expenses – Spesenvoranschlag)

* **Could you arrange for someone to meet me at the airport, please?**
  (Könnten Sie bitte veranlassen, dass mich jemand vom Flughafen abholt?)

* **My secretary has booked a room for me for tomorrow. It's in the name of Stefan Berger. I'll be checking in rather late, I'm afraid. At about midnight. Would you please hold the room for me?**
  (… . Ich fürchte, ich werde ziemlich spät ankommen. So gegen Mitternacht. Würden Sie bitte das Zimmer für mich freihalten?)

* **A: I've made a reservation for the fifteenth and now I'm afraid I'll have to cancel it. The conference in London has been called off.**
  (I'm afraid – leider / cancel – stornieren / call off – absagen)
  B: What name was the room booked under?
  A: It was booked in the name of Dr. Richard Lackner.

* **Good evening. I want a single room, please.**

* **I'd like two double rooms, please.**

* **A: I'm afraid we're full up.**
(Wir sind leider voll.)
B: Could you ring another hotel for me and ask if they have any vacancies?
(ring – anrufen / vacancy – freies Zimmer)

* **A: Have you got any vacancies for tonight?**
B: We have one double room on the second floor.
(floor – Stock)

* **A: How much is this room?**
B: £65 a night including breakfast.
(… inklusive Frühstück.)
A: What about the other meals?
(Und was ist mit den anderen Mahlzeiten?)
B: They are charged for separately.
(Für die muss man extra zahlen.)

* **How much do you charge per night?**
(charge – verlangen)

* **What's the surcharge for a single room?**
(surcharge – Zuschlag)

* **Is there an additional service charge or is service included in your rates?**
(additional service charge – Bedienungszuschlag / rate – Preis)

* **Have you got a room free on the top floor?**
(on the top floor – im obersten Stock)

* **Do you have a quiet room at the back?**
(quiet – ruhig / at the back – nach hinten hinaus)

* **Has the room got a view of the park?**
(view – Blick, Aussicht)

* **Is it a room with a view of the sea?**
  (… mit Blick aufs Meer?)

* **Have you got a twin room?**
  (Haben Sie ein Doppelzimmer mit Einzelbetten?)

* **I'd like one with a double bed.**

* **I'd like to havc a look at it, please.**

* **I'd rather have a room with a bath than one with a shower, if possible.**
  (rather – lieber)

* **A: Is this room big enough for you, sir?**
  (enough – genug)
  B: I suppose you haven't anything a little larger, have you?
  (suppose – annehmen / have you? – oder?)

* **All I want is a quiet room away from the noise of the traffic. I don't sleep very well.**
  (noise – Lärm / traffic – Verkehr)

* **I'll take it.**

* **I want to stay at least a week.**
  (at least – zumindest)

* **Do you want me to fill in this registration form right away?**
  (Soll ich dieses Anmeldeformular jetzt gleich ausfüllen?)

* **My company has been in touch with me this morning. They'd like me to stay on for two more days. I wonder if it's possible to extend my stay here until the sixth?**
  (Meine Firma hat mich heute morgen kontaktiert. … . / stay – bleiben / … . Wäre es möglich, bis zum 6. zu verlängern?)

AT THE RECEPTION

Am Empfang

* **Good evening, I've reserved a room. It's a double room with private bath. My name is Kreuz.**
(private bath – eigenes Bad)

* **A: Good afternoon. I believe you have two rooms booked for us: Dr. Baker and Dr. Schrempf.**
(believe – glauben)
B: Ah, yes. Rooms 225 and 226 on the second floor. Shall I call the porter?
(porter – Träger)
A: No, thank you, we've only got this hand luggage.
(hand luggage – Handgepäck)
B: And would you like newspapers in the morning?
A: Yes, we'd both like the Financial Times, please.

* **A: My name is Rolf Peterson, I've had a room booked for me from today for a week.**
(have room booked – Zimmer buchen lassen)
B: Yes, Mr. Peterson. It's Room 345 on the third floor. We'll have your luggage brought up immediately. Would you fill in the registration form, please.
(… . Wir werden Ihr Gepäck sofort hinaufbringen lassen. … .)
A: What do I fill in here?
B: I just need your signature and your passport number and we'll take care of the rest.
(just – nur / signature – Unterschrift / take care of – erledigen)

* **What do you mean you haven't got a room left? I booked four weeks in advance and I have your confirmation. Here it is.**
(what do you mean – was soll das heißen / left – frei / in advance – im Voraus)

* A: **Excuse me, where's room 543, please?**
B: **Come out of the lift on the fifth floor and turn down the corridor on the right. Room 543 is on the left.**
(… und gehen Sie nach rechts den Gang entlang. … .)

* **Please have the luggage taken up to my room.**
(Bitte lassen Sie das Gepäck in mein Zimmer hinaufbringen.)

* **Would it be possible for the porter to show me to my room?**
(show – bringen)

* **Can you arrange for my luggage to be collected, please? It is still at the airport.**
(Können Sie bitte veranlassen, dass mein Gepäck abgeholt wird? … . / still – noch immer)

* A: **Is your room all right?**
B: **Yes, it's fine, thanks.**

* **Could you tell me whether Mr. Bright has already checked in?**
(whether – ob)

* **Could you tell Mr. Bright when he checks in that I'll be waiting for him in the coffee lounge.**

* **Could you tell me what the voltage in the rooms is, please?**
(voltage – Stromspannung)

* **Do you have an adapter which I can use for my shaver?**
(adapter – Zwischenstecker / shaver – Rasierapparat)

* **Could you cash this traveller's cheque for me, please?**
(cash traveller's cheque – Reisescheck einlösen)

* **Could you look after these valuables for me, please?**
(Könnten Sie bitte diese Wertgegenstände für mich aufbewahren?)

* **Where can I deposit my valuables?**
(deposit – hinterlegen, aufbewahren)

* **Where can I post this letter?**
(post – aufgeben)

* **I'd like to book a table in the hotel restaurant for three at eight.**

* **Where is the dining room, please?**
(dining room – Speisesaal)

* **I'm expecting a long-distance call from Vienna. I'll be in the bar for an hour or so before I go up to my room.**
(expect – erwarten / long-distance call – Ferngespräch)

* **A: Can I make an international call from my room?**
B: Yes you can, but don't forget to dial 010 before the code of the country you're calling.
(dial – wählen / code – Vorwahl)

* **What is the country code for Austria for calls dialled from here?**
(country code – Landeskennzahl)

* **How do I get an outside line, please?**
(Wie kann ich bitte hinauswählen?)

* **I'd like an early morning call tomorrow at six thirty.**
(early morning call – Weckruf)

* **I'd like to be woken up in the morning at eight o'clock.**

* **I'd like to remind you to call me at seven tomorrow morning.**
(remind – erinnern)

* **I need a taxi tomorrow at nine thirty. Could you arrange that for me, please?**

* **I'd like to rent a car. Can you recommend where to go?**
(rent – mieten)

* **Could you call me a taxi, please?**

* A: **I'm staying at the hotel. I'd like to know where the car-park is, please.**
(car-park – Parkplatz, Parkgarage)
B: **It's behind the hotel, sir. You go round to the left.**
(behind – hinter)

* **Key to room 752, please. Is there any message for me?**
(key – Schlüssel / message – Nachricht)

* **Did anyone ask for me?**

* **Are there any letters for me?**
(Ist Post für mich da?)

* A: **I wonder if you'd be prepared to change rooms with another guest, sir? We appear to have made an error.**
(Wären Sie bitte bereit, mit einem anderen Gast Zimmer zu tauschen? Es scheint uns da ein Fehler unterlaufen zu sein.)
B: **I see no objection, provided that the room is of the same standard as my present one.**
(objection – Einwand / provided – vorausgesetzt / present – jetzig)

* A: **Would you object to Room 34, sir? It's very comfortable.**
(object to – etwas haben gegen)
B: **Well, I don't really want to change rooms. I asked for that room in particular.**
(in particular – speziell)

HOTEL SERVICES

* A: **I'd like to know something about the facilities that your hotel has to offer.**
(Könnten Sie mir bitte sagen, was das Hotel alles zu bieten hat?)
B: **We have two restaurants, a sauna, a heated swimming-pool, coffee shop and bar, and we offer free transport to the airport, exchange facilities, same-day laundry service, a hairdresser, souvenir shop, disco and cocktail bar.**
(exchange facilities – Möglichkeit, Geld zu wechseln / laundry – Wäscherei / hairdresser – Frisiersalon)

* A: **What facilities are there in the rooms?**
(facilities – [zusätzliche] Ausstattung)
B: **Each room has a mini-bar, colour television, separate WC, shower and bath.**
(separate – eigen)

* **Do all the rooms have air-conditioning and central heating?**

* **And what about evening entertainment?**
(evening entertainment – Abendunterhaltung)

* **How about restaurant facilities?**
(Welche Möglichkeiten gibt es hier zu essen?)

* **Do you have a swimming-pool or a sauna?**

* **Is there a fitness room?**

* A: **Do you have an in-house laundry service?**
B: **Yes. And an eight-hour dry-cleaning service.**
(dry cleaning – chemische Reinigung)

✳ **A: Where can I watch television?**
B: In the lounge straight over there.
(Im Aufenthaltsraum gleich dort drüben.)

✳ **Does anyone mind if I switch the TV on?**
(Stört es jemanden, wenn ich den Fernseher einschalte?)

✳ **Can you tell me where the gents is, please?**
(gents – Herrentoilette)

✳ **Where's the ladies, please?**
(ladies – Damentoilette)

✳ **Room Service, please. Could you send up a bottle of champagne and two glasses to room 432? And a small bottle of Perrier, please.**
(bottle – Flasche)

✳ **Room Service, please. I know it's pretty late, but would it still be possible to have a couple of sandwiches and a bottle of beer?**
(pretty late – ziemlich spät / still – noch / a couple of – ein paar)

✳ **Could you arrange to have these things washed for me, please?**
(Könnten Sie bitte diese Sachen für mich waschen lassen?)

✳ **I'd like to have my suits ironed before ten o'clock tomorrow.**
(Würden Sie bitte dafür sorgen, dass meine Anzüge … gebügelt werden.)

✳ **How long will it take to have my shirts pressed?**
(take – dauern / press shirt – Hemd bügeln)

BREAKFAST
Frühstück

* **What time do you serve breakfast?**
(breakfast – Frühstück)

* **I'd like breakfast in my room at eight thirty, continental breakfast, that is.**
(that is – und zwar)

* **Could you tell me where the breakfast buffet is, please?**

* **Where is the breakfast room, please?**

* **A: What would you like? Coffee or tea?**
B: I'd prefer tea, please.
(Ich möchte lieber Tee, bitte.)

* **A: How do you like your coffee?**
B: White, no sugar please.
(white – mit Milch)

* **Black with two sugars, please.**

* **A: Could I have scrambled eggs, please?**
(scrambled eggs – Rühreier, Eierspeise)
B: And two fried eggs for me, please.
(fried eggs – Spiegeleier)

* **Would you pass me the marmalade, please?**
(Würden Sie mir bitte die Orangenmarmelade geben?)

COMPLAINTS
Beschwerden

* **I'd like to see the manager, please.**
(see sbdy. – jemanden sprechen)

* **I'd like to lodge a complaint.**
(Ich möchte mich beschweren.)

* A: **What seems to be the trouble, sir?**
(Worum handelt es sich denn?)
B: **I'm not at all satisfied with the service in this hotel.**
(satisfied – zufrieden)

* **I wish to complain in the strongest terms about the service in this hotel.**
(Ich möchte mich ganz energisch … beschweren.)

* **I'm afraid I don't like my room. There's too much noise from the traffic outside. Could you find me a room that is a bit quieter, please?**
(I'm afraid – tut mir leid)

* **I'm not happy with my room. I didn't sleep at all last night.**
(not … at all – überhaupt nicht)

* **I'm afraid to have to report that I didn't get my early morning call and subsequently was late for a very important meeting.**
(report – mitteilen / subsequently – in der Folge / be late – zu spät kommen / meeting – Sitzung)

* **I'm sorry to say this, but the porter was rather rude to me just now.**
(rather rude – ziemlich unhöflich)

* **This key doesn't fit properly.**
(... passt nicht genau.)

* **The room hasn't been cleaned.**
(clean – reinigen)

* **The bed isn't made.**

* **There aren't any towels in my room.**
(towel – Handtuch)

* **The window doesn't shut properly.**
(Das Fenster schließt nicht ordentlich.)

* **The window doesn't open at all.**
(... lässt sich überhaupt nicht öffnen.)

* **The toilet won't flush.**
(Die Spülung funktioniert nicht.)

* **The light beside the bed doesn't work.**
(beside – neben / work – funktionieren)

* **The tap drips.**
(Der Wasserhahn tropft.)

* **There doesn't seem to be any hot water in my room.**
(Soweit ich das feststellen kann, gibt es kein Warmwasser in meinem Zimmer.)

* **The radio doesn't work.**

* **I can't seem to get the TV to work.**
(Irgendwie schaffe ich es nicht, den Fernseher einzuschalten.)

CHECKING OUT

Abreise

* **By what time do I have to check out?**
(Bis wann muss ich das Zimmer geräumt haben?)

* **When's check-out time?**

* **What time do we have to vacate the rooms?**
(vacate – räumen)

* **I'd like to check out, please.**
(Ich möchte bitte abreisen.)

* **I'm leaving tomorrow. Could you please have my bill ready.**
(Ich reise morgen ab. Könnten Sie bitte meine Rechnung fertig machen.)

* **Could you make up my bill, please. I'm leaving in an hour.**
(make up – fertig machen)

* A: **Would you prefer me to settle my bill now or after breakfast?**
(Möchten Sie lieber, dass ich meine Rechnung jetzt sofort oder nach dem Frühstück begleiche?)
B: **You can settle it right away, I have it ready. The rates include tax and service charge.**
(right away – jetzt gleich / tax – Steuer)

* **There must be a mistake. I didn't make that many telephone calls!**
(mistake – Irrtum)

* **Do you accept Eurocheques?**

* **Can I pay by Visa?**

* **I have to catch my plane to New York at five p.m. at Heathrow. Could you tell me the best way to get there in time?**
(catch plane – Maschine erwischen / five p.m. – 17 Uhr / in time – rechtzeitig)

* **Could you arrange for my luggage to be taken to the airport, please?**
(Könnten Sie bitte veranlassen, dass mein Gepäck zum Flughafen gebracht wird?)

* **Can I leave my things here until I get back?**
(leave – lassen)

BUSINESS FACILITIES

Leistungsangebot für Geschäftsleute

* **I'd need a bilingual secretary for some correspondence tomorrow afternoon. Could that be arranged?**
(bilingual – zweisprachig)

* **Do you have a copying service? I'd need fifteen copies tomorrow at nine. It is confidential, I might add.**
(confidential – vertraulich / add – hinzufügen)

* **Is there an in-house translation service?**
(in-house – hauseigen / translation – Übersetzung)

* **I'd need a room for a meeting tomorrow at two p.m.. The group will include about ten people.**

* **What are the dimensions of the room?**
(dimension – Ausmaß)

* **Does the room have a white board with markers?**
(board – Tafel / marker – Schreibstift)

* **Could you arrange a flip chart and markers for Room 305 at two p.m., please?**

* **I was wondering if our name cards and holders were ready yet?**
(Ich möchte wissen, ob unsere Namensschilder schon fertig sind.)

* **We need five rooms seating up to forty people each.**
(seat – Platz bieten)

* **What is the capacity of your Royal Garden Function Rooms?**
(capacity – Fassungsvermögen / function room – Veranstaltungsraum)

* **What about office support services? I suppose you have a fax, a photocopier and somebody that can help us with the preparation of the conference documents.**
(office support services – Bürodienste / suppose – annehmen, vermuten / preparation – Erstellung)

* A: **I'd need a fairly large room for a party of about thirty people the day after tomorrow from about seven p.m.. I'd like to show some slides first. Have you got a slide-projector and a screen?**
(fairly – ziemlich / party – Gruppe / slide – Dia / screen – Leinwand)
B: **Certainly. We can arrange that for you.**
(certainly – selbstverständlich)
A: **I'd like to try the equipment out tonight to make sure that everything is OK.**
(try out – ausprobieren / equipment – Geräte / tonight – heute abend / make sure – sich vergewissern)

* **We're looking for a hotel where we could hold a conference next March. Could I speak to the Conference and Banqueting Manager, please?**
(look for – suchen)

* **A: Have you got access to the Internet?**
(access – Zugang)
B: Certainly. You can use the computer in the Main Hall or the machines in the Business Centre on the first floor.
(floor – Stockwerk)

* **A: How are the conference rooms equipped?**
(equip – ausstatten)
B: The rooms are furnished with folding tables, comfortable chairs and an extensive range of AV facilities.
(furnish – ausstatten / folding table – Klapptisch / chair – Sessel / range – Auswahl / AV facilities – audio-visual facilities | audiovisuelle Einrichtungen)
A: You mean integrated sound systems with playback facilities for CDs and DVDs?
(sound – Ton, Laut / CD – Compact Disc / DVD – Digital Versatile Disc)
B: Yes, and of course overhead projectors for data and video projection.
A: You mean beamers?
B: Yes, that's what these projectors are often called.

VISITS AND PARTIES

Besuche und Parties

INVITATIONS

Einladungen

(see also "Restaurants, Bars, etc.: Invitations")

* A: **I don't know what your plans are, Brigitte, but would you like to have tea at my place on Bank Holiday Monday?**
(at my place – bei mir zu Hause)
B: **I've got nothing on so far, that'd be lovely. Thank you.**
(Ich habe bisher noch nichts vor, das wäre wirklich sehr nett. … .)

* A: **If you're free on Sunday, I'd like to invite you to have dinner with us at our house.**
(invite sbdy. to have dinner – jemanden zum Essen einladen)
B: **Yes I am free. That's very kind of you. When should I come?**
(kind – freundlich)

* A: **Well, if you're not doing anything on Tuesday evening, I was wondering if you'd perhaps like to join us for a meal?**
(… , möchten Sie vielleicht zu uns zum Essen kommen?)
B: **Thank you very much. I'd love to.**
(… , sehr gerne.)

* A: **Oh, by the way, we're throwing a little party tonight to celebrate Jim's promotion, Brendan. I do hope you can come.**
(by the way – übrigens / throw party – Party geben | veranstalten / celebrate – feiern / promotion – Beförderung / I do hope – ich hoffe sehr)
B: **That's very nice. I'd very much like to.**
A: **We'll be starting at around eight. Drop in any time you feel like it.**
(… . Komm vorbei, wann es dir passt.)

* **A: Have you got any plans for tomorrow evening?**
B: Nothing in particular, no. Why?
(Nichts Besonderes, … .)
A: Well, I was just wondering if you'd be interested in coming over to my place for supper? It'd give me a chance to repay some of the hospitality you gave us in Vienna last year.
(supper – Abendessen / hospitality – Gastfreundschaft)
B: I'd be delighted, Alan. Thank you very much, I'll look forward to it.
(Sehr gerne, … . / look forward to – sich freuen auf)

* **A: If you've nothing arranged this evening, Mr. Baines, I was wondering if you'd like to come round for a drink?**
(have nothing arranged – nichts vorhaben)
B: Thanks for the invitation, but I really don't think I'll be able to come. I've got so much preparation to do for tomorrow.
(invitation – Einladung / preparation – Vorbereitungen)

* **A: If you're free on Saturday, why not come round for a drink?**
B: Thank you very much, but unfortunately I won't be here at the weekend. What a pity!
(unfortunately – leider / won't – will not / what a pity – wie schade)

* **A: My wife and I thought it would be nice if you could come to lunch on Saturday. Would that suit you?**
(lunch – Mittagessen / suit – passen)
B: I'd really like to, Mr. Appleby, but I'm afraid I've just accepted an invitation to lunch with Chris. Thank you very much all the same.
(I'm afraid – leider / just – gerade / all the same – trotzdem)

* **A: Would you like to come to dinner at my house on Wednesday at around seven thirty?**
B: I'm terribly sorry, but I'm pressed for time at the moment. Perhaps we could make it next week?
(terrible – schrecklich / be pressed for time – unter Zeitdruck sein)

ARRIVAL

Eintreffen

* **A: Good evening, Mr. Baier. I'm so pleased you could come. Do come in.**
(… . Freut mich wirklich, dass Sie kommen konnten. Kommen Sie doch herein!)
B: Good evening. Thank you. What a nice place you have here.
(… . Sie haben es aber wirklich nett hier.)

* **A: Please come in.**
B: Thank you.
A: Take a seat wherever you like and make yourself feel at home.

* **A: Hi, Barbara. Brought you some flowers.**
B: Alex, they're gorgeous. I've never seen so many flowers!
(gorgeous – wunderschön)

* **A: Let me take your coat, Bruno.**
(coat – Mantel)
B: That's very kind of you, thanks.

* **A: I hope you found your way here without any trouble.**
B: Yes, no trouble at all, thank you.
(Ja, war überhaupt kein Problem, … .)

* **A: What a charming dress!**
(charming dress – bezauberndes Kleid)
B: Oh, thanks. Do you like it?

DRINKS

Getränke

(see also "Restaurants, Bars, etc.: Pubs/Pub Lunch; At the Bar")

* **A: While we're waiting, can I offer you a drink?**
  B: Thanks very much. What have you got?

* **A: Well, what would you like to drink?**
  B: Oh, Scotch, please.
  A: With ice?
  B: With ice please. On the rocks. Yes, that's fine.
  (on the rocks – mit Eis)

* **A: Could you give me a whisky, please?**
  B: Neat or with water?
  (neat – pur)

* **A: Would you care for a drink, Mr. Bammer?**
  (care for – mögen, wünschen)
  B: That's very kind of you. A glass of lager, please.
  (lager – Lagerbier)

* **Here's to you!**
  (Auf Ihr Wohl!)

* **A: Drink, Bethan?**
  B: Yes, an orange juice, please.
  C: Same for me, please.

* **A: You look as if you need a drink. What'll you have? Some more wine?**
  B: No, thanks. It's very good, but I've had enough.
  (enough – genug)

* **A: Let me get you a drink.**
(get – holen, bringen)
B: I'd like a soft drink, please. A coke with ice and lemon'll do fine.
(soft drink – alkoholfreies Getränk / lemon – Zitrone / will do fine – wäre fein)

* **A: May I have a tomato juice, please?**
B: I'm sorry, we've only got orange or grapefruit.

TEA / COFFEE

(see also "Visits and Parties: Drinks")

* **A: Would you like some tea or coffee?**
B: I'd prefer tea, please, if you don't mind.
(Ich möchte lieber Tee, wenn es leicht geht.)

* **A: Can I get you some tea, Bob?**
B: Only if you're having one.
(Nur wenn Sie sich auch einen holen.)

* **A: Would you care for a cup of coffee?**
(Möchten Sie gerne eine Tasse Kaffee?)
B: Mmm, I'd love a cup.

* **A: How do you like it?**
B: Black, no sugar, please.

* **White, two sugars, please.**
(white – mit Milch)

* **A: Ah, here's the coffee …**
B: Thanks.
A: Sugar, Bill?
B: Two please. Thanks.

* **A: Could I have the sugar, please?**
B: Yes, here you are.
(… , hier bitte!)
A: Thank you.

* **A: Please help yourself to coffee.**
(Bitte nehmen Sie sich Kaffee.)
B: Thanks, Alois, I will.

* **A: Won't you have another cup of tea, Bob?**
B: No, I'd rather not, thanks.
(Nein, eher nicht, … .)

* **A: Do you want another cup of coffee?**
B: No thanks, I'm fine.
(… , war sehr gut.)

* **A: How about a piece of cake?**
(Möchten Sie ein Stück Kuchen?)
B: Thank you, but no.

AT THE TABLE

Bei Tisch

(see also "Restaurants, Bars, etc.: During the Meal")

* **The food smells nice.**
(Das riecht aber gut.)

* **Doesn't this look lovely!**
(Das sieht aber gut aus.)

* **Do start, don't let it get cold.**
(do start – fangen Sie doch bitte an)

* **Would you mind passing the vinegar, please?**
(Würden Sie mir freundlicherweise den Essig geben?)

* **I wonder, could I have some mayonnaise or mustard, please?**
(Könnte ich bitte etwas Mayonnaise oder Senf haben?)

* **Help yourself to as much as you like, there's plenty more in the kitchen.**
(… , es gibt noch genug in der Küche.)

* **A: Have you had any salad?**
B: Yes, thank you.

* **A: Would you care for a bit more fish, Mr. Burrows?**
B: Not for me, thank you.

* **A: Another slice of roast beef?**
(slice – Scheibe)
B: No, thanks, really. It's delicious but I'm on a diet.
(delicious – ausgezeichnet)

* **A: You must have some more chicken.**
(have – nehmen / chicken – Huhn)
B: No, thanks. It tastes very good, but I'm supposed to be slimming.
(… . Es schmeckt sehr gut, aber ich soll eigentlich abnehmen.)
A: Can't I tempt you?
(tempt – verführen)
B: Well, maybe I could manage a very small piece.
(manage – vertragen)

* **A: Do have the rest of the mashed potato.**
(mashed potato – Kartoffelpüree)
B: It's delicious, but I don't think I ought to.
(… , aber ich glaube, ich soll eigentlich nicht mehr.)

* **A: Could I have a second helping, please?**
(helping – Portion)
B: Please help yourself.

* **A: Would you like some fruit salad to finish with?**
(Möchten Sie etwas Fruchtsalat zum Abschluss?)
B: That sounds very nice. Yes please.
(Das hört sich sehr gut an. … .)

* **I'll have to give in. That's too much for me.**
(give in – Handtuch werfen)

* **Can I bring you some coffee and a liqueur, perhaps?**

* **Oh dear, I am sorry, I've spilt some wine on the table-cloth.**
(spill – verschütten / table-cloth – Tischtuch)

AFTER THE MEAL

Nach dem Essen

(see also "Visits and Parties: Tea/Coffee")

* **Mmm, that was a delicious meal, Glenda.**

* **Oh, that was a lovely meal.**
(lovely – wunderbar)

* **A: Well, that was delicious! Thank you very much indeed. I didn't know you were such a good cook!**
B: Thank you. It's very kind of you to say so.
A: I could do the washing-up, if you like.
B: No, don't bother. I can put it all in the dishwasher.
(Nein, bemühen Sie sich nicht. … . / dishwasher – Geschirrspüler)

* **A: Would you care for some brandy?**
  B: That'd be just perfect.
  (Das wäre jetzt genau das Richtige.)

* **A: Mind if I smoke?**
  (Macht es Ihnen etwas aus, wenn ich rauche?)
  B: No, go ahead.
  (Nein, rauchen Sie nur.)

* **Well, actually, we'd prefer you not to. You can go out into the garden, though.**
  (Eigentlich wäre es uns lieber, Sie würden nicht rauchen. … . / though – aber)

* **Could I have an ashtray, please?**
  (ashtray – Aschenbecher)

* **A: Would you like a cigarette?**
  B: No thanks, I'm trying to give up.
  (give up – aufhören)

* **A: Could I scrounge a cigarette, please? I seem to have run out.**
  (scrounge – schnorren / … . Ich glaube, ich habe keine mehr.)
  B: Yes, of course. Here you are.

AT A PARTY

(see also "Restaurants, Bars, etc.: Smoking; Out on the Town")

* **A: Nice of you to come. Come in and join the party.**
  (join the party – mach mit)
  B: I can't stay long, I'm afraid.

* **Is Robin coming to the party?**

* **A: Hello, Brian, it's nice to see you here ... Who are all these people?**
B: Well, you know Sheila and Joy and the girl with the glasses is Louise.
(glasses – Augengläser, Brille)
A: Oh, I know. The receptionist.
(receptionist – Dame aus der Rezeption)

* **Fancy seeing you here! I haven't seen you for ages!**
(Was, du bist auch hier! … . / for ages – ewig)

* **A: Hello, Mr. Batten. I hope you're enjoying the party.**
(… . Ich hoffe, Sie unterhalten sich gut.)
B: Yes, very much.

* **A: Good party!**
B: It's all right.
A: Nice place!

* **A: Would you like a cheese sandwich?**
B: I'd love one, thanks.
C: Not for me, thanks.

* **A: Would you like something to eat?**
B: Yes, I'll have some cheese, please.

* **A: What's in this punch? It's pretty strong.**
(pretty – ziemlich)
B: Well, it's wine and fruit juice, mainly.
A: I feel quite tipsy!
(quite tipsy – ganz schön beschwipst)

* **A: What about trying a Guinness before you go home?**
(Möchten Sie noch einen Schluck Guinness-Bier, … ?)
B: Well, if you don't mind, I'd prefer not to have beer. Is there any wine left?
(… . Ist noch etwas Wein da?)

* **Excuse me, Helen. Have you got a light?**
(light – Feuer)

* **A: Cigarette?**
B: Oh yes, I'm dying for one.
(… , ich bin schon ganz süchtig nach einer.)

LEAVING AND THANKING FOR HOSPITALITY

Verabschiedung und Dank für die Gastfreundschaft

* **A: Thanks very much for the delicious meal, Mrs. Basinger.**
B: It was a pleasure to have you.
(Es war wirklich sehr nett, dass Sie uns besucht haben.)

* **A: Thanks for a lovely evening, Martin. It was most kind of you to invite me over.**
B: Very glad you could come.
(glad – froh)

* **Thank you so much for a pleasant evening.**
(pleasant – angenehm)

* **A: It's time we were off.**
(Es ist Zeit, dass wir gehen.)
B: What already? Won't you have another coffee?
A: I'd love to, but I have to be up early tomorrow. Thank you for a most enjoyable evening, though.
B: Not at all. Thank you for coming.
(not at all – aber bitte)

* **A: I'm afraid I really must be going now. Thanks for the coffee.**
B: Don't mention it.
(Bitte sehr!)

* **A: Thank you very much for organising this evening. I really appreciate your hospitality.**
(… . War wirklich sehr freundlich, dass Sie uns eingeladen haben.)
B: Not at all. Hope you can come again.

* **A: Thank you very much for all your hospitality. I really appreciate it.**
B: I'm glad you enjoyed it.
(Freut mich, dass es Ihnen gefallen hat.)

* **A: It really was very kind of you to invite me. I hope it hasn't been too much trouble.**
(… . Ich hoffe, es hat Ihnen nicht zu viele Umstände gemacht.)
B: Not at all. We've really enjoyed having you.
(Überhaupt nicht. Wir haben uns über Ihren Besuch wirklich sehr gefreut.)

* **A: Thank you very much for everything. It's been a very relaxing few days.**
(relaxing – erholsam)
B: It's a pity you can't stay longer.
(it's a pity – es ist schade)

* **A: If you'll excuse me, I really should be off now. Thank you so much for an excellent tea.**
B: Not at all. I hope you'll come and see us again soon. Drop in any time you feel like it.
(not at all – bitte sehr / see – besuchen)
A: Thank you, that's very kind of you.

* **A: Bobby, thanks very much for a wonderful party.**
B: Oh, Alison! Do you have to go? The party's just beginning.
A: Oh, I'm sorry. I've got to meet someone at the airport.
(meet – abholen)

RESTAURANTS, BARS, ETC.

Restaurants, Bars usw.

INVITATIONS

Einladungen

(see also "Visits and Parties: Invitations")

* **A: Why don't we discuss this over a meal?**
(over a meal – bei einem Essen)
B: What a good idea.

* **A: I'm feeling rather peckish, shall we go for something to eat?**
(rather peckish – ziemlich hungrig)
B: Sounds like a good idea.
(Ja, das ist eine gute Idee.)

* **A: May I invite you to lunch? We could discuss some of the points over a good meal.**
(invite – einladen / lunch – Mittagessen)
B: Thank you very much. That would be very nice.

* **A: How about something to eat?**
(Gehen wir etwas essen?)
B: Yes, I'm getting really hungry. Let's have a working lunch at The Swan.

* **A: Could we have lunch together tomorrow at the "Plaza"?**
(together – zusammen)
B: That's a good idea. Let's say twelve thirty at the bar?

* **A: I was wondering if you would care to have dinner with me at my hotel tonight, if you've got nothing planned.**
(Hätten Sie Lust, heute abend mit mir in meinem Hotel zu essen, … .)
B: I'd be delighted.
(be delighted – sich sehr freuen)

* **A: What are you doing this evening?**
B: Oh, nothing special.
A: We're going out to a "Heuriger". How about joining us?
(… . Kommen Sie doch mit.)
B: Yes, with pleasure. Thank you for inviting me. What is a "Heuriger", by the way?
(pleasure – Vergnügen / by the way – übrigens)
A: Well, it's a traditional Austrian wine tavern. The emphasis is on local new wines and there's usually a nice selection of food at the buffet.
(emphasis – Betonung / local new wine – Heuriger aus der näheren Umgebung / selection – Auswahl)

* **A: Would you like to come out to dinner with Dr. Venner and me tonight?**
B: Much as I'd like to, I'm afraid I'm already booked up for tonight.
(So gerne ich auch möchte, ich habe leider für heute abend schon etwas vor.)

* **A: To be quite honest I'm getting a bit hungry. We could go over to my hotel and have dinner there. Of course, you'd be my guest.**
(quite honest – ganz ehrlich)
B: Thank you for inviting me, but I'm afraid I can't come. I've already arranged something else.
(… . Ich habe bereits etwas anderes vor.)

* **A: Shall we grab a bite to eat?**
(Gehen wir eine Kleinigkeit essen?)
B: I'm afraid I've already made other arrangements for lunch.

* A: **I was thinking you might care for some lunch tomorrow, unless you're busy.**
(care for – mögen / unless – wenn nicht / busy – beschäftigt)
B: **That's very kind of you, Alice, but I don't think I can. It's my last day and I've still got a lot of work to do.**
(kind – freundlich / … und ich habe noch eine Menge Arbeit zu erledigen.)

* A: **Do you know any vegetarian restaurants around here?**
B: **Well, there is an Indian restaurant just down the road which has quite a wide range of vegetarian dishes. It's supposed to be quite good and very reasonable. Shall we give it a try?**
(quite a wide range – eine ziemlich große Auswahl / dish – Gericht, Speise / … . Es soll angeblich ganz gut sein und vernünftige Preise haben. … . / give sthg. a try – etwas versuchen)

* A: **Can you recommend a good restaurant near here?**
(recommend – empfehlen)
B: **The "La Grotta" is very good. It's an Italian restaurant. The food is excellent.**

PUBS / PUB LUNCH

(see also "Visits and Parties: Drinks")

* A: **What are you doing for lunch?**
B: **Let's go to the pub around the corner for a couple of sandwiches and a pint, shall we?**
(let's go … , shall we? – gehen wir doch / around the corner – um die Ecke / a couple of – ein paar / pint – Krügel Bier)

* **I'll just have a quick snack in a pub.**
(just – nur)

* **A: Let me get you a pint and a bite to eat down the Red Lion.**
(Ich lade dich auf ein Bier und eine Kleinigkeit zu essen im Red Lion ein.)
B: You're on.
(Okay, fein.)

* **What about a quick drink in the Cross Keys before we go back?**
(what about – wie wär's mit)

* **A: Let's find a table.**
B: There's nothing free.
A: Oh well, let's just stand at the bar till we find a place.

* **A: What can I get you?**
(get – bestellen)
B: I'd like a pint of bitter please, Adrian.
(bitter – dunkles englisches Bier)
A: What about you, Chris?
(Und dir, … ?)
C: The same, thanks.
A: Three pints of best, please.
(best – entspricht etwa der Qualität „Bockbier")

* **A: I could use a gin and tonic.**
(use – vertragen)
B: Me too.

* **A whisky would go down well.**
(… wäre das Richtige.)

* A: **I'm just going to the bar, can I get you a refill?**
(just – gerade / bar – Theke / … , noch einmal dasselbe für Sie?)
B: **I think I'll just have a half this time, thanks.**
(just – nur)
A: **And do you want any crisps?**
(crisps – Kartoffelchips)
B: **Yes please, get me a packet of cheese and onion, will you?**
(Ja bitte, bringen Sie mir bitte ein Packerl Chips mit Käse- und Zwiebelgeschmack.)

* A: **It's my round. What are you having?**
(… . Was nehmen Sie?)
B: **A Campari, please.**

* A: **Let me buy you a drink, Bob.**
B: **No thanks, I've just had one, and I need a clear head this afternoon.**

* A: **Do you fancy something to eat?**
(Möchten Sie etwas essen?)
B: **Yes, I think I'll have a ploughman's lunch.**
(ploughman's lunch – typisch englisches Gericht in einem Pub)
A: **I'm going to have a look and see what they've got in the way of bar meals.**
(what … in the way of – was für / bar meal – Essen, das man an der Theke bestellen und abholen muss)

* **Have they already rung for last orders?**
(ring – läuten / last order – letzte Bestellung vor der Sperrstunde)

* **It's closing time.**
(Es ist Sperrstunde.)

* **Keep the change.**
(Der Rest ist für Sie. | Stimmt schon.)

BOOKING A TABLE

Tischreservierung

* **A: What about dinner tonight at the Royal Crown?**
  B: Splendid, but don't you think we'd better book a table?
  (Ausgezeichnet, aber glauben Sie nicht, dass wir lieber einen Tisch reservieren sollten?)

* **I'd like to book a table for two for eight thirty tonight, please. My name is Mennel.**

* **Would you reserve us a table for six for this evening, please?**

* **A: I'd like to book a room for lunch next Thursday. I've got some people from head office coming. We'll be nine or ten.**
  (head office – Zentrale)
  B: Certainly. What kind of menu would you like?
  (certainly – gern / menu – Speisenfolge)
  A: Nothing particularly special – what do you suggest?
  (Nichts Besonderes … . / suggest – vorschlagen)
  B: Our regular menu, then – we normally do a starter followed by a main course and salad, cheese and a dessert.
  (regular – üblich / do – servieren / starter – Vorspeise / main course – Hauptgericht / dessert – süße Nachspeise)

* **Could you check with the restaurant whether the table is booked for Wednesday evening?**
  (check with – rückfragen in)

AT THE RECEPTION

* **Is it possible to have something to eat now?**

* **Do you do lunch?**
  (Kann man hier mittagessen?)

* **Is this table free?**

* A: **Would you like this table by the fireplace?**
  (fireplace – Kamin)
  B: **That'll be fine, thank you.**

* A: **A table for two, please.**
  B: **I'm afraid there's nothing free at the moment. But if you care to have a drink at the bar first, I think I can let you have the table by the window in about twenty minutes.**
  (I'm afraid – tut mir leid / about – etwa)

* **Let's go over to the bar and have a drink while we wait for our table.**
  (while – während)

* A: **I have booked a table for two people for eight o'clock. My name is Ammer.**
  B: **Ah yes. Your guest hasn't arrived yet. Would you care for a drink at the bar first?**
  (… . Ihr Gast ist noch nicht gekommen. Möchten Sie zuerst einen Drink an der Bar?)
  A: **Yes. Could you show her over when she comes? Her name is Hutchinson.**
  (show over – herführen)

AT THE BAR

(see also "Restaurants, Bars, etc.: Pubs/Pub Lunch" and "Visits and Parties: Drinks")

* **Let's have a drink, shall we?**
  (Wie wär's mit einem Drink?)

* **The usual dry Martini for you, Brigitte?**
  (dry – trocken)

* **The same again, please.**

* **It's on me.**
  (Das zahle ich. | Das geht auf meine Rechnung.)

* **Here's to the export deal. Cheers!**
  (Auf das Exportgeschäft! Zum Wohl!)

ORDERING

Bestellung

* **Waiter, the menu, please.**
  (Herr Ober, die Speisekarte bitte!)

* **A: Do you think you could ask the people at the next table if we could look at their menu?**
  B: Yes, of course. Excuse me, could you possibly let us see your menu?

* **Could I see the wine list, please?**
  (wine list – Weinkarte)

* **A: Would you like an aperitif before you order?**
  (order – bestellen)
  B: Yes, two dry sherries, please.

* **What's on the menu?**

* **A: What can you recommend?**
  (recommend – empfehlen)
  B: Why don't you try the "Tafelspitz"? It's an Austrian speciality. It's very tender, boiled beef.
  (tender – zart / boil – kochen)

* **A: Have you ever tried "Wienerschnitzel"? It's many Austrians' favourite meal – it's veal or pork fried in egg and breadcrumbs, served with chips or rice.**
  (favourite meal – Lieblingsgericht / veal – Kalbfleisch / pork – Schweinefleisch / fried in egg and breadcrumbs – paniert / chips – Pommes frites)
  B: I'm not sure because of my cholesterol level.
  (cholesterol level – Cholesterinspiegel)

* **A: What would you like to start with?**
  (Was möchten Sie als Erstes?)
  B: I think I'll have the prawn cocktail.
  (prawn cocktail – Shrimpscocktail)

* **Would you like an hors-d'oeuvre?**
  (hors-d'oeuvre – Vorspeise)

* **A: What would you like, Barbara?**
  B: I think I'll try the lamb chop. But I'll start off with the soup of the day.
  (lamb chop – Lammkotelett)

* **A: What's the soup of the day?**
  B: Cream of mushroom. Served with home-made rolls and butter.
  (cream of mushroom – Pilzcremesuppe / home-made rolls – selbstgemachte Brötchen)

* **A: What would you like as a main course?**
  B: I really don't know whether I fancy meat or fish.
  (whether – ob / fancy – nehmen sollen / meat – Fleisch)

* **A: What are you having?**
  (Was nehmen Sie?)
  B: I'm famished, I think I'll take the mixed grill.
  (Ich bin fast am Verhungern, … .)
  C: I think I'll just have something light.
  (just – nur)

* **A: I really like shellfish. But it's so incredibly expensive here.**
  (shellfish – Austern, Hummer, Langusten usw. / incredible – unglaublich / expensive – teuer)
  B: Yes, that's the trouble. I think I'll settle for the T-bone steak, myself.
  (trouble – Problem / settle for – sich entscheiden für)

* **A: Do you like seafood?**
  (seafood – Meeresfrüchte)
  B: I'm not overkeen, actually. And in fact I'm a bit allergic to it.
  (Eigentlich bin ich nicht allzusehr versessen darauf. … .)

* **Would you like boiled or fried potatoes?**
  (… Salz- oder Bratkartoffeln?)

* **A: Would you like red or white wine?**
  B: No wine for me thanks, I'm driving.
  (drive – mit dem Auto fahren)

- **A: May I take your order, sir?**
  (order – Bestellung)
  B: Could you come back in a moment? We haven't made up our minds yet.
  (… . Wir haben uns noch nicht entschieden.)

- **A: Are you ready to order now?**
  (order – bestellen)
  B: Yes, I'll have the roast beef with Yorkshire pudding and peas, please.
  (Yorkshire pudding – typisch englische nichtsüße Beilage / peas – Erbsen)

- **A: Would you like to order your wine, sir?**
  B: I've already ordered, thank you very much.

- **Can I order now, please?**

- **I'd like to order something to eat.**

- **A: I'll have avocado to start with, followed by a fillet steak.**
  B: How would you like your steak?
  A: Well done for me.
  (well done – gut durch)
  C: Medium to rare for me.
  (Halb durch bis blutig … .)

- **For starters we'll have two smoked salmon, followed by the pork dish.**
  (smoked salmon – Räucherlachs)

- **A: I think I'll have the roast lamb, please.**
  (roast lamb – Lammbraten)
  B: What vegetables would you like?
  (vegetables – Gemüse)
  A: What have you got?

* **What vegetables come with the fried plaice?**
(fried plaice – gebratene oder panierte Scholle)

* **Would you kindly tell us what Mexican dressing is?**
(kindly – bitte / dressing – Dressing, Salatsoße)

* **Do you do half portions for children?**
(Haben Sie Kinderportionen?)

* **Do you serve vegetarian food as well?**
(serve – haben)

* **What would you suggest as a sweet?**
(suggest – vorschlagen / sweet – süße Nachspeise)

* **How about freshly-made apple pie with cream?**
(how about – wie wär's mit / cream – Schlagobers)

* **I could recommend the "Milchrahmstrudel" – it's a type of strudle with cream cheese and custard. Delicious!**
(cream cheese – Topfen / custard – Vanillesoße / delicious – schmeckt ausgezeichnet)

* **A: Do you fancy a dessert?**
(fancy – Lust haben auf)
B: I'd love to, but I really feel full!

* **Well – I really shouldn't, but I will.**

* **No, I don't think I could manage one. You go ahead though.**
(Nein, ich glaub', es geht nicht mehr. Lassen Sie sich aber nicht abhalten.)

* **Could we see the sweet trolley, please?**
(sweet trolley – Dessertwagen)

* **For dessert I'll have a piece of Black Forest gâteau.**
(piece – Stück / Black Forest gâteau – Schwarzwälder Kirschtorte)

* **I'd like a selection from the cheeseboard, please.**
(selection from the cheeseboard – verschiedene Käsesorten)

* **Will it take long? We're in a bit of a hurry.**
(take – dauern)

DURING THE MEAL

Während des Essens

(see also "Visits and Parties: At the Table")

* **That's a very nice sherry.**

* **A: How's your meal?**
B: Fine. The trout is very good.
(trout – Forelle)

* **The sole is delicious.**
(sole – Seezunge)

* **What I like about British cooking is the vegetables.**

* **A: A little more wine?**
B: Just a little. I'm not used to drinking wine at midday.
(be used to – daran gewöhnt sein)

* **Would you pass me the salt, please?**
(pass – geben)

* **A: Could I borrow your salt and pepper?**
  (Könnte ich kurz Ihren Salz- und Pfefferstreuer haben?)
  B: Yes, certainly.
  (certainly – gern)

* **Could you try and catch the waiter's eye? I can't see him at all from here.**
  (Könntest du dem Kellner winken? … . / not … at all – überhaupt nicht)

* **Would you bring us another bottle of wine, please?**

* **A: I'd like to propose a toast to the new project.**
  (propose toast to – Toast ausbringen auf)
  All: To the new project!

* **A: Is the wine to your liking?**
  (Schmeckt Ihnen der Wein?)
  B: Yes, it's very good.

* **No, I'm afraid it's corked.**
  (… , er hat leider einen Korkgeschmack.)

* **Could we have a little more bread, please?**

* **Can I have a napkin, please?**
  (napkin – Serviette)

* **A: May I take this away now, sir?**
  B: Yes. Please do. My compliments to the chef. The lobster was delicious.
  (chef – Küchenchef / lobster – Hummer)

* **The service is very friendly and efficient, isn't it?**
  (efficient – flott / isn't it? – meinen Sie nicht auch?)

* **What a lovely place for a business lunch. The food is really excellent here. Do you come here often?**
(business lunch – Geschäftsessen)

SMOKING

* **A: Do you mind if I smoke?**
(Macht es Ihnen etwas aus, wenn ich rauche?)
B: I'd rather you didn't. I'm still eating.
(Es wäre mir lieber, Sie würden nicht rauchen. … . / still – noch)

* **A: Cigarette?**
B: No, thanks, not at the moment.

* **A: Have a cigarette.**
B: No, thanks. I've just put one out.
(put out – ausdämpfen)

* **No thanks. I'm trying to cut down.**
(… . Ich versuche, weniger zu rauchen.)

* **A: Would you care for a cigarette?**
B: No, thanks, I don't smoke.

* **Do you have a selection of cigars?**

* **A: Will you have a cigar?**
(Möchten Sie eine Zigarre?)
B: That's very kind of you, but I won't.
(kind – freundlich / won't – will not)

* **Have you got a light, please?**
(light – Feuer)

COMPLAINTS
Beschwerden

* **We need another fork and two more knives.**
(Wir brauchen noch eine Gabel und zwei Messer.)

* **A: Is everything all right?**
B: Not exactly. My steak is underdone. I asked for it medium. And I'm sorry to say this, but it's rather cold.
(underdone – zu wenig durch / medium – halb durch / rather – ziemlich)

* **Sorry, but we didn't order this.**

* **I'd like to speak to the head waiter, please. This is not the standard I've come to expect here.**
(head waiter – Oberkellner / expect – erwarten)

THE BILL
Die Rechnung

* **Waiter, the bill, please!**
(Herr Ober, die Rechnung bitte! | … , zahlen bitte!)

* **Could I have the bill, please?**

* **Put it on my bill, please. Room 485.**
(put – setzen)

* **All together, please.**
(Alles zusammen, … .)

* **It's my treat.**
(Sie sind mein Gast | meine Gäste.)

* **We'll split the bill next time, but this time it's on us.**
(split – teilen / … , aber dieses Mal bezahlen wir.)

* **I must insist that I pay for my own meal tonight.**
(insist that – bestehen darauf, dass)

* **Separate bills, please.**
(Getrennte Rechnungen, … .)

* **Shall we go Dutch on the bill?**
(Machen wir getrennte Rechnung?)

* **A: Is it customary to tip the waiter?**
(Ist es üblich, dem Kellner Trinkgeld zu geben?)
B: Yes, I think ten per cent of the bill is the normal tip.
(tip – Trinkgeld)

* **Thank you for this excellent meal. Let me take care of the tip, if you don't mind.**
(… . Ich erledige das mit dem Trinkgeld, wenn Sie nichts dagegen haben.)

* **Is service included?**

* **I don't think this is quite right. We didn't have any soup.**
(quite – ganz)

* **There must be a mistake. Could you check my bill again? You seem to have added the figures up wrongly.**
(mistake – Fehler, Irrtum / check again – nachrechnen / … . Sie dürften sich verrechnet haben.)

* **I'd like to pay by credit card, please.**

* **That's for you.**

AFTER THE MEAL

Nach dem Essen

(see also "Visits and Parties: Leaving and Thanking for Hospitality")

* **It was a good lunch. Thanks for inviting me.**

* **A: I hope you enjoyed your dinner.**
(Ich hoffe, das Essen hat Ihnen geschmeckt.)
B: Yes, I did, thank you. It was delicious.

* **Well, that was really most enjoyable, David. Thank you very much indeed.**

* **A: Thank you for inviting me, Mr. Baxter. I really enjoyed the meal.**
B: Good. I'm glad you liked it.
(be glad – sich freuen)

* **Thanks for asking me out, Jim. I've enjoyed myself a lot.**
(ask out – ausführen, einladen / … . Ich habe mich wirklich gut unterhalten.)

* **Would you like to go on somewhere else for a drink?**
(go on somewhere else – noch irgendwo anders hingehen)

* **A: I was thinking of going on to a jazz club now. Would you like to join me?**
(join sbdy. – mit jemandem mitgehen)
B: I'm rather tired, I think I'll go straight home, actually, we've got a hard day tomorrow.
(straight – gleich)

OUT ON THE TOWN

Nachtleben

(see also "Visits and Parties: At a Party")

* **We're thinking of going to a disco. Will you come with us?**

* **A: I'm really sorry, but I can't make it to the disco tonight.**
  (make – schaffen)
  B: Oh, that's a real shame.
  (Das ist aber wirklich schade.)

* **A: Shall we go to a night club? I know one where the music's really good.**
  B: I wouldn't mind going.
  (Ja, gern.)

* **We could go dancing somewhere, if you like.**

* **Do we have to pay to get in?**

* **Do you want to dance?**

* **Can I ask you for this dance?**

* **The music's a bit loud, shall we talk outside?**

* **A: I really must be going if I want to catch the last train back.**
  (catch – erwischen)
  B: I'll give you a lift back to your hotel, don't worry.
  (give sbdy. a lift – jemanden mit dem Auto mitnehmen / don't worry – kein Grund zur Eile)
  A: That'd be nice, thank you.

* **Can I walk you home?**
(Kann ich Sie nach Hause begleiten?)

* **May I see you home?**
(Darf ich Sie nach Hause bringen?)

* A: **Let me drive you home.**
(Darf ich Sie mit dem Auto nach Hause bringen?)
B: **Well, that's very nice of you, but only if it's not inconvenient.**
(… , aber nur, wenn es Ihnen keine Umstände macht.)
A: **It's no problem. It's on my way.**

FORMAL OCCASIONS

Offizielle Anlässe

TOASTS – GENERAL

Allgemeine Toasts

* A: **Your very good health, Mr. Bentley!**
  (Auf Ihr ganz spezielles Wohl, Herr Bentley!)
  B: **Thank you. And yours!**
  (… und auf das Ihre!)

* **At this point I should like to propose a toast to our good friend David. Here's to you, David!**
  (Hier möchte ich einen Toast auf unseren guten Freund David ausbringen. Auf dein Wohl, David!)

TOASTS – THANKING SOMEBODY

Toasts in Verbindung mit einem Dank

* **At this point I should like to propose a toast to a member of our working group, whom unforeseen circumstances force to leave us earlier than expected. Thank you very much for your valuable contributions Peter, and here's to your very good health!**
  (unforeseen – unvorhergesehen / circumstances – Umstände / force – zwingen / leave – verlassen / expect – erwarten / valuable – wertvoll / contribution – Beitrag)

* **Ladies and gentlemen, may I have your attention please for a moment. I just want to say thank you to all of you for the splendid job you've done in organising the presentation here in Brighton. I hope you will give me a chance to repay your hospitality next year. Here's to you all!**
(attention – Aufmerksamkeit / splendid job – großartigc Arbeit / repay hospitality – Gastfreundschaft erwidern / Here's to you all! – Auf Ihr Wohl!)

TOASTS – BEST WISHES FOR THE FUTURE

Toasts in Verbindung mit besten Wünschen für die Zukunft

* **I'm sure that this will be the start of a long period of mutually beneficial co-operation. Let us raise our glasses to Hunter Cement and Brown Construction and to everything the two companies stand for. May the new arrangement have a long and prosperous future!**
(mutually beneficial – für beide Seiten fruchtbringend / raise – erheben / stand for – repräsentieren / arrangement – Abmachung, Vereinbarung / prosperous – nutzbringend / future – Zukunft)

* **Excuse me, ladies and gentlemen. Before we break up I'd just like to say how glad we from Briars Ltd. are that we have finally managed to come to an agreement. Here's to many years of fruitful co-operation between our two companies!**
(break up – auseinandergehen / glad – froh / Ltd. – private limited company | etwa: GmbH in Großbritannien / finally – schließlich / manage – es schaffen / agreement – Abkommen / … . Auf viele Jahre fruchtbarer Zusammenarbeit zwischen unseren beiden Gesellschaften!)

∗ A: **Ladies and gentlemen, it is with the greatest pleasure that I invite you to raise your glasses to the future health and prosperity of Brown Construction. May the next hundred years be even more successful than the last. Brown Construction!**
(pleasure – Vergnügen / invite – einladen / future – zukünftig / health – Gedeihen / prosperity – wirtschaftlicher Erfolg / even – noch / successful – erfolgreich)
B: **Hear, hear!**
(Hört, Hört!)

TOASTS – CONGRATULATING PEOPLE

Toasts in Verbindung mit Gratulationen

∗ **I'd like to propose a toast! We have a lot to celebrate this evening. First, welcome back to Carl, who has just returned from the United States, where he negotiated a very complex information exchange agreement with UNEX Corp.. Here's to you, Carl!**
(a lot – viel / celebrate – feiern / return – zurückkehren / negotiate – aushandeln / information exchange – Informationsaustausch / Corp. – corporation | etwa: Aktiengesellschaft in den U.S.A.)

∗ **Next I'd like to raise my glass to John, who has successfully completed talks with the Science Secretary on a major R&D grant for our company. John!**
(complete – abschließen / Science Secretary – Wissenschaftsminister / major – größer / R & D – research and development | Forschung und Entwicklung / grant – Subvention; staatlicher Zuschuss)

∗ A: **And finally a toast to Eve, who has just won the company's first order in India. To Eve! Well done!**
(win – gewinnen; an Land ziehen / order – Auftrag)
B: **Eve!**

ANNOUNCEMENTS

Ankündigungen und Verlautbarungen

* **Ladies and gentlemen, welcome to Lancer Bikes. We have invited you because we want to make an important announcement.**
(invite – einladen / important – wichtig / announcement – Ankündigung, Verlautbarung)

* **Ladies and gentlemen, thank you all for having taken the trouble to come out here to Friars Ltd. in the middle of a busy week. I think the announcement I have to make will be of some interest to financial analysts covering the furniture industry.**
(trouble – Mühe / busy – arbeitsreich / analyst – Analyst, Wertpapierforscher / cover – bearbeiten / furniture – Möbel)

* **Unfortunately it is my sad duty to announce the closure of one of our plants.**
(Leider ist es meine traurige Pflicht, die Schließung eines unserer Werke anzukündigen.)

* **We have just received word from our representative in Cairo that we have been awarded a major government contract for the construction of fifteen truck service garages. The contract is the largest in the history of the company and if everything goes well, will make a major contribution to our profits.**
(receive word – Mitteilung erhalten / representative Vertreter / be awarded a government contract – den Zuschlag für einen öffentlichen Auftrag erhalten / truck – LKW / service garage – Service- | Reparaturwerkstätte / history – Geschichte / major contribution – wichtiger Beitrag)

* **Ladies and gentlemen, I am pleased to be able to report another successful year for FG plc. We are proud to say that we have managed to increase profits in spite of the downturn in the economy as a whole.**
(report – melden, berichten / plc – public limited company | etwa: Aktiengesellschaft in Großbritannien / proud – stolz / manage – es schaffen / increase – erhöhen / in spite of – trotz / downturn in the economy as a whole – Konjunkturabschwächung)

CELEBRATIONS
Feiern

* **We have come together here today to celebrate the 50th anniversary of Zorko plc, which from very humble beginnings in a small village in Shropshire has grown into a successful international group.**
(celebrate – feiern / anniversary – Jahresfeier, Jahrestag / humble – bescheiden / village – Dorf / grow – wachsen; sich entwickeln / successful – erfolgreich / group – Konzern)

* **I have called this impromptu gathering to tell you that we have just shipped our 5,000th lathe and I think this merits a little celebration.**
(call – einberufen / impromptu gathering – improvisierte Zusammenkunft / ship – ausliefern / lathe – Drehbank / merit – verdienen / celebration – Feier)

WELCOMING PEOPLE

Jemanden begrüßen

* **Ladies and gentlemen, I'd like to welcome you to our annual salesmen's conference, both on behalf of the Marketing Department and the Board of Directors.**
(annual salesmen's conference – Jahresversammlung des Vertriebspersonals / on behalf – im Namen / department – Abteilung / Board of Directors – Verwaltungsrat; Führungsgremium einer britischen | amerikanischen Kapitalgesellschaft)

* **In particular I would like to extend a cordial welcome to our guests of honour, above all to the Mayor of Telford, in whose city the new factory is to be located.**
(particular – besonders / extend cordial welcome to – herzlich begrüßen / guest of honour – Ehrengast / mayor – Bürgermeister / factory – Fabrik / locate – ansiedeln)

* **An especially cordial welcome to the representatives of the Birmingham Chamber of Commerce, who from the very beginning have stood behind our projects and without whose valuable help we probably would not be opening the new plant today.**
(especial – besonders / chamber of commerce – Handelskammer / valuable – wertvoll / probably – wahrscheinlich / plant – Werk)

THANKING FOR INVITATION

Dank für Einladung

* **I consider it a great honour to have been asked to award the Best Salesman's Trophy for 2007. The Evaluation Committee have nominated Mr. Boll. Mr. Boll, would you like to come up, please.**
(consider – betrachten / honour – Ehre / award – verleihen / evaluation – Bewertung, Selektion / come up – herauskommen, heraufkommen)

* **It is a great honour for me to have been invited to address the annual dealers' conference. The subject of my talk will be "Can selling be overdone?"**
(address a conference – das Wort an eine Konferenz richten / dealer – Händler / subject – Thema / overdo – übertreiben)

THANKING PEOPLE

Wie man sich bedankt

* **We are gathered here today to pay tribute to somebody who has given this company 25 years of uninterrupted valuable service, Mr. Grant Bruster, the well-known and well-liked Head of Marketing. Thank you very much, Mr. Bruster!**
(gather – zusammenkommen / pay tribute – Achtung zollen / uninterrupted – ununterbrochen / head – Leiter)

* **Grant, I would like to thank you, both on behalf of myself and of the Board of Directors, for all you have done for our company!**

* **Special thanks also go to Mr. Binner, who volunteered to host this sales conference in spite of the considerable pressure of work that his position involves.**
(special – besondere[r,s] / volunteer – sich freiwillig bereit erklären / host – als Gastgeber für … fungieren / in spite of – trotz / considerable – beträchtlich / pressure – Belastung / position – Stellung / involve – mit sich bringen)

* **Ladies and gentlemen, my colleagues have asked me to say a few words before we break up. I'd just like to say how grateful we are to you for all the help you have given us in the past three weeks. We thoroughly appreciate it.**
(break up – auseinandergehen / grateful – dankbar / in the past three weeks – in den letzten drei Wochen / thoroughly appreciate sthg. – etwas wirklich zu schätzen wissen)

* **Excuse me everyone. I don't want to make a formal speech or anything. But before I leave I'd just like to say how pleasant my stay has been. I hope that I will be able to repay some of your hospitality. Should you ever come to Vienna, don't fail to contact me.**
(speech – Rede / anything – etwas Derartiges / leave – abreisen / pleasant – angenehm / stay – Aufenthalt / ever – jemals / fail – es verabsäumen)

* **I just want to say a few words of thanks before I leave. I really appreciate how everyone has done their best to make me feel at home. I hope to see you all again as soon as I can arrange my next business trip.**
(appreciate – dankbar sein für; zu würdigen wissen / trip – Reise)

TV, RADIO, VIDEO, ETC.

Fernsehen, Radio, Video usw.

* A: **What do you do in your spare time?**
(spare time – Freizeit)
B: **Oh, nothing special. I watch TV or listen to the radio.**
(watch TV – fernsehen / listen to the radio – Radio hören)

* A: **Do you watch much TV?**
B: **Not really. I do always watch the news, though.**
(Eigentlich nicht. Ich sehe mir aber immer die Nachrichten an.)

* A: **Do you enjoy watching TV?**
(Sehen Sie gerne fern?)
B: **From time to time – it depends what's on. I like watching documentaries and nature programmes.**
(Gelegentlich – es hängt davon ab, was auf dem Programm ist. … .)

* A: **Do you like to watch TV?**
B: **We haven't got a TV – we think it's a bad influence on the kids.**
(influence – Einfluss / kid – Kind)

* **Do you ever watch telly?**
(ever – jemals / watch telly – fernsehen)

* A: **Is there anything interesting on the radio now?**
B: **I don't know, Adrian; here, have a look in the newspaper.**

* A: **What's on the radio this evening?**
B: **I think there's a concert being broadcast live from Vienna, if you like that kind of thing.**
(broadcast – übertragen, senden)

* **What wavelength is the BBC World Service on?**
  (wavelength – Wellenlänge)

* **What's on TV tonight?**

* A: **Is there anything worth watching on TV tonight?**
  (anything worth watching – irgend etwas Sehenswertes)
  B: **I think there's a film with Paul Newman on BBC 2. The write-up in the paper was excellent.**
  (write-up – Kritik, Besprechung / paper – Zeitung)
  A: **Sounds good. Let's watch it.**
  (sound – klingen)

* **There's an excellent quiz programme on tonight – you mustn't miss it.**
  (… – das dürfen Sie nicht verpassen.)

* A: **What's on TV this afternoon?**
  B: **They usually have sport on a Saturday afternoon.**

* A: **Would you mind if I don't come along with you to the pub tonight, there's something on TV I'd like to watch.**
  B: **No, not at all – if it's finished before closing time, why don't you come down and join us for last orders?**
  (closing time – Sperrstunde / join sbdy. for last orders – mit jemandem vor der Sperrstunde noch rasch etwas trinken)
  A: **I don't think it finishes before 11 o'clock actually.**

* A: **Do you mind if I switch over? The news is on the other channel.**
  (Haben Sie etwas dagegen, wenn ich umschalte? … .)
  B: **Not at all, I'd quite like to see it myself actually.**
  (not at all – ganz im Gegenteil; überhaupt nicht)

* A: **Do you know what channel the tennis match is on?**
  B: **I think it's on Channel 4.**

* **Don't you want to watch part two of the serial?**
(serial – Serie)

* **Does anyone mind if I watch the rugby?**

* **Would you mind turning it down a bit?**
(turn down – leiser stellen)

* **Could you turn it up a bit, please? I can't hear it properly.**
(turn up – lauter stellen / properly – ordentlich)

* A: **The picture is a bit blurred, isn't it?**
(Das Bild ist ein bisschen verschwommen, nicht wahr?)
B: **Yes it is, isn't it? I'll try and adjust the aerial.**
(aerial – Antenne)

* **The reception is really bad.**
(reception – Empfang)

* **Can you adjust the colour, please?**
(adjust colour – Farbe einstellen)

* **Have you seen the remote control?**
(remote control – Fernbedienung)

* **I find it very difficult to understand the dialects some of the actors are using.**
(actor – Schauspieler)

* **Do you mind if I switch it off?**
(switch off – abschalten)

* **Don't switch it off. I've been looking forward to this programme all day.**
(look forward to – sich freuen auf)

* **Has this set got teletext?**
(set – Apparat)

* **A: What are the TV programmes like in your country, Brian?**
(Wie sind die Fernsehprogramme … ?)
B: Not bad – compared with other countries.
(compare – vergleichen)

* **A: What about TV in your country, Berthold?**
B: Well, we have a public television service. It goes by the name of ORF and operates two channels.
(public – öffentlich rechtlich / ORF – Österreichischer Rundfunk | Austrian Broadcasting Corporation)
A: No private operators?
(operator – Betreiber)
B: Yes, of course, there are some. A special law was passed in 2001, and since then a number of private operators have entered the field. And then there is cable and satellite.
(law – Gesetz / pass – verabschieden / number – Reihe / enter the field – mitmischen)

* **A: Don't you have any soap operas on Austrian TV? Everyone here watches Heartbeat and even good old EastEnders and Coronation Street.**
(soap opera – Seifenoper)
B: Oh, I've never heard of those. We've just got some American soaps like Desperate Housewives, Sex and the City, and Reich und Schön.
A: That must be The Bold and the Beautiful, I would say.

* **A: Do you have many adverts on TV in Austria, Boris?**
(advert – Werbespot)
B: No, not too many – they have certain times during the day where you can advertise on TV, that's all. So none of the programmes are ever interrupted.
(advertise – werben / interrupt – unterbrechen)
C: That sounds much better than in England. I think there are more commercial breaks on ITV and Channel 4 than on ordinary TV programmes.
(commercial break – Programmunterbrechung zu Werbezwecken)

* A: **Have you ever tried TV advertising in your company?**
(advertising – Werbung / company – Firma, Gesellschaft)
B: **We did once, but without the right connections it's impossible to get enough slots to carry out an effective campaign – there are only a limited number available, I'm afraid.**
(once – einmal / connection – Verbindung / slot – Werbezeit / carry out – durchführen / available – verfügbar / I'm afraid – leider)
A: **My company is running two commercials at the moment. It's really expensive – I don't think it's a suitable medium for us, to be honest.**
(run commercial – Werbespot schalten / suitable – passend, geeignet / honest – ehrlich)

* **Have you got cable TV in your country?**

* **Have you seen one of the new digital models? Fantastic, I can tell you.**

* **I've got a fairly good TV set with about 40 channels and teletext. I can also use it as a home-banking terminal.**
(fairly – ziemlich)

* **The commercial stations show too many video clips for my taste.**
(commercial station – Privatsender / taste – Geschmack)

* A: **Have you got a DVD machine, Bill?**
(DVD – Digital Versatile Disc)
B: **Yes, I have. But I've found that although I record loads of things I'd like to watch, I never get round to watching them.**
(although – obwohl / record – aufnehmen / load – Menge / get round to sthg. – zu etwas kommen)

* **One of the best business programmes is on after midnight, so I usually tape it on my DVD recorder.**
(tape – aufnehmen)

* **A: Renting DVDs is still very popular here, in spite of the fact that it has become very easy to download films from the Internet.**
(rent – ausleihen / DVD – Digital Versatile Disc / still – noch immer / in spite of – trotz / download – herunterladen)
B: Yes, I've noticed this. The rental business isn't quite as large in Austria. I never rent DVDs, even though I do have a DVD player.
(notice – bemerken / rental business – Verleihgeschäft / quite – ganz / even though – obwohl)

* **A: So this is your new MP3 player – it looks pretty good.**
(… der sieht aber gut aus.)
B: Yes, very sleek and cool. And it's high quality – for both sound and video. By the way, do you know what MP3 stands for?
(sleek – schlank, elegant / sound – Ton / by the way – übrigens / know – wissen)
A: I think the abbreviation refers to a modern audio compression technology.
(abbreviation – Abkürzung / refer to – bezeichnen)

CINEMA, THEATRE, OPERA, CONCERTS AND MUSEUMS

Kino, Theater, Oper, Konzerte und Museen

CINEMA

* **Is there anything on at the cinema worth seeing this week?**
(be on – auf dem Programm sein / cinema – Kino / worth seeing – sehenswert)

* **What's on at the cinema this week?**

* **A: There's a very good Jane Fonda film on near here.**
B: I never have liked Jane Fonda, I'm afraid.
(I'm afraid – tut mir leid)

* **Are you going to be busy this evening? I was wondering if you might like to come to the cinema with me.**
(be busy – etwas vorhaben; beschäftigt sein / … . Möchten Sie vielleicht mit mir ins Kino gehen?)

* **A: Would you like to come to the pictures tonight?**
(pictures – Kino / tonight – heute abend)
B: I'd love to. What's on?
(Sehr gerne. … ?)

* **A: Shall we go to the pictures tonight?**
B: That's a good idea. I haven't been for ages.
(… . Ich bin schon eine Ewigkeit nicht gewesen.)
A: Fine. I'll come round and pick you up at your hotel.
(pick up – abholen)

* **A: What do you fancy seeing?**
(Was möchten Sie gerne sehen?)
B: I don't mind really. What film would you like to see?
(Das ist mir eigentlich gleich. … ?)

* **A: How about going to the cinema?**
(Gehen wir ins Kino?)
B: Oh, good idea. We could meet at the box-office. At quarter past seven?
(meet – sich treffen / box-office – Kassa / quarter past seven – Viertel nach sieben)
A: OK. Let's do that.

* **A: Could you come to the cinema tonight?**
B: I wish I could, but I've got this wretched meeting tomorrow.
(… , aber ich habe blöderweise diese Sitzung morgen.)

* **A: It really is a very good film.**
B: I'm sorry, it's not possible, maybe another evening?

* **A: Shall we go and see that new film with Robert de Niro tonight?**
B: Yes, that's great! Robert de Niro is one of my favourite actors.
(great – super / favourite actor – Lieblingsschauspieler)

* **When does the film start?**

* **How much are the tickets?**
(Wieviel kosten die Karten?)

* **A: What are you going to see?**
B: The new Kevin Costner film. Why don't you come as well?
(… . Kommen Sie doch auch mit.)
A: Oh, that would be nice, yes! … Oh, … oh dear, I'm busy tonight, I'm afraid. What about tomorrow night? Is that any good to you?
(… . Geht das bei Ihnen?)
B: Oh dear, no, I'm afraid I'm busy then myself.

* A: **Have you seen the new film at the Odeon?**
B: **No, not yet, but I was planning to go this week.**
(not yet – noch nicht)
A: **Why don't we go together, then?**
(Gehen wir doch gemeinsam.)
B: **Fine, how about on Wednesday?**
(how about – wie wär's)
A: **That's fine by me.**

* **Shall I get tickets in advance for the film? They're often sold out.**
(get tickets – Karten besorgen / in advance – im Voraus)

* A: **I didn't manage to get tickets. It's sold out.**
(Es ist mir nicht gelungen, Karten zu bekommen. … .)
B: **Oh, bad luck.**
(So ein Pech!)

* **Is this the queue for "The Godfather III"?**
(queue – Schlange / godfather – Pate)

* A: **Do you like French films?**
B: **Yes, though I prefer Italian ones.**
(though – obwohl / prefer – lieber haben; bevorzugen)

* **What do you think of German films?**

* A: **What do you think of "Switch"?**
B: **I don't know I haven't seen it yet. It's supposed to be fairly good, isn't it?**
(not … yet – noch nicht / … . Er soll angeblich recht gut sein, nicht?)
A: **Well, it's got good reviews here. And it's directed by Blake Edwards.**
(reviews – Kritiken / … . Und Blake Edwards führt Regie.)

* **A: Who's in it?**
(Wer spielt mit?)
B: Oh, Ellen Barkin.
A: Oh, great! I really like her. She's a good actress and she's got lovely legs.
(actress – Schauspielerin / legs – Beine)

* **Who stars in that new Alan Parker film?**
(Wer spielt … die Hauptrolle?)

* **Who plays the main part?**
(Wer spielt die Hauptrolle?)

* **I find Westerns rather boring.**
(rather boring – ziemlich langweilig)

* **I can't stand horror films.**
(stand – ausstehen)

* **I'm rather keen on comedies.**
(Ich sehe mir gerne Komödien an.)

* **I'm not overkeen on watching violent films.**
(Ich bin nicht allzu sehr versessen darauf, mir gewalttätige Filme anzusehen.)

——— ❖ ———

* **A: What did you think of that?**
B: Well, it was entertaining.
(entertaining – unterhaltsam)

* **The ending was a bit weak, wasn't it?**
(Der Schluss war ein bißchen schwach, nicht?)

* **I was expecting a completely different ending.**
(Ich habe mir ein völlig anderes Ende erwartet.)

* **I thought the story-line was a bit weak, but the photography was excellent.**
  (story-line – Handlung)

* **I thought Jack Nicholson was really overacting, didn't you?**
  (overact – übertrieben spielen / … , meinen Sie nicht auch?)

* **A: Did you like that?**
  B: Well, I thought it wasn't that good, actually.

* **A: Did you enjoy that?**
  (Hat Ihnen der Film gefallen?)
  B: Yes, indeed. I enjoyed it very much, thank you.

* **The film was really exciting.**
  (exciting – aufregend, spannend)

* **It has been nominated for 8 Oscars, you know.**

* **I hate films that are dubbed – I much prefer subtitles.**
  (dub – synchronisieren)

* **I thought it was too confusing with all the flashbacks.**
  (confusing – verwirrend / flashback – Rückblende)

* **A: Do you think it was filmed on location or at the studios?**
  (on location – an den Originalschauplätzen)
  B: Actually it said it was filmed on location.

* **I wonder what the critics will say about it in the papers tomorrow.**
  (wonder – neugierig sein / critic – Kritiker / paper – Zeitung)

THEATRE

* **A: I'm going out to the theatre tonight with some friends. Would you like to join us?**
(… . Möchten Sie mitkommen?)
B: I'd love to.

* **A: Should I get some tickets for the theatre?**
B: Yes, that'd be very kind of you.
(kind – freundlich, nett)

* **Would you prefer the matinee at 2 o'clock, or the evening performance?**
(prefer – vorziehen / matinee – Nachmittagsvorstellung / evening performance – Abendvorstellung)

* **A: If you're not doing anything special tonight, I was wondering if you would like to come to the theatre. I have some tickets.**
B: It's very kind of you to invite me, but I'm afraid I've already got something planned.
(invite – einladen)

* **A: If you're free tomorrow evening, would you like to go to the theatre? I've got a spare ticket.**
(… . Ich habe eine Karte übrig.)
B: Thank you very much. That would be very nice. I'll look forward to it.
(look forward to – sich freuen auf)

* **A: There's an excellent play on at the theatre. Shall I get some tickets for tomorrow?**
(play – Stück)
B: That's very kind of you but I've already made other arrangements.
(… , aber ich habe bereits etwas anderes vor.)

* **A: Is it still possible to get tickets for tonight?**
  B: Tonight is the premiere, so I doubt very much that there'll be any tickets left.
  (doubt – bezweifeln / there are tickets left – es sind noch Karten zu haben)

* **I'll try and get tickets for a play at the Vienna International Theatre.**

* **Would you be interested in going to an avantgarde theatre?**

* **Would you be interested in going to a typical Viennese cabaret?**

* **A: I'm thinking of going to the theatre while I'm here. Could you ring up and find out what's on?**
  (while – während / ring up – anrufen)
  B: Certainly. I'll give them a ring as soon as I've finished this.
  (Gern. Ich rufe an, sobald ich das hier fertig habe.)

* **Can you recommend a good play?**
  (recommend – empfehlen)

* **The play is really worth seeing.**

* **A: I like Shakespeare's plays.**
  B: Oh, so do I. They're doing Hamlet at the Royal Theatre next week.
  (do – aufführen)
  A: Shall we book some tickets, then?
  (book – vorbestellen)

* **Do you think we ought to book tickets?**
  (Glauben Sie, dass wir Karten vorbestellen sollten?)

* **I'd like to book two tickets for tomorrow, please.**

* **A: Do you have any tickets for tonight's performance, please?**
  B: I'm sorry, sir, they're all sold. But there are two cancellations for tomorrow, if you're able to come.
  (cancellation – Kartenrückgabe)

* **A: I'd like some tickets for tomorrow night's performance, please.**
  B: Sorry, madam, you'll have to go to the advance booking office. It's just opposite.
  (advance booking office – Vorverkaufskassa / just opposite – gleich gegenüber)

* **A: Do you have two seats left for tomorrow evening, please?**
  (left – noch frei)
  B: I've got two together in the dress circle at seven pounds fifty each. Or I've got two stalls at ten pounds.
  (two together – zwei nebeneinander / dress circle – erster Rang / stall – Parkettsitz)

* **There's nothing in the front row, is there?**
  (In der vordersten Reihe ist nichts mehr frei, oder?)

* **Where are the seats? Could you show me on the plan, please?**
  (plan – Sitzplan)

* **I'll have the two in the dress circle, please, in Row G.**

* **A: What time does the performance start?**
  B: At seven thirty. The doors open at seven.
  (… . Einlass ist um sieben.)

* **How long does the performance last?**
  (last – dauern)

* **Would you like me to try and change the tickets?**
  (change – umtauschen)

* A: **What should I wear to the theatre?**
  (wear – anziehen)
  B: **Well, it's an avantgarde theatre so you can really wear whatever you like.**

* **It doesn't really matter what you wear, but most people do wear a tie.**
  (Es ist eigentlich belanglos, … . / tie – Krawatte)

* **Where's the cloakroom, please?**
  (cloakroom – Garderobe)

* **Where can I buy a programme, please?**

* **Shall we go to the bar and have a drink?**

* **What time is the interval, please?**
  (interval – Pause)

——— ❖ ———

* **Where are the ladies, please?**
  (ladies – Damentoilette)

* A: **Could you tell me where the gents are, please?**
  (gents – Herrentoilette)
  B: **Down the corridor on the right-hand side.**
  A: **Thank you.**

* **I think the scenery is fantastic – it's really impressive.**
  (scenery – Bühnenbild, Dekoration / impressive – beeindruckend)

* **The acoustics aren't very good. – I'm finding it quite difficult to follow.**
  (quite – ziemlich)

* **Let's hope the second half is better!**

——— ❖ ———

* **A: What did you think of the play last night?**
  B: I enjoyed it very much.
  (Es hat mir sehr gut gefallen.)

* **I didn't think the acting was all that good myself.**
  (acting – schauspielerische Leistung)

* **After all we'd heard about it, we found the play a bit disappointing.**
  (disappointing – enttäuschend)

* **I thought the cast were brilliant – especially the leading actor.**
  (cast – Schauspieler / leading actor – Hauptdarsteller)

* **They must have rehearsed it for months.**
  (rehearse – proben)

* **It could have been worse.**
  (Es hätte schlimmer sein können.)

* **Frankly, I wish I'd stayed at home.**
  (Ganz ehrlich, ich hätte besser zu Hause bleiben sollen.)

OPERA

* **I was thinking of going to the opera tonight. Would you like to come?**

* **A: Would you like to go to the opera tomorrow evening?**
  B: Oh, thank you, that would be nice.

* A: **We could try and get tickets for the opera tomorrow.**
B: **What's on?**
(Was ist auf dem Programm?)
A: **Let's check the newspaper. It's The Magic Flute.**
(check – nachschauen in / Magic Flute – Zauberflöte)
B: **Yes, I'd love to see that. It's my favourite opera.**
(favourite opera – Lieblingsoper)

* A: **Do you know if it's possible to get tickets for the opera?**
B: **I'm not sure but I could try to find out for you, if you like.**
A: **That's very kind of you.**

* A: **They're doing "Carmen" at the Opera House. Does opera interest you at all?**
(do – spielen)
B: **Oh yes, it does. How can I get a ticket for it?**

* **No, actually I don't care much for opera.**
(… , eigentlich mache ich mir nicht allzu viel aus Opern.)

* A: **What do people wear to the opera?**
(wear – anziehen)
B: **People usually dress up for the opera. A dark suit or a dinner-jacket would be suitable.**
(dress up – etwas Schönes anziehen / dark suit – dunkler Anzug / dinner-jacket – Smoking / suitable – passend, geeignet)

* **Some ladies wear long dresses, but any smart dress or outfit would be fine.**
(… , aber irgendein anderes elegantes Kleid oder sonst etwas Elegantes zum Anziehen … .)

* **The first act was magnificent, wasn't it?**
(magnificent – großartig, glänzend / wasn't it? – nicht wahr?)

* **She's got a beautiful voice, hasn't she?**
(voice – Stimme / hasn't she? – nicht wahr?)

* **The conductor isn't much good, is he?**
(conductor – Dirigent / is he? – meinen Sie nicht auch?)

CONCERTS

* **A: By the way, I hear Elton John's coming to London soon.**
(Übrigens, … .)
B: That's right. I saw it advertised last week. I imagine it might be a bit difficult to get to see him.
(advertise – ankündigen / imagine – sich vorstellen)
A: Well, we can always try.
(Wir können es zumindest versuchen.)

* **A: Why don't you go to a show or something tonight?**
B: As a matter of fact, I thought Caroline might like to go to a concert.
A: Let's have a look and see what's on … You might try the Barenboim concert at the Royal Festival Hall.
B: That sounds interesting.
(sound – klingen)

* **A: Would you be free to come to a concert on Saturday evening?**
B: Thank you, but I'm afraid I've arranged to go out then.

* **A: Could you get me some tickets for the concert tomorrow?**
B: I'm afraid not. It's fully booked.
(Leider nicht. … .)

* **A: Do you think it'd be possible for you to get some tickets for the concert tomorrow?**
B: Of course, that's no problem.

* **How about going to a musical tonight?**
(Gehen wir heute abend in ein Musical?)

* **A: Would you be interested in going to a piano recital?**
(piano recital – Klavierabend)
B: Oh yes, that'd be great, thanks.
(great – sehr schön)

* **A: Is he a good pianist?**
B: Oh, not bad.

* **A: Shall we try and get tickets for U2? They're on at Wembley Stadium next weekend.**
(be on – auftreten)
B: Yes, that sounds great. Is that an open-air stadium?
(great – super)
A: Yes, so don't forget your umbrella!
(umbrella – Schirm)

* **A: How was the concert last night?**
B: It was great. I thoroughly enjoyed it.
(… . Es hat mir wirklich sehr gut gefallen.)

* **The newspaper reviews of the concert were very good indeed.**
(reviews – Kritiken)

MUSEUMS

* **A: Would you be interested in coming to the National History Museum?**
B: Thank you for the invitation, but I'm not sure if I can.
(invitation – Einladung)

* **A: We want to take you to the British Museum. You haven't been there before, have you?**
(have you? – oder?)
B: No, I haven't. I'd very much like to go.

* **A: I'd quite like to see the Chinese Exhibition while I'm here. Have you seen it yet?**
(quite – ganz / exhibition – Ausstellung / while – während / yet – schon)
B: No, I must admit I just haven't found the time, but I've heard it's well worth sceing.
(admit – zugeben / just – einfach / worth seeing – sehenswert)

* **A: By the way, may I ask you something? What's the National Gallery like? Do you think I ought to go there?**
(by the way – übrigens / … . Wie ist die National Gallery? … . / I ought to go – ich sollte gehen)
B: Well, there are lots of great paintings there, but I prefer the Tate Gallery myself. It's less like a museum.
(lots of – viele / great – großartig / painting – Gemälde / I prefer the Tate Gallery – mir ist die Tate Gallery lieber)

* **A: Don't you think that's an interesting picture?**
(picture – Bild)
B: Yes, it is, isn't it?

SPORTS AND OTHER LEISURE ACTIVITIES

Sport und andere Freizeitbeschäftigungen

* **A: What are your hobbies?**
B: I love playing tennis and squash.

* **A: What do you do in your spare time?**
(spare time – Freizeit)
B: There's nothing I enjoy more than gardening.
(Am liebsten arbeite ich im Garten.)

* **A: What's your favourite pastime?**
(Was machen Sie in Ihrer Freizeit am liebsten?)
B: My main interest is oil-painting.
(main – Haupt- / oil-painting – Ölmalerei)

* **A: What do you enjoy doing when you've got a spare moment?**
(spare moment – freie Minute)
B: I enjoy fishing.
(Ich fische gerne.)

* **What I particularly enjoy is going for a jog.**
(Was ich besonders gerne mache, ist laufen.)

* **A: And what do you do when you're not working?**
B: I'm very fond of skiing.
(Ich fahre sehr gern Schi.)

* **A: What are your interests?**
B: Well, I'm very keen on cooking.
(Ich koche sehr gerne.)

* **A: What are you interested in?**
B: I'm a bridge fan.
(bridge – Bridge)

* **A: Are you interested in riding?**
B: I've never tried it. But I'd like to have a go at it.
(… . Aber ich würde es gerne einmal probieren.)

* **A: Are people interested in skiing in England?**
B: Yes, it's becoming quite popular now.
(quite – ziemlich)

* **A: Do you take much interest in ballet?**
(ballet – Ballett)
B: Well, I'm not particularly interested in it actually.
(actually – eigentlich)

* **A: Do you like sport?**
B: Actually I'm not overkeen on it – I much prefer art.
(Eigentlich bin ich nicht allzu sehr versessen darauf – da interessiere ich mich wesentlich mehr für Kunst.)

* **A: Do you enjoy playing sports?**
(Betreiben Sie gerne Sport?)
B: As a matter of fact, I'm a very keen golfer and ice-skater.
(Eigentlich schon, ich spiele leidenschaftlich gern Golf und bin ein begeisterter Eisläufer.)

* **A: I'm not very keen on sport, are you?**
(Ich mache mir nicht sehr viel aus Sport, und wie ist es mit Ihnen?)
B: I don't mind watching it, but I'm not really into doing it myself.
(Ich sehe zwar ganz gern zu, aber selbst betreibe ich keinen.)

* **Formula One racing is my favourite spectator sport.**
(Am liebsten sehe ich mir Formel-1-Rennen an.)

* **A: By the way, do you like dancing?**
(by the way – übrigens)
B: Oh yes, I'm very fond of dancing.

* **A: Don't you like jogging?**
B: Actually I prefer swimming.

* **I've always liked cross-country skiing.**
(cross-country skiing – Langlauf)

* **I like to go mountaineering at weekends.**
(go mountaineering – bergsteigen gehen)

* **A: Do you play soccer?**
(Spielen Sie Fußball?)
B: Not any more, but I used to play when I was a student.
(… , aber früher einmal, als ich noch studierte, habe ich gespielt.)

* **Have you ever been water-skiing?**

* **A: Sailing is very enjoyable, don't you think?**
(Segeln ist ein netter Sport, meinen Sie nicht auch?)
B: I've never been sailing actually, but I'd love to give it a try sometime.
(… , aber ich würde es gerne irgendwann einmal versuchen.)

* **A: Which do you prefer, tennis or cycling?**
(prefer – lieber tun / cycle – radfahren)
B: I enjoy tennis more than cycling.

* **A: Do you prefer alpine skiing or cross-country?**
B: I like cross-country better than alpine.

* **A: Can you play any musical instruments?**
B: Well, I can play the piano a bit, but I'm pretty hopeless at it.
(… , aber ich bin ein ziemlich hoffnungsloser Fall.)

* **A: Are you keen on music?**
  (Sind Sie sehr an Musik interessiert?)
  B: I'm absolutely crazy about jazz.
  (Ich bin ganz verrückt nach Jazz.)

* **A: Are you into folk music at all?**
  (be into – gern haben; ein Fan sein)
  B: Well yes, but I like pop better.

* **A: Do you belong to any clubs or societies?**
  (belong to – Mitglied sein von / society – Gesellschaft, Verein)
  B: Actually I'm a member of the Lions Club.

——— ❖ ———

* **A: Would you care for a round of golf?**
  (Hätten Sie Lust zu einer Runde Golf?)
  B: Great! But I've only got time for 9 holes, is that O.K.?
  (great – super / hole – Loch)
  A: O.K. by me.

* **Would you be interested in coming sledging with us tomorrow?**
  (sledge – Schlitten fahren)

* **How about going for a cycle?**
  (Wie wär's mit einer Radtour?)

* **What about a game of darts at the pub?**
  (game of darts – Wurfpfeilschießen)

* **It'll be nice on the beach today. I think I'll go swimming.**

* **Let's go swimming.**

∗ **A: Why don't you join us for a game of tennis.**
(Gehen Sie doch mit uns Tennis spielen.)
B: I'd love to, thanks.
(Gern, danke.)

∗ **We could go for a walk in the Vienna Woods.**

∗ **Would you like to go for a good run in the Prater tomorrow?**

∗ **We could go to a sauna afterwards.**

∗ **A: What I'd really like is a good swim.**
B: Great, let's go to the swimming-baths tomorrow. Let's say at 11?
(swimming-baths – Hallenbad)

∗ **A: Do you fancy a game of snooker?**
(fancy – Lust haben auf / snooker – Snooker, eine Art Billard)
B: Sounds like a great idea!
(Klingt großartig.)

∗ **We might go to the races, if you like that kind of thing.**
(races – Pferderennen)

∗ **Well, John, perhaps you'd like to join me on Saturday? Spurs are playing Arsenal at home.**
(join sbdy. – jemanden begleiten; mit jemandem mitgehen / Spurs [Kurzform für Tottenham Hotspurs], Arsenal – zwei berühmte Londoner Fußballvereine)

∗ **What's the score?**
(Wieviel steht's? | Wie steht das Spiel?)

∗ **We could play table tennis or watch the tennis tournament on TV – it's up to you to decide.**
(Wir könnten Tischtennis spielen oder uns das Tennisturnier im Fernsehen ansehen – was immer Ihnen lieber ist.)

* **A: Which would you prefer: rowing or wind-surfing?**
(row – rudern)
B: I'd prefer wind-surfing.

SHOPPING

Einkaufen

* **I was thinking of taking a couple of hours off this afternoon to do some shopping, if you don't mind.**
  (take off – sich freinehmen / couple of – ein paar / if you don't mind – wenn es Ihnen nichts ausmacht)

* **I did some window-shopping last night in the High Street and quite a few things caught my eye. I think I'll go shopping on Saturday.**
  (do window-shopping – Schaufensterbummel machen / High Street – Haupteinkaufsstraße / quite a few – eine ganze Menge / catch one's eye – jemandem ins Auge springen)

* A: **There are a few odds and ends I'd like to buy before I go back this evening. What time do the shops close?**
  (odds and ends – verschiedene Kleinigkeiten / close – schließen)
  B: **Most shops close at about 6 o'clock, apart from the food shops, which usually stay open longer.**
  (apart from – außer)

* **What time does the off-licence on the corner shut?**
  (off-licence – Getränkehandlung / corner – Ecke / shut – schließen)

* **Can you recommend a good supermarket around here where I can get some food to take back with me?**
  (recommend – empfehlen)

* **Do you know a good bookshop where they have a wide selection of marketing literature?**
  (bookshop – Buchhandlung / wide selection – große Auswahl)

* A: **Where can I buy the Financial Times?**
  B: **There's a newsagent's just over the road.**
  (newsagent's – Zeitschriftenhandlung)

* **Is there a shop that specialises in photographic equipment near here?**
(photographic equipment – Fotoausrüstung)

* **Do you know any good department stores around here?**
(department store – Warenhaus, Kaufhaus)

——— ❖ ———

* **A: Can I help you?**
B: Yes, I wonder if you could tell me where to find a suit like the one in the window?
(I wonder if you could – könnten Sie bitte / suit – Anzug, Kostüm)

* **A: Are you being served?**
(serve – bedienen)
B: Yes, I'm being served, thank you.

* **I'm just looking, thank you.**

* **A: Could you point me in the right direction of the food department, please?**
(Könnten Sie mir bitte sagen, wie ich in die Lebensmittelabteilung komme?)
B: Go down the escalator over there to the basement, through the kitchenware department and it's straight ahead.
(escalator – Rolltreppe / over there – dort drüben / basement – Kellergeschoß / kitchenware department – Küchenabteilung / straight ahead – geradeaus)

* **Aren't there any baskets or trolleys left?**
(basket – Korb / trolley – Einkaufswagen)

* **Excuse me, where's the menswear department, please?**
(menswear department – Herrenabteilung)

* **I'm looking for the lingerie department.**
(look for – suchen / lingerie – Damenwäsche)

* **Is the sportswear on this floor?**
(sportswear – Sportbekleidung / floor – Stock)

* **A: Can you help me, please? I'm looking for a pure wool pullover.**
(pure wool pullover – Pullover aus reiner Wolle)
B: What size did you want?
(size – Größe)
A: Well, I'm not quite sure; medium I think.
(quite sure – ganz sicher / medium – mittel)

* **A: Are you looking for anything in particular?**
B: Yes, I'm interested in a silk tie, if you've got any.
(silk tie – Seidenkrawatte)

* **A: I wonder if you can help me. I'm looking for a blouse to match this skirt.**
(… . Ich suche eine Bluse, die zu diesem Rock passt.)
B: Well, I think something in red would go well with it, don't you?
(go with – passen zu / don't you? – meinen Sie nicht auch?)

* **I'd prefer something with a pattern – either stripes or checked or even spots – and not just a plain one.**
(prefer – bevorzugen / pattern – Muster / stripe – Streifen / checked – kariert / spot – Punkt / plain – ungemustert)

* **I'm looking for a shirt to match this jacket but I'm not sure of my collar size.**
(shirt – Hemd / collar size – Kragenweite)

* **A: I'd like to buy a pair of trousers for myself.**
(pair of trousers – Hose)
B: How much would you like to spend?
(spend – ausgeben)
A: That doesn't really matter, as long as they're not too expensive.
(Das ist eigentlich egal, solange sie nicht <u>zu</u> teuer ist.)

* **The trousers are a bit loose, can they be altered?**
(loose – weit / alter – ändern)

* **I'd like a pair of shoes in size 8 to go with this suit, please.**

* **I take size 38.**
(Ich habe Größe 38.)

* **I'm afraid they're too small. Do you do half sizes?**
(Ich fürchte, sie sind zu klein. Führen Sie Zwischengrößen?)

* **They're not really suitable. Can you show me anything else?**
(suitable – geeignet)

* **Excuse me, how much is this dress?**
(… , wieviel kostet dieses Kleid?)

* **A: Could I try this on, please?**
(try on – anprobieren)
B: Certainly, the changing room is over there.
(certainly – selbstverständlich / changing room – Umkleidekabine)

* **A: I'm afraid it doesn't fit – it's too tight around the waist. Have you got a bigger size?**
(fit – passen / tight – eng / waist – Taille)
B: I'm sorry, that's the last one but we should be getting some more in tomorrow.
(get in – hereinbekommen)

* **It's not quite what I was looking for.**

* **Do you really think this jacket suits me?**
(Glauben Sie wirklich, dass mir dieses Sakko | Jackett steht | passt?)

* **The sleeves are too long, can they be shortened?**
(sleeve – Ärmel / shorten – kürzen)

* **Do you have anything in different material? This seems to be a bit thick.**
(different material – anderer Stoff / seem – scheinen / thick – dick)

* **I'm not too keen on the colour – it's too dark.**
(keen on – begeistert von)

* **A: It's too big. Could I try the next size down?**
(next size down – nächstkleinere Größe)
B: I'm sorry, we're out of stock at the moment.
(be out of stock – keine haben)
A: Can you order one?
(order – bestellen)

* **It's a bit expensive, don't you think?**

* **Have you got anything cheaper?**

* **It fits very well. I'll take it. Do you take credit cards?**

* **What have you got in the way of leather handbags?**
(Was haben Sie an Lederhandtaschen?)

* **I need some films for my camera, please.**

* **20 Benson and Hedges, please.**

* **I'd like a carton of Rothmans, three packets of Marlboro and a lighter, please.**
(carton – Stange / packet – Schachtel, Päckchen / lighter – Feuerzeug)

* **A: Would you like anything else?**
B: No, thanks. That'll be all.

* **Have you got a map of the city, please?**
(map of the city – Stadtplan)

* **Could you make up a nice bunch of flowers for me, please? I need them as a birthday present.**
(make up – zusammenstellen / bunch of flowers – Blumenstrauß / present – Geschenk)

* **Do you stock health food?**
(Führen Sie Bio-Lebensmittel | Reformwaren?)

* **A: Do you have any whole-meal bread?**
(whole-meal bread – Vollkornbrot)
B: Sure, it's on the shelf over there.
(shelf – Regal)

* **Would it be possible to taste a small piece?**
(taste – kosten / piece – Stück)

* **Does the price include VAT?**
(VAT – value-added tax | Mehrwertsteuer)

* **A: How much does it come to altogether?**
(Wieviel kostet das alles zusammen?)
B: It comes to seventy-eight pounds and ninety-seven pence.

* **Where can I pay for these?**

* **Where's the cash desk?**
(cash desk – Kassa)

* **Can I pay at any checkout?**
(checkout – Supermarktkassa)

* **The queues are so long at the checkouts, isn't there an express one for just a few items?**
(queue – Warteschlange / express checkout – Schnellkassa / item – Artikel)

——— ❖ ———

* A: **Cash or charge?**
(Bar oder mit Kreditkarte?)
B: **I'd like to charge it. Here's my card.**

* **Put it on my credit card, please.**

* **I've got a credit card, would that be all right?**

* **Can I pay by Eurocheque?**

* A: **Would you be prepared to accept a Eurocheque?**
(Nehmen Sie auch Euroschecks?)
B: **Yes, if you can show me your cheque card and your passport.**

* **I'm willing to pay cash if you can give me a discount.**
(discount – Preisnachlass)

* **I'm sorry, I've only got a fifty-pound note, can you change it?**
(change a fifty-pound note – auf eine 50-Pfund-Note herausgeben)

* **I'm sorry but I haven't got any change.**
(change – Kleingeld)

* A: **Here's your change – fifty pence.**
(change – Wechselgeld)
B: **Sorry, that's not right, I gave you a ten-pound note.**
(ten-pound note – 10-Pfund-Note)

* **Would you count the change again, please? You seem to have made a mistake.**
(count again – nachzählen / change – Wechselgeld / … . Es dürfte Ihnen da ein Fehler unterlaufen sein.)

* **The bill comes to £6.50, and as I gave you a ten-pound note the change should be £3.50 and not £2.50.**
(come to – ausmachen)

——— ❖ ———

* A: **If it's not right, can I change it?**
(change – umtauschen)
B: **Yes, as long as you keep your receipt.**
(receipt – Kassenbeleg)

* **Could you gift-wrap it, please?**
(gift-wrap – als Geschenk verpacken)

* **Have you got any carrier-bags, please?**
(carrier-bag – Tragtasche)

* **Could you put it in a paper-bag, please?**

* A: **Would you like us to deliver this afternoon?**
(Möchten Sie, dass wir Ihnen die Sachen heute nachmittag zustellen?)
B: **Oh, yes please. That'd be lovely.**
(lovely – nett, freundlich)

* A: **I bought this from you yesterday and it's the wrong size. I was wondering if you could change it.**
B: **Have you got your receipt?**

* **I want to complain about this compact disc. When I got it home I realised I had the wrong disc inside the cover.**
  (complain – sich beschweren / realise – bemerken / cover – Hülle)

* **I got a real bargain at the sales last week.**
  (bargain – günstiger Kauf; Gelegenheitskauf / sales – Ausverkauf)

* **That was a really good buy. The price was reduced from forty-five to twenty-five pounds.**
  (buy – Kauf)

AT THE POST OFFICE

Auf der Post

* **Where is the nearest post office, please?**

* **Could you tell me where the nearest pillar-box is, please?**
  (pillar-box – Briefkasten)

* **Excuse me, how much is a letter to Austria?**
  (how much is – wie viel kostet)

* **How much does a postcard to Spain cost?**
  (postcard – Ansichtskarte)

* **How much do I have to put on a postcard to Scotland?**
  (put – kleben)

* **A: I want to send these letters and postcards to the United States. How much will they cost?**
  B: 56p for a letter. And 38p for a postcard.
  (p – pence)

* **What stamps do I need for an airmail letter to the United States?**
  (stamp – Briefmarke / airmail letter – Luftpostbrief)

* **A: What's the postage on these letters to Thailand, please?**
  (postage – Porto)
  B: I'll have to check. Do you need anything else?
  (check – nachschauen)

* **It's $2.44 for an airmail letter to Brazil, isn't it?**
  (isn't it? – nicht wahr?)

* **Five twenty pence stamps, please.**
  (twenty pence stamp – 20-Pence-Marke)

* **Six stamps for letters and five for postcards, please.**

* **Here's a ten-pound note. I'm sorry I haven't anything smaller.**
(ten-pound note – 10-Pfund-Note)

* **How long does a letter to Vienna take?**
(take – brauchen)

* **Could you weigh this letter, please?**
(weigh – abwägen)

* **Could you tell me the ZIP Code for Chicago, please?**
(ZIP Code – Postleitzahl in den U.S.A.)

* **What's the Postcode, please?**
(Postcode – Postleitzahl im Vereinigten Königreich)

* **I'd like to send this letter by airmail.**

* **I'd like to send this letter Express, please.**
(Als Expressbrief bitte! | Express bitte!)

* **I'd like to send this as a registered letter, please.**
(Eingeschrieben bitte!)

* **I want to send this parcel to Dublin, please.**
(parcel – Paket)

* **A: Would you please tell me how much this parcel to Austria is?**
B: Put it on the scales, please. Hm, that'll be four pounds fifty.
(scales – Waage)

* **Do I need a customs declaration?**
(customs declaration – Zollerklärung)

* **I'd like to send a money order for £100.**
(money order – Geldanweisung)

* **What does it cost to send a fax?**

* **How do I fill this in?**
  (fill in sthg. – etwas ausfüllen)

* **Could you help me fill in the form, please?**

* **A: Where can I post these letters?**
  (post letter – Brief aufgeben)
  B: There's a letter-box just around the corner.
  (letter-box – Briefkasten / just around the corner – gleich um die Ecke)

* **A: Are there any letters for me? My name is Maier. M-A-I-E-R.**
  (Ist Post für mich da? … .)
  B: Yes, there is something for you. Could I see your passport, please?

* **A: Where can I collect a parcel?**
  (collect – abholen)
  B: Counter four, please.
  (counter – Schalter)

* **I'd like to have a post-office box, please.**
  (post-office box – Postfach)

* **I would like to have my mail forwarded, please. This is my new address.**
  (have mail forwarded – Post nachsenden lassen)
* **A: Where can I make a telephone call, please?**
  B: There are a number of call-boxes just outside the post office.
  (call-box – Telefonzelle)

——— ❖ ———

* **I'd like to make a call to Vienna.**
  (call – Telefongespräch / Es sei darauf hingewiesen, dass in England die Postverwaltung keinen Telefondienst betreibt.)

* **The telephone directory, please.**
  (telephone directory – Telefonbuch)

* **How much is a call to Paris, please?**

* **What does a local call cost?**
  (local call – Ortsgespräch)

* **What coins do I need?**
  (coin – Münze)

* **Can you give me change, please? I need some 10p pieces.**
  (Können Sie mir bitte wechseln? Ich brauche ein paar 10-Pence-Stücke.)

TELEPHONING

Telefonieren

ANSWERING THE SWITCHBOARD

Telefonzentrale meldet sich

* **Good morning. Paper Mills plc. Can I help you?**
  (plc – public limited company | etwa: Aktiengesellschaft in Großbritannien)

* **Good afternoon. Stiegel Bräu Restaurant. May I help you?**

REQUESTING IDENTITY

Bitte um Namensnennung

PERSON/COMPANY CALLED REQUESTS IDENTITY

Angerufene Person oder Firma bittet um Namensnennung

* **Who is calling, please?**
  (Wer spricht bitte?)

* **Who is speaking, please?**

* **May I ask who is calling?**

* **Can I have your name, please?**

PERSON CALLING REQUESTS IDENTITY

Anrufer/in bittet um Namensnennung

* **Hello, is that the Brinely Garage?**

* **Hello, is that 564 321?**

* **Is that you, Mr. Mutter?**

CALLER IDENTIFIES HIMSELF/HERSELF IN REPLY TO A REQUEST FOR IDENTITY

Anrufer/in nennt auf Ersuchen hin seinen/ihren Namen

* **This is Jack Nickolson, of Briers Ltd.**

* **Brown, of Hertz & Co. I'm calling from Vienna about our Order No. 4567.**
  (… . Ich rufe aus Wien an, und zwar wegen unseres Auftrages Nr. 4567.)

* **This is Simone Weller calling from Munich.**

* **Peter Brittle speaking.**

* **Geoffrey Sellers here.**

PERSON CALLED ANSWERS THE PHONE

Angerufener/Angerufene meldet sich

* **Good morning, Peter File here.**
  (Guten Morgen. Peter File am Apparat.)

* **Hello, Ron Myers speaking.**
(Hallo. Hier spricht Ron Myers.)

* **A: Can I speak to Miss Baxter, please?**
B: Speaking.
(Am Apparat!)

* **Good afternoon, Fun Bikes Ltd., John Sage speaking.**
(Ltd. – private limited company | etwa: GmbH in Großbritannien)

* **Nancy Rhine's office.**

CALLER REQUESTS A PARTICULAR PERSON OR SERVICE

Anrufer/in verlangt eine bestimmte Person oder Abteilung

* **I'd like to speak to Mr. Brown, your export manager, please.**

* **May I speak to someone in the Sales Department, please? I have a complaint to make.**
(sales department – Verkaufsabteilung / complaint – Beschwerde, Reklamation)

* **Could I have the Research and Development Department, please?**
(Könnten Sie mir bitte die Forschungs- und Entwicklungsabteilung geben?)

* **Please connect me with the Export Department.**
(connect – verbinden)

* **Could you put me through to extension 715, please?**
(Könnten Sie mich bitte mit der Klappe 715 verbinden? / 715 – seven-one-five)

* **Can you put me on to someone in the Sales Department, please? I've got a couple of questions about your new filing system.**
(Könnten Sie mir jemanden aus der Verkaufsabteilung geben. Ich hab' ein paar Fragen zu Ihrem neuen Ablagesystem.)

* **This is John Weir speaking. Could I speak to Gert Moon on extension 567, please? I dialled his extension direct but there was no reply.**
(on extension 567 – auf Klappe 567 / dial an extension direct – eine Klappe durchwählen / there was no reply – niemand hat abgehoben)

* **Could you put me through as quickly as possible? I'm calling from Singapore and that's quite expensive.**
(possible – möglich / quite – ziemlich / expensive – teuer)

REACTION TO CALLER'S REQUEST FOR A PARTICULAR PERSON

Reaktion auf den Wunsch eines Anrufers / einer Anruferin, jemanden bestimmten zu sprechen

* **Hold the line, please. I'm putting you through.**
(Bleiben Sie am Apparat. Ich verbinde Sie.)

* **Hold on, please.**
(Bleiben Sie am Apparat, bitte.)

* **One moment, please. She'll be here in a minute.**

* **Hang on for a minute.**
(Bleiben Sie eine Sekunde dran!)

* **I'll put you through now. In case it shouldn't work, Mr. Sutter's extension is 345. You can dial it direct.**
(… . Falls es nicht funktioniert, die Klappe von Herrn Sutter ist 345. Sie können durchwählen.)

* **Well, normally dialling extensions direct works fine. But hold the line, I'll try to put you through.**

* **A: Mr. Brown's extension is engaged. Will you hold?**
  (engaged – besetzt / … . Wollen Sie warten?)
  B: Yes, I'll hold.
  (Ja, ich werde warten. | Ja, ich bleibe dran.)

* **Mr. Leer will be free in a minute. I'm putting you on hold.**
  (… . Wenn Sie bitte warten wollen.)

* **I've got Mr. Brown on the line for you.**
  (Ich habe Herrn Brown für Sie in der Leitung.)

* **A: Do you still want to hold?**
  (Wollen Sie noch länger warten?)
  B: Yes, I'm holding.

CALLER STATES HIS/HER BUSINESS

Anrufer/in gibt den Grund für seinen/ihren Anruf an

* **I'm calling about the consignment of electric power drills which you promised us by Thursday.**
  (about – wegen / consignment – Sendung / power drill – Bohrmaschine / promise – versprechen / by – bis spätestens / Thursday – Donnerstag)

* **My call is in reference to your stand at the Vienna Fair.**
  (Ich rufe im Zusammenhang mit Ihrem Stand auf der Wiener Messe an.)

* **I'm ringing you because we still haven't received any payment on our invoice A-1990 / 5432.**
  (ring – anrufen / still – noch / receive – erhalten / payment – Zahlung / on – für; in Zusammenhang mit / invoice – Rechnung)

* **The reason why I'm calling you is that I want to make a change in our last order. I hope it isn't too late.**
(Der Grund, warum ich Sie anrufe, ist, dass ich unseren letzten Auftrag abändern möchte. … .)

* **I'm calling on behalf of our Export Manager. He would like to know whether the last consignment has arrived in good order.**
(on behalf – für; im Auftrag von / whether – ob / arrive – ankommen / in good order – in gutem Zustand; gut)

* **I'm phoning because I don't think I'll be able to keep our appointment I'm afraid. I've got the flu.**
(keep appointment – Termin einhalten / I'm afraid – leider / flu – Grippe)

* **I'm phoning for some price information on Austrian wines.**

THE PERSON WANTED IS NOT AVAILABLE

Die gewünschte Person ist nicht erreichbar

* **I'm afraid she's not in at the moment. I'm a colleague of hers. Would you like to leave a message?**
(Leider ist sie im Augenblick nicht hier. … . Möchten Sie eine Nachricht hinterlassen?)

* **He's in a meeting with the Managing Director. If it's really important I could ask the operator to ring him there.**
(meeting – Sitzung / Managing Director – Generaldirektor / important – wichtig / operator – Telefonzentrale, Telefonist / in / ring – anrufen)

* **His secretary tells me that he won't be back before three p.m..**
(won't – will not / p.m. – am Nachmittag)

* **Mr. Brinner is away for a few days. He'll be back Friday afternoon. Can I take a message?**
(a few – ein paar)

* **I'm sorry, Ms. Moat has gone to London on business for a few days. Can I give her a message?**
(on business – geschäftlich)

* **Mr. Grout has just left for the factory. You can reach him there on 564 311 in about ten minutes.**
(Herr Grout ist gerade in die Fabrik gefahren. Sie können ihn dort in etwa 10 Minuten unter der Nummer … erreichen.)

* **Mrs. Ondine is on holiday. Perhaps I can help you.**

* **Mr. Brix is in another office at the moment. I could have the call transferred, if it's urgent.**
(transfer call – ein Gespräch umlegen | umleiten / urgent – dringend)

* **Can you tell me what you are calling about? Maybe I can help you.**
(call about sthg. – wegen etwas anrufen)

* **Would you like him to call you back?**
(Möchten Sie, dass er Sie zurückruft?)

* **Would you like to ring back later?**
(Möchten Sie später noch einmal anrufen?)

* **I'm afraid Mr. Lone is with a client at present.**
(at present – zur Zeit)

REACTING TO UNAVAILABILITY OF PARTY CALLED

Reaktion auf Nichterreichbarkeit des/der Angerufenen

- **Yes. That would be very kind. My number is 45673. The area code for Vienna is 01. But when calling from England leave off the 0 and dial 1 right after the country code, which is 43.**
  (kind – freundlich / area code – Vorwahlnummer, Ortskennzahl / leave off – auslassen / dial – wählen / right after – direkt nach / country code – Landeskennzahl)

- **Would you ask him to call me as soon as possible, please. It's urgent. My number is Norwich 546 781 extension 305.**

- **No, thank you. That's not necessary. Tell him that I called and that I'll call again at around four.**
  (at around four – um etwa vier Uhr)

- **It's very urgent. Are you sure Mr. Briner is not in the building? Have you tried paging him?**
  (building – Gebäude, Haus / page sbdy. – jmdn. anpiepsen; jmdn. mit dem Piepserl | Pager rufen; jmdn. ausrufen lassen)

- **When I call back, do I have to go through the operator or can I call straight through to his extension?**
  (call back – noch einmal anrufen / go through operator – die Vermittlung benötigen / straight through – direkt)

- **What is his extension?**

- **At what time can I phone him?**

- **When can I reach her?**
  (reach – erreichen)

* **Could you ask him to call me on 562 345, please. I'll be on that number until about 6 p.m..**
(on 562 345 – unter der Nummer 562 345)

* **Yes. Could he call me back? I'll be at 876 211 all day.**
(call back – zurückrufen / be at 876 211 – unter der Nummer 876 211 zu erreichen sein)

DIFFICULTIES IN UNDERSTANDING THE OTHER PARTY

Schwierigkeiten, den Gesprächspartner zu verstehen

* **Would you please repeat your name?**
(repeat – wiederholen)

* **Could you spell your name, please?**
(spell – buchstabieren)

* **I didn't catch your name. Would you please spell it?**
(catch – verstehen)

* **Ah, it's you Mr. Buttler. I didn't recognise your voice. The line's pretty bad. Sounds as if you're talking from the other end of the world.**
(recognise – erkennen / voice – Stimme / line – Leitung, Verbindung / pretty – ziemlich / sound – klingen)

* **Sorry, I couldn't hear what you said. Would you mind repeating the figure?**
(… . Würden Sie bitte die Zahl wiederholen.)

* **I didn't catch what you said. Could you repeat the last sentence, please?**

* **Could you speak a bit more slowly, please? My English is still a bit rusty.**
  (… . Ich bin im Englischen noch etwas aus der Übung.)

* **What was that? Did you really say 500 or have I got it wrong?**
  (get sthg. wrong – etwas falsch verstehen)

* **This is a very bad line, I'm afraid. I'll try to ring you again in half an hour.**
  (I'm afraid – tut mir leid)

* **Are you still there?**
  (Sind Sie noch dran?)

* **Can you hear me?**

SPELLING WORDS; NUMBERS AND OTHER DETAILS

Buchstabieren von Wörtern; Zahlen und andere Details

* **A: Could you spell the name for me, please?**
  B: Yes, certainly. D for Dora, I for Island, double N for Northpole, E for Edward, and R for Richard.
  (certainly – gern / D for Dora – D wie Dora)

* **Yes, it's five hundred. 5 double O.**
  (O – Null)

* **A: What is the order number?**
  (order – Auftrag)
  B: The number of the order in question is 5312 / A12. (five – three – one – two – stroke – capital A – one – two)
  (order in question – Auftrag, um den es sich handelt / stroke – [britisch] Schrägstrich / capital A – großes A; Großbuchstabe A)

* **A: Is it the number in the bottom line?**
(bottom line – letzte Zeile)
B: No, I mean the code in the top right-hand corner of the document. It should read 82(40)5 / 33.1-g (eight – two – open parenthesis – four – zero – close parenthesis – five – slash – three – three – point – one – hyphen – lower case g)
(top right-hand – rechts oben / corner – Ecke / read – lauten / open parenthesis – [U.S.] Klammer auf / close parenthesis – Klammer zu / slash – [U.S.] Schrägstrich / hyphen – Bindestrich / lower case g – kleines g)

* **The figure I want you to check is in column three, line four.**
(figure – Zahl / check – überprüfen / column – Spalte / line – Zeile)

* **The AWB number which I gave you a couple of hours ago is wrong. The last figure is a six and not – I repeat – and not a nine.**
(AWB – airway bill | Luftfrachtbrief / repeat – wiederholen)

* **The figure in the quantity column should read 2.6 tonnes, not 3.6 tonnes.**
(quantity – Menge / 2.6 – two point six | zwei Komma sechs / tonne – metrische Tonne)

* **The name is Holt & Frier: Capital H – o – l – t ampersand – capital F – r – i – e – r.**
(capital H – großes H / ampersand – Et-Zeichen)

* **A: The command you suggested for starting the program does not work.**
(command – Computerbefehl / suggest – vorschlagen / work – funktionieren)
B: That's strange. Are you sure you put in an asterisk?
(strange – seltsam / asterisk – Sternchen)

* **Put in a full stop after "now", a dash between "right" and "Waterfield", a colon after "price", and a semi-colon after "butter".** (put in – einfügen / full stop – Punkt / dash – Gedankenstrich / colon – Doppelpunkt / semi-colon – Strichpunkt)

RINGING OFF

Beendigung des Telefongesprächs

* **I must ring off now. But I'll get back to you soon.** (Ich muss jetzt auflegen. Aber ich melde mich bald wieder bei Ihnen.)

* **Thanks a lot. Goodbye.**

* **Sorry, I'll have to ring off now. I've got a call on the other line. Thank you for calling us.**

* **I think that's all. Bye, bye then.**

* **What time would it be convenient for me to call you again?** (Wann wäre es Ihnen angenehm, dass ich Sie wieder anrufe?)

* **I'll switch on the answering machine before I leave.** (switch on – einschalten / answering machine – Telefonanrufbeantworter / leave – weggehen)

* **Kind regards to your wife.** (Grüße an Ihre Frau.)

* **Remember me to your girl friend.** (Schöne Grüße an deine Freundin.)

TALKING ABOUT THE TELEPHONE

Gespräche rund um das Telefon

* **A: I've heard about these prepaid telephone cards. Since I'll have to make a lot of calls, do you think I should buy one?**
(prepaid telephone card – Telefonwertkarte / since – da / a lot of – viele; eine Menge)
B: Yes, cards are very convenient if you've got to make a lot of calls.
(convenient – praktisch)

* **A: How much is a telephone card?**
B: You can have one for £10, for £20, or for £50.

* **Are there enough public telephone boxes that will take a card?**
(telephone box – Telefonzelle)

* **You couldn't change a five-pound note, could you? I need some 50p coins for a telephone call.**
(change – wechseln / coin – Münze)

* **You can't use coins in a telephone box, you need special tokens.**
(token – Jeton, Wertmünze)

* **Can I borrow your telephone directory for a moment, please?**
(telephone directory – Telefonbuch)

* **He's not in the directory. He must have an unlisted number.**
(unlisted number | ex-directory number – Geheimnummer)

* **You have to press the button before you lift the receiver.**
(press button – Knopf drücken / lift receiver – Hörer abheben)

* **Dial 0 for external calls.**
(dial – wählen / call – Anruf)

* **Press the black button until you can hear a buzzing sound. Then lift the receiver.**
(buzzing sound – Summton)

* **The new push-button telephones are ever so much more convenient.**
(push-button telephone – Tastentelefon)

* **I've got the latest in telephone technology back home. My phone can store up to 50 numbers. It has an automatic redialling feature as well. Very convenient if the number you're calling is engaged.**
(store – speichern / redialling feature – Wählwiederholung [-svorrichtung] / engaged – besetzt)

* **No, you can't dial direct to Ghana. You've got to place your call through the international operator.**
(place call through operator – Anruf über die Vermittlung machen)

* **Where is the nearest pay phone, please?**
(pay phone – Telefonzelle, Münztelefon)

* **Could I use your phone for a moment?**

* **Mind if I use your phone to make a call to Germany?**
(Haben Sie etwas dagegen, … ?)

PERSONAL BANKING

Persönliche Bankgeschäfte

OPENING HOURS

Öffnungszeiten

* A: **What are the bank opening hours in this country?**
(opening hours – Öffnungszeiten)
B: **Banks are open from 9 a.m. to three thirty in the afternoon.**

* **When do your banks open?**

* **Some banks are open until twelve on Saturday mornings.**

* A: **What time do the banks close? I need to change some money.**
(close – schließen / need – müssen / change – wechseln, umwechseln)
B: **Banks close at three thirty. But there are quite a few exchange offices that are open much longer. I think there is even one at Victoria Station that's open round the clock.**
(quite a few – eine ganze Reihe von / exchange office – Wechselstube / even – sogar)

TRAVELLERS' CHEQUES

Reiseschecks

* A: **I'm travelling to Malaysia on business next week, what advice could you give me on taking money?**
(travel – reisen / on business – geschäftlich / advice – Rat)
B: **The best idea would be for you to take travellers' cheques denominated in dollars, because they can be cashed everywhere.**
(be denominated in – lauten auf / cash – einlösen / everywhere – überall)
A: **And what happens if I lose them?**
B: **You should report the numbers and amounts to the issuing institution without delay. Your money will be reimbursed, providing you haven't countersigned them.**
(report – melden / issue – ausstellen / without delay – unverzüglich / reimburse – rückerstatten / providing – vorausgesetzt / countersign – gegenzeichnen)

* **I'd like $1,000 in travellers' cheques, please. What denominations are available?**
(… . In welchen Beträgen sind sie erhältlich?)

* **Where should I put my signature?**
(signature – Unterschrift)

* **I'd like to cash some travellers' cheques, please.**

* **How much is your commission on cashing travellers' cheques, please?**
(commission – Provision)

* A: **Good morning. Can I cash this traveller's cheque here?**
B: **Yes, would you take it to the cashier at the foreign counter, please?**
(cashier – Schalterbeamter / foreign counter – Auslandsschalter)

* **A: Is it possible to cash travellers' cheques without any means of identification?**
(means of identification – Identitätsnachweis)
B: I'm afraid not, sir. I need to see your passport.
(Leider nein. … . / need – müssen)

* **Where should I countersign?**

EUROCHEQUES
Euroschecks

* **Do you cash Eurocheques?**

* **Would you kindly cash this Eurocheque?**
(kindly – bitte)

* **What is the maximum amount for one Eurocheque?**
(amount – Betrag)

* **Do I have to make it out in English or in German?**
(make out – ausstellen)

* **Should I endorse it?**
(endorse – auf der Rückseite unterschreiben; girieren)

ORDINARY CHEQUES

* **A: I'd like to cash this cheque, please.**
B: I'm afraid you can only pay this into an account, sir. It's a crossed cheque. Only open cheques are payable in cash.
(I'm afraid – tut mir leid / account – Konto / crossed cheque – gekreuzter Scheck; Verrechnungsscheck / open cheque – Barscheck / in cash – in bar)

* **Here is my cheque card.**

* **I'm sorry, I think I've forgotten my signature on the reverse side.**
(reverse side – Rückseite)

* **Should I sign it on the back?**
(Soll ich ihn auf der Rückseite unterschreiben?)

* **A: How would you like it, madam?**
B: Twenty-pound notes will do fine, thank you.
(Ich möchte gerne 20-Pfund-Noten.)

* **In fifties, please.**

* **Two notes of a hundred, please.**

* **Two twenties, five tens, a five and five one-pound coins, please.**

* **I seem to have mislaid my cheque card. What should I do?**
(Ich dürfte meine Scheckkarte verlegt haben. … ?)

* **A: Do you have crossed cheques in Austria?**
B: No, not really, but we have something very similar called 'Verrechnungsscheck'.
(similar – ähnlich)

* **A: By the way, you seem to use a lot more cheques than transfers here. And most of them are order cheques, aren't they?**
(Übrigens, es scheint, dass man hier viel mehr Schecks als Überweisungen verwendet. … . / order cheque – Namensscheck, Orderscheck / aren't they? – nicht wahr?)
B: What do you mean order cheques?
A: Well, cheques payable to a particular person, and not to bearer. We in Austria use mostly bearer cheques.
(particular – bestimmt / bearer – Inhaber / bearer cheque – Inhaberscheck)

CHANGING MONEY

Geld wechseln

* **I'd like to change euros into pounds, please.**
  (change – umwechseln)

* **How many pounds do I get for 2,000 euros, please?**

* **Could you change these Canadian dollars for me, please?**

* A: **I've got some Mexican pesos. I wonder whether you could change them for me, please?**
  (… . Könnten Sie sie mir bitte umwechseln?)
  B: **Certainly, madam. I'll just check the exchange rates.**
  (certainly – natürlich / just – nur / check – nachsehen / exchange rate – Wechselkurs)

* A: **Do you change foreign coins?**
  (foreign coins – ausländische Münzen)
  B: **No, I'm afraid we can't take foreign currency in small change.**
  (foreign currency in small change – ausländisches Kleingeld)

* **Can you give me £100 in euros, please?**

* **Can you change this fifty-pound note into dollars, please?**

* A: **Could you tell me the current rate of exchange for US dollars, please?**
  (current rate of exchange – heutiger Kurs)
  B: **Would you like to know the buying rate or selling rate?**
  (buying rate – Geldkurs, Ankaufskurs / selling rate – Briefkurs, Verkaufskurs)
  A: **Well, I'd like to buy dollars, so that's your selling rate, isn't it?**
  (isn't it? – nicht wahr?)

* **What's today's rate of exchange?**
(rate of exchange – Wechselkurs)

* **I'd like to know the rate for Swiss francs, please.**

* **A: I need $2,000 to take with me to the US, please.**
B: Would you like it in cash or in cheques?
(in cash – bar)
A: I'll have cash, please.

* **A: How would you like the money?**
B: In hundred-dollar notes, please.

* **Notes only, please.**

* **Some small change, too, please.**
(small change – Kleingeld)

* **I wonder if you could tell me whether there are any restrictions on taking foreign currency into the United States?**
(Könnten Sie mir bitte sagen, ob … . / foreign currency – Fremdwährung; ausländisches Geld)

——— ❖ ———

* **Do you think you could change this fifty-pound note for smaller notes, please?**
(change – wechseln)

* **Can you give me change, please?**
(Können Sie mir bitte wechseln?)

OPENING AND CLOSING AN ACCOUNT

Eröffnung und Schließung eines Kontos

* A: **I was thinking of opening an account over here as I'll probably be travelling back and forwards regularly from now on. Which bank could you recommend?**
(probably – wahrscheinlich / back and forwards – hin und her / regularly – regelmäßig / recommend – empfehlen)

B: **Well, if you just want a current account with the normal services, there isn't much to choose between the Big Four clearing banks, which are Nat West, Barclays, Lloyds and Midland. If you want to earn interest on your money then you're probably better off with an account at a building society, which can offer you attractive interest–bearing accounts with a cheque book and cash dispenser card, too.**
(current account – Kontokorrentkonto, Girokonto, Scheckkonto / there isn't much to choose between – es gibt kaum einen Unterschied zwischen / clearing bank – britische Geschäftsbank / earn interest – Zinsen bekommen / be better off – besser daran sein / building society – Bausparkasse / offer – anbieten / interest-bearing – verzinslich / cash dispenser – Geldausgabeautomat, Bankomat)

* A: **Do current accounts in Britain bear interest?**
(Werden Kontokorrenteinlagen … verzinst?)

B: **Usually only if you're more than £100 in the black.**
(Normalerweise nur, wenn Sie mehr als 100 Pfund auf dem Konto haben.)

* A: **I'd like to open a bank account, please.**
B: **Certainly. May I ask you what type of account you had in mind?**
(Gerne. Darf ich Sie fragen, an welche Art von Konto Sie gedacht haben?)
A: **A current account, I think.**
B: **Well, with our current account you have all the normal services such as free cheques, a £100 cheque guarantee card and cash card, plus a guaranteed overdraft of up to 50% of your salary and 9% interest is paid on every pound in your account.**
(cash card – Bezugskarte, Bankomatkarte / overdraft – Überziehungsmöglichkeit / salary – Gehalt / interest – Zinsen)

* **I'd like to open a deposit account, please.**
(deposit account – Sparkonto)

* **I'd like to transfer my account from this branch to your Manchester branch, please.**
(transfer – verlegen / branch – Filiale)

❖

* **I'm going back to Austria next week, so I won't be needing my current account any more. Could you close it and have the balance transferred to my account in Salzburg? Here's my account number.**
(won't – will not / close – schließen / have balance transferred – Überweisung des Guthabens veranlassen)

DEPOSITS
Einzahlungen

* A: **I'd like to pay some money into my account, please.**
B: **Certainly, sir. Could I have your account number, please?**
A: **Yes, here's my cheque card.**

* A: **I'd like to pay this crossed cheque in pounds sterling into my wife's account, please.**
  B: **Do you know the number of her account?**
  A: **Yes, here you are.**
  (… , hier bitte!)

* **May I have a paying–in slip, please?**
  (paying-in slip – Einzahlungsschein)

* **If I deposit this cheque today, when will the amount be credited to my account?**
  (deposit – einzahlen / amount – Betrag / credit – gutschreiben)

* A: **By the way, Bill, how much did you pay into our account with Midland Bank?**
  B: **I deposited £300 two weeks ago. Here's the receipt.**
  (receipt – Beleg)

WITHDRAWALS

Abhebungen

* A: **I'd like to take £50 out of my current account, please.**
  (take out – abheben)
  B: **Certainly, sir. Just make out a cheque payable to "Self" or "Cash".**

* A: **I'd like to withdraw some money from my savings account, please.**
  (withdraw – abheben / savings account – Sparkonto)
  B: **Certainly, how much would you like?**
  A: **Two hundred pounds.**
  B: **Could I have your passbook, please?**
  (passbook – Sparbuch)

* **A: I'd like to draw some money on my husband's account.**
(Ich möchte Geld vom Konto meines Gatten abheben.)
B: Have you got power of attorney, madam?
(power of attorney – Vollmacht)

* **Where should I sign?**

* **A: Your cash dispenser seems to have broken down. Could I withdraw £20 in cash, please?**
(… scheint kaputt zu sein. … ?)
B: Certainly. The easiest way is to make out a cheque, madam.

* **A: My cash dispenser card has been swallowed up.**
(swallow up – schlucken)
B: Did you key in the wrong PIN-code?
(key in – eingeben / PIN – Personal Identification Number | Bankomatcode)

TRANSFERS
Überweisungen

* **A: I would like to transfer £25.40 to this account, please.**
(transfer – überweisen)
B: Well, for such a small amount, and as it's a domestic transaction, it'd be much easier and less expensive for you to send a cheque.
(domestic transaction – Inlandstransaktion / expensive – teuer)

* **A: I'd like to pay a bill in Austria for 65 euros. Could I make a transfer?**
(bill – Rechnung / transfer – Überweisung)
B: Well, we could transfer the money for you, but for a small sum like that it's simpler to give you a cheque which you can send direct.

* A: **I'd like to transfer £450 from my current account to my deposit account, please.**
B: **Yes, could you sign here, please ... Thank you.**

* **Have the amount transferred by a bank.**
(Lassen Sie den Betrag von einer Bank überweisen.)

* A: **I've heard that the best way to transfer money abroad is by SWIFT, is that right?**
(abroad – ins Ausland / SWIFT – SWIFT | Society for Worldwide Interbank Financial Telecommunications)
B: **It is the quickest method, and in fact most of our international funds transfers are sent via SWIFT.**
(funds – Geld)

* A: **I'd like to transfer £300 to my mother in Innsbruck. Shall I pay cash or can you charge it to my account?**
(charge – anlasten, belasten)
B: **We'll make the payment and debit it to your account.**
(debit an amount to an account – ein Konto mit einem Betrag belasten)

* A: **Could you transfer £500 from my deposit account to this account in Germany, please?**
B: **Certainly. Would you like us to make the transfer by ordinary mail or by telex?**
(by ordinary mail – brieflich)

* **I'm expecting some money which was transferred to me about a week ago from Vienna. Is it in yet?**
(expect – erwarten / … . Ist es schon da?)

* **I'd like to arrange for my telephone bills to be paid by direct debit, please.**
(arrange for – veranlassen / direct debit – Abbuchungsverfahren, Lastschriftverfahren)

* **A: Could you arrange a standing order for £260 per month payable to this account, please?**
(standing order – Dauerauftrag)
B: Yes, that should be no problem. Could you just complete this form, please?
(complete form – Formular ausfüllen)

* **I'd like to transfer £250 on the first of each month, starting next month and until further notice, to my daughter, who's studying in Linz.**
(until further notice – bis auf Widerruf; bis auf Weiteres)

* **Could I cancel a standing order arrangement which I have for my rent? I'm leaving London to go back to Austria at the end of the month.**
(cancel – stornieren / rent – Miete / … . Ich gehe … nach Österreich zurück.)

OVERDRAFTS

Kontoüberziehungen

* **I wonder if it'd be possible to overdraw my account by up to £500 next month?**
(Wäre es möglich, dass ich mein Konto nächsten Monat bis zu 500 Pfund überziehe?)

* **A: How much would it cost for an overdraft of five hundred pounds?**
(overdraft – Überziehungskredit)
B: First of all there is a small commitment fee and then on top of that you'll have to pay interest.
(commitment fee – Bereitstellungsprovision / on top of that – zusätzlich)

* **What is the current rate of interest on an overdraft, please?**
(Wie hoch sind zur Zeit die Zinsen für … ?)

STATEMENTS AND BALANCE OF ACCOUNT

Kontoauszüge und Kontostand

∗ **Can you give me a statement, please?**
(statement – Kontoauszug)

∗ A: **Could you send me a statement at the end of each month?**
B: **Actually, you might find it more convenient to order statements as and when you need them from our ATMs using your cash card.**
(convenient – praktisch / order – abrufen / ATM – automated teller machine | automatischer Bankschalter / cash card – Bezugskarte, Bankomatkarte)

∗ A: **I'd like to know the balance of my account, please. It's number 4647839.**
(balance – Saldo, Stand)
B: **Ah, yes, you have a debit balance of £46.97.**
(debit balance – Minus)

∗ **Your account is overdrawn by £46.97.**

∗ A: **Could you tell me the balance on my account, please?**
B: **Your account shows a credit of £167.90.**
(credit – Guthaben, Plus)

CREDIT CARDS

Kreditkarten

∗ **Here is my credit card.**

∗ **Do you accept Visa credit cards?**

* **Can I withdraw cash with my credit card?**
  (withdraw cash – Geld abheben)

* **I wish to report that I've lost my credit card.**
  (report – melden)

* **Here are my credit card details. … Should I give you the expiry date, too?**
  (expiry date – Verfallsdatum)

MY JOB

Mein Job

WHAT DO YOU DO FOR A LIVING?

Wie verdienen Sie sich Ihren Lebensunterhalt?

* **What kind of job do you have?**

* **I'm a civil servant, with permanent tenure.**
  (civil servant – Staatsangestellter / permanent tenure – Pragmatisierung; unkündbare Stellung)

* **I work for the subsidiary of an American corporation.**
  (subsidiary – Tochtergesellschaft / corporation – [Kapital-]Gesellschaft, Konzern)

* **I'm a free-lance management consultant.**
  (Ich bin freiberuflicher Betriebsberater.)

* **I work as a software engineer for a large software house.**

* **I'm still a student.**
  (still – noch)

JOINING THE COMPANY

Eintritt in die Firma

* **I joined the company in 2005 as a management trainee.**
  (join company – in Firma | Gesellschaft eintreten / trainee – Praktikant, Trainee)

- **You won't believe it, but I've been with my present company for over 15 years.**
  (Sie werden es nicht glauben, aber ich bin schon seit über 15 Jahren bei meiner jetzigen Firma.)

- **I replied to an advertisement in 2006. They invited me for an interview and I got the job.**
  (reply to – antworten auf / advertisement – Anzeige / invite – einladen)

- **I met my present boss at the tennis club. That's how I got the job.**
  (meet – kennenlernen / present – jetzig, gegenwärtig / that's how – so; auf diese Weise)

- **I knew one of the managers from school.**
  (know – kennen)

- **I've worked for quite a few companies already. I think the one I'm with now is the sixth.**
  (quite a few – einige; nicht wenige / sixth – sechst)

WORKING HOURS AND WORKING CONDITIONS

Arbeitszeit und Arbeitsbedingungen

- **A: When do you start in the morning?**
  B: I have to start at nine.
  A: Nine? Well, that's rather late. In my country we start at eight. Some firms even at seven thirty.
  (rather – ziemlich / even – sogar)

- **It's not a nine-to-five job. As long as I meet my deadlines they don't bother too much about attendance.**
  (nine-to-five job – 08 / 15-Job / meet deadline – Termin einhalten / bother about – sich kümmern um / attendance – Anwesenheit)

* **I work long hours. And, if I've got a deadline to meet, I sometimes have to take work home with me over the weekend.**
(work long hours – oft sehr lange arbeiten; oft bis spät in die Nacht hinein arbeiten)

* **The official working week is 40 hours, but my company expect me to work up to 10 hours overtime.**
(working week – Arbeitszeit / expect – erwarten / overtime – Überstunden)

* **I did a lot of overtime last year.**
(a lot of – eine Menge; viel)

* **We've got a very rigid system. You have to get your card punched whenever you enter or leave the building.**
(rigid – starr / get card punched – [Stech-]Karte lochen | abstempeln lassen / enter – betreten / leave – verlassen / building – Gebäude)

* **We are on flexitime. This means I can start any time between 8 and 11 and leave between 4 and 7 in the afternoon, as long as I do my eight hours.**
(be on flexitime – gleitende Arbeitszeit haben / leave – weggehen)

* **I've got a nice office.**
(office – Büro)

SUPERIORS, SUBORDINATES AND COLLEAGUES

Vorgesetzte, Untergebene und Kollegen

* **My boss is very nice. Very constructive. Never tells you off, even if you've made a mistake.**
(tell sbdy. off – jmdn. heruntermachen / mistake – Fehler)

* **My boss is a woman actually. We've got a fairly large number of female managers.**
(fairly – ziemlich / female – weiblich)

* **A: I've never worked for a woman. What's it like?**
(... . Wie ist das?)
B: Well, at first it was a bit strange. But you get used to it, especially if the woman is a competent manager.
(strange – seltsam / get used to sthg. – sich an etwas gewöhnen / especially – besonders)

* **We've got lots of women managers in our company. It doesn't seem to make any difference.**
(seem – scheinen / difference – Unterschied)

* **My boss is a very difficult person to work with.**

* **He likes to show us who's the boss.**

* **Working under her was not much fun. But I learned a lot.**
(not much fun – nicht gerade lustig)

* **Most of the people in the Marketing Department are quite young and the atmosphere there is very relaxed.**
(quite – ziemlich / atmosphere – Klima / relaxed – locker)

* **Most of my colleagues are very nice people.**

——— ❖ ———

* **I report to the Marketing Manager.**
(report to sbdy. – jmdm. unterstellt sein)

* **I work under the Controller.**

* **My section comes under Materials Management.**
(Mein Referat gehört zur Abteilung Materialwirtschaft.)

* **I'm responsible for a team of about 50 sales reps.**
(responsible – verantwortlich, zuständig / sales rep – Vertreter, Reisender)

JOB DESCRIPTION AND DUTIES

Beschreibung des Arbeitsplatzes und Aufgaben

* **What exactly are your duties?**
(duty – Aufgabe)

* **What does your job involve?**
(Welche Tätigkeiten bringt Ihr Posten mit sich?)

* **I'm a sales engineer.**
(sales engineer – Verkaufsingenieur)

* **I'm responsible for maintaining contact with our advertising agency.**
(maintain – aufrechterhalten, halten / advertising agency – Werbeagentur)

* **I'm in charge of the Personnel Department.**
(Ich leite die Personalabteilung.)

* **I look after our overseas customers.**
(Ich betreue unsere ausländischen Kunden.)

* **I used to work as an account executive but transferred to the Personnel Department when they needed an assistant to the Personnel Manager.**
(Früher einmal habe ich als Kundenbetreuer | Kontakter gearbeitet, aber dann bin ich in die Personalabteilung übersiedelt, als ein Assistent für den Personalchef benötigt wurde.)

* **My main task is negotiating contracts with foreign suppliers.**
  (Meine Hauptaufgabe ist es, Verträge mit ausländischen Lieferanten auszuhandeln.)

* **The sales people negotiate the contract in outline. I'm responsible for the legal details.**
  (in outline – in groben Zügen; im Umriss / legal – juristisch)

* **My job involves a lot of travelling.**
  (Mein Posten ist mit sehr viel Reisen verbunden.)

* **I joined my company as a design engineer but switched to selling after four years.**
  (join company – in Firma | Gesellschaft eintreten / design engineer – Konstrukteur / switch – umsteigen)

* **I work in the field, selling specialised software to chemical companies.**
  (in the field – im Außendienst)

* **I'm mainly concerned with making insurance claims.**
  (Meine Hauptaufgabe ist die Anmeldung von Versicherungsansprüchen | das Melden von Schadensfällen.)

* **Currently I'm helping out in the Auditing Section.**
  (Zur Zeit helfe ich in der Innenrevision aus.)

* **I deal with the incoming German correspondence.**
  (deal with – bearbeiten)

JOB SATISFACTION

Arbeitszufriedenheit

* **Are you satisfied with your present job?**
  (satisfied – zufrieden / present – gegenwärtig, jetzig)

* **I like my present job.**

* **Yes, I enjoy my work, although it is a bit much sometimes.**
  (enjoy sthg. – etwas gerne tun | haben / although – obwohl)

* **What I like about my job is that I meet a lot of interesting people.**
  (meet – treffen; zusammenkommen mit)

* **What I particularly like about my job is that it involves a lot of travelling.**
  (particularly – besonders / involve – mit sich bringen / travel – reisen)

* **I don't like my present job.**

* **I hate sitting in the office all day. I'd prefer to travel and meet people.**
  (hate – hassen / all day – den ganzen Tag / prefer – vorziehen)

* **I don't like what I'm doing right now. Too much of a grind.**
  (right now – zur Zeit; gerade jetzt / grind – Mühe, Plackerei)

* **I've a lot of independence.**
  (independence – Unabhängigkeit)

* **What I can't stand is the paperwork.**
  (Was ich nicht leiden kann, ist der Papierkram.)

LEAVING THE COMPANY AND LOOKING FOR A NEW JOB

Ausscheiden aus der Firma und Suche nach einem neuen Arbeitsplatz

* **I'm thinking of leaving the firm.**
  (leave firm – aus Firma ausscheiden)

* **I'm planning to move to another company.**
  (move to – wechseln zu)

* **Unless I get promotion within the next year or two I might move on.**
  (unless – wenn nicht / promotion – Beförderung / move on – weiterziehen; sich beruflich verändern)

* **I'm between jobs. I left the company after a row with my immediate superior.**
  (row – Krach / immediate superior – unmittelbare[r] Vorgesetzte[r])

* **I was fired when they found out that I had a second job.**

* **I'm looking for a job.**
  (look for – suchen)

* **I've handed in my resignation.**
  (Ich habe meinen Rücktritt eingereicht. | Ich habe gekündigt.)

* **I'm still working for them because there is a six-week period of notice in my contract of employment.**
  (still – noch immer / period of notice – Kündigungsfrist / contract of employment – Arbeitsvertrag)

* **I'm going to hand in my notice next week.**
  (hand in – einreichen / notice – Kündigung)

* **I'm still trying to find something suitable in public relations or advertising.**
  (suitable – geeignet, passend / advertising – Werbung)

* **I'm going to retire in three years.**
(retire – in Pension gehen)

* **I'm not what you might call a job-hopper, but I've worked for quite a few companies already. I'm always interested in a new challenge.**
(job-hopper – jemand, der häufig den Job wechselt / quite a few – ziemlich viele / challenge – Herausforderung)

* **No, I wouldn't dream of leaving my firm. I really like it there. It's like a second home to me.**
(Nein, mir würde es nicht im Traume einfallen, … .)

* **A: Ever thought of setting up your own business?**
(Jemals daran gedacht, sich selbständig zu machen?)
B: I briefly toyed with the idea of setting up a partnership or a company with a couple of friends.
(briefly – kurz / toy – spielen / partnership – Personengesellschaft / company – Kapitalgesellschaft / a couple of – ein paar)

* **One of my colleagues left the firm to join a workers' co-operative. Earns much less there but finds it more rewarding to work for an organisation that is owned and controlled by its own workers.**
(join – eintreten in; sich anschließen / workers' co-operative – Betrieb in Arbeiterselbstverwaltung / earn – verdienen / rewarding – lohnend / owned by – im Eigentum von / control – führen)

COMPENSATION
Entlohnung

* **A: How much do you make?**
(make – verdienen)
B: That's a good question.

* **I don't mind telling you how much I earn. But in my country people don't usually talk about their salaries, not even with fairly close friends.**
(Es macht mir nichts aus, … . / salary – Gehalt / not even – nicht einmal / fairly close friends – ziemlich gute Freunde)

* **My basic salary is around £40,000. And then I get about £10,000 in commissions, and the usual benefits of course.**
(basic salary – Grundgehalt / around – ungefähr / commission – Provision / benefits – Nebenleistungen, Sozialleistungen)

* **I make about €3,500 a month, that is before tax and national insurance.**
(Ich verdiene rund 3.500 Euro im Monat, und zwar vor Abzug der Steuern und Sozialabgaben.)

* **They gave me a company car last year.**
(company car – Firmenauto)

* **To make it comparable with a British salary you would have to multiply that by 14.**
(comparable – vergleichbar)

* **Yes 14. Because we are paid 14 monthly salaries a year. Sounds odd, I know, but makes sense for tax reasons.**
(sound odd – seltsam | komisch klingen / make sense – sinnvoll sein / for tax reasons – aus steuerlichen Gründen)

* **The statutory minimum holiday in Austria is five weeks.**
  (Der gesetzlich vorgeschriebene Mindesturlaub in … .)

* **If you want to compare this figure with a British or American salary, you would have to take into account the number of salaries paid per year, the longer paid holidays, the larger number of public holidays and, of course, the higher taxes.**
  (compare – vergleichen / figure – Zahl / take into account – berücksichtigen / number – Anzahl / public holiday – Feiertag / tax – Steuer)

* **The gross figure looks quite good. But with all the deductions, take-home pay isn't much to write home about, especially if you consider the high rate of inflation.**
  (gross – brutto / quite – ganz / deduction – Abzug / take-home pay – ausbezahlter Betrag / sthg. is not much to write home about – mit etwas ist es nicht weit her / consider – berücksichtigen)

* **The meals in the works cafeteria are subsidised.**
  (works cafeteria – Werkskantine / subsidised – subventioniert)

* A: **Do you have a share option scheme for managers in your company?**
  (share option scheme – Aktienbezugsrechtsprogramm)
  B: **Share option schemes for managers are not very common in Austria. But we do have a share-save scheme for ordinary employees.**
  (common – häufig / share-save scheme – Ansparprogramm für Aktien / employee – Mitarbeiter, Arbeitnehmer)

PROMOTION
Beförderung

* **I'm after the Sales Manager's job.**
  (be after – aussein auf)

* **I'm waiting for the Controller to retire. I think I've got a good chance of getting his job.**
  (retire – in Pension gehen)

* **I'm in line for the position of Sales Manager.**
  (be in line – in Warteposition sein)

* **I was promoted last month.**
  (promote – befördern)

* **He is being groomed for moving into the top spot.**
  (Er wird auf eine Übersiedlung ins Chefzimmer vorbereitet.)

* **I'm number two now in the Sales Department.**

* **A: I have just been promoted to the position of Office Manager.**
  B: Congratulation!

* **They offered me the top spot in the Advertising Department.**
  (top spot – Leiterstelle)

* **I was promoted to Procurement Manager last week.**
  (Procurement Manager – Leiter des Beschaffungswesens)

* **I was given a job higher up the ladder.**
  (ladder – Hierarchie)

* **The pay is lousy, but I've got good career prospects.**
  (pay – Bezahlung, Entlohnung / career prospects – Aufstiegschancen)

* **Mine has been a fairly typical career pattern.**
  (Ich habe eine ziemlich typische berufliche Laufbahn.)

* **I've been invited to join the Management Board of my company.**
  (Man hat mir einen Sitz im Vorstand meiner Gesellschaft angeboten.)

YOUR BUSINESS HERE IN BRITAIN

Zweck Ihres Aufenthaltes in Großbritannien

* **I've come over for a job interview.**
  (job interview – Einstellungsgespräch)

* **I'm trying to find a firm to represent my company in England and Wales.**
  (represent – vertreten)

* **I'm doing an IBM internship in London.**
  (internship – Praktikum)

* **My company has sent me over to attend a language course.**
  (attend – besuchen / language course – Sprachkurs)

* **I've been sent over to audit our branch in Brighton.**
  (audit – Revision durchführen in / branch – Filiale)

* **My assignment is to call on some of our important customers.**
  (Ich habe den Auftrag, einige unserer wichtigen Kunden zu besuchen.)

* **The main purpose of my visit is to inspect the books of our British licensee.**
  (main purpose – Hauptzweck / inspect – inspizieren, prüfen / licensee – Lizenznehmer)

* **My mission is to negotiate a licensing agreement with a company in Oxford.**
(mission – Auftrag, Aufgabe / negotiate – aushandeln / licensing agreement – Lizenzabkommen)

EDUCATIONAL BACKGROUND

Bildungsweg

SECONDARY EDUCATION

Höhere Schulen, „Mittelschulen“

* **A: What school did you go to?**
  B: I attended what we call a "Commercial Academy". This is a high school with a strong business element in its curriculum.
  (attend – besuchen / high school – [US] höhere Schule; „Mittelschule“ / curriculum – Lehrplan, Studienprogramm)

* **I went to a grammar school with special emphasis on modern languages.**
  (grammar school – [brit.] Gymnasium; allgemeinbildende höhere Schule; „Mittelschule“ / emphasis – Betonung / language – Sprache)

* **I did my Matura – approximately equivalent to your A levels – in 1982.**
  (do [exam] – [Prüfung] ablegen / approximately – ungefähr / be equivalent to sthg. – einer Sache entsprechen)

* **After doing my A levels I began my studies at the University of Vienna.**

* **I dropped out of grammar school when I was 15. I simply didn't see any point in going on at that time.**
  (drop out – ausscheiden, austreten / simple – einfach / point – Sinn)

* **I became apprenticed to a bookseller and went back to school when I was 19.**
  (Ich bekam eine Lehrstelle bei einem Buchhändler … .)

* **A: Is your school system really all that different from ours?**
(all that – so / different – verschieden)
B: I think the main difference between British grammar schools and our equivalent – called "Gymnasium" – is that we have a much broader curriculum. There is much less specialisation, particularly in the higher forms.
(main – wichtigst, Haupt … / curriculum – Lehrangebot, Lehrplan / particularly – besonders / form – Klasse)

* **The final exam is also different. Above all it's not a national exam. It is set by your own teachers.**
(final exam – Abschlussprüfung / national exam – einheitliche Prüfung für ein ganzes Land / set exam – Prüfung erstellen)

* **The greatest cultural difference is certainly the students' attitude towards cheating.**
(attitude – Einstellung / cheat – schwindeln)

* **Cribbing and cheating in exams are a national pastime. They are not considered dishonourable.**
(Abschreiben und Schwindeln bei Prüfungen sind ein Volkssport. … . / be considered – gelten als / dishonourable – unehrenhaft)

* **As a matter of fact, you are regarded as a sissy if you don't cheat or help your friends in exams.**
(be regarded as – gehalten werden für / sissy – „Seicherl", Schwächling)

ACCESS TO UNIVERSITIES

Zulassung zum Universitätsstudium

* **A: Is it difficult to get a place at a university in your country?**
B: Well, up to a few years ago access to universities was not restricted.
(up to a few years ago – bis vor wenigen Jahren / access – Zutritt / restricted – beschränkt)

* **Provided you managed to get through secondary school successfully, you were entitled to a place at a university of your choice. They couldn't turn you down.**
(provided – vorausgesetzt / manage – es schaffen / secondary school – höhere Schule; „Mittelschule“ / successful – erfolgreich / be entitled to – Anspruch haben auf / choice – Wahl / turn down – ablehnen)

* **There were no admission exams, not even interviews.**
(admission exam – Aufnahmsprüfung, Zulassungsprüfung / not even – nicht einmal)

* **Obviously this system created a lot of problems. Overcrowding and a high drop-out rate, you know. That's why universities are now allowed to impose restrictions in some of the more popular courses.**
(obviously – klarerweise / create – mit sich bringen; führen zu / a lot of – viele; eine Menge / overcrowding – Überfüllung / drop-out rate – Ausfallsquote / impose – einführen, auferlegen / course – Studienrichtung)

DEGREES

Akademische Grade

* **What is your academic background?**
(Was haben Sie für eine akademische Ausbildung?)

* **I graduated from the University of Economics and Business Administration in Vienna in 1989.**
(graduate from university – Studium an Universität mit akademischem Grad abschließen / University of Economics and Business Administration – Wirtschaftsuniversität / economics – Volkswirtschaftslehre / business administration – Betriebswirtschaftslehre)

* **I earned a Master's degree in Business Administration. That's not an MBA, because in my country the Master's degree is the first university degree, while the MBA is post-graduate.**
(earn degree – akademischen Grad erwerben / MBA – Master of Business Administration / post-graduate [degree] – zweiter | ranghöherer akademischer Grad)

* **A: What does M.A. on your business card stand for?**
(business card – Visitenkarte / stand for – stehen für)
B: I hold a Master of Arts degree.
(hold degree – akademischen Grad innehaben / Master of Arts – etwa: Magister der Philosophie)

* **Are you a graduate of the London School of Economics?**
(graduate – Absolvent)

* **I majored in Business Administration.**
(Mein Hauptfach war Betriebswirtschaftslehre.)

* **I did what I think the Americans call a double major. I read Law at the University of Vienna and I did Business Administration at the University of Economics and Business Administration in the same city.**
(double major – doppeltes Hauptfach; Doppelstudium / read – studieren / law – Rechtswissenschaften, Jus)

* **My brother is a university-trained chemist.**
(Mein Bruder ist ein akademisch ausgebildeter Chemiker | Diplomchemiker.)

* **Only the big companies have a policy of hiring graduates.**
(policy – Politik / hire – anstellen, einstellen / graduate – Akademiker)

* **I'm thinking of going back to university and doing a Social Science Doctorate in Operations Research.**
(social science – Sozialwissenschaft)

STUDIES AND EXAMINATIONS

Studium und Prüfungen

* **We had to attend a number of seminars. In most of them you had to write a fairly long paper and present it either alone or together with some other students.**
  (attend – besuchen / fairly – ziemlich / paper – Referat / present – präsentieren, halten)

* **Maths was my favourite subject, both in high school and at university, but I didn't like Law.**
  (maths – mathematics / favourite subject – Lieblingsgegenstand / both … and … – sowohl … als auch …)

* **I liked university. Might even have stayed on and gone in for an academic career if a suitable opening had turned up.**
  (even – sogar / stay on – dort bleiben / go in for – sich entscheiden für / suitable opening – geeignete freie Stelle / turn up – sich ergeben)

* **Under the new regime, which was adopted in 1985, languages and Computer Science became much more important.**
  (under – im Rahmen / regime – [Studien-]Ordnung / adopt – einführen / language – Sprache)

* **As I enrolled for the Commerce Course I had to do two languages. One in Part I of the Course only and the other both in Part I and in Part II.**
  (enrol for – inskribieren; sich anmelden für / Commerce Course – handelswissenschaftliche Studienrichtung / Part I – erster Studienabschnitt)

* **My university offers a number of courses. The most popular one is Business Administration, followed by Commerce. Economics and Business Education are less important.**
(course – Studienrichtung / business administration – Betriebswirtschaftslehre / commerce – Handelswissenschaften / economics – Volkswirtschaftslehre / business education – Wirtschaftspädagogik / important – wichtig)

* **In Part II, I specialised in Materials Management.**
(materials management – Materialwirtschaft)

* **A: When did you take your final exams?**
B: I sat for my finals in 1985.
(sit for an exam – zu einer Prüfung antreten / final – final examination | Abschlussprüfung)

* **The final exams are quite tough. In many subjects you have a four-hour written exam and, if you pass that, a short oral one.**
(quite – ziemlich / tough – streng, schwer / subject – Gegenstand / pass exam – Prüfung bestehen / oral exam – mündliche Prüfung)

* **The course covered a wide range of subjects, some quite irrelevant to what I did later, like Constitutional Law, Commoditology, Financial Accounting and Cost Accounting.**
(Das Programm der Studienrichtung umfasste eine breite Palette von Gegenständen, wovon einige für das, was ich später machte, ganz irrelevant waren, wie z. B. Verfassungsrecht, Warenkunde, Finanzbuchhaltung und Kostenrechnung.)

* **Some of the teachers were a pain in the neck.**
(pain in the neck – kaum auszuhalten)

* **I had a couple of very good teachers. One of them even made it internationally.**
(a couple of – ein paar / even – sogar / make it – reüssieren; Erfolg haben)

* **The subject of my master's thesis was "The Property Market in Vienna".**
(subject – Gegenstand / master's thesis – Diplomarbeit / property market – Immobilienmarkt)

* **I developed a model of the car market in Austria as part of my master's thesis. Sold it to a big car dealer after I had graduated.**
(develop – entwickeln, erstellen / sell – verkaufen / car dealer – Autohändler)

FINANCE

Finanzierung des Studiums

* **A: How much does it cost you a year to study at a university?**
B: Well, there is a modest tuition fee, that is modest by international standards, and there is talk that universities will be allowed to charge more to foreign students.
(modest – moderat / tuition fee – Studiengebühr / by – gemessen an; im Vergleich zu / there is talk – man spricht darüber / charge to – verlangen von / foreign – ausländisch)

* **The other costs – like everywhere – depend a lot on your personal circumstances.**
(depend on – abhängen von / a lot – stark / circumstances – Umstände, Verhältnisse)

* **I managed to get a place in a hall of residence, which was much cheaper than renting private accommodation.**
(manage – es schaffen / hall of residence – Studentenheim / cheap – billig / rent – mieten / accommodation – Unterkunft)

* **I shared a small flat with two friends. That helped to keep down our cost of living.**
(Ich hatte eine kleine Wohnung gemeinsam mit zwei Freunden. … . / keep down – niedrig halten)

* **Since I am from Vienna, I continued to live with my parents when I started university.**
(since – da / continue to live – weiterhin wohnen / parents – Eltern)

* **We have means-tested student grants. That is, you can get a grant if your parents don't earn too much money.**
(means-tested – an einen Bedürftigkeitsnachweis gebunden / grant – Unterhaltsstipendium)

* **Then there are scholarships for which you need a good grade average.**
(scholarship – [Begabten-]Stipendium / grade average – Notendurchschnitt)

* **My parents gave me quite a generous monthly allowance so I didn't have to do any part-time jobs.**
(quite – ziemlich / generous – großzügig / allowance – geldliche Zuwendung / part-time job – Teilzeitbeschäftigung)

* **I had to interrupt my studies because my father died and so I had to earn some money to finish the Course.**
(interrupt – unterbrechen / die – sterben / earn – verdienen / finish – abschließen / course – Studienprogramm [einer bestimmten Studienrichtung])

* **I worked my way through College, doing part-time jobs during the academic year and working full-time in the holidays.**
(Ich war ein Werkstudent, und zwar war ich während des Studienjahres teilzeit- und während der Ferien ganztags beschäftigt.)

* **In Austria, regular full-time students enjoy a number of benefits. One is reduced fares for public transport. Moreover, most banks offer free student accounts.**
(regular full-time student – ordentlicher Hörer / enjoy – in den Genuss kommen von; erhalten / number – Reihe / benefit – Vergünstigung / fare – Beförderungsentgelt, Fahrpreis / public – öffentlich / moreover – außerdem / offer – anbieten / free – gebührenfrei / account – Konto)

CONDITIONS AT UNIVERSITY

Studienbedingungen

✻ **A: What was life like at your university?**
B: Since I went to one of the small universities, conditions were not too bad.
(since – da / condition – Verhältnis)

✻ **Some of our universities are grossly overcrowded. Classes are large and the drop-out rate is very high.**
(grossly overcrowded – krass überbelegt / drop-out rate – Ausfallsquote)

✻ **Registering for major exams sometimes involved waiting in queues for hours on end.**
(register – sich anmelden / major – größer / involve – bedeuten, heißen / queue – Schlange / for hours on end – stundenlang)

✻ **What you learn is how to survive under pressure.**
(survive – überleben / pressure – Druck)

✻ **Since there are so many students and not enough teachers, it was very difficult to find a supervisor for my master's thesis.**
(enough – genug / supervisor for master's thesis – Diplomarbeitsbetreuer)

✻ **The student-teacher ratio was appalling.**
(student-teacher ratio – Betreuungsverhältnis / appalling – schrecklich)

STUDY RECORD

Studienergebnisse

* **I had fairly good grades.**
  (fairly – ziemlich / grade – Note)

* **I was among the top two per cent of the class graduating in 1989.**
  (class – Jahrgang)

* **I must admit my marks were not that good.**
  (admit – zugeben / mark – [brit.] Note)

* **In Austria, most people don't take the grades they earn at university too seriously.**
  (earn – bekommen / serious – ernst)

* **It took me seven years to get my degree. I must admit I didn't work very hard in the first two years. It was so exciting being in Vienna. There were lots of things to do apart from studying.**
  (it took me – ich brauchte / exciting – aufregend / lots of – eine Menge / apart from – abgesehen von)

* **You are not thrown out if you fail an exam. You can sit most exams three or four times before you get into trouble.**
  (throw out – hinauswerfen / fail exam – bei Prüfung durchfallen / three times – dreimal / trouble – Schwierigkeiten)

STUDYING ABROAD

Studium im Ausland

* **I studied abroad for a year and my university gave me credit for some of the work I had done there.**
(abroad – im Ausland / give credit for sthg. – etwas anrechnen)

* **Unfortunately they did not give me any credit for the courses I completed in the United States. There was some administrative snag I did not understand.**
(unfortunately – leider / complete course – Lehrveranstaltung absolvieren / snag – Haken, Schwierigkeit)

* **I managed to get a scholarship and did a year in France at one of the Grandes Ecoles. That's why my French is much better than my English.**
(manage – es zuwege bringen; es schaffen / scholarship – Stipendium)

EXTRACURRICULAR ACTIVITIES

Außeruniversitäre Aktivitäten

* **I was a representative of the Students' Union and organised a couple of large conventions, one on post-cold-war marketing issues.**
(students' union – Hochschülerschaft / convention – Kongress / issue – Problem)

* **I edited the students' magazine for two years.**
(edit – herausgeben)

* **I worked part-time at a bank while I was still at the university.**
(work part-time – teilzeitbeschäftigt sein / while – während / still – noch)

* **I attended a Spanish course in 1988.**

* **I did several traineeships during the summer vacations.**
(traineeship – [Ferial-]Praxis / vacations – Ferien)

* **I was lucky to be accepted by IBM Vienna for an internship in the summer before I graduated.**
(be lucky – Glück haben / for an internship – für ein Praktikum; als Praktikant)

POST UNIVERSITY

Nach dem Studienabschluss

* **After I had finished university, I spent a year abroad working for a company in France.**
(finish – beenden / spend – verbringen / company – Gesellschaft)

* **I was hired straight from university.**
(Ich wurde direkt von der Universität weg eingestellt.)

* **I went on a world tour after I had graduated.**

* **Unfortunately I had to do my military service before I could start looking for a job.**
(unfortunately – leider / look for – suchen; sich umsehen um)

* **I dithered around for a time after I had finished. Didn't really know what to do until I got this interesting offer.**
(dither around – unentschlossen sein; zögern / know – wissen / until – bis / offer – Angebot)

MY COMPANY

Meine Firma

TYPE, SIZE, LOCATION, OWNERSHIP, HISTORY, ETC.

Art, Größe, Standort, Eigentumsverhältnisse, Geschichte usw.

* **What kind of company do you work for?**
(kind – Art / company – Gesellschaft)

* **Where is your company based?**
(Wo hat Ihre Gesellschaft ihren Sitz?)

* **I work for a medium-sized steel company based in Vienna.**
(medium-sized – mittelgroß / steel – Stahl)

* **My company is a wholly-owned subsidiary of an American corporation. It is fairly large, at least by Austrian standards.**
(wholly-owned subsidiary – 100%ige Tochter / corporation – [US] Gesellschaft, Kapitalgesellschaft, Konzern / fairly – ziemlich / by – gemessen an / standards – Verhältnisse, Normen)

* **Our Headquarters is in Vienna, but we've got subsidiaries and branches in most European countries.**
(headquarters – [Konzern-]Zentrale / branch – Zweiganstalt, Filiale)

* **We're thinking of opening a representative office in New York.**
(representative office – Repräsentanz)

* **We were taken over by a U.S. corporation last year.**
(take over – übernehmen, aufkaufen)

* **We fought the take-over bid tooth and nail because we thought they would replace the whole management. In the end they allowed us to continue much as before.**
(fight – bekämpfen / take-over bid – Übernahmeangebot / tooth and nail – ganz energisch; mit Klauen und Zähnen / replace – ersetzen / in the end – letzten Endes / continue – weitermachen)

* **We went public last year, because we needed to raise more capital.**
(go public – an die Börse gehen / need – müssen / raise – aufbringen)

* **Most of our shareholders are small private investors.**
(shareholder – Aktionär)

* **A couple of months ago an American corporation acquired a 30 per cent stake in our company.**
(a couple of – ein paar / acquire – erwerben / stake – Beteiligung)

* **There are rumours that the public corporation I work for is going to be privatised next year.**
(rumours – Gerüchte / public corporation – [brit.] verstaatlichte Gesellschaft / privatise – privatisieren, entstaatlichen)

* **Just imagine, our major shareholder is planning to take the company private.**
(imagine [sthg.] – sich [etwas] vorstellen / major shareholder – Hauptaktionär / take private – von der Börse abziehen)

* **We are a fairly small private company.**
(fairly – ziemlich / private company – etwa: GmbH; kleine Familien-AG)

- **Originally the firm was established as a partnership. But when one of the partners died in 1984, we converted into something that corresponds fairly closely to your private limited company.**
  (originally – ursprünglich / establish – errichten, gründen / partnership – Personengesellschaft / partner – Teilhaber / die – sterben / convert – sich umwandeln / correspond to – entsprechen / close – genau / private limited company – [brit.] etwa: GmbH)

- **No, an Austrian GmbH is not exactly the same as a private limited company. One important difference is that in Austria there is a fairly high minimum capital requirement.**
  (important – wichtig / minimum capital requirement – Mindestkapitalerfordernis)

- **We'll probably make a major acquisition later this year.**
  (probably – wahrscheinlich / major – größer / acquisition – Firmenerwerb)

- **We are considering merging with an American chemical firm.**
  (consider – in Erwägung ziehen / merge – fusionieren)

- **We've got outlets in all European countries, including Russia.**
  (outlet – Laden, Verkaufsgeschäft)

- **Irish tax breaks are so generous that we decided to locate the new facility on an industrial estate near Dublin.**
  (tax break – steuerliche Vergünstigung / generous – großzügig / decide – beschließen; sich entscheiden / locate – ansiedeln / facility – Produktionsstätte, -einrichtung / industrial estate – Industriepark, Industriezone)

- **We have done our sums and are relocating to Scotland.**
  (Wir haben die Sache durchgerechnet und übersiedeln nach Schottland.)

* **We have one green-field site development going at the moment.**
(green-field site – [Bauplatz] auf der grünen Wiese / development – Bauvorhaben / have sthg. going – etwas laufen haben)

* **Are you an independent company or part of a larger group?**
(independent – unabhängig / group – Konzern)

* **Our parent company keeps us on a fairly short leash.**
(parent company – Muttergesellschaft / keep on a short leash – eng an der Kandare halten)

* **We shall probably need five new distribution depots to serve the new retail outlets.**
(distribution depot – Auslieferungslager / serve – beliefern / retail outlet – Einzelhandelsgeschäft)

PRODUCTS AND ACTIVITIES

Produkte und Tätigkeitsbereiche

* **Our main activity is prospecting for oil.**
(main activity – Hauptgeschäftsbereich / prospect for – suchen; schürfen nach)

* **We are a highly diversified group, a conglomerate in fact.**
(highly diversified – stark diversifiziert / conglomerate – Mischkonzern)

* **Our product range includes machine tools and mini-computers.**
(product range – Sortiment, Produktionsprogramm / machine tool – Werkzeugmaschine)

* **My company has been engaged in manufacturing high-pressure valves since it was founded thirty years ago.**
(be engaged in – sich befassen mit / manufacture – erzeugen / high-pressure valve – Hochdruckventil / found – gründen)

* **We trade in plastic and steel semis.**
(trade in – handeln mit / semis – Halbzeug)

* **We represent several American and Japanese companies in Europe.**
(represent – vertreten)

* **We are subcontractors to two German car manufacturers.**
(subcontractor – Zulieferer / car manufacturer – Autohersteller)

* **We have decided to farm out the manufacture of some key components.**
(decide – beschließen / farm out – an eine andere Firma vergeben / key component – wichtiger Bauteil)

* **My company specialises in buying and selling commercial property.**
(specialise in – spezialisiert sein auf / commercial property – Büro- und Geschäftsimmobilien)

* **More than half of our turnover is achieved abroad.**
(turnover – Umsatz / achieve – erzielen / abroad – im Ausland)

* **Our export ratio has always been very high, around 90 per cent in most years.**
(export ratio – Exportquote / around – rund)

* **Last year exports accounted for 85 per cent of total sales.**
(Voriges Jahr entfielen 85% des Gesamtumsatzes auf Exporte.)

* **At the last board meeting it was decided to commit a large sum to the development of bauxit deposits in Western Australia.**
(board – Verwaltungsrat; Führungsgremium einer brit. / US Kapitalgesellschaft / meeting – Sitzung / commit to – verbindlich vorsehen für; binden für / development – Erschließung / deposit – Lagerstätte)

ORGANISATIONAL STRUCTURE AND MANAGEMENT

Organisationsstruktur und Management

* **In Austria we have a two-tier system. This means my company has two separate boards: a supervisory board – similar to your non-executive directors – and a management board.**
(two-tier system – zweistufiges System / board – Führungsgremium / supervisory board – Aufsichtsrat / non-executive director – nichtgeschäftsführendes Mitglied des brit. / US [einstufigen] Führungsgremiums / management board – Vorstand)

* **The main difference to your system is that in Austria a director cannot be an executive at the same time. The directors are all non-executive.**
(director – Mitglied des Aufsichtsrates / executive – [hochrangiger] Manager)

* **Yes, the management board are appointed by the directors. But, as I've already said, they are not allowed to appoint one of their own members.**
(appoint – bestellen)

* **Our organisation chart is pretty complicated. But basically we are organised on functional not on divisional lines.**
(Unser Organigramm ist ziemlich kompliziert. Aber im Wesentlichen sind wir nach dem funktionalen und nicht nach dem Geschäftsspartenprinzip gegliedert.)

* **Our organisational structure was revamped two years ago. We got rid of a whole layer of middle managers. We are now what Drucker calls a "flat organisation" and much leaner and more efficient.**
(revamp – völlig neu gestalten / get rid of – loswerden / layer – Schichte / flat – flach / lean – mager; ohne unnötiges Fett)

* **A: In my company Production Scheduling comes under Materials Management.**
(In meiner Gesellschaft untersteht die Arbeitsvorbereitung der Materialwirtschaft.)
B: That's interesting. And to whom is the Materials Manager responsible?
(… . Und wem untersteht der Leiter der Materialwirtschaft?)

* **I'm in charge of Personnel and report directly to who you in the States would probably call the President.**
(be in charge of – Leiter sein von; leiten / Personnel – Personalabteilung / report to – unterstehen / president – Verwaltungsratsvorsitzender; Vorstandsvorsitzender [mit gleichzeitiger Aufsichtsratsfunktion] einer US-Kapitalgesellschaft; „Generaldirektor")

* **A: We have a fairly large Market Research Section, which is part of the Marketing Department.**
(market research – Marktforschung / section – Abteilung, Referat)
B: Does this mean that you do most research in-house?
A: Yes, although we do farm out the really large surveys.
(although – obwohl / do farm out – natürlich extern vergeben / survey – Erhebung, Studie)

CURRENT CONDITIONS

Gegenwärtige Lage

ORDERS AND CAPACITY UTILISATION

Aufträge und Kapazitätsauslastung

* **We can't complain. We have a satisfactory order book that will keep us busy for the next three months.**
(Wir können uns nicht beklagen. Wir haben einen zufriedenstellenden Auftragsbestand, der uns für die nächsten drei Monate beschäftigen wird.)

* **Can't grumble. We're working flat out to meet the demand for the new printer.**
(grumble – sich beklagen / work flat out – volles Rohr fahren / meet demand – Nachfrage decken)

* **I'm a bit worried about capacity utilisation. It's been stuck at around 60 per cent and that's just not good enough in the long run.**
(be worried – besorgt sein / capacity utilisation – Kapazitätsauslastung / be stuck – steckenbleiben; hängen / around – ungefähr / in the long run – auf lange Sicht)

* **Orders are down on last year but still at a satisfactory level.**
(order – Auftrag / be down on – niedriger sein als / still – noch immer / satisfactory – zufriedenstellend / level – Höhe, Niveau)

* **I don't think we will be awarded the contract. Our prices are probably too high.**
(Ich glaube nicht, dass wir den Zuschlag bekommen werden. … . / probably – wahrscheinlich)

* **We managed to land a couple of large, profitable contracts.**
(manage – es schaffen / land – an Land ziehen / a couple of – ein paar / contract – Auftrag)

COMPETITION

Konkurrenz

* **We won the tender against keen competition from Japanese firms.**
(Wir haben die Ausschreibung gegen starke Konkurrenz seitens japanischer Firmen gewonnen.)

* **Competition is getting tougher by the hour.**
(Die Konkurrenz wird mit jedem Tag härter.)

* **The Japanese are our keenest competitors. They are difficult to beat because they come up with new products all the time.**
(keenest competitor – härtester Konkurrent / beat – schlagen / come up with – daherkommen mit; sich einfallen lassen / all the time – die ganze Zeit; immer)

* **We've been under a lot of pressure lately from German competitors. Their products are really good and not too expensive.**
(be under a lot of pressure – stark unter Druck stehen / lately – in der letzten Zeit / expensive – teuer)

* **We can handle domestic competition but we simply cannot match the prices of Third World competitors.**
(handle – fertig werden mit / domestic – inländisch / match prices – mit Preisen Schritt halten)

* **We are probably fourth or fifth in our line, in terms of sales, that is.**
(Wir liegen in unserer Branche wahrscheinlich an vierter oder fünfter Stelle, und zwar gemessen am Umsatz.)

* **We used to be number one in banknote printing machines but have now fallen back to third place. Two Dutch companies have overtaken us.**
(Wir waren früher einmal die Nummer eins bei Banknotendruckmaschinen … . / Dutch – holländisch / overtake – überholen)

* **We are number two, breathing down the industry leader's neck.**
(breathe down sbdy.'s neck – jmdm. dicht auf den Fersen sein / industry leader – Branchenführer)

* **Our industry is dominated by a couple of big firms. We belong to the small fry.**
(industry – Branche / dominate – beherrschen / a couple of – ein paar / belong to – gehören zu / small fry – Kleingemüse)

* **We are a typical niche operator.**
(Wir sind ein typisches Beispiel für eine Firma, die sich in einer Marktnische etabliert hat.)

* **We are in a mature market, where you can increase market share only at the expense of competition.**
(Wir sind auf einem gesättigten Markt, wo man Marktanteile nur auf Kosten der Konkurrenz erhöhen kann.)

* **We managed to obtain a foothold in the market in the teeth of cut-throat competition from a couple of Korean firms.**
(Es ist uns gelungen, trotz härtester Konkurrenz seitens einiger koreanischer Firmen auf dem Markt Fuß zu fassen.)

* **We are worried about cheap imports.**
(be worried – sich Sorgen machen / cheap – billig)

* **A competitor managed to lure away two of our key accounts last month.**
(manage – es zuwege bringen / lure away – weglocken, abwerben / key account – wichtiger Großkunde)

* **We have got a lot of catching up to do.**
(Wir haben eine Menge aufzuholen.)

* **If prices stay depressed for much longer, we'll have to get out of domestic appliances altogether.**
(stay depressed – gedrückt bleiben / get out of – aussteigen bei / domestic appliances – Haushaltsgeräte / altogether – gänzlich)

* A: **How much is your market share?**
(Wie hoch ist Ihr Marktanteil?)
B: **We have about five per cent of the British soap market.**
(soap market – Seifenmarkt)

* **Dumping by Japanese firms has hit our sales badly.**
(hit – treffen / badly – hart, stark)

SALES

Umsatz/Absatz

* **Sales have been a bit slack lately. We have commissioned a survey to find out why.**
(slack – flau, lustlos / lately – in der letzten Zeit / commission – in Auftrag geben)

* **Strangely enough, sales are holding up pretty well considering that we are in a recession. It's a bit of a surprise. We didn't expect it.**
(strangely enough – seltsamerweise / hold up – sich halten / pretty – ziemlich / considering – wenn man bedenkt / surprise – Überraschung / expect – erwarten)

* **Our new advertising campaign has really paid off. It's pushed sales up by all of 20 per cent.**
(advertising campaign – Werbekampagne / pay off – sich auszahlen / push up – in die Höhe treiben / by all of 20 per cent – um ganze 20%)

* **We are still relying on a couple of old brands.**
(Wir stützen uns noch immer auf ein paar alte Marken | Markenartikel.)

* **We haven't put anything new on the market for quite a long time. That's bound to hit sales sooner or later.**
(Wir haben schon ziemlich lange nichts mehr Neues auf den Markt gebracht. Das muss sich zwangsläufig früher oder später negativ auf den Umsatz auswirken.)

* **Sales of big-ticket items have been hit hardest.**
(Den Absatz der teuren Artikel hat es besonders hart erwischt.)

* **Exports have not been doing too well lately, mainly because of the lower dollar.**
(do well – gut abschneiden / mainly – hauptsächlich / lower dollar – niedrigerer Dollarkurs)

* **It's becoming increasingly difficult to export to that country. They are short of foreign exchange and countertrade is very complicated.**
(Es wird immer schwieriger, in dieses Land zu exportieren. Es herrscht dort eine Devisenknappheit, und Gegengeschäfte sind sehr kompliziert.)

* **Half our sales come from services.**
(Die Hälfte unseres Umsatzes entfällt auf Dienstleistungen.)

* **Exports have always accounted for more than two thirds of our sales.**
(account for – ausmachen)

* **Last year we actually exceeded our sales target. This year is going to be much more difficult. We'd be glad if we could get anywhere near it.**
(Voriges Jahr haben wir tatsächlich unser Umsatzziel übertroffen. Heuer wird es viel schwerer werden. Wir wären froh, wenn wir irgendwo in die Nähe kommen könnten.)

* **The sales target we set ourselves last year was much too ambitious.**
(set – setzen / too ambitious – zu hoch gegriffen)

* **Our sales were right on target last year.**
(Wir haben im Vorjahr unser Umsatzziel genau erreicht.)

PROFITS AND LOSSES

Gewinn und Verlust

* **We managed to maintain profits in spite of lower sales.**
(Es gelang uns, die Gewinne trotz eines niedrigeren Umsatzes zu halten.)

* **Our profits have been hit by the increase in interest rates.**
(be hit – beeinträchtigt werden / increase – Erhöhung / interest rate – Zinssatz)

* **Last year was really terrible. We lost a packet because the dollar slumped and we hadn't hedged our open currency positions.**
(terrible – schrecklich / lose a packet – einen Haufen Geld verlieren / slump – abstürzen / hedge – absichern / open currency position – offene Währungsposition)

* **We managed to get back into the black in fiscal 2005 by cutting costs wherever possible.**
(get back into the black – zurück in die Gewinnzone kommen / fiscal – Geschäftsjahr / cut – senken / wherever possible – wo immer es möglich war)

* **Our pre-tax profits were higher than last year, but there was also a higher tax charge and so the bottom line was about the same.**
(pre-tax – vor Steuern / tax charge – Steuerbelastung / bottom line – Reingewinn, Endergebnis / about – ungefähr)

* **Our main financial ratios are O.K..**
(Unsere wichtigsten finanzwirtschaftlichen Kennzahlen sind in Ordnung.)

* **I wouldn't really know what our Return on Investment is. I would have to check with our Controller's Department.**
(return on investment – [Gesamt-]Kapitalrentabilität / check with – nachfragen | rückfragen bei)

* **Our profits were caught in a squeeze: labour costs went up and prices fell due to slack demand.**
(Wir gerieten in die Kosten-Preis-Schere: Die Lohnkosten stiegen und die Preise fielen aufgrund der flauen Nachfrage.)

* **We have been in the red for far too long.**
(Wir stecken schon viel zu lange in der Verlustzone.)

* **We had a fairly large exchange loss last year.**
(exchange loss – Wechselkursverlust)

* **We now break even at only 40 per cent of capacity.**
(break even – ausgeglichen bilanzieren)

* **We went nearly bust but were bailed out by the government. Couldn't allow us to go under because of the jobs involved.**
(go bust – pleite gehen / bail out – retten / go under – zugrunde gehen / the jobs involved – die Arbeitsplätze, die auf dem Spiel standen)

COSTS

Kosten

* **We have started a cost-cutting drive.**
(Wir haben eine Kostensenkungskampagne gestartet.)

* **Our overheads are much too high. Administration is probably a bit top-heavy.**
(Unsere Gemeinkosten sind viel zu hoch. Wahrscheinlich ist unsere Verwaltung etwas zu kopflastig.)

* **We installed a new cost-control system last year.**
(install – installieren, einführen)

* **The thing is, too much of our capital is tied up in stocks. The interest expense involved takes a big bite out of our profits.**
(Die Sache ist, dass wir zu viel Kapital in den Lagerbeständen gebunden haben. Der damit verbundene Zinsaufwand frisst einen beträchtlichen Teil unseres Gewinnes auf.)

* **We tried JIT in an effort to reduce inventories. Didn't work because our suppliers weren't reliable enough.**
(JIT – just in time / effort – Bemühung / inventory – Lagerbestand / work – funktionieren / supplier – Lieferant / reliable – verlässlich)

* **We are handicapped by some of the highest labour costs in Europe. It's not so much the hourly rates themselves but the high supplementary wage costs, such as paid holidays, national insurance contributions, maternity benefits, etc.**
(Wir sind durch Lohnkosten, die zu den höchsten in Europa zählen, belastet. Dabei sind es nicht so sehr die Stundenlöhne an sich als die hohen Lohnnebenkosten, wie z. B. bezahlter Urlaub, Sozialversicherungsbeiträge, Mutterschaftsgeld usw.)

* **We have decided to partly automate our production line to cut labour costs and increase productivity.**
(automate – automatisieren / production line – Fertigungsstraße / cut – senken / increase – erhöhen)

* **We had to cut back on fringe benefits last year, which were, however, very generous anyway.**
(Wir mussten voriges Jahr die Nebenleistungen | Sozialleistungen kürzen. Die waren aber ohnehin sehr großzügig.)

* **Headquarters put in a new Controller, who cut R&D expenditure drastically to stop the red ink.**
(headquarters – [Konzern-]Zentrale / put in – einsetzen / R&D – Research & Development | Forschung & Entwicklung / expenditure – Aufwand, Ausgaben / red ink – rote Zahlen; Verluste)

* **We have got a fairly high debt-equity ratio, so our profits are very sensitive to changes in interest rates.**
(Wir haben einen ziemlich hohen Verschuldungsgrad, sodass unser Gewinn sehr empfindlich auf Zinsänderungen reagiert.)

* **Our gearing is much too high. As long as interest rates are as low as they are that's not a problem. But even a moderate increase could wipe out our profits.**
(gearing – Verschuldungsgrad / interest rate – Zinssatz / even – selbst / moderate – mäßig / increase – Erhöhung / wipe out – zum Verschwinden bringen)

FINANCING

Finanzierung

* A: **We have been ploughing back a fairly high percentage of our profits to strengthen our equity position.**
(Wir führen [seit einiger Zeit] einen ziemlich hohen Prozentsatz unseres Gewinnes den Rücklagen zu, um unsere Eigenkapitalbasis zu stärken.)
B: **What do your shareholders say to that?**
(shareholder – Aktionär)
A: **Well, since our share price has risen quite sharply, they don't seem to mind too much.**
(since – da / share price – Aktienkurs / rise – steigen / quite – ziemlich / seem – scheinen / mind – [etwas] dagegen haben)

* **At yesterday's closing price our shares are on a multiple of 25.**
(at – auf der Basis / closing price – Schlusskurs / be on a multiple of … – ein Kurs-Gewinn-Verhältnis von … aufweisen)

✳ **Interest rates are so low at the moment that we've decided to refinance part of our debt.**
(refinance – umschulden / debt – Schulden)

✳ **We are planning a rights issue for later this year. We will use the money to make a major acquisition.**
(rights issue – Ausgabe von jungen Aktien [auf Bezugsrechtsbasis] / major acquisition – größerer Firmenerwerb)

HUMAN RESOURCES / EMPLOYEES

Personalressourcen / Mitarbeiter

✳ **We have 600 employees. 200 white-collar, or salaried, employees, and around 400 blue-collar workers.**
(employee – Mitarbeiter, Arbeitnehmer / white-collar employee – Angestellter / blue-collar employee – Arbeiter)

✳ A: **Unfortunately we had to make 100 people redundant last year as part of a cost-cutting exercise.**
(unfortunately – leider / make redundant – [brit.] abbauen / cost-cutting exercise – Kostensenkungsaktion)
B: **Ah, you mean you had to lay them off.**
(lay off – [US] abbauen)

✳ **We have two employee directors on the supervisory board. It's a statutory requirement for large companies.**
(employee director – Arbeitnehmervertreter [im Aufsichtsrat] / statutory requirement – gesetzliches Erfordernis)

✳ **We are planning to expand our work-force.**
(work-force – Belegschaft)

✳ **We do our recruiting through a special consulting firm.**
(recruiting – Personalbeschaffung / consulting firm – Beratungsfirma)

* **We have been experimenting with worker participation for a number of years.**
(worker participation – Arbeitnehmermitbestimmung)

* **Employee participation works well on the shop-floor but it's a problem further up, in particular at board level.**
(work – funktionieren / shop-floor – unmittelbarer Produktionsbereich; „Werkbank" / further up – weiter oben / level – Ebene / board – Verwaltungsrat; Führungsgremium einer brit. / US-Kapitalgesellschaft)

* **The trade unions are not the main problem. But workers are represented through a second channel, a body called "Betriebsrat".**
(trade union – Gewerkschaft / represent – vertreten / body – Gremium)

* **Generally speaking, we get along quite well with our workers. We've never had a strike and we've always managed to reach a compromise.**
(generally speaking – im Allgemeinen / get along – auskommen / manage – es schaffen)

* **I'm glad to say that our labour turnover has always been very low.**
(glad – froh / labour turnover – Mitarbeiterfluktuation)

* **The trade unions are pushing for a shorter working week again.**
(push for – drängen auf / shorter working week – Arbeitszeitverkürzung)

* **What with the fairly long holidays with pay and the large number of public holidays – also with pay –, I don't think that this is really an important issue.**
(what with – angesichts / holidays with pay – bezahlter Urlaub / public holiday – Feiertag / important – wichtig / issue – Problem, Thema)

* **We have a very keen equal opportunities employment policy. As a result, quite a few of our managers are women.**
(keen – engagiert, radikal / equal opportunities employment policy – auf dem Gleichbehandlungsprinzip basierende Personalpolitik / quite a few – ziemlich viele)

PREMISES

Räumlichkeiten, Betriebsstätte

* A: **Would you like me to show you round our premises?**
(Möchten Sie, dass ich Ihnen unsere Räumlichkeiten zeige | Sie durch unsere Räumlichkeiten führe?)
B: **Yes, very much so.**

* A: **The building seems very new. When was it built?**
(building – Gebäude)
B: **Well, this particular office block was put up in 1986. Before that we were in a suburb on the other side of the river.**
(office block – Bürogebäude / put up – errichten / suburb – Vorstadt / river – Fluss)

* **We've leased the building from a property company. It's a more flexible arrangement than buying your own property.**
(property company – Immobiliengesellschaft / own – eigen / property – Gebäude, Immobilie, Liegenschaft)

* A: **The warehouse is over there.**
(warehouse – Lagerhaus)
B: **Is that where you store the heavy machines?**
(store – lagern)

* **A: This is the new machine shop. We put in a flexible manufacturing system two years ago. Would you like to take a look at it?**
(machine shop – Maschinenhalle / manufacturing system – Fertigungssystem / take a look at sthg. – etwas anschauen)
B: Yes. I'd be very interested. We're thinking of switching to FM ourselves.
(switch to – umsteigen auf / FM – flexible manufacturing)

* **The R&D Section is on the third floor. Let's take the lift.**
(R&D – Research and Development | Forschung und Entwicklung | F&E / section – Abteilung, Referat / floor – Stockwerk)

* **A: What you see over there in the far corner is our loading bay. We deliver most of our orders in our own trucks.**
(far corner – Ecke ganz hinten / loading bay – Verladezone / deliver – liefern / truck – Lastwagen)
B: Do you have a big fleet of trucks?
(fleet of trucks – LKW-Fuhrpark, LKW-Flotte)
A: Yes. I wouldn't know the exact number though.
(though – aber, doch)

COMPUTERS

Computer

* **I bought myself a PC before I came over.**
(PC – PC | Personalcomputer / come over – herüberkommen)

* **It's very user-friendly. It didn't take me more than a couple of hours to get the hang of it.**
(Er ist sehr benutzerfreundlich. Ich brauchte nur ein paar Stunden um zu kapieren, wie er funktioniert.)

* **The manual is terrific. Explains everything step by step. So you can't go wrong.**
(manual – Handbuch / terrific – super / explain – erklären / step by step – Schritt für Schritt / go wrong – sich verirren; Fehler machen)

* **A: What application programs do you use?**
(application program – Anwendungsprogramm)
B: The latest Google programs for word-processing, spreadsheets and that sort of thing.
(word-processing – Textverarbeitung / spreadsheet – Tabellenkalkulation / that sort of thing – dergleichen)

* **I don't use pirate copies any more. Had a virus once and lost umpteens of important files. It's not worth it.**
(Ich verwende keine Raubkopien von Programmen mehr. Hatte einmal einen Virus und verlor zig wichtige Dateien. Zahlt sich nicht aus.)

* **I'm going to swap my desk-top model for a laptop. Laptops are much more convenient, and the features are the same as on a regular PC.**
(swap – umtauschen, eintauschen / desk-top model – Tischmodell / convenient – praktisch / feature – Leistungsmerkmal / regular – normal)

* **Look, I bought myself a new laptop. It has a 1 GB working memory, a 60 GB hard disk, Bluetooth, Wi-Fi, and mobile broadband. The Li-ion battery is good for up to 5.7 hours of operation.**
(GB – Gigabyte / working memory – Arbeitsspeicher / hard disk – Festplatte / Wi-Fi – Wireless Fidelity / mobile broadband – mobiles Breitband / operation – Betrieb)

* **I had a head crash last year. Fortunately I had made back-up copies of everything on the hard disk. Otherwise I don't know what I would have done.**
(Voriges Jahr stürzte mir die Festplatte ab. Glücklicherweise hatte ich Back-up-Kopien von allem gemacht, was auf der Festplatte war. Sonst weiß ich nicht, was ich getan hätte.)

* **Don't know what I would do without my computer and access to the Internet! It's such a convenient source of information.**
(Ich weiß nicht, was ich ohne meinen Computer und Zugang zum Internet täte. … . / convenient – praktisch / source of information – Informationsquelle)

* A: **The things are getting cheaper by the day. I think I'll take the plunge and buy one too.**
(cheap – billig / by the day – Tag für Tag / take the plunge – den Sprung wagen)
B: **Yes, you can get a very good configuration for under three hundred pounds: computer, operating system, monitor, ink-jet printer, the lot. Most firms throw in a couple of application programs as well.**
(configuration – Konfiguration / operating system – Betriebssystem / monitor – Bildschirm, Monitor / ink-jet printer – Tintenstrahldrucker / the lot – einfach alles, was dazugehört / throw in – draufgeben)

* **I'm not satisfied with the new Windows Vista. Too many features I don't need. Have decided to go back to Windows XP. Or I might try one of the open-source operating systems.**
(feature – Leistungsmerkmal / decide – sich entschließen / open source – mit offenem Quellcode)

* **Macs are fun to use, but compatibility with other machines is still a bit of a problem.**
(Mac – Macintosh / fun to use – lustig zu benutzen / compatibility – Kompatibilität)

* **I get a headache if I sit in front of the computer for more than two hours. Don't understand how our VDU workers can stand it.**
(headache – Kopfschmerzen / in front of – vor / VDU worker – Bildschirmarbeiter / stand sthg. – etwas aushalten)

* **It may sound odd, but some of my colleagues hate computers. Can't seem to get used to them.**
(sound – klingen / odd – seltsam / hate – hassen / … . Sie können sich anscheinend nicht daran gewöhnen.)

* **My son sits in front of the computer all day long. He is so interested that he will be an expert by the time he's twelve.**
(all day long – den ganzen Tag / by the time – wenn)

* **Paperless office, my foot! We have to shuffle more paper than before the introduction of the new system.**
(paperless office – papierloses Büro / my foot – oder sonst noch was / shuffle – herumschieben / introduction – Einführung)

* **We had to call in a consultant to sort out our computer problem. The manual didn't help.**
(call in – beiziehen / consultant – Beratungsfirma / sort out – lösen; in Ordnung bringen / manual – Handbuch)

* **We have decided to install a mainframe. In spite of the latest improvements in micros and minis, they still couldn't handle the vast amounts of data we have to process.**
(decide – sich entschließen / mainframe – Großrechner / in spite of – trotz / micro – Mikrocomputer, PC / mini – Minicomputer / still – noch / handle – verarbeiten, manipulieren / vast amount – ungeheure Menge / process – verarbeiten)

* **Yes, you're right. Computer fraud is a problem. One of our employees nicked our customer file and sold it to a competitor.**
(computer fraud – Computerkriminalität / employee – Mitarbeiter / nick – klauen / customer file – Kundendatei / competitor – Konkurrent)

NEGOTIATING CONTRACTS

Vertragsverhandlungen

CHAT PHASE

Vorgeplänkel

(see also "Weather" and "Meeting People")

* **A: I hope you had a good flight.**
(flight – Flug)
B: Yes, the weather was fine and there was no turbulence.

* **A: Is this your first time in England?**
(Sind Sie zum ersten Mal in England?)
B: No. I attended a language course in Brighton when I was sixteen. But I've never been here on business before.
(attend – besuchen / language – Sprache / on business – geschäftlich)

* **A: I hope the hotel room we reserved for you is all right.**
B: Yes, I've got a very nice and quiet room. And I had a good night's sleep, which means I'm going to be a very tough negotiator today.
(quiet – ruhig / mean – bedeuten / tough – hart / negotiator – Verhandler)

* **A: Sorry, I'm a bit late, but my taxi got stuck in a traffic jam.**
(sorry – tut mir leid / get stuck – steckenbleiben / traffic jam – Stau)
B: I'm sorry to hear that. Must have been something exceptional. The rush-hour is normally over by 10 o'clock.
(rush-hour – Verkehrsspitze / by – bis [längstens])

* **Would anybody like a cup of coffee before we start?**

∗ **Would you care for coffee or something else to drink?**
(care for sthg. – etwas mögen | wollen)

∗ **I've asked Reception to serve some tea at ten, if that's O.K. with you.**

OPENING THE DISCUSSION

Eröffnung der Diskussion

∗ **Let's begin, shall we?**
(Fangen wir doch an.)

∗ **We might as well get down to business.**
(Wir könnten eigentlich anfangen.)

∗ **If you agree, I'd say let's get straight to the point without wasting any time on preliminaries.**
(agree – zustimmen / get straight to the point – gleich zur Sache kommen / waste – verschwenden / preliminaries – Vorgeplänkel)

∗ **May I suggest that we first discuss the less controversial points and leave the thorny knots, like price, for tomorrow?**
(suggest – vorschlagen / controversial – kontroversiell, umstritten / leave – lassen / thorny knot – kniffliger Punkt)

∗ **I think you will have received and read my proposals.**
(receive – erhalten / proposal – Vorschlag)

∗ **May I suggest a procedure for this first meeting?**
(procedure – Vorgangsweise / meeting – Sitzung)

* **A: I don't think we should aim for too much at this first meeting. I see it mainly as a chance to explore areas of agreement and disagreement.**
  (aim for – erreichen wollen / … . Ich sehe die Sitzung in erster Linie als Möglichkeit, herauszufinden, wo wir übereinstimmen und wo nicht.)
  B: I see it that way too. Let's leave serious bargaining for tomorrow.
  (Ich sehe das auch so. Verhandeln wir die wesentlichen Punkte erst morgen.)

* **I don't think that we need a formal agenda.**
  (agenda – Tagesordnung, Verhandlungsplan)

* **May I suggest that we first agree on the main points to be discussed today?**
  (agree on – sich einigen auf / main point – Hauptpunkt)

DELIVERY, DELIVERY DATES AND TRANSPORT

Lieferung, Liefertermine und Transport

* **We can live with the other terms, but the delivery date is too tight.**
  (terms – Bedingungen / delivery date – Lieferdatum, -termin / tight – knapp)

* **Couldn't you make it six weeks instead of eight? That would give us enough time to assemble the machine and meet the deadline set by our customer.**
  (instead of – anstatt / enough – genug / assemble – zusammenbauen, montieren / meet deadline – Termin einhalten / set – festsetzen / customer – Kunde)

* **I don't think we can meet the delivery date you suggest.**
  (suggest – vorschlagen)

* **Couldn't you extend the delivery period by a week or so? That would make things much easier for us.**
(extend – verlängern / delivery period – Lieferfrist / by – um)

* **Yes, I think we could bring the date forward by a week or so. But I'd have to check with Headquarters before I can give you a firm promise.**
(bring forward – vorziehen / check with sbdy. – bei jmdm. rückfragen / headquarters – [Firmen-]Zentrale / firm promise – feste Zusage)

* **Now, as far as delivery dates are concerned, there shouldn't be any problems.**
(Nun, was die Liefertermine betrifft, … .)

* **You mustn't let us down on delivery dates.**
(Sie dürfen uns bei den Lieferterminen nicht im Stich lassen.)

* **We can let you have the first batch in six weeks and the balance in about three months, from today, that is.**
(batch – Teilmenge, Stapel / balance – Rest; restliche Artikel / about – ungefähr / from today, that is – und zwar von heute an gerechnet)

* **O.K., that's agreed then. 20 in six weeks and the rest in early July.**
(Gut. Also abgemacht. … . / in early July – Anfang Juli)

* **We wouldn't mind paying a bit more, if you could let us have the material by the end of next week.**
(Wir hätten nichts dagegen, etwas mehr zu zahlen, … .)

* **You would have to give us a bit more time to make the modifications you require.**
(modification – Änderung / require – benötigen, verlangen)

* **I need the ball-bearings very urgently.**
(ball-bearing – Kugellager / urgent – dringend)

* **The import licence is valid only until March 31. This means that delivery would have to be effected by March 15 to leave some margin for unexpected delays.**
(valid – gültig / be effected – erfolgen / by – bis [spätestens] / margin – Spielraum / unexpected – unerwartet / delay –Verzögerung)

* **The only obstacle I see is availability of shipping-space. We have to book two months ahead.**
(obstacle – Hindernis / availability – Verfügbarkeit / shipping-space – Frachtraum / ahead – im Vorhinein)

* **As I pointed out right at the beginning: we are working flat out and cannot promise more than two tonnes per month.**
(point out – feststellen / right – gleich / work flat out – voll ausgelastet sein / promise – versprechen)

* **Yes, we would be prepared to make some concessions as far as delivery dates are concerned.**
(be prepared – bereit sein / concession – Zugeständnis / concern – betreffen)

* **The penalty for late delivery is much too stiff. Our marketing people won't buy that.**
(penalty for late delivery – Pönale für Lieferverzug / stiff – „geschmalzen", hoch / buy – akzeptieren)

* **I don't think I can get our people to accept the penalty clause.**
(get – dazu bringen / clause – Klausel, Paragraph)

* **A: Transport might be a problem. I don't think the machine would fit on a normal lorry.**
(fit – passen / lorry – LKW)
B: Don't worry about transport. It can be shipped in pieces.
(worry – sich Sorgen machen / ship – versenden / in pieces – in [ihre] Bestandteile zerlegt)

* **There won't be any delay. The machine can be assembled and put into operation in a matter of hours.**
(won't – will not / assemble – zusammenbauen, montieren / put into operation – in Betrieb nehmen / in a matter of hours – innerhalb von [wenigen] Stunden)

* **We'll arrange for somebody to accompany the consignment and to help you install the machine.**
(Wir werden veranlassen, dass jemand die Sendung begleitet … .)

* **Delivery would have to be effected within two weeks of signing the contract.**
(sign – unterzeichnen)

* **We'd prefer to collect the goods from your premises ourselves. So give us a quotation ex works.**
(prefer – vorziehen / collect – abholen / premises – Geschäftsräume, Betriebsgelände / quotation – Preisangabe / ex works – ab Werk)

* **Both FOB and CIF terms would be acceptable to us.**
(FOB – free on board | frei an Bord / CIF – cost, insurance, and freight | Kosten, Versicherung, Fracht)

* **No, we couldn't shorten the delivery date. It's not so much that we have a fairly full order book at the moment but that we depend on a subcontractor for some essential components.**
(shorten – verkürzen / fairly – ziemlich / order book – Auftragsmappe, Auftragsbestand / depend on sbdy. for sthg. – hinsichtlich einer Sache auf jemanden angewiesen sein / subcontractor – Zulieferer, Subunternehmer / essential – wesentlich, wichtig / component – Bauteil)

* A: **Basically I'm in favour of part-shipments, but they will push up the cost of transport.**
(basically – im Prinzip / in favour of – für / part-shipment – Teillieferung / push up – in die Höhe treiben)
B: **You do have a point there, because the question is who will bear the higher transport charges.**
(have a point – recht haben / question – Frage / bear – tragen, übernehmen / charges – Kosten)

* **The best plan would be to ship the dyes by air.**
(ship by air – als Luftfracht versenden / dye – Farbe)

QUANTITIES
Mengen

* **Could we now move on to discussing quantities?**
(move on to – dazu übergehen)

* **We'll probably need another 50 tonnes early next year.**
(probably – wahrscheinlich / another – weitere / early next year – Anfang nächsten Jahres)

* **Could you give us some idea of your annual requirements?**
(Könnten Sie uns eine ungefähre Vorstellung Ihres Jahresbedarfes geben?)

* A: **How many would you need?**
B: **Fifty. Maybe sixty at the outside.**
(at the outside – wenn's hoch kommt; im äußersten Fall)

* **I really can't say at this stage. Around 600 probably.**
(stage – Zeitpunkt / around – ungefähr)

* **500 is only an estimate, though. We cannot bind ourselves to this figure. It could be 10 per cent more or 10 per cent less.**
(estimate – Schätzung / though – jedoch / bind oneself – sich binden / figure – Zahl)

* **We'll need 300, give or take 10.**
(Wir brauchen 300, 10 auf oder ab.)

* **Quantities would be no problem. We could probably supply any number you might require from stock.**
(supply – liefern / require – benötigen / from stock – vom Lager; sofort)

* **Correct me if I'm wrong, but did you say the maximum you can supply in any given month would be 60?**
(be wrong – Unrecht haben; sich irren)

* **We have prepared a detailed bill of quantities. Let me give everybody a copy.**
(prepare – erstellen, vorbereiten / bill of quantities – Mengengerüst)

PRODUCTS, QUALITY AND MODIFICATIONS

Produkte, Qualität und Modifikationen

(see also "Product Presentations")

* A: **If you can match the sample here, it's a deal.**
(Das Geschäft gilt, wenn Sie etwas diesem Muster hier Entsprechendes anbieten können.)
B: **Can I have a look at the specifications? … That should be no problem.**
(specifications – [technische] Angaben)

* **We have tested your machine. It's suitable for what we have in mind.**
(suitable – geeignet / have in mind – vorhaben; im Sinn haben)

* **This is a technical question which I would have to refer to our Production Department. I'll make a note of it.**
(refer to – weiterleiten an / make a note of sthg. – sich etwas notieren)

* A: **The feeder assembly would have to be modified.**
(feeder assembly – Beschickungsvorrichtung)
B: **I don't think that would be a problem. Production will come up with something.**
(come up with sthg. – sich etwas einfallen lassen)

* **No, you can forget the RX34. It's much too slow. We need something faster.**
(slow – langsam / fast – schnell)

* A: **We would need something with at least double the rated capacity of this model.**
(at least – zumindest / double – doppelt / rated capacity – Nennleistung)
B: **Well, then I'd suggest the RTV-7, which is capable of turning out 600 units per hour.**
(suggest – vorschlagen / be capable of – in der Lage sein / turn out – produzieren / unit – Stück)
C: **Sorry to interrupt you Ben, but don't you think that the GTV-8 would be even more suitable?**
(interrupt – unterbrechen / even – sogar noch)

TERMS OF PAYMENT

Zahlungsbedingungen

* **Our standard terms of payment are included in our General Terms of Sale. I don't think this point will require a lot of discussion.**
(terms of payment – Zahlungsbedingungen / General Terms of Sale – Allgemeine Geschäftsbedingungen / require – erfordern / a lot of – viel)

* **I'd appreciate it if you would pay for the first 10 machines in advance.**
(Ich wäre Ihnen verbunden, wenn Sie für die ersten zehn Maschinen im Voraus bezahlen wollten.)

* **I could allow you the usual terms, i.e. thirty days net, if you give us the usual references.**
(allow – einräumen, gewähren / usual – üblich / terms – Zahlungsbedingungen, Zahlungsziel / i.e. – that is / net – Kassa netto ohne Abzug / reference – Referenz, Referenzadresse)

* **Sorry, I've not been authorised to discuss credit terms.**
(authorise – ermächtigen / credit terms – Zahlungsziele)

* **I hope you will understand that I cannot offer you open account terms at once.**
(open account terms – offenes [d. h. unbesichertes] Ziel; Lieferung gegen offene Rechnung / at once – sofort)

* **I hope you don't mind paying in advance on this order.**
(Ich hoffe, es macht Ihnen nichts aus, bei diesem Auftrag im Voraus zu bezahlen.)

* **Forget L/Cs. Too complicated and too expensive, you know. We'd be willing to pay in advance, if you reduce the price by two per cent.**
(L/C – Letter of Credit | Akkreditiv / expensive – teuer / pay in advance – im Voraus zahlen / reduce by senken um)

* **No, I'm sorry but D/A on your first order is out of the question. We don't want to set a precedent.**
(D/A – documents against acceptance | Dokumente gegen Akzept / be out of the question – nicht in Frage kommen / set precedent – Präzedenzfall schaffen)

* A: **How about 20 per cent in U.S. dollars and the balance in the form of premium vodka?**
(balance – Restbetrag / premium vodka – Spitzenwodka)
B: **Sounds intriguing. But 20 per cent is not good enough. Wouldn't know what to do with so much vodka. Make it 40 per cent in dollars.**
(sound – klingen / intriguing – interessant, verlockend / be good enough – reichen)
A: **I couldn't go higher than 30 per cent. Where, do you think, are we going to get so many dollars? And even if you agree to 30, I would have to check with my boss.**
(even – sogar / agree to – zustimmen / check with – rückfragen bei)

* **You must not forget that this machine would be built to your exact specifications. So we must insist on at least 40 per cent down when you place the order.**
(build – bauen / to specifications – nach Angaben / insist on – bestehen auf / down – als Anzahlung / place order – Auftrag erteilen)

* A: **May I suggest a compromise? 10 per cent when you place the order, another 10 per cent on delivery, and the remainder payable in eight semi-annual instalments.**
(suggest – vorschlagen / on delivery – bei Lieferung / remainder – Restbetrag / semi-annual instalment – Halbjahresrate)
B: **Well, I suppose that's a reasonable compromise.**
(Ja, das scheint mir ein vernünftiger Kompromiss zu sein.)

* A: **I have to insist on an advance payment guarantee issued by a reputable bank, though.**
(advance payment guarantee – Anzahlungsgarantie / issue – ausstellen / reputable – renommiert / though – jedoch, aber)
B: **My people would consider a guarantee a slur on their reputation.**
(consider – betrachten / slur – Flecken)

* **I would need more detailed specifications before I can quote a firm price.**
(quote – angeben, anbieten / firm – fest, bindend)

* **A: If I get you right, you are saying that if we agree to pay the bank charges, we have a deal?**
(Wenn ich Sie recht verstehe, so sagen Sie, dass wir ins Geschäft kommen, wenn wir uns bereit erklären, die Bankspesen zu übernehmen?)
B: Yes. Maybe I've not expressed myself clearly enough. But that's what I've been saying all along.
(express – ausdrücken / … . Aber das sage ich schon die ganze Zeit.)

——— ❖ ———

* **If you really insist on invoicing in your own currency, we would have no alternative but to call the whole thing off.**
(invoice – fakturieren / currency – Währung / but – als / call sthg. off – etwas abblasen)

* **We are not prepared to bear the exchange risk.**
(prepared – bereit / bear – übernehmen, tragen / exchange risk – Wechselkursrisiko)

* **Why don't we insert a currency escalator clause?**
(insert – einfügen / currency escalator clause – Kurssicherungsklausel)

PRICES AND COMMISSIONS

Preise und Provisionen

* **Let's concentrate on prices first.**

* **The next point is price then.**

* **Well, I think it's about time that we got down to discussing prices.**
(Ich glaube, es ist nun eigentlich an der Zeit, dass wir über die Preise zu reden beginnen.)

* **I want to make it quite clear from the very beginning that we are not authorised to negotiate a final price.**
  (Ich möchte gleich zu Beginn eindeutig klarstellen, dass wir kein Pouvoir haben, einen endgültigen Preis auszuhandeln.)

* **Frankly, your prices are simply too high. I can get a much better deal from some of your competitors.**
  (frankly – offen gesagt / simple – einfach / deal – Geschäft, Angebot, Preis / competitor – Konkurrent)

* **Sorry but I'll have to restrict negotiations to the simpler models. The more sophisticated ones with the additional features are right outside our range.**
  (restrict – beschränken / sophisticated – kompliziert; technisch höherstehend / additional – zusätzlich / feature – Leistungsmerkmal / right – gänzlich / range – [Preis-]Bereich, Vorstellungen)

* **Quality is not the main consideration in our market. We sell – and therefore have to buy – on price.**
  (main consideration – wichtigstes Verkaufsargument / market – Sparte / sell on price – über den Preis verkaufen)

* **I don't see why you can't match the prices quoted by your main competitors. You must have much the same cost structure.**
  (Ich verstehe nicht, warum Sie nicht mit den Preisen Ihrer Hauptkonkurrenten mithalten können. Sie müssen doch in etwa dieselbe Kostenstruktur haben.)

* **If this is your last word on price, the deal's off, and, there won't be any more orders.**
  (be off – geplatzt sein / won't – will not / order – Auftrag)

* **Well, I don't think I can go much lower.**

* **I need at least a small concession on price to show to Headquarters.**
  (at least – zumindest / concession on price – Zugeständnis beim Preis / headquarters – [Firmen-]Zentrale)

* **I cannot accept your offer. Your prices are simply not competitive.**
  (offer – Angebot / competitive – konkurrenzfähig)

* **There's a good chance that we shall place further orders if you can make some concession on price.**
  (further – weiter / place orders – Aufträge erteilen)

* **Frankly, I'm a bit disappointed at what you are suggesting in terms of prices. Don't forget we are one of your best customers.**
  (frankly – offen gesagt / disappointed – enttäuscht / in terms of – hinsichtlich / customer – Kunde)

* **Even for a good product the price is much too high.**
  (even – sogar, selbst)

* **Yes, I admit that our prices are higher than those of our competitors. It would be silly to say otherwise. But you have to look at the overall situation. Just consider the savings in fuel and maintenance that our machines make possible.**
  (admit – zugeben / silly – unsinnig / otherwise – etwas anderes / overall situation – Gesamtsituation / consider – betrachten; in Rechnung stellen / saving – Einsparung / fuel – Treibstoff / maintenance – Wartung)

* **I don't think that I can persuade Headquarters to accept your price. But I'll give it a try.**
  (persuade – überreden / give sthg. a try – etwas versuchen)

* **Let me repeat what I said an hour ago: $400 per tonne is as far as we can go.**
  (repeat – wiederholen)

* **I'll have trouble explaining that to my boss, but to show you our goodwill we'll reduce the price by another two per cent.**
  (trouble – Schwierigkeiten / explain – erklären / by another two per cent – um weitere zwei Prozent)

* **Well, we know pretty well what our competitors charge. Their prices for the small units range from £300 to £350.**
(pretty – ziemlich / charge – berechnen, verlangen / unit – Gerät / range from … to … – zwischen … und … liegen)

* **If I go any lower, we'd make a loss on the deal.**
(on – bei / deal – Geschäft)

* **This is about as far as we could go. Any further concessions would leave us no profit.**
(concession – Zugeständnis / leave – lassen)

* **Please don't forget that I can't go beyond the limits set by Headquarters. I'm not a free agent.**
(go beyond sthg. – über etwas hinausgehen / limit – Grenze / headquarters – [Firmen-]Zentrale / I'm not a free agent – ich bin gebunden)

* **You're driving a hard bargain. You don't want to see us go bankrupt, do you?**
(drive a hard bargain – beinhart verhandeln / do you? – oder?)

* **A: No, you charge too much for this.**
B: But against our higher price you must set the longer warranty period and the lower service charges we offer.
(Aber unserem höheren Preis müssen Sie zum Vergleich die längere Garantiefrist und die niedrigeren Servicekosten, die wir bieten, gegenüberstellen.)

* **Don't you think that the higher quality justifies the slightly higher prices?**
(justify – rechtfertigen / slightly – etwas, leicht)

* **$3,000 for 12 units sounds reasonable. I think I can accept that.**
(unit – Stück, Gerät / sound – klingen / reasonable – vernünftig)

* **£450? Now you're talking.**
(… ? Das lässt sich hören.)

* **Let's compromise. I think I can let you have the drills for $650 each, including packing and delivery.**
(compromise – Kompromiss machen | eingehen / drill – Bohrmaschine, Bohrer / each – pro Stück / including – einschließlich)

* **We seem to be deadlocked on price. What would you say to discussing something less controversial for a while and coming back to prices later?**
(be deadlocked – festgefahren sein / on – bei)

——— ❖ ———

* **The price is net of VAT.**
(net of – ohne, abzüglich / VAT – value-added tax | Mehrwertsteuer)

* **What else is included in the price?**

* **The price includes export packing and delivery to the Vienna Air Freight Terminal.**

* **Let's get this clear. Does this figure include delivery or not?**
(get sthg. clear – etwas klarstellen / figure – Zahl, Preis)

* **Could you itemise the price for the PX51 drilling machine? I'd like to see how it is made up.**
(itemise – aufschlüsseln / drilling machine – Bohrmaschine / be made up – zusammengesetzt sein)

* **I've prepared a detailed quotation for the scrubber. Here you are.**
(Ich habe ein detailliertes Angebot für die Rauchwaschanlage erstellt. Hier ist es.)

* **Packing would be charged at cost.**
(at cost – zum Selbstkostenpreis)

* A: **What about insurance? Is that included or not?**
(insurance – Versicherung)
B: **Our prices here are quoted FOB Hull. This means insurance would have to be covered by your firm.**
(Unsere Preise hier verstehen sich FOB Hull. … . / cover – abdecken)

* **Sorry, I seem to have got lost. Are we talking about the price of the basic model or of the souped-up version?**
(get lost – den Faden verlieren / basic model – Grundversion / soup up – auffrisieren)

——— ❖ ———

* **Five per cent on sales is not good enough. I need at least eight per cent to break even and 10 per cent for a slim profit margin.**
(sales – Umsatz / be good enough – ausreichen / break even – glatt aussteigen; ausgeglichen bilanzieren / slim – knapp, niedrig / margin – Spanne)

* A: **Our commission would be 10 per cent on net sales. But in addition you would have to agree to pay us a minimum of $5000 per month even if sales do not warrant it.**
(commission – Provision / in addition – zusätzlich / agree – sich verpflichten; sich bereit erklären / even – selbst, sogar / warrant – rechtfertigen)
B: **Let me make a counter-proposal: we'll give you 12 per cent, but without a guaranteed minimum.**
(counter-proposal – Gegenvorschlag)

DISCOUNTS

Preisnachlässe

* **A: What about a good discount for an old customer?**
(Wie wäre es mit einem anständigen Preisnachlass ... ?)
B: Well, we could give you the quantity discount we normally allow for 300 units and over. That would be six per cent.
(quantity discount – Mengenrabatt / allow – gewähren, einräumen / unit – Stück, Gerät / over – darüber)
A: Couldn't you make that 10 per cent?
B: No. 10 per cent is too high. Seven is as far as I can go. But there is always a two per cent cash discount if you pay within a week.
(cash discount – Skonto)

* **Look, if you increase your order to 50 units, we could actually give you the 10 per cent you asked for.**
(increase – erhöhen / actually – tatsächlich)

* **Don't you run any special discounts for early purchases?**
(run – anbieten / special discount – Sonderrabatt / early – vorgezogen / purchase – Einkauf, Kauf, Bezug)

* **Normally we get a better discount on repeat orders. Three per cent really is not good enough.**
(repeat order – Nachbestellung)

* **Couldn't you give us a better discount for such a large quantity?**

* A: **Your discount period is a bit on the short side, just five days. Couldn't you make it ten?**
(discount period – Skontofrist / be a bit on the short side – eher kurz sein)
B: **That's one of the things that might be a bit difficult to change because it's part of our General Terms of Business. But I'll see what I can do.**
(change – ändern / General Terms of Business – Allgemeine Geschäftsbedingungen)

* **I'd have to check with Headquarters before I say yes or no.**
(check with – rückfragen in | bei / headquarters – [Firmen-]Zentrale)

* **I admit two per cent off doesn't sound much. But don't forget that in contrast to our competitors we have held last year's list price.**
(admit – zugeben / two per cent off – Preisnachlass von zwei Prozent / sound – klingen / in contrast – im Gegensatz / competitor – Konkurrent / hold – halten; nicht ändern)

* **We can offer you a better discount if you decide to place your order before May 1.**
(decide – sich entschließen / place order – Auftrag erteilen)

* A: **What is your quantity discount?**
B: **That depends on how much you order. Our discount system operates on a sliding scale. For one hundred units it would be six per cent, eight per cent if you order 200 or more.**
(depend on – abhängen von / … . Unsere Rabatte werden nach einem Staffelsystem berechnet. … .)

* **I think I can meet you halfway: I can give you seven and a half per cent if you increase your order to 100 units.**
(meet sbdy. halfway – jmdm. auf halbem Wege entgegenkommen)

* **A: What are your discounts for selling to the trade?**
(trade – Handel, Wiederverkäufer)
B: Our trade discount to bona fide dealers is 35 per cent, plus an extra five per cent off the list price on orders for 400 units or more.
(trade discount – Wiederverkäuferrabatt, Stufenrabatt / bona fide dealers – Käufer, die ihren Händlerstatus nachweisen können; Käufer mit Gewerbeschein)

* **All our prices are net. We don't allow any cash discount.**
(Alle unsere Preise sind Nettopreise. Wir gewähren kein Skonto.)

TERM AND TERMINATION

Vertragslaufzeit und Beendigung des Vertragsverhältnisses

* **I have gone through the draft agreement you gave me yesterday. The only objection I have is that the agreement should run for an initial period of five years instead of four.**
(draft agreement – Vertragsentwurf / objection – Einwand / run for an initial period of … – eine anfängliche Laufzeit von … haben)

* **A: What about the period of notice? Is 12 months all right?**
(notice – Kündigung)
B: Yes, I think 12 months is standard for agency agreements.
(standard – Norm / agency agreement – Handelsvertretervertrag)

* **The main sticking point seems to be termination.**
(Es scheint sich hauptsächlich bei der Klausel über die Beendigung des Vertragsverhältnisses zu spießen.)

* **Don't worry, we have obtained a legal opinion on this point.**
(Da brauchen Sie sich keine Sorgen zu machen. Wir haben zu diesem Punkt ein Rechtsgutachten eingeholt.)

DRAFT CONTRACTS, LEGAL AND TECHNICAL POINTS

Vertragsentwürfe, juristische und technische Details

* **I've studied the draft contract you sent me. It's a good starting point, but no more than that.**
(draft contract – Vertragsentwurf)

* **Did I send you a copy? No? I've got one with me. Could you have it photocopied and study it for our next meeting on Thursday?**
(meeting – Sitzung)

* **May I call your attention to Clause 4 of the Draft Agreement?**
(call attention to – Aufmerksamkeit lenken auf / clause – Klausel, Paragraph)

* **I think there is a mistake in Section 3. The first sentence should read: "In the absence of any other clause ... ."**
(mistake – Fehler / section – Paragraph / read – lauten / in the absence of – mangels)

* **I have strong reservations about Paragraph b.**
(reservation – Vorbehalt / paragraph – Absatz, Abschnitt)

* **I hope you will understand that Subsection 8 will have to be amended.**
(subsection – Ziffer / amend – abändern)

* **A: I think Clause 5 is substantially the same as Clause 8. I think we could delete it. Any objections?**
(substantially – im Wesentlichen / delete – streichen / objection – Einwand)
B: No. You're right of course.

* **In Clause 6 there is a reference to Schedule I in connection with the goods to be supplied under the Contract. I couldn't find Schedule I anywhere. You must have forgotten to attach it to the draft.**
(reference – Verweis / schedule – Vertragsanhang / connection – Zusammenhang / the goods to be supplied under the contract – die aufgrund des Vertrages zu liefernde Ware / attach – anheften, anfügen)

* **I think the wording of Clause 9 is misleading and should be changed. It seems to suggest that we would be responsible for collecting the goods.**
(wording – Formulierung / misleading – irreführend / seem – scheinen / suggest – die Interpretation nahelegen / responsible – verantwortlich / collect – abholen)

* **I think we should include a Force Majeure Clause.**
(include – inkludieren, hereinnehmen / force majeure – höhere Gewalt)

* **What struck me about Clause 10 is that no mention is made of demurrage.**
(Was mir bei Paragraph 10 auffiel, ist, dass kein Liegegeld erwähnt wird.)

* **I think that Clause 1 does not reflect what we agreed last Friday.**
(reflect – widerspiegeln, entsprechen / what – das | dem, was)

* **A: Don't you agree that the wording of Clause 1 is not very clear?**
(Meinen Sie nicht auch, dass die Formulierung von Paragraph 1 nicht sehr klar ist?)
B: Yes, you're right. I think it will have to be redrafted.
(redraft – neu formulieren; umschreiben)

* **Could you explain what the last sentence on page four of the draft means? It doesn't seem to make sense.**
(explain – erklären / page – Seite / mean – bedeuten / make sense – Sinn ergeben)

* A: **In my opinion we should add a standard arbitration clause. Is that O.K. with you?**
(opinion – Meinung / standard arbitration clause – übliche Schiedsklausel)
B: **Yes, of course. Why don't we use the standard ICC clause?**
(ICC – International Chamber of Commerce | Internationale Handelskammer)

* **The next point to be discussed is Clause 6. I think it's on page four.**

BREAKS, NEXT MEETING, FINISHING

Pausen, die nächste Sitzung, Abschluss der Verhandlungen

* **I think we could all do with a break. Coffee, tea anybody?**
(do with – brauchen / break – Pause)

* **What about a coffee-break? That would give me a chance to call Headquarters about the contract currency.**
(what about – wie wär's mit / call – anrufen / headquarters – [Firmen-]Zentrale / contract currency – Vertragswährung)

* **We have reached agreement on a number of important points today. I think we could finalise the contract next Monday, if that's O.K. with you.**
(reach agreement – Übereinstimmung erzielen / number – Anzahl, Reihe / important – wichtig / finalise – finalisieren)

* **We seem to be fairly close to agreement on most of the points. I think we can finish the whole thing in a couple of hours. So why not meet again after dinner?**
(seem – scheinen / fairly – ziemlich / close to – nahe an / finish – beenden / a couple of – ein paar / dinner – Essen)

* **A: Would it be possible to have another meeting the day after tomorrow? I might be able to clarify some of the points you raised by then.**
(clarify – klären / raise point – Frage aufwerfen / by – bis [spätestens])
B: That would be Friday, wouldn't it? Yes, Friday would be O.K..
(wouldn't it? – nicht wahr?)
A: Two o'clock again?
B: Yes, two is fine.

* **See you again on Thursday then. Don't forget to bring the draft contract with you.**

* **Could you draft a suitable clause to cover this point for the next meeting?**
(draft – entwerfen, konzipieren / suitable – geeignet / cover – erfassen, abdecken)

* **I'll have the contract typed out. It will be ready for signature by about three this afternoon.**
(Ich werde den Vertrag tippen lassen. … . / ready for signature – unterschriftsreif / about – etwa)

* **I think that's all. I'll get our lawyers to check the draft to make sure we haven't overlooked anything.**
(get to check – veranlassen zu prüfen / lawyer – Jurist / make sure – sicherstellen / overlook – übersehen)

* **So, that's it then. Let's go and have a drink on it.**
(So, das wär's dann. Gehen wir einen darauf trinken.)

MEETINGS

Sitzungen

(see also “Conferences” and “General Presentations”)

STARTING THE MEETING

Sitzungseröffnung

* **O.K., let’s get started.**
  (Okay, fangen wir an.)

* **Let’s get started, shall we?**
  (Fangen wir also an.)

* **Shall we begin?**
  (Wollen wir anfangen?)

* **Right then. Let’s get down to business, shall we?**
  (Gut, fangen wir also an.)

* **May I have your attention, please, ladies and gentlemen?**
  (Darf ich um Ihre Aufmerksamkeit bitten, … ?)

* **I call the second meeting of the Investment Committee to order.**
  (Ich eröffne hiermit die zweite Sitzung des Investitionsausschusses.)

* **I declare the meeting open.**
  (Ich erkläre die Sitzung für eröffnet.)

∗ **We have a new member here today, Miss Briar from Auditing. I'd like to welcome her very cordially. Miss Briar is an experienced accountant and I'm looking forward to her contributions.**
(member – Mitglied / Auditing – Revisionsabteilung / cordially – herzlich / experienced – erfahren / accountant – [Bilanz-] Buchhalterin / look forward to – sich freuen auf / contribution – Beitrag)

∗ **Since most of the members don't know each other, I've asked my secretary to prepare name cards. Would you please check whether you have the right card in front of you?**
(since – da / prepare – vorbereiten, erstellen / whether – ob / in front of – vor)

∗ **May I remind you that we agreed last time not to smoke in meetings. I suggest that we have a break after an hour or so to give smoking members a chance to indulge in their vice in the adjacent room.**
(remind – [daran] erinnern / agree – sich einigen / suggest – vorschlagen / break – Pause / indulge in vice – Laster frönen / adjacent room – Zimmer nebenan)

∗ **What about the minutes of the last meeting? Any queries? Can we take them as read?**
(Wie steht es mit dem Protokoll der letzten Sitzung? Irgendwelche Einwendungen? Gilt es als angenommen?)

∗ **I have received apologies for absence from Frank Finley and Anne Foley. They are both in London on business.**
(receive – erhalten / apology for absence – Entschuldigung wegen Abwesenheit / on business – geschäftlich)

∗ **I have received apologies from Jeff Wright, who is unable to attend because of other urgent commitments.**
(attend – teilnehmen / urgent – dringend / commitment – Verpflichtung)

SETTING THE AGENDA

Festlegung der Tagesordnung

* **We've three items of business on the agenda this morning.**
  (Die Tagesordnung für die Sitzung heute morgen umfasst drei Punkte.)

* **There are four main topics on the agenda.**
  (main topic – Hauptthema)

* **There are four things we've got to discuss today.**

* **The agenda this morning consists of two items.**
  (consist of – bestehen aus; umfassen)

* **First let's look at the request for more funds submitted by the Marketing Department.**
  (look at sthg. – sich etwas ansehen; etwas behandeln / request – Ersuchen / funds – Mittel / submit – vorlegen, unterbreiten)

* **The big question we have to tackle today concerns the results of the cost-cutting drive.**
  (question – Frage, Problem / tackle – angehen; sich befassen mit / concern – betreffen / cost-cutting drive – Kostensenkungsprogramm)

* **The major problem we've got to discuss is the high labour turnover in the Accounts Department.**
  (major problem – Hauptproblem; wichtigstes Problem / labour turnover – Fluktuation / accounts department – Buchhaltungsabteilung)

* **I'd like to continue where we left off last week.**
  (Ich möchte dort fortsetzen, wo wir letzte Woche aufgehört haben.)

* **There is still some unfinished business from the last meeting.**
  (Es gibt da noch ein paar Punkte, die in der letzten Sitzung nicht abgeschlossen wurden.)

* **Any additions to the formal agenda?**
(addition – Zusatz; zusätzlicher Punkt)

INVITING CONTRIBUTIONS AND ASKING FOR OPINIONS

Bitte um Diskussionsbeiträge und Meinungsäußerungen

* **Now Mr. Rider has the floor.**
(Jetzt hat Herr Rider das Wort.)

* **It's your turn now, Ms. Green.**
(Sie sind jetzt an der Reihe, … .)

* **Yes, why don't you start, the floor is yours.**
(… , Sie sind am Wort.)

* **Would you like to comment on this, Peter?**
(Möchtest du etwas dazu sagen, Peter?)

* **Is this O.K. with you, Susan?**
(Geht das in Ordnung bei dir, Susan?)

* **What's your view on this, Fred?**
(Was ist deine Ansicht dazu, Fred?)

* **How do you see this, Anne?**
(Wie siehst du die Sache, Anne?)

* **How do you feel about this, Paul?**
(Wie ist deine Meinung zu dieser Sache, Paul?)

* **What is your opinion about the new schedule, Mr. Baxter?**
(Was halten Sie vom neuen Terminplan, Herr Baxter?)

* **Isn't there anybody who would like to say a few words in favour of the proposal?**
(a few – ein paar / in favour of – zugunsten / proposal – Vorschlag)

* **Judith, could you outline the pros and cons of the project, please?**
(outline – kurz umreißen / the pros and cons – das Für und Wider)

* **So what are <u>your</u> suggestions?**
(Was schlagen <u>Sie</u> vor?)

* **Has anyone anything further to add?**
(Hat noch jemand etwas dazu zu sagen?)

AGREEING AND DISAGREEING

Zustimmung und Ablehnung

* **I go along with that.**
(Dieser Meinung | Diesem Vorschlag schließe ich mich an.)

* **I'm not sure I agree. We have to weigh the pros and cons more carefully.**
(Ich bin mir da nicht ganz sicher, ob ich derselben Meinung bin. Wir müssen das Für und Wider sorgfältiger abwägen.)

* **I think you're right. We should put more emphasis on public relations.**
(put emphasis on sthg. – etwas betonen | in den Vordergrund stellen)

* **I couldn't agree more.**
(Da bin ich ganz und gar Ihrer Meinung.)

* **I agree.**
(Dem kann ich zustimmen. | Ich bin auch dieser Meinung.)

* **I disagree.**
(Da bin ich anderer Meinung. | Dem kann ich nicht zustimmen.)

* **I agree up to a point.**
(Dem kann ich bis zu einem gewissen Punkt zustimmen. | Dem kann ich mich mit gewissen Einschränkungen anschließen.)

* **I think we are in agreement on bringing forward the completion date.**
(Ich glaube, wir sind uns darin einig, das Fertigstellungsdatum vorzuziehen.)

* **The proposal to farm the job out to a specialist has my full support.**
(proposal – Vorschlag / farm out – extern vergeben / support – Unterstützung)

* **Do you agree that this is a non-starter?**
(be a non-starter – keinerlei Erfolgschancen haben; aussichtslos sein)

* **I don't accept that. In my view, we should go ahead.**
(in my view – meiner Ansicht nach / go ahead – anfangen)

* **I'm not sure whether I can go along with you here.**
(whether – ob / go along with sbdy. – mit jmdm. mitgehen; jmdn. unterstützen)

* **I'm afraid I don't agree with Harry.**
(Leider bin ich da anderer Meinung als Harry.)

* **I completely disagree. We can't wait. We have to act now.**
(Da bin ich gänzlich anderer Meinung. … . / wait – warten / act – handeln)

* **I'm not convinced that this is a good idea.**
(convince – überzeugen)

* **I couldn't possibly support such a move.**
  (Ich könnte so einen Schritt nie unterstützen.)

* **On balance, I think it's not the right time for the move.**
  (on balance – per Saldo; alles in allem)

* **That's oversimplifying it.**
  (oversimplify – zu stark vereinfachen)

PERSUADING AND CONVINCING

Überreden und überzeugen

* **Couldn't you reconsider your stance, Frank?**
  (reconsider – noch einmal überlegen / stance – Standpunkt)

* **Can't this persuade you either?**
  (not … either – auch nicht)

* **I think this is an irrefutable argument.**
  (irrefutable – unwiderlegbar)

* **Don't you think that it's time to do something about the loss of reach?**
  (loss of reach – Reichweitenverlust)

* **Have a look at this letter. Maybe this will convince you that we can't delay the decision any longer.**
  (letter – Brief / convince – überzeugen / delay – aufschieben / decision – Entscheidung)

* **Wouldn't you agree that the proposal is quite reasonable?**
  (proposal – Vorschlag / quite – durchaus, ganz / reasonable – vernünftig)

* **I can't understand why it should be so difficult to come round to our view.**
(come round to our view – sich unserer Meinung anschließen)

* **I do hope you will change your mind.**
(Ich hoffe wirklich, dass Sie Ihre Meinung ändern werden | dass Sie sich anders besinnen werden.)

* **Can't you give an inch just once?**
(Können Sie nicht wenigstens einmal nur ein bisschen nachgeben?)

SUGGESTIONS AND REACTIONS

Vorschläge und Reaktionen darauf

* A: **I suggest that we examine each of these plans in detail.**
(Ich schlage vor, dass wir jeden einzelnen dieser Pläne detailliert prüfen.)
B: **Yes, I think that's a good idea.**

* A: **I think we should take a closer look at the details.**
(Ich glaube, wir sollten uns die Details genauer ansehen.)
B: **I'd say so, too.**

* A: **I recommend that we take his objections very seriously.**
(Ich empfehle, dass wir seine Einwände sehr ernst nehmen.)
B: **Yes, I agree. After all, he is the expert.**
(after all – schließlich)

* A: **I recommend dropping the charge.**
(drop charge – Anschuldigung fallenlassen | nicht weiter verfolgen)
B: **No, I couldn't go along with that. That would be a bit premature.**
(go along with – mitgehen / premature – voreilig)

✻ A: **How about deferring the next item until we have clarified the details?**
(Wie wäre es, wenn wir die Behandlung des nächsten Tagesordnungspunktes aufschieben, bis wir die Einzelheiten geklärt haben?)
B: **I don't think that would be a good idea.**

✻ A: **What about offering them a special discount?**
(Wie wäre es, wenn wir ihnen einen Sonderrabatt anbieten?)
B: **Well, I'm not sure whether that will clinch it. But it's worth a try.**
(whether – ob / clinch sthg. – etwas zu einem endgültigen Abschluss bringen / worth a try – einen Versuch wert)

✻ A: **I propose calling in an expert.**
(Ich schlage vor, einen Experten beizuziehen.)
B: **No, I think that would be a waste of time. The matter isn't all that important.**
(Nein, ich glaube, das wäre Zeitverschwendung. So wichtig ist die Sache auch wieder nicht.)

✻ A: **What I would suggest is that the financial aspects of the deal should be investigated much more closely.**
(deal – Geschäft / investigate – untersuchen / close – genau)
B: **Yes, that's what we should do.**

✻ A: **Listen, why don't we send somebody over there to sort out the problem on the spot?**
(listen – zuhören / sort out – lösen / on the spot – an Ort und Stelle; vor Ort)
B: **Yes, why not? Although I'm not sure whether the expense would be really justified.**
(although – obwohl / expense – Aufwand / justified – gerechtfertigt)

* **A: My suggestion would be that we concentrate on the premium end of the market.**
(premium end – Hochpreissegment, Luxussegment)
B: Do you really think that would work? It might be a bit risky.
(work – funktionieren)

* **A: My suggestion is to call for a second opinion.**
(call for – einholen / opinion – Gutachten)
B: I'd support that.
(support – unterstützen)

* **A: Don't you think it would be better to waive the penalty?**
(waive – verzichten auf / penalty – Pönale)
B: With respect Peter, you have missed the point.
(Bei allem Respekt, Peter, aber du hast nicht verstanden, worum es geht | aber du hast den springenden Punkt nicht kapiert.)

CONCEDING POINTS

Zugeständnisse machen

* **I think you've got a point there. There is a strong case for not splitting the department.**
(Ich glaube, da hast du recht. Es gibt starke Argumente, die gegen eine Aufspaltung der Abteilung sprechen.)

* **You may be right there, but we must not forget that interest rates have risen in the meantime.**
(be right – recht haben / interest rate – Zinssatz / rise – steigen; sich erhöhen / meantime – Zwischenzeit)

* **You could have a point there. On the other hand I still think the financial aspects are more important.**
(Da könntest du recht haben. Andererseits glaube ich trotzdem, dass die finanziellen Aspekte wichtiger sind.)

* **I think you're on to something here, but in my view the financial angle should be explored first.**
(Ich glaube, da haben Sie den Finger auf einen wichtigen Punkt gelegt, … . / view – Ansicht / angle – Aspekt / explore – untersuchen, analysieren)

CLARIFYING
Klarstellungen

* **So, please, let me get this clear. We do not intend to merely license our invention.**
(Ich möchte das bitte ganz klar zum Ausdruck bringen. Wir beabsichtigen nicht, unsere Erfindung bloß in Form von Lizenzen zu verwerten.)

* **Could you clarify what you have just said? I don't think I fully understand you.**
(clarify – näher erläutern / just – gerade)

* **What exactly do you mean by "special requirements"?**
(Was genau verstehen Sie unter „Sondererfordernissen"?)

* **Could you be a bit more specific?**
(specific – konkret, spezifisch)

* **I'm sorry, but could you explain this in a little more detail?**
(Entschuldigen Sie, aber könnten Sie das etwas genauer erklären?)

* **Sorry, probably I haven't made myself entirely clear.**
(Tut mir leid. Ich habe mich wahrscheinlich nicht ganz klar ausgedrückt.)

* **I'd like to make it quite clear that I will not support the scheme.**
(quite – ganz / support – unterstützen / scheme – Projekt, Aktion)

* **I'm afraid there seems to have been a slight misunderstanding. This isn't quite what I meant.**
  (Ich fürchte, da scheint es ein kleines Missverständnis gegeben zu haben. Das habe ich eigentlich nicht ganz so gemeint.)

* **Actually, what I was trying to say is that we need more information.**
  (Was ich eigentlich sagen wollte, ist, … .)

* **From what you have just said I'm not quite sure whether you are in favour or against the proposal.**
  (whether – ob / in favour – dafür / proposal – Vorschlag, Antrag)

INTERRUPTIONS AND DEALING WITH INTERRUPTIONS

Unterbrechungen und wie man damit umgeht

* **May I interrupt you for a moment? I think you have forgotten to allow for the period of grace.**
  (interrupt – unterbrechen / allow for – berücksichtigen / period of grace – tilgungsfreier Zeitraum)

* **Excuse me. May I come in here?**
  (Entschuldigen Sie. Darf ich an dieser Stelle etwas [dazu] sagen?)

* **Now hold on. Even if your projections are right, we won't reach the break-even point before 2010.**
  (Moment mal. Selbst wenn Ihre Prognosen stimmen, werden wir die Gewinnschwelle erst 2010 erreichen.)

* **Excuse me. Before you go on, could I just say this?**
  (Entschuldigen Sie. Bevor Sie fortfahren, könnte ich nur kurz etwas sagen?)

* **Excuse me for interrupting you. But before we go on, we have to clarify the cost position.**
  (clarify – klären)

* **Can I just make a brief comment here?**
(Kann ich nur kurz etwas dazu sagen?)

——— ❖ ———

* **Excuse me, Miss Friar, I think Mr. Greer would like to make a point.**
(make a point – eine Anmerkung machen)

* **A: If you don't mind, Brian, could Anne just briefly tell us what she heard in the Ministry? I think that would be very relevant here.**
(if you don't mind – wenn es Ihnen nichts ausmacht / brief – kurz)
B: Yes, certainly. Anne, go ahead.
(Ja, natürlich. Schieß los, Anne.)

——— ❖ ———

* **Sorry, can I continue now? I haven't finished yet.**
(continue – fortfahren / … . Ich bin noch nicht fertig.)

* **I'll come back to this later, if you don't mind.**

* **That's an interesting point, but I'd rather deal with it later on.**
(I'd rather – ich möchte lieber / deal with – behandeln)

* **I'd rather comment on this later on.**
(Ich möchte mich lieber später dazu äußern.)

——— ❖ ———

* **Could you hold back until Peter has finished?**
(Könntest du warten, bis Peter fertig ist?)

* **Sorry Mr. Fisher, you'll have to wait a little. We must let Ms. Bunter finish first.**

* **Be brief Thomas, because strictly speaking Mr. Gower has the floor.**
(Fass dich kurz, … . / strictly speaking – genaugenommen, eigentlich / have the floor – am Wort sein)

MOVING THE DISCUSSION FORWARD

Überleitung zum nächsten Tagesordnungspunkt

* **Well, let's move on to the environmental aspects of the project.**
(Gehen wir jetzt zu den ökologischen Aspekten des Projektes über.)

* **Now, let's move on to item two on the agenda.**
(Wenden wir uns nun dem zweiten Tagesordnungspunkt zu.)

* **Can we next deal with the legal implications of the move?**
(Können wir als nächstes die juristischen Implikationen des Schrittes behandeln?)

* **Now, let's turn our attention to the question of discounts.**
(Wenden wir uns nun der Frage der Preisnachlässe zu.)

* **Could we now discuss item three?**

* **I think this leads us to the next point.**
(lead – bringen, führen)

* **The next item on the agenda is the Environmental Impact Assessment.**
(Der nächste Tagesordnungspunkt ist die Umweltverträglichkeitsprüfung.)

* **Any objections to bringing Item 6 forward? I think it would be better to deal with it right now.**
(Spricht etwas dagegen, dass wir den Punkt 6 vorziehen? … .)

KEEPING THE DISCUSSION ON TRACK

Wie man Abweichungen vom Thema verhindert

* A: **Excuse me, Frank, I know this is a very interesting question but it is not our main concern today.**
  (question – Frage / main concern – Hauptthema, Hauptanliegen)
  B: **You're right of course. Let's leave it for the next meeting.**
  (leave – lassen)

* **No, I don't agree. I think what I've been saying is very relevant to our main topic.**
  (main topic – Hauptthema)

* **Let's not stray too far from our main concern. Our time is limited anyway.**
  (stray – abschweifen / limited – beschränkt / anyway – ohnehin)

* **Let's not lose sight of the main point.**
  (lose sight of sthg. – etwas aus dem Auge verlieren)

* **I'm afraid we are getting side-tracked.**
  (Ich fürchte, wir kommen da auf ein Nebengleis.)

* **May I remind you that the issue under discussion is the new marketing plan and not the marketing manager.**
  (remind – [daran] erinnern / issue – Thema)

HANDLING AWKWARD QUESTIONS AND BEING EVASIVE

Wie man mit unangenehmen Fragen umgeht und Ausflüchte macht

* **I'm afraid I can't give you a definite answer at present.**
  (Tut mir leid, aber ich kann Ihnen zum gegenwärtigen Zeitpunkt keine endgültige Antwort geben.)

* **It's hard to say at the moment. It all depends on how our competitors react to our move.**
(depend on – abhängen von / competitor – Konkurrent / react to – reagieren auf / move – Schritt)

* **Sorry to sound evasive, but there is no straightforward answer to that.**
(Tut mir leid, wenn es nach einer Ausflucht klingt, aber die Frage kann nicht so einfach beantwortet werden.)

* **I'd need more information to answer your question.**

* **It's too soon for a final judgement.**
(final judgement – endgültige Bewertung; endgültiges Urteil)

* **I can't really say more at present. Anything I add might jeopardise the negotiations with the syndicate.**
(add – hinzufügen / jeopardise – gefährden / negotiation Verhandlung / syndicate – Konsortium)

* **I hope you will understand, but to answer your question I would have to divulge classified information.**
(divulge – preisgeben / classified – geheim)

* **I'm sorry but I have not been authorised by the Board to disclose more.**
(authorise – ermächtigen / board – Verwaltungsrat; Führungsgremium einer brit. / US-Kapitalgesellschaft / disclose – offenlegen, mitteilen)

* **You seem to be avoiding my question.**
(seem – scheinen / avoid – ausweichen)

SUMMARISING

Zusammenfassungen

* **In a nutshell, what I'm saying is that costs are too high.**
  (Der langen Rede kurzer Sinn ist, dass … .)

* **To summarise, in my view, there are too many uncertainties.**
  (Um das Ganze zusammenzufassen: meiner Meinung nach gibt es zu viele Unsicherheiten.)

* **Let me sum up what has been agreed so far.**
  (sum up – zusammenfassen / agree sthg. – sich auf etwas einigen)

* **Let me recap on what has been decided so far.**
  (recap on – zusammenfassen / decide – entscheiden, beschließen)

* **Let me pull together the main strands of the argument.**
  (pull together – zusammenziehen / strand – Linie, Faden)

* **A: Does this summarise your present position?**
  (present – gegenwärtig, aktuell)
  B: Yes, that's an accurate summary.
  (accurate – genau / summary – Zusammenfassung)

FORMAL MOTIONS AND VOTING

Formelle Anträge und Abstimmungen

* **I think everyone has had their say now. We cannot discuss the pros and cons interminably. Let's have a motion and vote on it.**
  (Ich glaube, alle haben jetzt etwas dazu gesagt. Wir können das Für und Wider nicht endlos diskutieren. Irgend jemand muss einen formellen Antrag stellen, und dann stimmen wir ab.)

* **I don't think we see eye to eye on this at all. Let's put it to the vote.**
(Ich glaube nicht, dass wir die Sache auch nur im entferntesten gleich sehen. Stimmen wir also darüber ab.)

* **Mr. Chairman, I'd like to move that the project be postponed until the financial details have been clarified.**
(Herr Vorsitzender, ich möchte beantragen, dass das Projekt bis zur Klärung der finanziellen Einzelheiten aufgeschoben wird.)

* **I would like to propose that Ms. Gold should be asked to stay on.**
(propose – vorschlagen / stay on – in der Firma bleiben)

* **All right then. Let's put it to the vote.**

* **Perhaps we should take a vote on this.**
(take a vote on sthg. – über etwas abstimmen)

* **How many are in favour of postponing the project? How many against?**
(Wie viele sind für den Aufschub des Projektes? … ?)

* **All those in favour? … five. Those against? … four.**

* **Any abstentions?**
(Enthält sich irgend jemand der Stimme? | Stimmenthaltungen?)

* **Can I ask for a show of hands?**
(Könnten Sie bitte aufzeigen?)

* **The motion to postpone the project has been carried by five votes to two.**
(Der Antrag, das Projekt aufzuschieben, ist mit fünf zu zwei Stimmen angenommen worden.)

* **The motion has been rejected.**
(reject – ablehnen)

* **Five in favour, five against. I'll have to use my casting vote. I'm against the proposal. This means that the motion has been defeated.** (… . Ich muss von meinem Dirimierungsrecht Gebrauch machen. … . / proposal – Antrag / mean – heißen, bedeuten / defeat – ablehnen)

* **It's a draw.** (Die Abstimmung ist unentschieden ausgegangen.)

* **Are we all agreed on this then?** (Sind wir da alle einer Meinung?)

* **Agreed.** (Ja, einer Meinung.)

* **If everyone agrees … .**

* **A: Since this is a very sensitive matter I suggest that we have a secret ballot.** (Da das eine sehr heikle Angelegenheit ist, schlage ich vor, dass wir geheim darüber abstimmen.)
B: I don't think the Rules of Procedure say anything about a secret ballot. I'm against it. (Ich glaube nicht, dass die Geschäftsordnung eine geheime Abstimmung vorsieht. Ich bin dagegen.)

* **A: This motion cannot be put to the vote since nobody has seconded it.** (second – formell unterstützen)
B: Requiring formal support for a motion is British and not Continental practice. (Das Erfordernis einer formellen Unterstützung für einen Antrag ist nur in Großbritannien, nicht aber auf dem Kontinent üblich.)
A: I see. Are you sure that there is nothing about this in the Rules of Procedure?
B: I'm positive. I drew them up myself. (Ganz sicher. Ich habe sie selbst erstellt.)

MINUTES

Das Protokoll

* **Don't put that in the minutes, please. It would make a bad impression on outsiders.**
  (Schreiben Sie das bitte nicht ins Protokoll. Es würde einen schlechten Eindruck auf Außenstehende machen.)

* **Walter, will you draft suitable minutes about these two proposals, please?**
  (Walter, würdest du bitte diese beiden Anträge für das Protokoll entsprechend formulieren?)

* **My suggestion is – and I want this to be minuted – that we first talk to the trade union representatives.**
  (Mein Vorschlag ist – und ich möchte, dass das protokolliert wird –, dass wir zuerst mit den Gewerkschaftsvertretern reden.)

* **I must insist that my objections are put in the minutes. I want to make it quite clear where I stand on this matter.**
  (Ich muss darauf bestehen, dass meine Einwände ins Protokoll aufgenommen werden. Ich möchte meine Haltung in dieser Sache eindeutig klarstellen.)

CLOSING THE MEETING

Wie man eine Sitzung schließt

* **All right. Time is getting on and I'd like to wind the meeting up now.**
  (… . Es wird langsam spät, und ich möchte die Sitzung jetzt zu einem Abschluss bringen.)

* **I think it's time we finished.**
  (Ich glaube, es ist Zeit, dass wir Schluss machen.)

* **Is there any other business?**
  (Etwas unter Allfälliges?)

* **If we are all agreed then, I'd like to close the meeting.**
  (close – schließen)

* **We are running out of time and I think we should break up now.**
  (Die Zeit wird langsam knapp, und ich glaube, wir sollten jetzt Schluss machen.)

* **I suggest that we adjourn and leave the last two items on the agenda for the next meeting. There is no point in rushing them through. They can wait until next week.**
  (adjourn – [sich] vertagen / leave – lassen / there is no point – es hat keinen Sinn / rush through – durchpeitschen)

* **Bye, see you all in two weeks' time.**

POST MEETING

Nach der Sitzung

* **Would you be willing to chair the next meeting, Mary? I have to attend a business function in Paris and I don't think I'll be able to make it.**
  (chair meeting – bei Sitzung Vorsitz führen / attend – teilnehmen an / business function – geschäftlich wichtige Veranstaltung / make it – es schaffen)

* **Giles, could I have a copy of the minutes by tomorrow afternoon?**
  (by – bis [spätestens])

* **Geoffrey, could you get the minutes typed and distributed to the members as soon as possible?**
  (get sthg. typed – etwas tippen lassen / distribute – verteilen)

* **Could I have a word with you in my office, Anne?**

* **I don't think the meeting went too well. There was a lot of unnecessary bickering.**
(a lot of – viel / unnecessary – unnötig, überflüssig / bickering – Gezänke)

* **Yes, some of the contributions were simply too long and partly irrelevant.**
(contribution – Beitrag / simply – einfach / partly – teilweise)

* A: **Charles Miller can be a real pain in the neck.**
(… kann einem wirklich auf die Nerven gehen.)
B: **I agree. He is so stubborn and just refuses to see somebody else's point of view.**
(stubborn – stur / just – einfach / refuse – sich weigern / point of view – Standpunkt)

* A: **Ah, that was a great meeting! Most of the participants were very constructive and spoke only to the point.**
(participant – Teilnehmer / speak to the point – zum Thema sprechen)
B: **Yes, but part of the credit goes to you. You handled the meeting very well. I particularly liked the way in which you dealt with the ramblings of Peter Read.**
(part of the credit goes to you – das ist teilweise dein Verdienst / handle – führen, leiten / particularly – besonders / deal with – fertigwerden mit / ramblings – zielloses Geschwätz)

CONFERENCES

Konferenzen

(see also "Meetings" and "General Presentations")

REGISTRATION AND GENERAL INFORMATION

Anmeldung und allgemeine Informationen

* **I'd like to register for the Conference on the Internalisation of External Effects, please.**
  (register – anmelden)

* **A: Could I have my tag and the copies of the conference papers?**
  (tag – Namensschild / conference papers – Konferenzunterlagen)
  B: Here you are, sir.
  (Hier bitte!)

* **A: What? You can't find my name on the list? I registered months ago and paid the full fee.**
  (fee – Gebühr)
  B: When did you say you registered?

* **I wonder if you could tell me whether Mr. Vetter has already arrived, please.**
  (Könnten Sie mir bitte sagen, ob Herr Vetter schon angekommen ist.)

* **No, you're right. I didn't book a hotel through your organisation because I'm staying with friends.**
  (stay with – wohnen bei)

——— ❖ ———

* **Can you tell me where Dr. Minor's talk will be held?**
  (talk – Vortrag)

* **Excuse me, could you tell me where the leaders of the working groups are meeting this afternoon?**
(leader – Leiter / working group – Arbeitsgruppe / meet – sich treffen)

* **When does the plenary session start this afternoon?**
(plenary session – Plenarsitzung)

* **I'd like to join the working party on Materials Management. Where are they meeting?**
(join – mitmachen bei / working party – Arbeitsgruppe / materials management – Materialwirtschaft)

* **A: Could you tell us where to register for the working groups, please?**
B: Yes, certainly. The office is on the second floor at the end of the corridor.
(certainly – gern / office – Büro / floor – Stock)

* **No, it can't be Room No. 34. I went there just a minute ago and it's occupied by the Cost Accounting people.**
(occupied – besetzt / cost accounting – Kostenrechnung)

* **A: Excuse me, is this the working party on Corporate Culture?**
(corporate culture – Unternehmenskultur)
B: No, we are the Operations Research people. The Corporate Culture people are meeting in Room 234. This is Room 134.

* **A: Excuse me, I'm afraid I'm a bit late. My plane was held up in Manchester because of fog. Could I still join your working party?**
(I'm afraid – ich fürchte / plane – Flugzeug / fog – dichter Nebel / still – noch)
B: Certainly. Come in and have a seat. What is your name?

* A: **What a pleasant surprise, Brian! I didn't know that you were coming, too. Great to see you again.**
(pleasant – freudig / surprise – Überraschung / great – schön)
B: **Hello Andrew. Great to see you too. Didn't know myself that I'd be coming until a week ago. But the man my company originally wanted to send fell ill.**
(originally – ursprünglich / fall ill – krank werden)

* A: **Yes, I'm going to read a paper on environmental audits.**
(read paper – Referat halten / environmental audit – Umweltbilanz)
B: **I didn't know that you were an expert in that field.**
(field – Gebiet)

OPENING CONFERENCES AND INTRODUCING SPEAKERS

Eröffnung von Konferenzen und Vorstellung von Vortragenden

* **Ladies and gentlemen, on this note, I declare the 4th Conference on "The Diffusion of Technology" open.**
(on this note – in diesem Sinne / declare open – für eröffnet erklären)

* **Ladies and gentlemen, I have great pleasure in introducing Dr. Holmes, an expert on environmental matters and a specialist in business law.**
(have great pleasure – sich sehr freuen; das Vergnügen haben / introduce – vorstellen / environmental matters – Umweltfragen, -angelegenheiten / business law – Wirtschaftsrecht)

* **It gives me great pleasure to welcome our next speaker, Mr. Van Dyke from Rotterdam.**

* **Our first speaker, Professor Blue, will talk on "The Cost Centre Concept".**
(cost centre – Kostenstelle)

* **Ladies and gentlemen, we are pleased to have with us today Mr. Brown from the Confederation of British Industry. Mr. Brown's talk will be on "The British Strike Record".**
(Confederation of British Industry – britischer Unternehmerverband / strike record – Streikbilanz)

* **Mr. Potter's subject today is "The Role of the Stock Exchange".**
(subject – Thema / stock exchange – [Wertpapier-]Börse)

SPEAKER THANKS CHAIRMAN

Vortragende/r dankt Vorsitzender/m

* **Thank you very much for your kind words, although you've made it very difficult for me to meet the expectations you have aroused.**
(kind – freundlich / although – obwohl / meet expectations – Erwartungen erfüllen / arouse – erwecken)

* **That was very kind of you, Ms. Chairperson.**
(Ms. – neutrale Form für Miss oder Mrs. / chairperson – Vorsitzende / r)

SPEAKER INTRODUCES SUBJECT

Vortragende/r stellt ihr/sein Thema vor

* **The subject of my paper is "Countertrade with Bulgaria".**
(countertrade – Gegengeschäfte)

* **In the course of the next 30 minutes we shall be analysing some of the new financial derivatives.**
(course – Verlauf / financial derivatives – derivative Finanzprodukte)

* **Ladies and gentlemen, as you have already heard, I'll be talking about "Cost Accounting Problems in Flexible Manufacturing Systems".**
(flexible manufacturing system – flexibles Fertigungssystem)

SPEAKER INTRODUCES FIRST POINT

Vortragende/r präsentiert ersten Punkt

* **I'd like to begin by giving you a brief outline of my paper.**
(brief outline – Kurzfassung / paper – Referat)

* **Let us begin with a summary of the major points I shall be considering.**
(summary – Zusammenfassung / major point – wichtigster Punkt / consider – erörtern, behandeln)

* **The first aspect to be considered is the motivation behind the new government policy.**
(government – Regierung / policy – Politik)

SPEAKER MOVES ON TO NEXT POINT/S

Vortragende/r leitet zum nächsten Punkt / zu den nächsten Punkten über

* **Let us move on to the next point then.**
(move on to – übergehen zu)

* **The second main point is how middle management can be involved in the scheme.**
(involve – einbinden / scheme – Projekt)

* **We are now in a position to consider the second major aspect, viz. the tax implications.**
(in a position – in der Lage / viz. – namely | nämlich / tax – Steuer)

* **The second element in the mix we shall investigate is off-shore manufacturing.**
(investigate – untersuchen / off-shore manufacturing – Produktion im Ausland)

* **Now I'd like to turn to the next point.**
(turn to – sich zuwenden)

CONCLUDING REMARKS

Schlussbemerkungen

* **Finally I'd like to summarise the chief points I've made.**
(finally – zum Abschluss / summarise – zusammenfassen / chief point – wichtigste Aussage)

* **By way of conclusion let me once again stress the importance of obtaining government support.**
(by way of conclusion – zum Abschluss / once again – noch einmal / stress – betonen / importance – Wichtigkeit / obtain – erhalten, erlangen / support – Unterstützung)

* **A few closing remarks … .**
(closing remark – Schlussbemerkung)

* **I should now like to conclude by highlighting the crucial aspects once again.**
(conclude – schließen / highlight – herausstreichen / crucial – entscheidend)

* **Let me end on a note of optimism.**
(Ich möchte den Vortrag optimistisch ausklingen lassen. | Lassen Sie mich zum Schluss noch etwas Optimistisches sagen.)

* **In conclusion let me quote the doyen of marketing theory, Professor Kotler.**
(in conclusion – zum Abschluss / quote – zitieren / doyen – Doyen)

THANKING SPEAKER, INITIATING DISCUSSION, CLOSING CONFERENCE OR SESSION

Dank an die/den Vortragende/n, Eröffnung der Diskussion, Abschluss der Konferenz oder Sitzung

* **I'm sure I'm speaking for everyone when I say how grateful we are to Dr. Miller for his extremely interesting lecture.**
(grateful – dankbar / extremely – äußerst / lecture – Vortrag)

* **I'd like to thank Mr. Fallow for his thoroughly provoking paper.**
(thoroughly provoking – äußerst anregend / paper – Referat)

* **Are there any questions for the Speaker?**
(question – Frage / speaker – Redner)

* **Yes, the gentleman at the far end of the room. Would you identify yourself, please?**
(at the far end – ganz hinten / … . Würden Sie uns bitte Ihren Namen sagen?)

* **Mr. Fallow, would you like to answer this point?**
(point – Einwurf, Frage)

* **Could the paper also be made available in German?**
(make available – zur Verfügung stellen)

* **I now declare this meeting closed. We'll meet again in the plenary session here at 17.00 hours.**
(Ich erkläre nun die Sitzung für beendet. … . / plenary session – Plenarsitzung / 17.00 hours – seventeenhundred hours)

GENERAL PRESENTATIONS (INCLUDING QUANTITATIVE STATEMENTS AND DIAGRAMS)

**Allgemeine Präsentationen
(unter besonderer Berücksichtigung von quantitativen Aussagen und Diagrammen)**

(see also "Meetings" and "Conferences")

INTRODUCTIONS

Einleitende Worte

SIGNALLING THE START

Beginn der Präsentation

* **May I have your attention, please, ladies and gentlemen?**
(attention – Aufmerksamkeit)

* **Right then, ladies and gentlemen, shall we begin?**

* **Right. Is everyone ready?**

* **OK. Can we start, gentlemen?**

* **Right then. Let's get down to business, shall we?**

* **OK everybody, let's get started.**

* **Let's get started, shall we?**

* **Let's begin, shall we?**

* **Are we ready to begin?**

PRESENTING ONESELF

Referent/in stellt sich vor

* **I'd like to introduce myself. My name is Jane Baxter and I am from the Goldman-Capel Consultancy.**
(introduce – vorstellen / consultancy – Beratung[-sfirma])

* **May I introduce myself: I'm Gary Brown, Production Manager of Electrovans PLC, London.**

* **Hello, let me introduce myself. My name is Tom Redford and I'm Head of Personnel here.**
(head – Leiter / Personnel – Personal[-abteilung])

* **Right, ladies and gentlemen, I should like to introduce myself. I'm Susan Brannigan from General Motors Detroit. I'm in charge of the Truck Division.**
(in charge of – verantwortlich für; zuständig für / truck – LKW / division – Sparte, Geschäftsbereich)

* **Good morning. For those of you who don't already know me, I'm James Colby from Marketing.**

* **Ladies and gentlemen, please allow me to introduce myself. My name is Linda Carter, Advertising Manager for Clyde Petroleum.**

SETTING THE SCENE

Beschreibung der Rahmenbedingungen

* **Good morning, I have been commissioned by your President to analyse the purchasing activities of your company and to make some constructive suggestions on how to streamline procurement.**
  (commission – beauftragen / president – Generaldirektor, Vorstandsvorsitzender / purchasing – Einkauf, Beschaffung / suggestion – Vorschlag / streamline – rationalisieren, effizienter machen / procurement – Beschaffung)

* **In case anyone present does not know, I was asked two months ago to outline Marketing's views on our planned move into the East European markets.**
  (outline – kurz darlegen / view – Ansicht / move – Schritt, Eintritt)

* **Briefly, our company's initial successes with the new line of phosphate-free detergents have not been sustained this year.**
  (brief – kurz / initial – anfänglich / success – Erfolg / line – [Produkt-]Linie, Artikelgruppe / detergent – Waschmittel / be sustained – anhalten)

* **Ladies and gentlemen, as you may know, our company is in a difficult position. To put it simply, if we don't cut costs, profits will continue to fall.**
  (to put it simply – einfach gesagt / cut – senken)

* **The euro has declined, exports have gone up and imports have gone down. To put it briefly, the Balance of Trade – latterly also called the *Goods Account* – has improved considerably.**
  (decline – fallen, sinken / to put it briefly – kurz gesagt / balance of trade – Handelsbilanz, Warenverkehrsbilanz / latterly – jüngst; in letzter Zeit / call – bezeichnen / improve – sich verbessern / considerable – beträchtlich)

* **Well, the situation is like this: in spite of a rise in sales, profits have dropped sharply.**
(in spite of – trotz / rise in sales – Umsatzsteigerung / drop – fallen / sharp – stark, dramatisch)

EXPRESSING PURPOSE

Zweck der Präsentation

* **I'm here today to report on new developments in the American market.**
(report on – Bericht erstatten über / development – Entwicklung)

* **Ladies and gentlemen, as you all know, R&D have completed their work on the new speed control. The question now is how to exploit this invention. It will be my task to present a number of options.**
(R&D – Research & Development [Department] | Forschung[-s] und Entwicklung[-sabteilung] / speed control – Geschwindigkeitsregler / exploit – [wirtschaftlich] verwerten / invention – Erfindung / task – Aufgabe / number – Reihe, Anzahl)

* **What I want to do today is report our findings and help you formulate an appropriate strategy.**
(findings – [Untersuchungs-]Ergebnisse / appropriate – geeignet, passend, zielführend)

* **The purpose of this presentation is to analyse our countertrade activities.**
(countertrade – Gegengeschäfte)

* **My objective this morning is to demonstrate and explain our new range of copiers.**
(objective – Ziel, Aufgabe / demonstrate – vorführen / explain – erklären / range – Palette, Sortiment)

* **The main reason I am here today is to introduce our latest product.**

DESCRIBING THE STRUCTURE

Aufbau der Präsentation

* **First I'd like to outline the present situation, then I'm going to present the alternatives open to us, and finally I shall be recommending which of these alternatives we should take.**
  (outline – skizzieren; kurz darstellen / recommend – empfehlen)

* **First I'd like to discuss various environmental impacts on tourism and tourists, second I'm going to examine the positive and negative impact of tourism on the natural environment, and finally I shall be offering some practical suggestions on how to minimise any unfavourable effects.**
  (impact – Auswirkung / examine – analysieren / natural environment – Umwelt / offer – machen / suggestion – Vorschlag / unfavourable – negativ, ungünstig)

* **To start with, I'd like to look at the history of my company, secondly I want to review the current situation, after that I shall focus on our competitors, and finally I shall be considering the future.**
  (to start with – zuerst / history – Geschichte / review sthg. – einen Überblick über etwas geben / current – aktuell, gegenwärtig / competitor – Konkurrent / consider – betrachten)

* **I'd like to begin by giving you a brief outline of my presentation. Firstly I want to examine the nature of job stress and burn-out and explain how the structure of the organisation and attributes of the job contribute to or ameliorate stress. Next I'm going to identify and analyse in detail the many forces and factors that cause job stress, such as downsizing, reorganisation and changing technology. And finally I will present some models for job stress intervention at both the individual level and the organisational and policy levels.**
  (brief – kurz / outline – Überblick / burn-out – Burnout[syndrom]; psychische Erschöpfung / attribute – Merkmal, Eigenschaft / contribute – beitragen / ameliorate – verbessern; günstig beeinflussen / force – Einfluss / downsizing – Gesundschrumpfen, Personalreduzierung, Downsizing / intervention – Eingriff, Lenkungsmaßnahme / level – Ebene)

* **Let me begin with a summary of the major points I shall be considering. Firstly, I want to explore the pricing of pharmaceutical products in domestic and international markets. Secondly, I'm going to deal with the forces affecting competition in world markets. Thirdly, I will show how competition affects risks in research and development. And fourthly, I will describe the ways in which cost-effective research and information are used to promote pharmaceuticals.**
(summary – Zusammenfassung / major – wichtigst, Haupt- / pricing – Preisbildung / domestic – heimisch / deal with – sich befassen mit / force – Einfluss / affect – beeinflussen; einwirken auf / competition – Konkurrenz, Wettbewerb / research and development – Forschung und Entwicklung / promote – [Absatz] fördern)

INTRODUCING A TOPIC

Einführung eines Themas

NAMING THE TOPIC

Benennung des Themas

* **In the course of the next 30 minutes I shall be analysing some of the new financial derivatives.**
(course – Verlauf / financial derivatives – Finanzderivative; derivative Finanzinstrumente)

* **Ladies and gentlemen, as you've already heard, I'll be talking about Strategic Total Quality Management.**

* **The major problem I want to discuss is the high staff turnover in the Accounts Department.**
(staff turnover – Mitarbeiterfluktuation / Accounts Department – Buchhaltungsabteilung; Abteilung Rechnungswesen)

* **Unfortunately it is my sad duty to announce the closure of one of our plants.**
(Leider ist es meine traurige Pflicht, Sie über die [bevorstehende] Schließung eines unserer Werke zu informieren.)

* **Ladies and gentlemen, I am pleased to be able to report another successful year for Amstrad plc. I am proud to say that we have managed to increase profits in spite of the downturn in the economy as a whole.**
(successful – erfolgreich / proud – stolz / manage – es schaffen / increase – erhöhen / in spite of – trotz / downturn in the economy as a whole – Konjunkturabschwung)

* **I'm going to present my case for raising the funds from a syndicate of major banks rather than from our shareholders.**
(case – Argumente / raise funds – Mittel aufbringen / syndicate – Konsortium / major bank – Großbank / shareholder – Aktionär)

* **My company has just introduced a new range of application programs for materials handling. I'd like to show you what the new programs can do for you.**
(range – Palette / application program – Anwendungsprogramm / materials handling – innerbetrieblicher Transport)

* **If you agree, it is my intention to look at the main organizational risk factors responsible for job stress.**
(if you agree – mit Ihrer Zustimmung / intention – Absicht / responsible – verantwortlich)

* **I'd like to examine the nature and purposes of the different types of part-time employment.**
(purpose – Zweck / part-time employment – Teilzeitbeschäftigung)

* **I shall go over the results of our cost-cutting drive.**
(go over – durchgehen, besprechen / cut – senken, reduzieren / drive – Aktion, Programm)

* **Let me explain how automation can assist you in reducing costs and improving efficiency.**
  (assist in – beitragen zu / improve – verbessern)

* **The subject of my presentation is "Business Ethics".**
  (subject – Thema / business ethics – Wirtschaftsethik)

HYPOTHESISING

Diskussion von Annahmen

* **It is interesting to ask oneself what would happen if the strikes continued beyond next week.**
  (continue – sich fortsetzen / beyond X – über X hinaus)

* **Suppose we lowered our prices by 20 per cent all round. What would that do for our market share?**
  (suppose – nehmen wir einmal an / all round – insgesamt / market share – Marktanteil)

* **For argument's sake, let us assume that the market became saturated in half the time we expect. What would the result be for our projected turnover?**
  (for argument's sake – nur einmal als Hypothese / assume – annehmen / saturated – gesättigt / expect – erwarten / project – prognostizieren / turnover – Umsatz)

* **At this point, one might wonder whether such a situation would have arisen if we had been more aware of what was going on around us.**
  (wonder – sich fragen / arise – entstehen / be aware of sthg. – sich einer Sache bewusst sein)

ASKING RHETORICAL QUESTIONS

Rhetorische Fragen

* **This raises the question of who is responsible for this unfortunate situation.**
  (raise – aufwerfen / responsible – verantwortlich / unfortunate – bedauerlich)

* **It's really a question of whether we attempt to stop the losses in our components plant or move over to outsourcing.**
  (whether – ob / attempt – versuchen / component – [Original-] Bestandteil; Bauteil / plant – Werk / move over to – umsteigen auf / outsourcing – Outsourcing, Auslagerung)

* **The question now foremost in everyone's mind is: where did we go wrong?**
  (be foremost in sbdy.'s mind – sich aufdrängen)

* **The dilemma is: do we ignore the drawbacks of our chosen strategy or do we do our best to prevent them derailing the whole project?**
  (drawback – Nachteil, Schattenseite / chosen – gewählt / prevent – verhindern / derail – zum Entgleisen bringen)

* **The firm finds itself with an accumulated deficit of £4 million. So how did things deteriorate so far without anyone noticing?**
  (deteriorate – sich verschlimmern; sich verschlechtern / notice – bemerken)

SEQUENCING
Ablaufgestaltung

MOVING ON, LOOKING BACK, DIGRESSING
Übergang zum nächsten Punkt, Rückschau, Exkurs

* **If you agree, I should like to move on to my next section.**
(if you agree – wenn es Ihnen Recht ist / move on to – sich zuwenden)

* **I would now like to jump for a moment to my final point.**
(jump to – vorwegnehmen)

* **This brings me to my next point.**

* **This is the overall picture. Let us now consider the details.**
(overall picture – Gesamtbild)

* **Let's look back over the arguments invoked so far.**
(invoke – vorbringen)

* **I'd like to digress here and look at our competitors' performance.**
(digress – sich kurz einem anderen Thema zuwenden / competitor – Konkurrent / performance – Abschneiden, Leistung, Resultat)

* **I'd just like to mention in passing that the market has become more competitive in the last three years.**
(just – nur / mention – erwähnen / in passing – nebenbei / competitive – hart umkämpft; konkurrenzbetont)

* **Let's consider a different perspective on the question: what are the shareholders likely to think of such a reversal of policy?**
(perspective – Aspekt, Sichtweise / shareholder – Aktionär / likely – wahrscheinlich / reversal – Kehrtwendung, Kurswechsel)

* **Let me return to my main argument.**

* **To get back to the previous topic, our firm should be thinking in terms of a drastic overhaul of its production strategy.**
(previous – vorherig, früher / think in terms of sthg. – sich etwas überlegen / overhaul – Revision, Neugestaltung)

* **Right, let me get back to the point I was discussing.**

COMING TO THE POINT

Zur Sache kommen

* **Let me come to the point: because of shrinking cash flow, this company will be bankrupt in one year unless it adopts a more customer-oriented approach.**
(shrink – schrumpfen, sinken / bankrupt – bankrott / adopt – ergreifen / approach – Ansatz, Methode)

* **Ultimately, the crux of the matter is that the bank is unwilling to extend our credit line beyond next week. In addition, it is threatening to have the receivers sent in unless we agree to its suggestions regarding the composition of the Board.**
(ultimately – letztlich / crux – entscheidender Punkt / extend – [weiter] aufrechterhalten / beyond sthg. – über etwas hinaus / threaten – drohen / receiver – Konkursverwalter / unless – wenn nicht / suggestion – Vorschlag / regarding – betreffend / composition – Zusammensetzung / board – Verwaltungsrat)

* **What I am getting at is this: there is no evidence that our competitors are doing any better than we are.**
(Worauf ich hinauswill … . / evidence – Beweis[-e])

* **The upshot of all this is that we shall have to be more careful about our image in future.**
(upshot – Fazit)

∗ **Putting it in a nutshell, the firm faces bankruptcy unless it can find a way to cut costs dramatically within the next six months.**
(Um es kurz zu sagen, … . / face sthg. – sich mit etwas konfrontiert sehen / bankruptcy – Konkurs, Ausgleich, Bankrott / unless – wenn nicht / cut – senken)

(See also section DESCRIBING THE STRUCTURE above)

MAKING RECOMMENDATIONS / STATING TARGETS

(Empfehlungen / Zielvorgaben)

∗ **Our first major recommendation is that you should seriously consider moving production to a low-wage country. Alternatively, you should investigate ways of reducing wage and other costs so as to achieve a reasonable level of competitiveness before the end of next quarter.**
(major recommendation – wichtige Empfehlung / serious – ernsthaft / consider – in Erwägung ziehen / move – verlegen / low-wage country – Niedriglohnland / investigate – untersuchen / achieve – erreichen, erzielen / reasonable – angemessen / competitiveness – Wettbewerbsfähigkeit / quarter – Quartal)

∗ **We would recommend you to envisage a rights issue as a matter of urgency.**
(envisage – ins Auge fassen / rights issue – Emission von jungen Aktien [auf Bezugsrechtsbasis] / urgency – Dringlichkeit, Vorrang)

∗ **I strongly urge you to react to this challenge to your market position before your situation becomes too undermined by your main competitors' aggressive marketing strategy.**
(urge – drängen / react to – reagieren auf / challenge – Angriff / undermine – unterminieren)

∗ **We are convinced that the correct policy is to play a waiting game for now. Moreover, we can eliminate the other proposed strategies as too expensive to be implemented unless the situation is really critical.**
(convinced – überzeugt / play a waiting game – abwarten / for now – fürs Erste einmal / moreover – überdies / propose – vorschlagen / expensive – kostspielig, teuer / implement – implementieren, umsetzen, verwirklichen / unless – wenn nicht)

* **We think you should try to raise commitment levels among all sections of the workforce, otherwise the outlook is bleak.**
(raise commitment levels – Engagement verstärken; Einsatz erhöhen / workforce – Belegschaft / outlook – Aussichten / bleak – düster)

* **Clearly you ought to be taking a longer-term perspective on this question, as short-term fixes will only put off the day of reckoning while making no real contribution to a solution of the problem.**
(ought to – sollten / longer-term – längerfristig / fix – Lösung / put off – hinausschieben / day of reckoning – Tag der Abrechnung, „Zahltag" / contribution – Beitrag)

——— ❖ ———

* **One major long-term target that we simply have to achieve is to raise the profit margins on all our product lines by at least 30 per cent.**
(target – Ziel, Vorgabe / profit margin – Gewinnspanne, Umsatzrentabilität / product line – Produktlinie, Artikelgruppe)

* **The firm's first priority must be to ensure that Return on Investment quickly reaches a satisfactory figure.**
(ensure – sicherstellen / Return on Investment – [Gesamt-]Kapitalrentabilität / satisfactory – zufrieden stellend / figure – Höhe, Prozentsatz)

* **Our main objective should be to achieve 12 per cent compound growth of profits over the next five years.**
(objective – Ziel / achieve – erzielen, erreichen / compound growth – kumulative Steigerung)

* **It is essential that we either acquire the patents or negotiate a licensing agreement that covers the next ten years.**
(essential – wesentlich, entscheidend / acquire – erwerben / negotiate – aushandeln / licensing agreement that covers the next ten years – Lizenzvertrag für die nächsten zehn Jahre)

* **The company must do its damnedest to get back into the black. What's more, it must at the same time be careful not to cut back on spending for future growth.**
(Die Gesellschaft muss alles nur Erdenkliche unternehmen … . / black – Gewinnzone / cut back on sthg. – etwas kürzen / spending – Ausgaben)

SUMMING UP AND CONCLUDING

Zusammenfassung und Schlussbemerkungen

* **I should like to recapitulate my main points.**
(recapitulate – zusammenfassen, rekapitulieren)

* **At this point, I should like to summarise my recommendations.**
(summarise – zusammenfassen)

* **Let me now draw the various threads of my argument together.**
(draw together – zusammenführen / thread – [Argumentations-]Linie)

* **With hindsight, one can see that these developments form part of a pattern of degenerating communications between management and the workforce that has been gradually taking place over the last three years.**
(with hindsight – im Nachhinein / development – Entwicklung / pattern – Muster, Struktur / degenerate – immer schlechter werden / workforce – Belegschaft / gradual – schrittweise)

* **Summing up, there are four main reasons why we find ourselves in this mess.**
(mess – Patsche; schwierige Lage)

* **To recap, then, we have examined three alternative strategies. Since we rule out the first as too expensive and reject the second as unrealistic, that leaves the third as the only possible way out of this crisis.**
(recap – rekapitulieren, wiederholen / rule out – ausschließen; nicht in Betracht ziehen / reject – ausscheiden, ablehnen)

——— ❖ ———

* **This brings me to the final part of my presentation here this morning.**

* **Let me end by saying that it has been a pleasure to be asked to speak to you today and I should be very happy to answer any questions you may have.**

* **Finally, may I just underline that the results of our deliberations are strictly confidential.**
(underline – betonen, unterstreichen / deliberations – Überlegungen / strictly confidential – streng vertraulich)

* **In conclusion, I would just like to stress that analysis is an important step, but what really counts is action. In other words, we have to tackle the underlying problems and do so quickly.**
(in conclusion – zum Abschluss / stress – betonen / step – Schritt / count – zählen / tackle – in Angriff nehmen)

* **Finally, I'd just like to say that the future looks bright provided we really apply ourselves to resolving our current problems.**
(bright – freundlich, hell / provided – vorausgesetzt / apply oneself to – sich anstrengen / resolve – lösen / current – derzeitig)

* **Thank you for your attention. Are there any questions?**
(attention – Aufmerksamkeit)

* **Well, that's all I have to say for now. Thank you.**

OTHER USEFUL FUNCTIONS AND THEIR EXPONENTS

Weitere nützliche kommunikative Funktionen und ihre sprachlichen Ausprägungen

DIRECTING ATTENTION

Aufmerksamkeitslenkung

* **May I call your attention to page nine of our Annual Report.**
(call – lenken / attention – Aufmerksamkeit / Annual Report – Jahresbericht)

* **It will not have escaped your notice that we now recycle close to 50 per cent of the solid waste generated in our plants.**
(escape – entgehen / notice – Aufmerksamkeit / close to – knapp unter / solid waste – feste Abfallstoffe / be generated – anfallen / plant – Werk, Anlage)

* **If you refer to the bar chart on page six of the hand-out, you will see that we are no longer number one in our industry in terms of operating margins.**
(refer to – anschauen / bar chart – Säulen-, Balkendiagramm / hand-out – Unterlage, Tischvorlage / industry – Branche, Wirtschaftszweig / in terms of – hinsichtlich; was betrifft / operating margin – Umsatzrendite auf der Basis des Betriebsergebnisses; Betriebsmarge)

* **If you compare the blue segments in the two pie charts, you will immediately see that the share of services in total sales has increased.**
(compare – vergleichen / pie chart – Kreisdiagramm / immediately – sofort, gleich / share – Anteil / services – Dienstleistungen / total sales – Gesamtumsatz / increase – sich erhöhen)

* **If you look at column four in the table, you will see quite clearly that foreign direct investment has gone up considerably in the past few years.**
(column – Spalte / table – Tabelle / quite clearly – ganz eindeutig / foreign direct investment – ausländische Direktinvestitionen / considerable – beträchtlich)

* **As you can see from the figures on the flip chart, it cost us €15 million to meet the stricter emission standards. But we developed most of the equipment in-house and this has given us a lead in filter technology.**
(figure – Zahl / meet – einhalten / strict – streng / develop – entwickeln / equipment – Geräte / in-house – firmenintern / lead – Vorsprung)

* **If we look at GNP, we can see that Austria has had a higher growth rate than most other OECD countries, of course with the exception of the United States.**
(GNP – gross national product | Bruttosozialprodukt / growth rate – Wachstumsrate / OECD – Organization for Economic Cooperation and Development / exception – Ausnahme)

* **You will note that, as far as sales are concerned, the situation has improved.**
(note – bemerken, feststellen / as far as X is concerned – was X betrifft / sales – [wertmäßiger] Umsatz / improve – sich verbessern)

* **As we can see, the fall in profits was caused by high labour costs.**
(cause – verursachen / labour costs – Arbeitskosten)

* **As you see, our market share has been falling, whereas ATB's has been rising rapidly.**
(market share – Marktanteil / rise – steigen; sich erhöhen)

* **As you will notice, the drop in revenue was the result of new competition.**
(notice – feststellen, bemerken / drop – Rückgang / revenue – [Umsatz-]Erlöse / competition – Konkurrenz)

EXPRESSING OPINIONS

Meinungsäußerungen

* **It is our firm conviction that the audit will show our books to be in order.**
(firm – fest / conviction – Überzeugung / audit – [Buch-]Prüfung)

* **We believe that the market has peaked and that a shakeout will ensue rapidly.**
(believe – der Meinung sein / peak – den Höhepunkt überschreiten / shakeout – Rezession, Ausleseprozess, Konsolidierungsprozess / shakeout ensues – Rezession stellt sich ein; es kommt zu einer Rezession)

* **One might incline to the view that this strategy was misplaced, since the resultant increase in turnover was negligible.**
(incline to – sich zugeneigt fühlen / view – Ansicht / misplaced – fehl am Platz; ungeeignet / resultant – sich daraus ergebend / increase in turnover – Umsatzsteigerung / negligible – vernachlässigbar)

* **It is difficult to avoid the conclusion that we should abandon this market segment.**
(avoid – vermeiden; sich entziehen / conclusion – Schlussfolgerung / abandon – aufgeben)

* **It seems to me that this phenomenon is duc to factors beyond the company's control.**
(seem – scheinen / due to – zurückzuführen auf / beyond the company's control – außerhalb der Einflusssphäre der Gesellschaft)

* **In my opinion, the price ought to be increased at least in line with inflation.**
(opinion – Meinung / ought to – sollte / at least – zumindest / in line with inflation – im Ausmaß der Inflationsrate)

* **We think that no dividend should be paid this year.**

FORECASTING

Präsentation von Prognosen

* **Our forecasts show that the idea of capturing waste heat will cut our fuel bill by more than 40 per cent.**
(forecast – Prognose / capture – nutzen / waste heat – Abwärme / cut – senken / fuel bill – Heiz- und Treibstoffkosten)

* **We are confident that we will reach break-even point before 2010.**
(confident – absolut sicher / break-even point – Break-Even-Punkt, Gewinnschwelle)

* **My projection is that the show will attract over 5,000 trade visitors.**
(projection – Prognose / attract – anlocken / trade visitor – Firmenkunde)

* **The Munich-based Ifo economic research institute forecasts that the recession in the building industry will reach Germany next year.**
(Munich-based – mit Sitz in München / building industry – Baubranche)

* **Receipts from tourism are forecast to drop by approximately 5 per cent next year.**
(receipts – Einnahmen / forecast – prognostizieren / drop – zurückgehen / approximately – annähernd)

* **It is forecast that the budget deficit will exceed the 50-billion mark.**
(exceed – übersteigen / billion – Milliarde / mark – Grenze)

* **Experts forecast a dramatic increase in international business crime in the next five years.**
(business crime – Wirtschaftskriminalität)

* **The aggregate current account deficit of LDCs is expected to be around 60 billion dollars this year.**
(aggregate – aggregiert, Gesamt- / current account – Leistungsbilanz; Bilanz der laufenden Posten / LDCs – least developed countries | die ärmsten Entwicklungsländer / expect – erwarten / around – ungefähr)

* **It is expected that exports, already up from 6 to 10 million euros, will continue to rise.**
(Man erwartet, dass die Exporte, die schon von 6 auf 10 Millionen Euro gestiegen sind, weiterhin steigen werden.)

* **I expect that our sales will flatten out next year.**
(sales – Umsatz / flatten out – sich abflachen)

* **Economists expect a decline in industrial production, exports and personal consumption.**
(economist – Volkswirt / decline – Rückgang)

* **Market analysts predict that M3 will overshoot the central bank target by a whopping 10%.**
(predict – vorhersagen, prognostizieren / M3 – [Geldmengendefinition] M3 / overshoot – überschreiten / target – Ziel[-vorgabe], Vorgabe / whopping – saftig, ganz)

* **Our marketing department anticipates a slight fall in spending on infrastructure projects.**
(anticipate – erwarten, vorhersagen / slight – leicht, geringfügig)

INTERPRETING INFORMATION

Interpretation von Informationen

* **This seems to suggest that the survey was skewed somehow.**
(seem – scheinen / suggest – [Vermutung] nahe legen / survey – Erhebung, Studie / skewed – verzerrt)

* **These figures could be interpreted as proving that the public is not concerned about the environmental impact of fossil fuels.**
(figures – Zahlen / prove – beweisen, nachweisen / public – Öffentlichkeit / be concerned – beunruhigt sein / environmental impact – Auswirkung auf die Umwelt / fuel – Brenn-, Treibstoff)

* **It would seem, from the information we have received, that other companies operating in the services sector are encountering similar difficulties.**
(receive – erhalten / services sector – Dienstleistungssektor / encounter sthg. – sich mit etwas konfrontiert sehen)

* **The figures for last year show that, while overall demand for consumer goods declined by three per cent, the electronics sector expanded rapidly.**
(overall demand – Gesamtnachfrage / decline – zurückgehen)

* **Our results indicate that there is a clear market niche for designer hi-fi equipment. Moreover, it is clear that a considerable price premium can be realistically expected by those first in the market.**
(indicate – zeigen / moreover – außerdem / considerable – beträchtlich / price premium – Höherpreis, Preisaufschlag)

* **It is obvious from the figures that the money we spent on R&D last year has paid off handsomely.**
(obvious – offenkundig, evident / R&D – Research and Development | Forschung und Entwicklung / pay off handsomely – sich ordentlich rentieren)

INTRODUCING EVIDENCE/DIAGRAMS

Präsentation von Beweismaterial/Diagrammen

* **I'd like to support my findings by a number of charts.**
(support – stützen / finding – Ergebnis / number – Anzahl, Reihe / chart – Diagramm)

* **I'd like to begin by analysing the chart on page six of the hand-out.**
(page – Seite / hand-out – [verteilte] Broschüre, Mappe)

* **Let me show you two charts to highlight some of the points I've made.**
(highlight – herausstreichen / make point – Aussage machen; Feststellung treffen)

* **Here's a diagram illustrating what I've just said.**
(just – gerade)

* **This graph here relates advertising expenditure to sales.**
(graph – Graph, Linie, Graphik / relate – in Beziehung setzen / advertising expenditure – Werbeausgaben, -aufwand / sales – Umsatz)

* **In the first chart here, annual sales from 1995 to 2005 are shown as bars.**
(annual sales – Jahresumsatz / show – darstellen / bar – Balken, Säule)

* **Let's move on to the next table, which compares the contribution margins of different product groups.**
(move on to – weitergehen zu / table – Tabelle / compare – vergleichen / contribution margin – Deckungsbeitrag / different – verschieden)

* **I'd like you to look at this pie chart.**
(pie chart – Kreisdiagramm, Tortendiagramm)

* **Let's have a look at this PowerPoint slide.**

* **Just look at this matrix.**
(Schauen Sie sich nur einmal diese Matrix an.)

* **Have a look at the flip chart.**

* **If you look at this diagram, you will see that profits rose to 15 million dollars in 2007.**

PRESENTING CALCULATIONS

Präsentation von Berechnungen

* **Our calculations show that our competitors are clearly practising price dumping in the hope of squeezing us out of the market.**
(competitor – Konkurrent, Mitbewerber / clear – eindeutig / squeeze out of the market – aus dem Markt verdrängen)

* **My figures so far indicate that we are on course to achieving our output targets for the current year.**
(figures – Zahlen / indicate – zeigen / be on course – [gut] unterwegs sein / achieve – erreichen / target – Ziel[-vorgabe] / current – laufend)

* **Our latest estimates suggest that a recovery in consumer demand has already started.**
(estimate – Schätzung / suggest – vermuten lassen / recovery – Aufschwung, Erholung / demand – Nachfrage)

* **I calculate that we should reach break-even point within six months of starting production.**
(I calculate that – meinen Berechnungen nach / break-even point – Break-Even-Punkt, Gewinnschwelle)

QUANTITATIVE STATEMENTS AND DIAGRAMS

Quantitative Aussagen und Diagramme

INTRODUCING DIAGRAMS

(See INTRODUCING EVIDENCE/DIAGRAMS above)

BREAKDOWNS AND PERCENTAGE SHARES

Aufgliederungen und Prozentanteile

* **This is a breakdown of our exports by country of destination, and this is an analysis according to commodity.**
  (breakdown – Aufschlüsselung, Aufgliederung / by – nach / country of destination – Bestimmungsland / analysis – Aufgliederung, Aufschlüsselung / according to – nach / commodity – Ware)

* **As you can see, the share of exports in total sales has declined.**
  (share of exports in total sales – Exportquote / decline – fallen, sinken)

* **The pie chart top left shows that exports account for just under fourteen per cent of total sales.**
  (Das Kreisdiagramm oben links zeigt, dass nur knapp 14% des Gesamtumsatzes auf Exporte entfallen. / …, dass Exporte nur knapp 14% des Gesamtumsatzes ausmachen.)

DESCRIBING THE BEHAVIOUR OF VARIABLES

Beschreibung des Verhaltens von Variablen

* **The broken line shows that exports of big-ticket items have been increasing since 2001.**
  (broken line – strichlierte Linie / big-ticket item – Hochpreisartikel / have been increasing since – steigen seit)

* **Now let's turn to page six of the booklet, where you can find a time series showing the development of the market shares of our competitors. Brior Corp.'s increased by all of 15 per cent.**
(turn to – sich zuwenden / booklet – Broschüre / time series – [statistische] Zeitreihe / development – Entwicklung / market share – Marktanteil / competitor – Konkurrent / Corp. – corporation [US] | [etwa] Kapitalgesellschaft, Aktiengesellschaft / by all of 15 per cent – um ganze 15%)

* **The figures speak for themselves. Sales 30 per cent down on the year and pre-tax profits up 15 per cent.**
(figure – Zahl, Ergebnis / … . Der Umsatz ist gegenüber dem Vorjahr um 30% gefallen und der Gewinn vor Steuern um 15% gestiegen.)

* **As you can see, in early 2007 sales recovered.**
(in early 2007 – Anfang 2007 / recover – sich erholen)

* **Surprisingly, our exports soared in the middle of a world recession, as you can see from the time series on page five.**
(surprisingly – überraschenderweise / soar – stark steigen)

* **Now let's look at the red column in the table. This represents sales of large units. Not very encouraging, is it? They fell by more than ten per cent in both 2003 and 2004.**
(column – Spalte / table – Tabelle / unit – Gerät / encouraging – ermutigend / is it? – oder? / both … and … – sowohl … als auch …)

* **At the beginning of 2008, we experienced a drastic fall in profits, as you can see from the dip in the line here.**
(experience – erleben / dip – [kurzes] Absacken)

* **The share price dropped suddenly in the middle of 2006. It picked up slightly in the third quarter, but since then has fallen gently.**
(share price – Aktienkurs / drop – fallen / suddenly – plötzlich / pick up – sich erholen / slightly – geringfügig, etwas / quarter – Quartal / gently – leicht)

* **In 2007, interest income plummeted, dropping by no less than 76 per cent. That's on page four.**
(interest income – Zinserträge / plummet – abstürzen / drop – zurückgehen, fallen)

* **Fortunately, sales bottomed out sooner than expected. As you can see, the decline began levelling out as early as June. They hit bottom in September and, as you can see, are now back to their 2004 level and rising.**
(fortunately – glücklicherweise / bottom out – Tiefpunkt erreichen und wieder steigen / expect – erwarten / decline – Rückgang / level out – abflachen; sich verflachen / as early as – schon / hit bottom – Tiefpunkt erreichen / level – Niveau / rise – steigen)

* **Our profits decreased dramatically at the end of 2005. The situation improved in the first half of 2006, and after this they rose steadily until the final quarter of last year.**
(decrease – fallen / improve – sich verbessern / steady – stetig, kontinuierlich)

* **The dividend has remained unchanged for the past five years. The development of dividends is shown on the last page of the booklet.**
(remain unchanged – unverändert bleiben / development – Entwicklung / page – Seite / booklet – Broschüre)

* **The depreciation charge has been fairly constant in the past few years. You can see the line's almost level.**
(depreciation charge – Abschreibungsaufwand / fairly – ziemlich / in the past few years – in den letzten paar Jahren / level – eben)

* **Sales have been flat in the past two years.**
(be flat – stagnieren)

* **Our projection is that provisions will peak out next year.**
(projection – Prognose / provision – Rückstellung, Wertberichtigung / peak out – Höhepunkt überschreiten)

* **Inexplicably, there was a bulge in orders in early May. That's the fifth bar in the chart.**
(inexplicably – unerklärlicherweise / bulge – plötzliche starke Ausweitung / order – Auftrag / fifth – fünft / bar – Säule, Balken / chart – Diagramm)

DESCRIBING RANKINGS
Beschreibung von Rangordnungen

* **With regard to sales, they have ranked first for the past five years.**
(with regard to sales – was den Umsatz betrifft / rank first – an erster Stelle rangieren)

* **The next graph shows that our company has fallen back to third place in terms of output.**
(graph – Graph, Graphik / in terms of – gemessen an; hinsichtlich)

* **The ranking on page five is very interesting. It shows that Boots PLC has moved up to fourth place, overtaking both us and our main competitor in the European market.**
(ranking – Rangordnung / move up to – vorstoßen auf / overtake – überholen / main competitor – Hauptkonkurrent)

* **From the next chart it is quite clear that ATB will continue to head the list by a wide margin.**
(quite – ganz / continue to head the list – weiterhin an erster Stelle liegen / by a wide margin – mit großem Abstand)

* **The following table is a projection for the next five years – and it raises an interesting point: although the division is expected to continue to rank first in terms of sales, it will no longer be number one in cash flow.**
(projection – Prognose / raise point – Frage aufwerfen / although – obwohl / division – Sparte, Geschäftsbereich / expect – erwarten / continue to rank first – weiterhin an erster Stelle rangieren)

MISCELLANEOUS
Sonstiges

* **On the vertical axis you can see the total amount of capital employed. The horizontal axis measures the return, i.e. profits plus financing costs expressed as a percentage of total capital employed.**
(amount – Betrag, Summe / capital employed – eingesetztes [Gesamt-]Kapital / measure – messen / return – Rentabilität / i.e. – that is / express – ausdrücken / percentage – Prozentsatz)

* **I've plotted the inventory levels in a diagram to emphasise my argument.**
(plot in a diagram – in ein Diagramm eintragen / inventory level – Höhe [oder Wert] des Lagerbestandes / emphasise – unterstreichen, betonen)

* **The vertical axis represents the share price. The horizontal axis shows time.**
(share price – Aktienkurs)

* **From year five on, the curve slopes steeply upwards.**
(slope steeply upwards – sich steil nach oben neigen)

* **The interesting point about the curve is its slope. It's very steep in periods one to five but then begins to level off and goes into a gentle decline after period ten.**
(slope – Neigung, Steigung / level off – sich abflachen / go – übergehen / gentle decline – sanfter Rückgang)

* **As you can see from the broken line, in period two (1995 to 2005) overheads settled down at around 13 per cent of sales.**
(broken line – strichlierte Linie / overheads – Gemeinkosten / settle down – sich einpendeln / around – rund)

* **The dotted line stands for sales, the solid line for operating expenses.**
(dotted line – punktierte Linie / solid line – durchgezogene Linie / operating expenses – betrieblicher Aufwand)

* **The hatched area between the two curves requires further explanation.**
(hatched – schraffiert / require – erfordern / further – weiter / explanation – Erklärung)

* **What does the shaded segment stand for?**
(shaded – getönt, dunkel)

* **Now look here, where the two lines intersect. This is the point where the joint venture begins to show a better return on investment than the licensing strategy.**
(intersect – sich schneiden / return on investment – [Gesamt]Kapitalrentabilität)

* **Now, let's take a closer look at the topmost ray emanating from the origin. It represents production process A.**
(take a closer look at sthg. – sich etwas genauer anschauen / topmost – oberst / ray – Strahl / emanate – ausgehen / origin – Ursprung)

* **Let's examine the price index on page three and the volume indices on page five in greater detail.**
(examine in greater detail – näher betrachten / volume index – Mengenindex)

* **Very briefly, the matrix here shows the performance of our products in terms of market growth (on the vertical axis) and relative market share (on the horizontal axis).**
(brief – kurz / performance – Abschneiden, Leistung / growth – Wachstum / market share – Marktanteil)

* **The power drills are down here in the cash cow quadrant. But here in the top right-hand quadrant, we have our lawnmowers with a negligible share of a rapidly expanding market segment.**
(power drill – Bohrmaschine / cash cow – Cashcow, Melkkuh / top right-hand – rechts oben / lawnmower – Rasenmäher / negligible – geringfügig / share – Anteil)

PRODUCT PRESENTATIONS

Produktpräsentationen

INTRODUCTION

Einleitung

* **Ladies and gentlemen, I'm pleased to present our new range of humidifiers.**
  (be pleased – sich freuen / present – vorstellen, präsentieren / range – Sortiment / humidifier – Luftbefeuchter)

* **Ladies and gentlemen, thank you for giving me the opportunity to present our latest training package for salesmen.**
  (opportunity – Gelegenheit / latest – neuest / training package – Ausbildungsprogramm / salesman – Verkäufer, Reisender)

* **I'm sure you will find our new range of skin care products interesting.**
  (skin care – Hautpflege)

* **I'm Frank Brinner of Goller plc and I'm here today to demonstrate and explain our new range of copiers.**
  (plc – public limited company | [brit.] etwa: Aktiengesellschaft / demonstrate – vorführen / explain – erklären)

* **Ladies and gentlemen, my company has come up with a radically new solution to your filing problems. Let me explain how the new ROMFI-system can assist you in reducing costs and improving efficiency.**
  (come up with sthg. – sich etwas einfallen lassen / solution – Lösung / filing – Ablage, Registratur / assist – helfen / improve – verbessern)

* **My company has just introduced a new range of application programs for materials handling. I'd like to show you what the new programs can do for you.**
(introduce – einführen / application program – Anwendungsprogramm / materials handling – innerbetrieblicher Transport)

* **You might be wondering what something called "Ideofix" and produced by a chemical company could have to offer to a financial service company.**
(wonder – sich fragen / offer – bieten, anbieten)

MATERIALS AND COMPOSITION

Materialien und Zusammensetzung

* **The casing consists of a new type of bonded material, which is very strong and very light.**
(casing – Gehäuse / consist of – bestehen aus / bonded material – Verbundmaterial)

* **The cream contains only natural ingredients.**
(cream – Creme / contain – enthalten / ingredient – Bestandteil, Inhaltsstoff)

* **None of the ingredients has been tested on animals.**
(Keiner der Inhaltsstoffe ist in Tierversuchen getestet worden.)

* **We use only the best raw materials available.**
(available – erhältlich, verfügbar)

* **It's made of high-quality materials.**

* **The synthetic rubber used in the product is extremely hard-wearing.**
(rubber – Gummi / hard-wearing – strapazierfähig)

* **Our products are all hand-made from fir harvested from sustainably managed forests.**
  (fir – Kiefernholz / harvest – schlägern / sustainably managed – nachhaltig bewirtschaftet / forest – Wald)

PROPERTIES AND QUALITY

Eigenschaften und Qualität

* **It's resistant to abrasion.**
  (resistant to abrasion – abriebfest)

* **The watch is waterproof to a depth of 90 feet.**
  (watch – Uhr / waterproof – wasserdicht / depth – Wassertiefe / foot – Fuß [30,48 cm])

* **The main benefits of the measuring device are its accuracy and speed.**
  (main – Haupt … / benefit – Nutzen / measuring device – Messvorrichtung / accuracy – Genauigkeit / speed – Geschwindigkeit)

* **The "Securior" safe will certainly live up to its name.**
  (Der Securior-Safe hält sicherlich, was sein Name verspricht.)

* **The material will not warp, even if exposed to very high temperatures.**
  (warp – sich werfen / even if – selbst wenn / expose – aussetzen)

* **The cloth irons well.**
  (Das Tuch lässt sich gut bügeln.)

* **The soap is lighter than water and will float.**
  (will float – schwimmt)

* **The product is carefully finished down to the minutest detail.**
  (… bis ins kleinste Detail sorgfältig ausgeführt.)

* **What you will particularly like about the machine is its reliability.**
(particularly – besonders / reliability – Verlässlichkeit)

* **I'd like to draw your attention to the excellent workmanship of our products.**
(draw attention to – Aufmerksamkeit lenken auf / workmanship – Verarbeitung)

* **It's state of the art all the way.**
(Es entspricht in jeder Hinsicht dem neuesten Stand der Technik.)

* **The ink-jet printer is fully compatible with all leading software.**
(ink-jet printer – Tintenstrahldrucker / leading – führend)

* **The computer runs on a new type of long-life battery.**
(run on – betrieben werden mit)

* **The chip will accelerate the performance of practically all popular software packages by up to five times.**
(accelerate – beschleunigen / performance – Leistung / by up to five times – bis um das Fünffache)

* **To demonstrate how confident we are of the quality and reliability the new product carries a three-year warranty.**
(be confident of – fest glauben an / carry sthg. – mit etwas ausgestattet sein / warranty – Garantie)

* **We sell only premium wines.**
(premium – Spitzen …)

* **The machine can be assembled and put into operation in a matter of hours.**
(assemble – zusammenbauen / put into operation – in Betrieb nehmen / in a matter of hours – innerhalb weniger Stunden)

HANDY SIZE AND FLEXIBILITY

Praktische Größe und Flexibilität

* **The machine fits easily into your brief-case.**
  (fit into – hineinpassen in / brief-case – Aktentasche)

* **It can be folded and does not take up much storage space in winter.**
  (fold – zusammenlegen / take up – brauchen / storage space – Raum zum Aufbewahren)

* **The new filing system is very economical of space.**
  (filing system – Ablagesystem / economical of space – raumsparend)

* **The height can be adjusted very easily.**
  (height – Höhe / adjust – verstellen)

* **It adjusts to any height.**
  (Es lässt sich auf jede beliebige Höhe – d. h. stufenlos – einstellen.)

* **The vehicle can be fitted with an additional shock absorber.**
  (vehicle – Fahrzeug / fit – ausstatten / additional – zusätzlich / shock absorber – Stoßdämpfer)

* **The device plugs into any standard wall socket.**
  (Das Gerät kann an jeder normalen Steckdose angesteckt werden.)

* **Our system allows you to link up computer products from different manufacturers.**
  (link up – miteinander verbinden / different – verschieden / manufacturer – Erzeuger, Produzent)

BENEFICIAL ENVIRONMENTAL CONSEQUENCES

Positive ökologische Auswirkungen

* **The device could reduce your electricity bill by as much as 15 per cent.**
(electricity bill – Stromrechnung / by as much as 15% – um ganze 15%)

* **Another advantage is that the container can easily be recycled.**
(advantage – Vorteil / container – Behälter, Verpackung)

* **The product is environmentally benign.**
(Das Produkt ist umweltfreundlich.)

* **The standard model is fitted with a catalytic converter.**
(be fitted with – ausgestattet sein mit / catalytic converter – Katalysator)

* **A special filter reduces emissions to below the mandatory standard.**
(mandatory – gesetzlich vorgeschrieben / standard – Grenzwert)

* **The plastic used in the bag is biodegradable.**
(biodegradable – biologisch abbaubar)

CUSTOMER ACCEPTANCE

Kundenakzeptanz

* **The new lotion will go down well with your younger customers.**
(lotion – Gesichtswasser / go down well with – gut ankommen bei / customer – Kunde)

* **Test-marketing has shown that the new drink is very popular with teenagers.**

* **Your customers will love it.**

* **I'm sure it will find a ready market.**
  (… wird sich gut verkaufen.)

* **The new brand has established itself in the market in an incredibly short time.**
  (brand – Marke, Markenartikel / establish oneself – sich etablieren / incredible – unglaublich)

* **Our newly developed sprinkler sells very well in Germany and Austria.**
  (develop – entwickeln / sprinkler – Sprinkler, Rasensprenger / sell – sich verkaufen)

* **Although it has been on the market for only three months, the glue has built a strong franchise.**
  (although – obwohl / glue – Klebstoff / build franchise – Gefolgschaft aufbauen; Kundenakzeptanz erreichen)

* **The article will help you to build volume.**
  (build volume – Absatzmenge steigern; Umsatzvolumen ausbauen)

* **The new stylus will satisfy even your most discriminating customers.**
  (stylus – Abspielnadel / satisfy – zufriedenstellen / even – selbst / discriminating – kritisch, wählerisch)

PRICE AND PERFORMANCE

Preis und Leistung

* **The product is excellent value for money.**
  (Das Produkt ist äußerst preiswert.)

* **It is not very expensive.**
  (expensive – teuer)

* **You won't find a better product at this price.**
(won't – will not)

* **And don't forget the low price.**

* **The two new cameras are very reasonably priced.**
(be reasonably priced – einen vernünftigen Preis haben)

* **It has an excellent price-performance ratio.**
(performance – Leistung / ratio – Verhältnis)

PACKING
Verpackung

* **The opener comes in a superbly finished leather-case.**
(opener – Flaschenöffner / come – geliefert werden / finish – ausführen / leather-case – Lederetui)

* **It's supplied in a reusable container.**
(supply – liefern / reusable – wiederverwendbar / container – Behälter, Verpackung)

* **We've reduced packaging to what is absolutely necessary to protect the article. I think that might help you win points with the green consumer.**
(packaging – Verpackung, Aufmachung / necessary – notwendig / protect – schützen / points – Gutpunkte / with – bei / consumer – Konsument)

MEASUREMENTS AND WEIGHTS

Abmessungen und Gewichte

* **The casing measures 6" by 4" by 2".**
  (… six by four by two inches. / Das Gehäuse misst 6 mal 4 mal 2 Zoll. [1 Zoll = 2,54 cm])

* **It is less than three feet wide and one foot high.**
  (wide – breit)

* **The screen measures 60 cm across.**
  (Der Bildschirm ist 60 cm breit.)

* **The machine weighs slightly over 50 kilos.**
  (slightly over – etwas mehr als)

* **The pipes are 3.5 cm in diameter.**
  (Der Durchmesser der Röhren beträgt 3,5 cm.)

IMPROVEMENTS

Verbesserungen

* **This is a much improved version of our standard XTX model.**
  (much improved – stark verbessert)

* **We have added a number of new features.**
  (Wir haben das Gerät mit einer Reihe von neuen Leistungsmerkmalen ausgestattet.)

* **The new model is even more economical in consumption.**
  (even – noch; sogar noch / economical – wirtschaftlich, sparsam / consumption – Verbrauch)

* **The new model is even more user-friendly than the old one.**
  (user-friendly – benutzerfreundlich)

* **The new features make the new model even better value than the old one.**
  (make sthg. better value – etwas preiswerter machen)

* **We have miniaturised several components and thus reduced the weight by as much as 50 per cent compared with the old version.**
  (miniaturise – miniaturisieren, verkleinern / several – einige / component – Bauteil, Bestandteil / thus – so / weight – Gewicht / by as much as 50% – um ganze 50% / compare – vergleichen)

* **We have succeeded in reducing fuel consumption by all of 30 per cent.**
  (Es ist uns gelungen, den Treibstoffverbrauch um ganze 30% zu verringern.)

* **We have shrunk the size of the machine so that it can easily be mounted on a rail carriage.**
  (shrink – verringern / size – Größe / mount – montieren, befestigen / rail carriage – Eisenbahnwaggon)

VARIETY

Vielfalt des Angebots

* **The unit comes in three different sizes: small, medium, and large.**
  (come – zu haben sein; geliefert werden / different – verschieden)

* **The model can be supplied in four different colours.**
  (supply – liefern / colour – Farbe)

* **The basic design is available in three different materials.**
  (basic design – Grundmodell / be available – zu haben sein)

* **We stock also a note-book size version.**
(stock – führen / note-book size – Taschenformat)

* **We are planning to introduce a model in a slightly different shade.**
(introduce – einführen / shade – Farbton, Farbnuance)

SUITABILITY AND MODIFICATIONS

Eignung und Modifikationen

* **I think this model, the PRS2, would be the most suitable for the application you have in mind.**
(suitable – geeignet / application – Anwendung, Verwendungszweck / have sthg. in mind – an etwas denken; etwas im Auge | Sinn haben)

* **We can alter our standard model to your specifications.**
(alter – ändern / to your specifications – nach Ihren Angaben)

* **We have a basic version which can be customised to meet individual requirements.**
(Wir haben eine Grundversion, die modifiziert werden kann, um den individuellen Kundenwünschen zu entsprechen.)

* **I think this is exactly what you need.**

* **I think the X23 will fit your bill.**
(Ich glaube, das Modell X23 wird Ihren Vorstellungen entsprechen.)

COMPARISON WITH COMPETING PRODUCTS

Vergleich mit Konkurrenzprodukten

* **Our product cannot be beaten for quality.**
(… ist unübertrefflich, was die Qualität betrifft.)

* **The new PX4 is certainly much better than anything on the market.**
(certainly – sicherlich)

* **Our new pump is second to none.**
(Unsere neue Pumpe braucht keinen Vergleich mit einem Konkurrenzprodukt zu scheuen.)

* **You won't find a better valve at this price.**
(won't – will not / valve – Ventil)

* **Our competitors will have a lot of catching up to do before they can match our printer.**
(Die Konkurrenz wird sich sehr anstrengen müssen, bevor sie mit unserem Drucker gleichziehen kann.)

* **Our new correction fluid compares well with anything on the market.**
(correction fluid – Korrekturflüssigkeit / compare well – bei einem Vergleich gut abschneiden)

* **The machine is much faster than competing products.**
(fast – schnell / competing product – Konkurrenzprodukt)

* **In contrast to most competing models ours requires next to no maintenance.**
(in contrast – im Gegensatz / require – erfordern / next to no – fast keine / maintenance – Wartung, Wartungsarbeiten)

* **It's definitely the best recorder on the market.**
(definitely – ganz entschieden)

DEMONSTRATIONS AND ILLUSTRATIONS

Vorführungen und Illustrationen

* **Now I'd like to demonstrate the new machine.**
  (demonstrate – vorführen)

* **This is how you can control the speed. You just have to turn this knob.**
  (control – regeln / speed – Geschwindigkeit / turn – drehen / knob – Knopf)

* **The controls are over there on the other side of the machine.**
  (control – Steuervorrichtung)

* **Here's a short video showing the machine in operation.**
  (in operation – in Betrieb)

* **Let me show you a few slides to illustrate what I've said about the new product.**
  (slide – Diapositiv)

* **If you take a look at the leaflet which we have distributed, you will immediately see what I mean by "flexibility".**
  (leaflet – Handzettel / distribute – verteilen / immediately – sofort / mean by – verstehen unter)

* **I'll now show you a few slides of the new model to give you an idea of what it looks like on the factory floor.**
  (give an idea – einen Eindruck vermitteln / factory floor – Fabrik, Produktionsbereich)

* **May I refer you to the brochure for further technical details.**
  (Nähere technische Details sind bitte der Broschüre zu entnehmen.)

* **If you come over here I can show you a scale-model of the URU-34.**
  (scale-model – maßstabgetreues Modell)

TRADE FAIRS

Messen

ABOUT FAIRS AND FAIR PREPARATIONS

Gespräche über Messen und Vorbereitungsarbeiten

* **A: We are thinking of participating in the London International Menswear Fair.**
(participate – teilnehmen / menswear – Herrenbekleidung)
B: When is it?
A: I think it's always held in mid-September.
(hold – abhalten)

* **You shouldn't leave it too late before you apply for your space requirements. They were sold out by June last year.**
(leave sthg. late – sich mit etwas Zeit lassen / apply for – anmelden / space requirements – Platzbedarf / sold out – ausverkauft)

* **It's a large event with about 450 exhibitors from all over the world.**
(event – Veranstaltung / exhibitor – Aussteller)

* **They claim in their brochure that the show attracted over 5,000 trade visitors last year.**
(claim – behaupten / show – Schau, Ausstellung / attract – anlocken / trade visitor – Firmenkunde)

* **A: Has your company ever participated in the Hanover Fair?**
(company – Firma, Gesellschaft / ever – jemals)
B: No, we actually prefer smaller events. They're more suitable for the type of goods we handle.
(prefer – vorziehen / suitable – geeignet / handle – führen)

* **We would need about 3,000 square metres of uninterrupted exhibition space in a central location in London.**
(square metre – Quadratmeter / uninterrupted – durchgehend; ohne Trennwände / exhibition space – Ausstellungsfläche / central location – zentrale Lage)

* A: **I phoned the Austrian Trade Representative in London and he said that the London Arena would be a suitable venue for our trade show. What do you say?**
(phone – anrufen / Trade Representative – Handelsdelegierter der Bundeswirtschaftskammer / venue – Veranstaltungsort / trade show – Fachausstellung, Fachmesse)
B: **I think he's right. I know the place because we staged an exhibition there once.**
(stage – veranstalten / exhibition – Ausstellung / once – einmal)

* **It's centrally located and easily accessible by road and rail.**
(centrally located – zentral gelegen / be easily accessible by road and rail – gute Straßen- und Bahnverbindungen haben)

* A: **What about parking facilities?**
(Wie steht's mit den Parkmöglichkeiten?)
B: **That should be no problem. They must have around 600 parking-spaces on site and there's a car-park within two minutes' walking distance from the main hall.**
(around – ungefähr / on site – auf dem Gelände / car-park – Garage, Parkhaus, Parkplatz / main hall – Haupthalle)

* **Their catering service is also very good.**
(catering – Catering; Angebot an Speisen und Getränken)

* **What is the total cost per square metre?**

* **We might get a subsidy from our local Chamber of Commerce towards the cost of participating in the fair.**
(subsidy – Subvention / chamber of commerce – Handelskammer / towards – zur teilweisen Abdeckung)

* **I don't have any particular wishes regarding location, except maybe that the stand shouldn't be in a remote corner.**
(particular – besondere / wishes regarding location – Platzwünsche / except – außer / remote corner – entlegene Ecke)

* **I've still got one prime location. Look here on this layout plan. It's next to the main entrance.**
(still – noch / prime location – Vorzugsplazierung / layout plan – Lageplan, Grundriss / main entrance – Haupteingang)

* **I think we'll opt for the shell stand. It's obviously less original than a designer-built stand but ever so much cheaper.**
(opt for – sich entscheiden für / shell stand – Einheitskoje / obviously – offensichtlich / ever so much cheaper – um so viel billiger)

* A: **Where is the Organisers' Office, please?**
(organisers – Messeveranstalter)
B: **It's at the other end of the exhibition site. It's a ten minutes' walk. Alternatively, you could phone them on 5678.**
(exhibition site – Ausstellungsgelände / alternatively – oder … auch / phone on 5678 – unter der Nummer 5678 anrufen)

* **We would need the address of a fair contractor. Do you know a reliable firm you could recommend?**
(fair contractor – Messebaufirma / reliable – verlässlich / recommend – empfehlen)

ON THE STAND

Am Messestand

CONVERSATIONS WITH OTHER STAFF MEMBERS

Gespräche mit anderen Mitarbeitern

* **Make sure that there are at least two people on the stand at all times.**
(make sure – sicherstellen / at least – zumindest)

* **Could you please keep an eye on the exhibits while I go for a cup of coffee?**
(keep an eye on sthg. – etwas im Auge behalten / exhibit – Ausstellungsgegenstand, Exponat / while – während)

* **Will you call the Cleaning Service and make sure that they get their work finished <u>before</u> the Fair opens, please.**
(call – anrufen / cleaning service – Reinigungsdienst / finish – beenden)

CONVERSATIONS WITH VISITORS

Gespräche mit Besuchern

* **Can I help you? You seem to be interested in our new lawn-mower.**
(seem – scheinen / lawn-mower – Rasenmäher)

* **The engineer who actually designed this machine will be back on the stand in about an hour. He will be pleased to answer any technical questions you might have. Could you come back at around three?**
(engineer – Ingenieur / design – konstruieren / about – ungefähr / be pleased – sich freuen / question – Frage / at around – zirka um)

* **I'm authorised to grant a special discount of ten per cent on all orders placed during the fair.**
(Ich bin ermächtigt, auf alle während der Messe erteilten Aufträge einen Sonderrabatt von zehn Prozent zu gewähren.)

* **I think the best model for the application you have in mind is this one over here, the GRT-23.**
(application – Anwendung / have sthg. in mind – an etwas denken; etwas im Auge | Sinn haben)

* **May I offer you a glass of orange juice? Or maybe something a little stronger?**
(offer – anbieten)

* **Sit down for a moment. Mr. Primer, our chief design engineer, will be available when he has finished his phone call.**
(chief design engineer – Chefkonstrukteur / be available – zur Verfügung stehen)

* **I saw the machine at the Bristol Engineering Show last year, but you seem to have added several new features.**
(seem – scheinen / add – zusätzlich ausstatten mit / several – einige / feature – Leistungsmerkmal)

* **If you come back at three one of our engineers will be giving a demonstration of this machine.**
(demonstration – Vorführung)

* **We are going to have a reception for our most important customers at the Plaza Hotel tomorrow evening. We would be delighted if you could come.**
(reception – Empfang / important – wichtig / customer – Kunde / be delighted – sich sehr freuen)

* **We are planning to hold a short seminar for our customers at the Convention Centre tomorrow from six to eight p.m..**
(hold – abhalten / convention centre – Konferenzzentrum / p.m. – am Abend)

* **Can I give you my business card? We shall be pleased to welcome you to our company if you should ever go to Vienna.**
(business card – Visitenkarte / ever – je, jemals)

* **If you give me your telephone number, I'll call you right after the fair and arrange for one of our sales engineers to visit you.**
(right after – gleich nach / arrange for – veranlassen, dass / sales engineer – Verkaufsingenieur)

* **We actually have a second stand on the ground floor in the video section. Ask for Mr. Gummer, he's the expert.**
(ground floor – Erdgeschoß / video section – Videoabteilung)

* **I'm sorry about the mistakes in the brochure. We should have had it translated by a local service.**
(Tut mir leid wegen der Fehler in der Broschüre. Wir hätten sie von einem Büro vor Ort übersetzen lassen sollen.)

CONVERSATIONS WITH FAIR CONTRACTORS AND WORKERS

Gespräche mit Messebaufirmen und -arbeitern

* **We need a floral contractor to spruce up the stand a bit. Could you recommend a reliable firm?**
(floral contractor – Florist / spruce up – herausputzen / recommend – empfehlen / reliable – verlässlich)

* **Could you please get the X-4 up to our stand on the second floor as soon as the goods lift has been repaired.**
(get up – hinauftransportieren / floor – Geschoß, Stock / goods lift – Warenaufzug)

* **The lights on our stand don't work. Could you do something about them right away?**
(work – funktionieren / do about – sich kümmern um / right away – sofort; gleich jetzt)

* **A fuse must have blown. Where's the fuse-box?**
(fuse – Sicherung / blow – durchbrennen / fuse-box – Sicherungskasten)

* **Is there a bottle-bank anywhere on the site?**
(bottle-bank – Glascontainer / site – [Messe-]Gelände)

* **Can you arrange for the stand to be dismantled and shipped to Toronto? We have booked a place there at the InterFur. Here's the address.**
(Können Sie veranlassen, dass der Stand abgebaut und nach Toronto geschickt wird? … .)

* **Please make sure that the exhibits are carefully packed.**
(make sure – sicherstellen / careful – sorgfältig)

POST MORTEM

Nach der Messe – Analyse und Bewertung

* **A: How was the trade fair in Brighton?**
B: Not too bad. About two hundred trade visitors contacted us and we managed to book a fairly large number of orders.
(trade visitor – Firmenbesucher / manage – können / fairly – ziemlich / order – Auftrag)

* **Well, the Pump Makers' Exhibition in Hull was a complete flop. We distributed tons of promotional material but we didn't make a single sale.**
(distribute – verteilen / promotional material – Werbematerial / sale – Verkauf)

* **I haven't analysed the records yet, but from what I saw at the stand I'd say that participating was a good investment.**
(not … yet – noch nicht / records – Aufzeichnungen / participate – teilnehmen)

* **I was against taking part right from the beginning, but nobody listened to me. Now we are about €30,000 out of pocket and haven't much to show for it.**
(take part – teilnehmen / right from the beginning – von allem Anfang an / listen to – hören auf / … . Nun haben wir rund 30.000 Euro ausgegeben und können kaum Resultate vorweisen.)

* **The exhibition itself was O.K., but we had so much trouble getting the exhibits back to Austria. There was something wrong with the ATA carnet and Customs wanted us to pay the normal import duty.**
(trouble – Schwierigkeiten, Mühe / exhibit – Ausstellungsgegenstand / ATA carnet – Carnet ATA; Dokument für den Vormerkverkehr / Customs – Zollbehörde / import duty – Importzoll)

* **We shouldn't have taken part in the group display. If you want to attract visitors you really need a separate stand.**
(group display – Gemeinschaftsstand / attract – anziehen / separate – eigen)

* **We didn't book too many orders during the fair but the press did give us a good write-up, so I'm still optimistic about the follow-up business.**
(press gives sthg. a good write-up – etwas hat eine gute Presse / still – noch immer / follow-up business – Nachmessegeschäft)

CONTACTS WITH ADVERTISING AGENCIES

Kontakte mit Werbeagenturen

REACTIONS TO SUGGESTIONS AND CONCEPTS

Reaktionen auf Vorschläge und Konzepte

* **We are not satisfied with your suggestions for the new campaign.**
  (satisfied – zufrieden / suggestion – Vorschlag)

* **The visual concept is good, but I think the slogan you suggested needs to be improved.**
  (visual concept – Bildidee / suggest – vorschlagen / need – müssen / improve – verbessern)

* **I think you will have to come up with something more lively.**
  (come up with sthg. – sich etwas einfallen lassen / lively – lebendig, lebhaft)

* **I'm not sure, but maybe our sales promotion efforts should have been supported by a series of TV spots.**
  (sales promotion – Verkaufsförderung / effort – Bemühung / support – unterstützen / series – Reihe)

* **We are not at all satisfied with the results of your latest campaign.**
  (not at all – überhaupt nicht)

* **No, that's too flashy. We want to project a more sedate image. Don't forget we are selling industrial equipment.**
  (flashy – knallig, protzig / project – ausstrahlen / sedate – gesetzt / industrial equipment – Anlagegüter, Investitionsgüter)

* **I think you still don't understand what our company stands for.**
(still – noch immer / company – Gesellschaft, Firma)

* **No, that wouldn't do for the type of product we sell.**
(do – gehen; geeignet sein)

* **I think the copy is much too long. People don't have time to read a whole page of text.**
(copy – Werbetext / page – Seite)

* **Splendid! That's the idea.**
(Großartig! Genau das brauchen wir.)

* **Yes, I particularly like the new slogan. Brilliant idea.**
(particularly – besonders)

* **That's exactly what we need to reach our target group.**
(reach – erreichen / target group – Zielgruppe)

* **That looks like an award winner.**
(Das sieht nach einer Auszeichnung aus.)

* **It's hilarious. I hope the audience won't forget that it's an ad for our product.**
(hilarious – zum Schreien lustig / audience – Publikum / won't – will not / ad – advertisement | Annonce, Werbung)

DISCUSSING ADVERTISING POLICIES – MEDIA SELECTION

Diskussion werbepolitischer Konzepte – Medienauswahl

* **We are probably not putting enough emphasis on TV spots.**
(probably – wahrscheinlich / put emphasis on – Nachdruck legen auf / enough – genug, ausreichend)

* **I don't think that advertising on TV would be suitable for this product, quite apart from the fact that it's much too expensive.**
(advertising on TV – Fernsehwerbung / suitable – geeignet / quite – ganz / apart from – abgesehen von / expensive – teuer)

* **No, this channel wouldn't have the necessary reach.**
(reach – Reichweite)

* **So far we have advertised only in the trade press. But for some of the products we've added to our range the national press might be more suitable.**
(advertise – werben, annoncieren / trade press – Fachpresse / range – Produktpalette / national press – die großen Tageszeitungen und Zeitschriften mit landesweiter Verbreitung)

* **No, not in the tabloids. That would hurt our image.**
(tabloids – Boulevardpresse / hurt – schaden)

* **Why don't we try radio commercials for a change? They are much cheaper and easier to produce than TV spots. If you give us the O.K., we could be on the air in a week.**
(try – versuchen / commercial – Werbespot, Werbesendung / for a change – zur Abwechslung / cheap – billig / be on the air – auf Sendung sein)

* **We'll shift part of our advertising budget into direct marketing.**
(shift – umschichten / advertising budget – Werbebudget)

* A: **Would you be interested in organising a mail shot for us?**
(mail shot – Mailing, Direktwerbung)
B: **We don't do mail shots ourselves. But we have a trade investment in a company which specialises in that sort of thing. They are very reliable. Shall I put you on to them?**
(trade investment – Beteiligung / reliable – verlässlich / put sbdy. on to sbdy. – für jmdn. Kontakt mit jmdm. herstellen; jmdn. an jmdn. weiterreichen)

* **We need to change our promotional mix and put more emphasis on direct mail shots.**
(need – müssen / promotional mix – kommunikationspolitischer Mix)

* **Why don't we try a teaser campaign?**
(teaser – Teaser, „Neckwerbung")

* **Let's start with the packaging. I think it will have to be redesigned. I don't like it any more. Looks too stolid.**
(packaging – Verpackung, Aufmachung / redesign – neu gestalten / stolid – fad, gesetzt)

* **Yes, I agree. You should develop a global advertising strategy.**
(agree – zustimmen; derselben Meinung sein / develop – entwickeln)

* **I'm against translating the copy. It should be recreated by a local copy-writer.**
(translate – übersetzen / recreate – neu kreieren / copy-writer – Werbetexter)

* **A: Don't you think that we need more information before we can decide on a new advertising strategy? We simply don't know enough about our target group.**
(decide on – sich entscheiden für / simply – einfach / target group – Zielgruppe)
B: Definitely, a new survey is an absolute must. The results of the old one are out of date. Also, if I remember correctly, it had a very low response rate.
(definitely – absolut richtig / survey – Erhebung, Studie / out of date – veraltet, überholt / remember – sich erinnern / response rate – Rücklaufquote; Prozentsatz der beantworteten Fragebögen)
A: Good. So we are agreed. Let's commission a new survey then and make sure that the questionnaires are designed very carefully.
(be agreed – einer Meinung sein; sich geeinigt haben / commission – in Auftrag geben / make sure – sicherstellen / questionnaire – Fragebogen / design – zusammenstellen, entwerfen / careful – sorgfältig)

TECHNICAL DETAILS, SCHEDULES AND DEADLINES

Technische Details, Zeitpläne und Termine

* **The deadline for the roughs is Monday.**
(deadline – letzter Termin / rough – Entwurf)

* **I know it will be tough to meet our deadline, but we have to bc ready for the Christmas business.**
(tough – hart, schwierig / meet deadline – Termin einhalten / ready – bereit, fertig / business – Geschäft)

* **Why don't you let me have a look at the storyboard?**
(storyboard – Storyboard)

* **I mustn't forget to tell you: the meeting with the new account executive has been rescheduled for next Tuesday.**
(must not – nicht dürfen / meeting – Sitzung / account executive – Kontakter, Etatdirektor / reschedule for – verlegen auf)

* **Has the script already been submitted for approval?**
(script – Drehbuch / submit – vorlegen / approval – Billigung, Genehmigung)

* **The tape will be released to the radio stations a week from today.**
(tape – Band / release – zum Senden freigeben)

* **Can you let me have a sketch of the new poster?**
(sketch – Skizze / poster – Plakat)

* **My suggestion is to run the ad three times a week – Tuesdays, Thursdays and Fridays – for two months.**
(suggestion – Vorschlag / run ad – Annonce schalten / three times – dreimal)

TERMINATING AGREEMENT WITH AGENCY

Beendigung des Vertragsverhältnisses mit der Agentur

* **The latest campaign was a complete flop. So we have decided to put our account up for review.**
(decide – sich entschließen; beschließen / account – Account, [Werbe-]Etat / put account up for review – verschiedene Agenturen zu einer Wettbewerbspräsentation für einen Etat einladen)

* **I think we'd better part company. Our ideas of what the advertising for our firm should be like differ simply too much.**
(Ich glaube, das beste wäre, wenn wir uns trennen. … . / differ – sich unterscheiden / simply – einfach)

* **Our agency has lost one of its best creative people. We are thinking of switching our account.**
(switch – anderweitig vergeben)

* **We are considering terminating the relationship with our agency.**
(consider – überlegen, erwägen / terminate – beenden / relationship – [Vertrags-]Verhältnis)

COMPLAINTS

Reklamationen

BUYER MAKES A COMPLAINT

Käufer beschwert sich / reklamiert

GENERAL/UNSPECIFIC COMPLAINTS

Allgemeine/unbestimmte Reklamationen

* A: **I've got a complaint to make.**
(Ich habe eine Reklamation. | Ich muss mich beschweren.)
B: **What is it about?**
(Welche Sache betreffend? | Worum handelt es sich denn?)
A: **It's about the brochures you printed for us.**
(print – drucken)

* A: **I'm afraid I have a serious complaint to make.**
(I'm afraid – leider; ich fürchte / serious – ernst, schwerwiegend)
B: **I'm sorry to hear that. What's gone wrong?**
(… . Was ist schiefgelaufen?)

* A: **I've got a complaint to make.**
B: **Oh, not again. What is it this time?**
(this time – dieses Mal)

* A: **Listen, we are not satisfied with the way you handled our last order.**
(listen – hören Sie mal / satisfied – zufrieden / way – Art und Weise / handle – erledigen, ausführen / order – Auftrag)
B: **Sorry to hear that. What's the problem?**

FAULTY OR DAMAGED GOODS

Mangelhafte oder beschädigte Ware

* **A: I have to complain about the pocket calculators you sent us last week.**
(complain about – sich beschweren über / pocket calculator – Taschenrechner)
B: What seems to be the trouble?
(Was ist denn das Problem?)
A: They are just not working. Not a single one.
(just – einfach / work – funktionieren / single one – einziger)

* **The last batch we received from you was faulty.**
(batch – Posten, Teilmenge / receive – erhalten / be faulty – Mängel aufweisen)

* **The goods arrived damaged.**
(Die Ware kam beschädigt an.)

* **The sugar content of the jam is way below what we had agreed. Here's the certificate of analysis by an independent agency.**
(sugar content – Zuckergehalt / jam – Marmelade / way below – weit unter / agree – sich einigen auf; vereinbaren / independent – unabhängig / agency – Stelle)

* **25 plates were found to be broken when we opened the case.**
(Wir stellten fest, dass 25 Teller zerbrochen waren, als wir die Kiste öffneten.)

* **The goods you sent us do not correspond with the sample we gave you. Our customers would never buy such poor-quality stuff.**
(correspond – übereinstimmen / sample – Muster / customer – Kunde / poor-quality – minderwertig / stuff – Zeug)

* **You sent us ten defective drive belts. That's not good enough!**
(defective – schadhaft / drive belt – Transmissionsriemen / … . So geht's wirklich nicht!)

* **Although your people have replaced several defective parts, the lathe is still not working properly.**
(although – obwohl / replace – ersetzen / several – einige / part – Teil / lathe – Drehbank / still – noch immer / proper – richtig, ordentlich)

* **The program you developed for us is full of bugs.**
(develop – entwickeln / bug – Fehler)

* **The report you sent us about our new customer is too superficial. We are very disappointed.**
(report – Bericht / superficial – oberflächlich / disappointed – enttäuscht)

WRONG GOODS

Falsche Ware

* **You don't seem to understand: you sent us the wrong goods. We didn't order any valves.**
(seem – scheinen / order – bestellen / valve – Ventil)

* **There's a serious problem. The case contained completely different goods from the ones we ordered.**
(serious – ernst / case – Kiste / contain – enthalten / different – andere)

* **You supplied a thicker material by mistake.**
(supply – liefern / by mistake – irrtümlicherweise)

* **You sent us DC5s instead of DC7s. It's a damn nuisance because we need them to complete a job for a very important customer.**
(instead of – anstatt / a damn nuisance – verdammt ärgerlich / complete – fertigstellen / job – Auftrag)

* **There seems to have been a mix-up. I ordered 26 of your heavy-duty RFC-I tyres and you sent me 62 of the much smaller RFC-Vs.**
(seem – scheinen / mix-up – Verwechslung / heavy-duty tyre – Hochleistungsreifen)

* **The containers are not the size and shape we ordered.**
(container – Gefäß, Behälter, Verpackung / size – Größe / shape – Form, Gestalt)

WRONG QUANTITY

Falsche Menge

* **Three typewriters are missing from the consignment.**
(typewriter – Schreibmaschine / be missing from – fehlen bei | aus / consignment – Sendung)

* **You haven't sent us all the goods we ordered.**

* **You've forgotten to include a manual.**
(manual – Handbuch)

* **I ordered 75 and you sent me 57. Are your shipping clerks dyslexic, or something?**
(shipping clerk – Expedient, Versandsachbearbeiter / dyslexic – legasthenisch / or something – oder was)

* **The last consignment has been shortshipped.**
(Die letzte Sendung wurde nicht vollständig geliefert.)

DELAY IN DELIVERY

Lieferverzug

* **We haven't received the goods yet.**
(receive – erhalten / not … yet – noch nicht)

* **Our order P2345 / 11 / 91 is already two weeks overdue. What's the matter?**
(overdue – überfällig / what's the matter? – was ist los?)

* **Can you tell me why the transparencencies we ordered six weeks ago haven't arrived yet? I wish you'd keep the deadlines we have fixed.**
(transparency – Overheadfolie / arrive – ankommen / keep deadline – Termin | Frist einhalten)

* **The consignment we complained about last week did not arrive until today. We have no use for it any more.**
(did not arrive until today – kam erst heute an)

* **Our progress chaser has been unable to get an explanation as to why the ball-bearings we ordered on May 2 have not been delivered yet. Could you look into the matter and report back by tomorrow?**
(Unserem Terminjäger ist es nicht gelungen eine Erklärung zu bekommen, warum die Kugellager, die wir am 2. Mai bestellten, noch nicht geliefert worden sind. Könnten Sie der Sache nachgehen und sich bis morgen wieder melden?)

* **We're wondering why there is such a long delay. Have the compressors left the factory yet?**
(Wir möchten gerne wissen, … . / delay – Verzug / leave – verlassen / factory – Fabrik / yet – schon)

* **You seem to have overlooked our order. We should have received the disk drives last week.**
(overlook – übersehen / disk drive – Platten-, Diskettenlaufwerk)

* **What's happened to our crank-shafts? We are still waiting for them. Yes, that's order No. 451 / 2 / 90.**
  (happen to – geschehen mit / still – noch immer / crank-shaft – Kurbelwelle)

* **It's the third or fourth time that you've failed to meet the delivery date. The sales manager is furious.**
  (the [third] time – das [dritte] Mal / fail to meet – nicht einhalten / furious – wütend)

PACKING

Verpackung

* **I have to complain about the really careless packing of the last consignment.**
  (careless – schlampig; nicht sehr sorgfältig)

* **You've done it again. This time it's inadequate packing.**
  (Sie können es nicht lassen! Diesmal ist es die unzureichende Verpackung.)

* **You did not secure the cartons with metal straps as we had suggested.**
  (secure – verstärken / metal strap – Metallband / suggest – vorschlagen)

* **I'm surprised at the way in which you packed the machine.**
  (surprised – überrascht / way – Art und Weise)

* **You should have used stronger cardboard boxes for such a heavy item.**
  (cardboard – Pappe / box – Schachtel / item – Artikel)

* **Your packers apparently left out the padding and that's why the casing on the printer is cracked.**
(apparently – offenbar / leave out – weglassen, vergessen / padding – Füllmaterial / casing – Gehäuse / printer – Drucker / crack – bersten, springen)

* **The sacks were not strong enough. So some of them burst and the contents ran out.**
(enough – genug / burst – platzen / contents – Inhalt / run out – auslaufen)

* **The flaps on most of the cartons came unstuck. You must have used a poor-quality glue.**
(flap – Klappendeckel / come unstuck – aufgehen; sich lösen / poor-quality – minderwertig / glue – Klebstoff)

BUYER SUGGESTS PLAN OF ACTION

Käufer schlägt Regelung vor

* **Well, we have no use for the spanners you sent us. We can either return them at your expense or keep them until you have them collected.**
(have use for sthg. – etwas brauchen können / spanner – Schraubenschlüssel / either … or – entweder … oder / at sbdy.'s expense – auf jmds. Kosten / have sthg. collected – etwas abholen lassen)

* **We are returning the goods.**

* **The important thing is that you send us a replacement as soon as possible. We'll discuss the rest next week.**
(important – wichtig / replacement – Ersatzlieferung / as soon as possible – so bald wie möglich)

* **We must have the replacement by Tuesday at the latest. So you will have to send it by air – at your expense, of course.**
(by … at the latest – bis spätestens … / by air – als Luftfracht)

* **We would be prepared to keep the goods if you reduce the price by 15 per cent.**
(be prepared – bereit sein / keep – behalten / by – um)

* **We are willing to extend the delivery period by a week. But that's the limit. After that we would have to activate the penalty clause.**
(extend – verlängern / delivery period – Lieferfrist / penalty clause – Pönaleklausel)

BUYER MAKES THREATS

Käufer droht

* **If it happens again we'll simply have to look for another supplier.**
(happen – passieren / simple – einfach / look for – sich umsehen um / supplier – Lieferant)

* **This is no way to handle a first order! You will understand that we are no longer interested in doing business with you.**
(So kann man doch nicht mit einem Erstauftrag umgehen! … . / do business – Geschäfte tätigen)

* **I'm inclined to lodge a formal complaint with the Commercial Section of your Embassy.**
(be inclined – gute Lust haben / lodge – einbringen / commercial section – Handelsabteilung / embassy – Botschaft)

SELLER'S REACTION TO COMPLAINT, INVESTIGATION AND INSPECTION

Reaktion des Verkäufers auf Reklamation, Untersuchung und Inspektion

* **Well, that sounds serious. I'll send one of our service staff over first thing tomorrow morning.**
(sound – klingen / serious – ernst / staff – Personal / first thing – gleich)

* **I've come over to investigate your complaint personally.**
(come over – herüber [nach England] kommen / investigate – untersuchen)

* **Since you are such an important customer I jumped on the next plane. Here I am. Could I have a look at the defective home trainers?**
(Da Sie ein so wichtiger Kunde sind, nahm ich gleich das nächste Flugzeug. … . / defective – schadhaft)

* A: **Can I inspect the consignment?**
(inspect – inspizieren / consignment – Sendung)
B: **Yes, of course, it's in the warehouse by the factory gate.**
(warehouse – Lagerhaus / factory gate – Fabrikstor)

* A: **Why don't you have a look yourself? The VDUs are over there.**
(VDU – visual display unit | Bildschirm; optische Anzeige)
B: **You're absolutely right. They seem to have been banged about quite badly.**
(… . Sie scheinen wirklich ziemlich unsanft behandelt worden zu sein.)

SELLER'S ADMISSION OF FAULT AND APOLOGIES

Verkäufer nimmt Schuld auf sich und entschuldigt sich

* **Sorry to hear that. Something obviously has gone wrong.**
  (obviously – offensichtlich / go wrong – schiefgehen)

* **Your complaint is perfectly justified.**
  (Ihre Reklamation ist absolut gerechtfertigt.)

* **We're very sorry for this delay. It won't happen again.**
  (delay – Verzug, Verzögerung / won't – will not / happen – passieren, geschehen)

* **Yes, I think it was partly our fault.**
  (partly – teilweise / fault – Schuld)

* **I do have to apologise. It seems that our shipping department is to blame for the scratches across the top of the desk.**
  (Ich muss mich wirklich entschuldigen. … . / seem – scheinen / shipping department – Versandabteilung / be to blame for sthg. – an etwas schuld sein / scratch – Kratzer / across – quer über / top – [Schreib-]Platte, Arbeitsplatte / desk – Schreibtisch)

* **Yes, it's our fault all right. But couldn't you waive the penalty?**
  (Ja, es stimmt schon, dass es unsere Schuld ist. Aber könnten Sie nicht auf das Pönale verzichten?)

* **There has been a mistake at our end, I'm afraid. Let me explain what happened.**
  (mistake – Fehler / at our end – bei uns hier / I'm afraid – leider / explain – erklären)

∗ **Yes, you were right. Our warehouse people are responsible for the delay.**
(be right – recht haben / warehouse – Lagerhaus, Lager / responsible – verantwortlich)

∗ **I do understand that you are angry.**
(Ich verstehe wirklich, dass Sie wütend sind.)

∗ **Sorry again. We'll make every effort to prevent similar mistakes in the future.**
(Nochmals Entschuldigung. … . / effort – Anstrengung, Mühe / prevent – verhindern / similar – ähnlich / future – Zukunft)

∗ **That was just not good enough. I'll have to have a word with the lads in the packing department.**
(Das war wirklich nicht in Ordnung. Ich werde mit den Burschen in der Verpackungsabteilung ein ernstes Wort sprechen müssen.)

∗ **I must apologise. We really should have rung you up to tell you. But the lorry drivers are on strike so we can't get the goods to the airport.**
(apologise – sich entschuldigen / ring up – anrufen / lorry driver – Lastwagenfahrer / be on strike – streiken; im Ausstand sein)

SELLER SUGGESTS OR ANNOUNCES SETTLEMENT

Verkäufer schlägt Regelung vor oder kündigt eine an

∗ **Would it be acceptable if I sent somebody over to respray the consoles? In addition, we would offer you a five per cent reduction to compensate you for the trouble we have put you to.**
(respray – neu spritzen | lackieren / console – Konsole, Bedienungsplatz / in addition – zusätzlich / offer – anbieten / compensate – entschädigen / the trouble we have put you to – die Unannehmlichkeiten, die wir Ihnen bereitet haben)

* **We had a fire in the warehouse which destroyed most of our stock. We hope you don't mind if we send you only half the order next Monday. The balance would go out in two weeks' time.**
(warehouse – Lagerhaus / destroy – zerstören / stock – Lagerbestand / you don't mind – es macht Ihnen nichts aus / order – Auftrag / balance – Rest / go out – geliefert werden / in two weeks' time – in zwei Wochen)

* **What would you say to a 50 per cent price reduction if you agree to keep the unsuitable items?**
(agree – sich bereit erklären / keep – behalten / unsuitable – nicht geeignet / item – Artikel)

* **We are rushing out a new consignment today.**
(Wir beeilen uns und schicken Ihnen noch heute eine neue Lieferung.)

* **We are sending you a few extra units to make up for the inconvenience.**
(a few – ein paar / make up for – [jmdn.] entschädigen / inconvenience – Unannehmlichkeiten)

* **One of our customers has more of the components in question than he needs at the moment. I'll ask him to send you 50 right away so that you can continue production.**
(the components in question – die gegenständlichen Bauteile / right away – sofort / continue production – weiterproduzieren)

* **Yes, we are willing to repair the machine free of charge, though, strictly speaking, the guarantee period has already expired.**
(free of charge – kostenlos / though – obwohl / strictly speaking – genaugenommen / expire – ablaufen)

* **Why don't you return the defective items carriage forward and we'll send you a credit note right away.**
(return – zurücksenden / defective – schadhaft / item – Artikel / carriage forward – unfrei / credit note – Gutschriftsanzeige)

* **The replacement should reach you by Friday at the latest.**
(replacement – Ersatzlieferung / reach sbdy. – bei jmdm. ankommen / by … at the latest – bis spätestens …)

BUYER REACTS TO SELLER'S SUGGESTIONS

Käufer reagiert auf Vorschläge des Verkäufers

* **Yes, that seems acceptable. But please make sure that it doesn't happen again.**
(seem – scheinen / make sure – sicherstellen / happen – passieren, geschehen)

* **No, we can't accept that. That's not good enough.**
(Wir können das nicht akzeptieren. Das ist nicht ausreichend.)

* **Well, I don't know. Ten per cent is not a very generous offer. It'll have to be at least 15.**
(generous – großzügig / at least – zumindest)

* **Well, I suppose I can accept that. Sounds reasonable.**
(suppose – glauben / sound – klingen / reasonable – angemessen, vernünftig)

SELLER DOES NOT ACCEPT COMPLAINT

Verkäufer weist Reklamation zurück

* **What was that? Deep scratches across the top? I can't believe it.**
(scratch – Kratzer / across – quer über / top – Schreibplatte, Arbeitsplatte / believe – glauben)

* **We are surprised to hear that you are not satisfied with the last consignment we sent you. What's the matter?**
(surprised – überrascht / satisfied – zufrieden / consignment – Lieferung / what's the matter? – was ist los?)

* **The defect is quite clearly not due to faulty materials or workmanship. That's why it is not covered by our warranty.**
(quite – ganz / be due to – zurückzuführen sein auf / workmanship – Verarbeitung / cover – decken / warranty – Garantie)

* **We checked the material very carefully prior to shipment. Here's the inspection record.**
(careful – sorgfältig / prior to – vor / shipment – Versand / inspection record – Prüfprotokoll)

* **You don't seem to have followed our operating instructions carefully enough.**
(seem – scheinen / operating instructions – Bedienungsanleitung / enough – genug)

* **Well, we have been discussing your claim now for over two hours and I'm still not convinced that it is justified.**
(Nun, wir diskutieren Ihre Reklamation jetzt schon über zwei Stunden, und ich bin noch immer nicht überzeugt, dass sie gerechtfertigt ist.)

* **The inspection showed that your staff used the wrong kind of transparency for the copying job.**
(staff – Personal / kind – Art / transparency – Overheadfolie / job – Auftrag, Arbeit)

* **To be quite honest, I think you are making this complaint to get a reduction in price. It's really not justified.**
(quite – ganz / honest – ehrlich)

* **The goods seem to have been damaged in transit. Since they were sold ex works the damage can't well be our responsibility.**
(damage – beschädigen / in transit – während des Transportes / since – da / sell – verkaufen / ex works – ab Werk / responsibility – Verantwortung, Schuld)

* **We handled the case very carefully at our end. So it must be your or the carrier's fault.**
(handle – umgehen mit; behandeln / case – Kiste / at our end – bei uns hier / carrier – Frachtführer / fault – Schuld)

* **You seem to have forgotten to adjust the voltage before you switched on the machine.**
(adjust – umstellen / voltage – elektrische Spannung / switch on – einschalten)

* **There's no need to be worried. There is a second switch at the back of the machine.**
(Sie brauchen sich keine Sorgen zu machen. … . / switch – Schalter / back – Rückseite)

* **We can't understand the delay you're complaining about. The spare parts were dispatched by parcel post on March 23, and should have reached you long ago.**
(spare part – Ersatzteil / dispatch – versenden / by parcel post – als Postpaket)

SELLER'S OR BUYER'S SUGGESTIONS OR THREATS IF THERE IS NO AGREEMENT

Vorschläge oder Drohungen seitens des Verkäufers oder Käufers im Falle der Nichteinigung

* **We don't seem to be able to agree on whose fault it is. So why don't we submit the whole thing to arbitration? I think there is something about this in the Contract of Sale anyway.**
(agree – sich einigen / submit sthg. to arbitration – etwas einem Schiedsgericht übergeben / contract of sale – Kaufvertrag / anyway – ohnehin)

* **If you really refuse to budge, I'll have to ask my lawyer what I should do. The amount of money involved is simply too large.**
(Wenn Sie sich wirklich weigern, auch nur ein kleines Zugeständnis zu machen, werde ich meinen Rechtsanwalt konsultieren müssen. Die Summe, um die es geht, ist einfach zu groß.)

* **Let's see if our respective lawyers can reach an agreement.**
(respective – jeweilig / reach agreement – Einigung erzielen)

* **If you cannot come up with a better offer, I'm afraid we will have to place our orders elsewhere.**
(come up with sthg. – etwas auf den Tisch legen / be afraid – fürchten / place order – Auftrag vergeben / elsewhere – anderswo; an eine andere Firma)

* **If this is your last word, we shall have to hand the matter over to our solicitors.**
(hand over to – übergeben / matter – Sache, Angelegenheit / solicitors – Rechtsanwalt[-skanzlei])

* **We'll have to sue you for damages, I'm afraid.**
(sue for damages – auf Schadenersatz klagen)

* **I think we have no alternative left but to take you to court.**
(… es bleibt uns nichts anderes übrig, als Sie zu klagen.)

BUYER ACCEPTS RESPONSIBILITY

Käufer übernimmt Verantwortung

* **I have to admit that it was our fault.**
  (admit – zugeben / fault – Schuld)

* **The foreman confessed that the workers dropped two of the heavy cases when unloading the consignment.**
  (foreman – Vorarbeiter, Meister / confess – eingestehen / drop – fallen lassen / heavy – schwer / unload – abladen / consignment – Sendung)

* **I hope you don't bear us a grudge for blaming you first.**
  (Ich hoffe, Sie tragen es uns nicht nach, dass wir Ihnen zuerst die Schuld gegeben haben.)

* **All I can do, apart from saying that I'm sorry, is promise a couple of large orders for next month. Though, to be quite honest, we would have placed them with you anyway.**
  (apart from – abgesehen von / promise – versprechen / a couple of – ein paar / though – obwohl / place order with sbdy. – jmdm. einen Auftrag erteilen)

TALKING ABOUT THE ECONOMY

Gespräche über die Wirtschaft

ECONOMIC SITUATION

Konjunkturlage

* A: **What is the economic situation like in your country at the moment, Peter?**
(economic situation – Konjunkturlage)
B: **Not too bad, actually. The economy is expanding nicely, unemployment is fairly low, and so is inflation.**
(nicely – ordentlich / unemployment – Arbeitslosigkeit / fairly low – ziemlich niedrig)

* **The forecasts for next year have been revised downwards. The consensus opinion seems to be zero growth or worse.**
(forecast – Prognose / revise downwards – nach unten hin korrigieren / consensus opinion – übereinstimmende Meinung [der Experten] / zero growth – Nullwachstum)

* **Our economy is not doing well at the moment. Just look at the economic data published yesterday. GDP growth is flat and prices are still rising.**
(do well – gut abschneiden / GDP – gross domestic product | Bruttoinlandsprodukt / growth – Wachstum / be flat – stagnieren / still – noch immer / rise – steigen)

* **We've not been hit by a really serious slump since the war. Of course, there have been a few rough patches.**
(hit – treffen / slump – starke Rezession / rough patch – schwierige Zeit; Durststrecke)

* **A: I've just had a look at the latest figures. Most leading indicators are pointing downwards.**
(figure – Zahl / leading indicator – Frühindikator / point downwards – nach unten weisen)
B: Not a pretty sight! What I find particularly worrying is the development of manufacturing order books. They are at a six-month low.
(sight – Anblick / worrying – beunruhigend / development – Entwicklung / manufacturing order books – Auftragsbestand in der Fertigungsindustrie / low – tiefster Stand)
A: Yes, but there is one bright spot, and that is new orders. I think they give a better indication of what is ahead.
(bright spot – Lichtblick / new orders – Auftragseingang / what is ahead – was vor uns liegt)

* **Both industrial production and personal consumption are set to decline. We are heading for a recession, and no mistake.**
(personal consumption – privater Konsum / X is set to decline – alles deutet darauf hin, dass X zurückgehen wird / head for – zusteuern auf / and no mistake – ohne Zweifel)

* **A: Would you believe it? Overall capacity utilisation is running close to 100 per cent.**
(believe – glauben / overall – Gesamt- / capacity utilisation – Kapazitätsauslastung)
B: This means that there will be supply bottlenecks and higher prices. Not a pretty prospect!
(supply bottleneck – Versorgungsengpass / pretty prospect – schöne Aussichten)

* **A: How did retail sales fare in September?**
(retail sales – Einzelhandelsumsatz / fare – abschneiden)
B: They were 0.3 per cent up on the previous month.
(be up on – höher sein im Vergleich zu)

* **This may come as a surprise, but we have a higher growth rate than most other OECD countries.**
(surprise – Überraschung / growth rate – Wachstumsrate / OECD – Organization for Economic Cooperation and Development)

* **A: I think Germany ranks fairly high in terms of per capita GDP.**
(rank – rangieren / fairly – ziemlich / in terms of – gemessen an / per capita – pro Kopf)
B: Yes, you are among the richest countries in the EU, with Ireland at the top of the list.
(among – unter / at the top of the list – an erster Stelle)

* **The strange thing is that unemployment has been creeping up in spite of satisfactory economic growth. Nevertheless, it's still on the low side by OECD standards.**
(strange – seltsam / unemployment – Arbeitslosigkeit / creep up – sich schleichend erhöhen / in spite of – trotz / satisfactory – zufriedenstellend / nevertheless – nichtsdestotrotz / still – noch immer / on the low side – eher niedrig / by OECD standards – gemessen an den OECD-Werten)

* **A: Our unit labour costs have been falling steadily since the early nineties. And, what is more important, they have been declining faster than in other European countries.**
(unit labour costs – Lohnstückkosten / steady – stetig / nineties – die Neunzigerjahre / decline – zurückgehen)
B: Does this mean your country has become more competitive internationally?
(competitive – konkurrenzfähig)
A: Yes, that's what lower unit labour costs indicate.

ECONOMIC AND SOCIAL POLICIES

Wirtschafts- und Sozialpolitik

* A: **I think it's time to kickstart the economy.**
(kickstart – [wieder] in Schwung bringen)
B: **I agree. There is a strong case for reflation. Government should have boosted spending on infrastructure long ago.**
(agree – zustimmen / there is a strong case for – vieles spricht für / reflation – Konjunkturbelebung / boost – kräftig erhöhen / spending – Ausgaben)

* A: **The government spokesman has said it will increase taxes and cut expenditures to reduce the budget deficit.**
(spokesman – Sprecher / increase – erhöhen / tax – Steuer / cut – senken / expenditure – Ausgabe, Ausgaben)
B: **I don't believe a word. They have made similar promises before without living up to them.**
(believe – glauben / promise – Versprechen / live up to – einhalten)
A: **Yes, but we will have to meet the Maastricht criteria somehow sooner or later.**
(meet – erfüllen)

* A: **The budget deficit for next year is now estimated at 44 billion euros. That's five billion more than they said it would be only two months ago.**
(estimate at – schätzen auf / billion – Milliarde)
B: **Well, even 44 billion does not seem too bad for such a large economy.**
(even – sogar, selbst)
A: **True as far as it goes, but don't forget that the federal deficit is just the tip of the iceberg. The overall public sector deficit is much, much bigger.**
(true as far as it goes – das ist schon richtig / tip – Spitze / overall – Gesamt- / public – öffentlich)
B: **What do you mean by *overall*?**
A: **Well, it's the total deficit. It includes not only the federal government but also the Länder, local authorities and special funds.**
(local authorities – Bezirke und Gemeinden / fund – Fonds, Kasse)

* **The official budget deficit is not too high, although, like in most other countries, there is a lot of off-budget financing.**
(although – obwohl / a lot of – eine Menge / off-budget – außerbudgetär)

* A: **Did you see the national debt clock on Times Square when you were in New York?**
(national debt – Staatsschuld / clock – Uhr)
B: **You must mean the one that shows the increase per second. No. But I was there in 2000 when it was shut down, as far as I know.**
(increase – Erhöhung / shut down – abschalten)
A: **Yes, you are right there. They restarted it in 2002. Had to, because the surplus accumulated by Clinton had turned into a huge deficit under Bush.**
(surplus – [Budget-]Überschuss / accumulate – ansammeln, erwirtschaften / turn – sich verwandeln)

* **In 1995 the federal government had to take over the debt of the old East-German state. This added another DM40 billion in interest cost to the budget every year.**
(debt – Schulden / add – hinzufügen / interest – Zinsen)

* **The unification with East Germany cost us more than we had anticipated, much more as a matter of fact.**
(unification – Vereinigung / anticipate – erwarten / as a matter of fact – eigentlich)

* **What really worries me is that a large chunk of government expenditure goes on items that are more or less fixed: public-sector wages, subsidies and the debt service. Only a small portion is still discretionary.**
(worry – Sorgen machen / chunk – Brocken / go on – entfallen auf / public – öffentlich / wages – Löhne & Gehälter / subsidy – Subvention / debt service – Schuldendienst / portion – Teil / still – noch / discretionary – frei disponierbar)

* **Our national debt is around 160 billion euros, that's roughly equivalent to 60 per cent of GDP.**
(national debt – Staatsschuld / billion – Milliarde / roughly – ungefähr / be equivalent to – entsprechen / GDP – gross domestic product | Bruttoinlandsprodukt)

* **The present government is certainly not prepared to fight unemployment at all costs. You can imagine that the trade unions are not too happy about this.**
(present – jetzig, gegenwärtig / certainly – sicherlich / prepared – bereit / fight – bekämpfen / at all costs – um jeden Preis / trade union – Gewerkschaft)

* A: **The austerity programme which was announced yesterday is patently unfair. Most of the burden will fall on small earners.**
(austerity programme – [drastisches] Sparprogramm / announce – ankündigen, verlautbaren / patently – ausgesprochen / burden – Last, Bürde / small earner – Kleinverdiener)
B: **Yes, and government hasn't dared to touch the tax breaks granted to big companies last year.**
(dare – wagen / touch – anrühren / tax break – steuerliche Vergünstigung / grant – gewähren)

* A: **The unions might accept pay restraint and spending cuts if government were to raise taxes on high earners.**
(union – Gewerkschaft / pay restraint – Zurückhaltung bei Löhnen und Gehältern / spending cut – Ausgabenkürzung / raise – erhöhen / tax – Steuer / high earner – Großverdiener)
B: **But the Minister of Finance is said to be against soaking the rich.**
(is said to be … – soll angeblich … sein / soak – schröpfen, ausnehmen)

* **Another thorny problem is revenue-sharing with the Länder.**
(thorny – heikel, schwierig / revenue-sharing – Finanzausgleich)

* **Our monetary policy used to shadow what the Germans were doing. When their central bank pushed up interest rates we usually followed suit.**
(monetary policy – Geld- und Kreditpolitik / used to shadow – hielt sich früher eng an / central bank – Zentralbank, Notenbank / push up – erhöhen / interest rate – Zinssatz / follow suit – nachziehen)

* **Some people blame the government for not cutting the budget deficit and leaving the central bank to do all the inflation fighting.**
(blame – beschuldigen / leave – überlassen / fight – bekämpfen)

* **I'm afraid we will have to resign ourselves to high interest rates for some time to come. The ECB is unlikely to cut rates before there is hard evidence that inflation is under control.**
(resign oneself to – sich abfinden mit / ECB – European Central Bank | Europäische Zentralbank / is unlikely to cut – wird wahrscheinlich nicht senken / evidence – Beweise)

* A: **Many people feel that the ECB has been too restrictive lately.**
(feel – der Meinung sein / lately – in jüngster Zeit)
B: **I disagree. I don't think we should take any chances with inflation.**
(disagree – anderer Meinung sein / take chances – sich auf ein Risiko einlassen)

* **The problem is that the central bank has failed to control M3, which is our main monetary measure. It is expected to overshoot the target set a few years ago by a whopping 10%.**
(fail – es verabsäumen / control – unter Kontrolle halten / monetary measure – Geldmengendefinition / overshoot – übersteigen / target – Ziel / whopping – saftig, riesig)

* A: **You have a very generous state pension system in Austria, don't you? But can you really afford it?**
(generous – großzügig / don't you? – oder? / afford sthg. – sich etwas leisten)

B: **Well, it's ultimately a political decision how much money you want to spend on your oldies. But even with our positive attitude towards senior citizens, the official retirement age is bound to go up in the next few years, I fear.**
(ultimately – letztlich / decision – Entscheidung / spend – ausgeben / oldies – ältere Generation / even – selbst / attitude – Einstellung / senior citizens – Senioren / retirement age – Pensionsalter / is bound to go up – wird zwangsläufig in die Höhe gehen)

* A: **We opted for a mandatory long-term care insurance model for the entire German population as long ago as 1995.**
(opt for – sich entscheiden für / mandatory – gesetzlich [vorgeschrieben] / long-term care insurance – Pflegeversicherung / entire – gesamt / population – Bevölkerung / as long ago as – schon, bereits)

B: **Wow! This sounds great, but how do you finance it?**
(sound – klingen)

A: **The system is based on employers' and employees' contributions.**
(… Arbeitgeber- und Arbeitnehmerbeiträge.)

B: **And it really covers everybody?**
(cover – erfassen)

A: **Yes, but about 10 per cent of those eligible have decided to opt out of the public system and purchase private LTC services.**
(those eligible – Anspruchsberechtigte / decide – sich entscheiden / opt out – freiwillig ausscheiden / purchase – kaufen / LTC – long-term care insurance)

* **A:** **Do you really believe that there is a case for treating the unemployed more harshly?**
(believe – glauben / a case for – Argumente für / treat – behandeln / the unemployed – die Arbeitslosen / harsh – hart)

B: **I certainly do. High unemployment benefits encourage people to stay on the dole longer than necessary and thus increase the unemployment rate.**
(uncmployment benefits – Arbeitslosengeld / encourage – veranlassen, ermutigen / stay on the dole – Arbeitslosengeldbezieher bleiben / necessary – notwendig / increase – erhöhen)

A: **You may have a point there, but the real reasons for the large number of jobless are different.**
(Da mögen Sie ja Recht haben, aber die eigentlichen Gründe für die hohen Arbeitslosenzahlen … .)

TAXES

Steuern

* **Our taxes are much too high, and there are too many of them.**
(tax – Steuer, Abgabe, Gebühr)

* **A:** **Of course, we've got a progressive income tax. At 50 per cent, the top tax rate is higher than in many other countries. But there are a lot of exceptions. The effective burden is only around 40 per cent.**
(top tax rate – Spitzensteuersatz / exception – Ausnahmeregelung / effective burden – tatsächliche Belastung)

B: **What about corporate income tax?**
(corporate income tax – Körperschaftsteuer)

A: **That's a flat-rate tax and much lower. It was cut to 25 per cent a few years ago to attract foreign direct investment.**
(flat-rate tax – Einheitssteuer, Pauschalsteuer / attract – anlocken / foreign direct investment – ausländische Direktinvestitionen)

* **Our tax brackets are not linked to the inflation rate. This means there are hidden tax increases every year.**
(Unsere Progressionsstufen sind nicht an die Inflationsrate gebunden. Das heißt, dass es jedes Jahr versteckte Steuererhöhungen gibt.)

* **A: I read somewhere that you have a special tax on current investment income.**
(tax on current investment income – Kapitalertragsteuer)

B: Yes, that's correct. It's called *Kapitalertragsteuer*. It means, for example, that banks are obliged to withhold 25% of the interest on deposits and pay it over to the revenue authorities.
(obliged – verpflichtet / withhold – einbehalten / interest – Zinsen / deposit – Einlage / pay over to – abführen an / revenue authorities – Fiskus, Steuerbehörde)

A: You mean 25% irrespective of the amount of interest earned?
(irrespective – unabhängig / amount – Betrag / earn – verdienen)

B: Yes, it's a flat-rate tax. Another important point is that income taxed this way does not have to be included in your income tax return.
(flat rate – einheitlicher Steuersatz / tax – besteuern / income tax return – Einkommensteuererklärung)

* **A: I'm sure you are not taking the planned tax increase lying down.**
(..., dass Sie die geplante Steuererhöhung nicht einfach hinnehmen werden.)

B: You can bet on that. Everybody is busy exploring the loopholes and a lot of money is being diverted abroad.
(Darauf können Sie wetten. ... . / be busy exploring – eifrig erforschen / loophole – Schlupfloch, Gesetzeslücke / divert – umlenken / abroad – ins Ausland)

* **A: True, the Austrian corporation tax rate is not very high. But there is a 25 per cent withholding tax on dividends paid out of taxed profits.**
(true – stimmt / corporation tax – Körperschaftsteuer / withholding tax [on dividends] – Kapitalertragsteuer, Quellensteuer)

B: In my country, President Bush reduced the rates attracted by dividends.
(rates attracted by X – die auf X entfallenden Steuersätze)

* **Austrian VAT is on the high side. The standard rate is 20 per cent, and there is a reduced rate of ten per cent for books, foodstuffs and such like.**
(VAT – value-added tax | Mehrwertsteuer / on the high side – eher hoch / standard rate – Normalsteuersatz / foodstuffs – Lebensmittel / and such like – und Ähnliches)

* **The German standard VAT rate went up from 16% to 19% with effect from January 1, 2007.**
(with effect from – mit Wirkung vom)

* **I'm all for green taxes – provided that they don't increase the overall tax burden. The additional revenues should be used to reduce social security taxes.**
(all – sehr / provided – vorausgesetzt / increase – erhöhen / overall – gesamt / tax burden – Steuerbelastung / additional – zusätzlich / revenues – Steueraufkommen / social security tax – Sozialversicherungsabgabe)

* **Why don't we impose a hefty environment tax on all car sales, like in Denmark?**
(impose – einführen, auferlegen / hefty – saftig / environment tax – Umweltsteuer / car sales – Autoverkäufe)

ECONOMIC SYSTEM AND INDUSTRIAL STRUCTURE

Wirtschaftssystem und Wirtschaftsstruktur

(see also "Politics")

* **The transition from a centrally planned economy to a free market economy is proving quite difficult.**
(transition – Übergang / centrally planned economy – Zentralverwaltungswirtschaft / prove – sich erweisen als)

* **I think the concept of a socially-oriented free market economy was invented here in Germany. And tempering capitalism with a dose of social responsibility has proved a successful recipe, hasn't it?**
(invent – erfinden / temper – mildern, abschwächen / dose – Dosis / responsibility – Verantwortung / successful – erfolgreich / recipe – Rezept / hasn't it? – oder?)

* A: **What makes you think that Austria has a centrally planned economy similar to the former Eastern-bloc countries?**
(make – veranlassen / similar to – ähnlich)
B: **How would you characterise your economic system, then?**
A: **Basically we have a free market economy, but one with a strong public sector. Also social security has always been very important in our system.**
(basically – im Prinzip / public – öffentlich / social security – soziale Sicherheit / important – wichtig)

* **In Austria, business firms are organised in Chambers of Commerce, workers in Chambers of Labour, and farmers in Chambers of Agriculture. What strikes most foreigners as odd is that membership in these organisations is compulsory.**
(chamber of commerce – Handelskammer / labour – Arbeiter[-schaft] / agriculture – Landwirtschaft / strike as odd – seltsam empfinden / foreigner – Ausländer / membership – Mitgliedschaft / compulsory – verpflichtend)

* **Parallel to this there are organisations with voluntary membership, such as trade unions.**
(voluntary – freiwillig / trade union – Gewerkschaft)

* **Actually, quite a few people attribute the low rate of inflation to our system of industrial relations, the much talked about "social partnership". It has certainly had a moderating influence on wage claims.**
(attribute – zuschreiben / industrial relations – Arbeitgeber-Arbeitnehmerbeziehungen / moderating – mäßigend, dämpfend / influence – Einfluss / wage claim – Lohnforderung

* **A: What about your strike record?**
(Wie steht's mit eurer Streikbilanz?)
B: Well, there are hardly any strikes in Austria. Usually industrial disputes are settled by negotiations.
(hardly – kaum / industrial dispute – Arbeitskonflikt / settle – regeln, lösen / negotiations – Verhandlungen)

* **I'd say strikes are not really a problem, although we had some big ones in the past.**
(although – obwohl / past – Vergangenheit)

* **German employers are not afraid of hitting back and locking out workers.**
(employer – Arbeitgeber / be afraid of – sich scheuen / hit back – zurückschlagen / lock out – aussperren)

* **On the negative side, Austria's economy is still heavily regulated. One example is business licensing. In spite of a lot of deregulation in recent years, there are still too many administrative hurdles for new businesses.**
(still – noch immer / heavily regulated – stark regelmentiert / business licensing – [etwa] Gewerberecht / in spite of – trotz / deregulation – Liberalisierung, Deregulierung / in recent years – in den letzten Jahren / hurdle – Hürde / business – Firma, Unternehmen)

* **A: What about price controls?**
(price controls – Preisregelung)
B: Well, in the past there were quite a few of them. But now, very few prices are still controlled.
(past – Vergangenheit / quite a few – eine ganze Menge / control – regeln, lenken)

* **You won't be surprised to hear that our agriculture is heavily protected and subsidised. Whose isn't?**
(won't – will not / surprise – überraschen / agriculture – Landwirtschaft / protect – schützen / subsidise – subventionieren)

* **Like in most industrialised countries, services account for a large chunk of our GDP, around 70 per cent, if I'm not mistaken.**
(account for – ausmachen / chunk – Teil, Stück / GDP – gross domestic product | Bruttoinlandsprodukt / be mistaken – sich irren)

* A: **You may not believe it, but Austria is actually ahead of Germany and Britain in the economic stakes. We are the fourth richest country in the EU.**
(believe – glauben / be ahead of – liegen vor / economic stakes – Wirtschaftswettlauf)
B: **You mean your per capita GDP is higher than ours?**
(per capita – pro Kopf)

* **In contrast to many other European countries, there aren't any really big privately-owned groups in Austria. With a few exceptions, Austrian companies are small or medium-sized.**
(privately-owned – in Privatbesitz / group – Konzern / exception – Ausnahme / medium-sized – mittelgroß)

* A: **Do you still have nationalised industries in Austria?**
(nationalised – verstaatlicht)
B: **Yes, we do, although most of them have been privatised. But back in the sixties, there were around 70 state-owned enterprises in my country.**
(although – obwohl / the sixties – die Sechzigerjahre / state-owned enterprise – Staatsbetrieb)

* **Political meddling and mismanagement triggered a crisis in the late seventies. The group of nationalised industries made a record loss.**
(meddling – Einmischung / trigger – auslösen / loss – Verlust)

* **Basically, the new management have done a good job refocusing the nationalised industries. The emphasis on basic materials like steel has gone. High-tech products with a higher percentage of value added are getting more attention now.**
(basically – im Prinzip / do a good job – erfolgreich sein bei / refocus – neu ausrichten / emphasis – Betonung / go – verschwinden / percentage – Prozentsatz / value added – Wertschöpfung / attention – Aufmerksamkeit)

* **Recently, several smaller companies have been privatised, and some of the state-owned companies have gone into partnership with private-sector firms.**
(recently – in der letzten Zeit / several – mehrere, einige / state-owned – im Staatseigentum / go into partnership with sbdy. – sich mit jmdm. verbünden; sich mit jmdm. zusammenschließen)

* **Well, you know, in some cases government has restricted private equity participation to 49 per cent or retained a golden share.**
(case – Fall / restrict – beschränken / equity participation – Beteiligung / retain – zurückbehalten / golden share – goldene Aktie; Aktie, die Stimmenmehrheit sichert)

* A: **Is it really true that in 2002 your government bailed out a telecommunications company with an emergency loan?**
(bail out – retten / emergency loan – Notkredit)
B: **Yes, unfortunately you're right. Governments always seem to give in to the temptation to bail out hopeless cases just to protect jobs.**
(unfortunately – leider / seem – scheinen / give in – nachgeben / temptation – Versuchung / just – nur / protect – schützen, retten / job – Arbeitsplatz)

——— ❖ ———

* **The car industry is of course still very important. Last year, motor vehicles ranked first in terms of output, just ahead of chemicals.**
(vehicle – Fahrzeug / rank first – an erster Stelle rangieren / in terms of – gemessen an / just ahead of – knapp vor)

* **Germany is very strong in electrical and mechanical engineering, although some of our companies have trouble in keeping up with foreign competitors. Medium-sized machine tool makers would be an example.**
(Deutschland ist sehr stark im Elektro- und Maschinenbau, obwohl einige unserer Gesellschaften Schwierigkeiten haben, mit der ausländischen Konkurrenz Schritt zu halten. Mittelgroße Werkzeugmaschinenfirmen wären ein Beispiel.)

* **I don't know whether you are aware of the fact that we are completely dependent on imports for oil. I think we have to import 98 per cent of our requirements.**
(whether – ob / be aware of – sich bewusst sein / dependent on – abhängig von / requirements – Bedarf)

* A: **Germany has several nuclear power stations, but in 1998 it was decided to phase them out.**
(several – einige / nuclear power station – Atomkraftwerk / decide – sich entschließen / phase out – auslaufen lassen)
B: **You mean you are not building any new ones?**
A: **Yes, but the original tough decision was watered down in 2000. Also, there is a lot of international pressure on Germany to reconsider its position. After all, atomic power plants don't have any CO_2 emissions.**
(tough – hart, streng / water down – verwässern / reconsider – überdenken)

* A: **You probably did not know that none of our electricity here in Austria comes from nuclear power stations. We rely exclusively on hydroelectric power and coal- or oil-fired facilities.**
(rely on – sich stützen auf / hydroelectric power – Wasserkraft / facility – Anlage)
B: **But I have heard that you're secretly importing nuclear electricity from neighbouring countries.**
(secret – heimlich / nuclear electricity – Atomstrom)

* **As a matter of fact, we do have a nuclear power plant. It was completed in 1978, but never went on line. We have a law prohibiting the generation of electricity by nuclear fission.**
(as a matter of fact – eigentlich; genau genommen / go on line – ans Netz gehen / law – Gesetz / prohibit – verbieten / generation – Erzeugung / fission – Spaltung)

* **Did you know that the basic oxygen process was developed in Austria? It's probably still the most important steel-making technology. It has earned us a lot in licence fees as a matter of fact.**
(basic oxygen process – L.D.-Verfahren / develop – entwickeln / probably – wahrscheinlich / still – noch immer / earn – einbringen, verdienen / fee – Gebühr)

* **We are also quite good at producing special metals.**
(quite – ganz, ziemlich)

* **Paper – as you might expect – is another important industry.**
(expect – erwarten)

INTERNATIONAL ECONOMIC RELATIONS

Internationale Wirtschaftsbeziehungen

* **Next year is going to be difficult. The appreciation of our currency is bound to affect our exports, at least in the short run.**
(appreciation – Aufwertung / currency – Währung / be bound to affect – sich zwangsläufig negativ auswirken auf / at least in the short run – zumindest auf kurze Sicht)

* **The opening up of the markets in the former Eastern bloc is a mixed blessing. Exports are up alright, but, on the other hand, cheap imports represent a real threat to some industries.**
(former – ehemalig / mixed blessing – nicht nur positiv / be up – gestiegen sein / alright – das stimmt sicherlich / cheap – billig / threat – Bedrohung / industry – Wirtschaftszweig, Branche)

* **The current WTO negotiations seem to have been dragging on for ages. It's a pity because we could really do with a stimulus to world trade.**
(Die laufenden WTO-Verhandlungen scheinen sich schon endlos lang hinzuziehen. Das ist schade, weil wir einen Anreiz für den Welthandel gut brauchen könnten.)

* **Usually our current account is in surplus. But last year we slipped into the red. We hope to be back in the black next year.**
(current account – Leistungsbilanz / in surplus – aktiv / slip – abrutschen / red – Defizit; rote Zahlen / in the black – aktiv)

* **Everybody is talking about opportunities in Russia. What I see when I look at Russia is mainly unpaid bills. They owe us billions of euros.**
(opportunity – Chance / mainly – vor allem / bill – Rechnung / owe – schulden / billion – Milliarde)

* **A: Do you think your government will forgive Iraq its debt?**
(forgive – erlassen / debt – Schulden)
B: Well, to be honest, given the high budget deficit, this is not very likely. Maybe a small portion.
(honest – ehrlich / given – angesichts / likely – wahrscheinlich / portion – Teil)

* **These countries account for less than two per cent of German exports.**
(Auf diese Länder entfallen … .)

* **Our economy is heavily dependent on foreign trade, both in goods and services.**
(dependent on – abhängig von / foreign trade – Außenhandel / both … and … – sowohl … als auch … / service – Dienstleistung)

* **Exports did very well last year, partly because our unit labour costs had risen less sharply than those of our competitors.**
(do well – gut abschneiden / partly – teilweise / unit labour costs – Lohnstückkosten / rise – steigen / competitor – Konkurrent)

* **Well, Austria used to have a fairly large trade deficit. We usually managed to offset it by selling enough services to foreigners. But thanks to the surge of exports to Eastern Europe, the Goods Account tends to be in the black now.**
(used to have – hatte früher einmal / fairly – ziemlich / trade deficit – Handelsbilanzdefizit / manage – es schaffen / offset – ausgleichen / enough – genügend / foreigner – Ausländer / thanks to – dank, wegen / surge – starke Erhöhung / Goods Account – Warenverkehrsbilanz, Handelsbilanz / be in the black – aktiv sein; einen Überschuss aufweisen)

* **Yes, tourism is of course very important. It brings in a lot of the foreign exchange we need to buy foreign goods.**
(foreign exchange – Devisen / foreign – ausländisch)

* **Germany's services account always shows a large deficit, partly as a result of heavy spending on foreign tourism.**
(services account – Dienstleistungsbilanz / heavy spending – hohe Ausgaben)

* **As a matter of fact, tourism in Austria contributes more to GNP than in any other country of the world, in percentage terms, of course.**
(contribute – beitragen / GNP – gross national product | Bruttonationalprodukt / in percentage terms – prozentmäßig)

——— ❖ ———

* **We have no car industry worth speaking of. We import all of our cars, most of them from Germany and Italy.**
(worth speaking of – nennenswert)

* **On the other hand, we are very strong in subcontracting, especially to the German motor industry. As a matter of fact, exports of automobile components match imports of German cars in value terms.**
(on the other hand – andererseits / subcontracting – Zuliefergeschäft / motor industry – Autoindustrie / component – Bauteil, Bestandteil / match – entsprechen / in value terms – wertmäßig)

* **The composition of our exports has changed a lot over the past ten years. Finished goods now account for a much higher percentage of the total.**
(composition – Zusammensetzung / change – sich ändern / a lot – sehr, stark / finished goods – Fertigwaren / account for – ausmachen / percentage – Prozentsatz / total – Gesamtsumme)

* **Did you know that timber is still one of our staple exports?**
(timber – Holz / still – noch immer / staple export – Hauptausfuhrartikel)

* **Then we've got some star performers in highly specialised fields. One example is Plasser & Theurer. They are the world's main supplier of railway-track equipment.**
(star performer – Spitzenfirma / field – Gebiet, Sparte / main supplier – Hauptlieferant / railway-track equipment – Bahnbaumaschinen)

* **As you might imagine, a lot of our imports come from – and a lot of our exports go to – Germany.**
(imagine [sthg.] – sich [etwas] vorstellen / a lot of – eine Menge)

* **Because of our geographical position we also do a lot of trade with eastern European countries. That's why so many of the world's best countertrade specialists are based in Vienna.**
(because of – wegen / do trade – Handel treiben / countertrade – Gegengeschäfte / be based in Vienna – [ihren] Sitz in Wien haben)

——— ❖ ———

* **German foreign direct investment has increased considerably in the past few years, but we are still far behind countries like the Netherlands in per capita terms.**
(foreign – Auslands- / increase – sich erhöhen; steigen / considerable – beträchtlich / in per capita terms – auf Pro-Kopf-Basis)

* **More and more Austrian firms are setting up branches or subsidiaries abroad. But this is not a one-way street: foreign companies are doing the same in Austria, in many cases to serve the eastern European markets.**
(set up – errichten / branch – Zweigstelle / subsidiary – Tochtergesellschaft / abroad – im Ausland / one-way street – Einbahnstraße)

* **Of course, joint ventures are also very popular, especially in eastern European countries and China.**

——— ❖ ———

* A: **What about your currency?**
(Wie steht's mit Ihrer Währung?)
B: **Today, we are part of the eurozone. But we used to have our own currency, the Austrian schilling – which was, however, tied to the German mark.**
(used to have – hatten früher einmal / be tied to – gebunden sein an)
A: **Does this mean that you pursued a hard currency policy?**
(pursue – verfolgen)
B: **Yes, definitely. It helped us to keep down inflation. And that offset some of its negative impact on export prices.**
(definitely – ganz entschieden / offset – ausgleichen / impact – Auswirkungen)

* A: **How did you weather the ERM crisis in 1992?**
(weather – überstehen / ERM – Exchange Rate Mechanism | EU-Wechselkursmechanismus)
B: **Well, actually not too badly. Of course, being a minor currency and being tied to the Deutschmark did not do any harm.**
(actually – eigentlich / minor – weniger wichtig / do harm – schaden)

——— ❖ ———

* **I've got to admit that we do not spend all that much on development aid. I'm ashamed even to mention the figure. Well, I should not have said *development aid. Development co-operation* is the politically correct term.**
(admit – zugeben / spend on – ausgeben für / all that much – allzu viel / development aid – Entwicklungshilfe / be ashamed – sich schämen / mention – erwähnen / figure – Zahl / development co-operation – Entwicklungszusammenarbeit / term – Ausdruck, Bezeichnung)

* **Helping developing and least developed countries is not just a matter of throwing money at them. Technology transfer and free access to our markets are at least as important.**
(developing countries – Entwicklungsländer / least developed countries – die ärmsten Entwicklungsländer / be not just a matter of – nicht einfach bedeuten / throw money at sbdy. – jmdm. einfach Geld geben / free access – ungehinderter Zutritt / at least – zumindest)

* **A: In 2006 Germany spent around 10 billion dollars on development co-operation projects. This makes it the fifth-largest donor country worldwide.**
(donor country – Geberland)
B: Yes, but it ranks only 13th if this expenditure is expressed as a percentage of GNI.
(rank – rangieren / expenditure – Ausgabe[n] / express – ausdrücken / GNI – gross national income | Bruttoinlandseinkommen)

* **A: One of the most important trends is that governments have started to outsource development co-operation projects to NGOs.**
(outsource – outsourcen, auslagern / NGO – non-governmental organisation | Nichtregierungsorganisation)
B: Probably because they have the required know-how.
(required – erforderlich)

EUROPEAN UNION
Europäische Union

* **A: Austria easily met the criteria set for full participation in EMU.**
  (meet – erfüllen / set – festsetzen / EMU – Economic and Monetary Union | Wirtschafts- und Währungsunion)
  B: You mean the five Maastricht criteria?

* **As a member of the EU, Austria finds it more difficult to restrict the movement of lorries through its territory. Free movement of goods and all that, you know. Switzerland is in a much better position in this respect.**
  (member – Mitglied / restrict – beschränken / movement through – Durchfahrt durch / lorry – Lastkraftwagen, LKW / free movement of goods – Freizügigkeit des Warenverkehrs / and all that – und so weiter / respect – Hinsicht)

* **You mustn't forget that we had a free trade agreement with what was then the EC. Since the end of the transitional period in 1977, industrial goods have entered Austria duty free.**
  (must not – nicht dürfen / agreement – Abkommen / transitional period – Übergangszeit / enter – eingeführt werden / duty free – zollfrei)

* **No, the EEA is not a customs union, but it adds the free movement of capital, services and labour to the existing agreement between EFTA and the EU.**
  (EEA – European Economic Area | Europäischer Wirtschaftsraum / customs union – Zollunion / add – hinzufügen / free movement of capital – Freizügigkeit des Kapitalverkehrs / labour – Arbeitskräfte / EFTA – European Free Trade Association | Europäische Freihandelsassoziation)

* **It will take the new members years to catch up. The gap is just too wide to be closed in a short time.**
  (Die neuen Mitglieder werden Jahre brauchen … . / catch up – aufholen / gap – Lücke / just – einfach / close – schließen)

* A: **In spite of reforms, there is still a lot wrong with the EU's common agricultural policy.**
(in spite of – trotz / still – noch immer / a lot – eine Menge / agricultural policy – Landwirtschaftspolitik)
B: **Quite so, export subsidies are still too high and too much of the EU budget goes on agriculture.**
(quite so – ganz recht / subsidy – Subvention)

* A: **I can't help feeling that the whole CAP is a disaster. Don't you think that something should be done about the high subsidies and import duties?**
(feel – der Meinung sein / CAP – Common Agricultural Policy [of the EU] | Gemeinsame Landwirtschaftspolitik [der EU] / disaster – Katastrophe / import duty – Importzoll)
B: **They have been cut somewhat under WTO pressure, but probably not enough. The EU tariff on sugar imports is still a mindboggling 256 per cent, and export subsidies are ruining farmers in developing countries.**
(cut – senken / somewhat – etwas / WTO – World Trade Organization | Welthandelsorganisation / pressure – Druck / probably – wahrscheinlich / tariff – Zoll / still – noch immer / mind-boggling – irre, unglaublich / developing country – Entwicklungsland)

* A: **Why has Britain refused to introduce the euro?**
(refuse – sich weigern / introduce – einführen)
B: **Well, I think that this has a lot more to do with political sentiments than with economic sense. The pound is still a symbol of Britain's separate identity.**
(sentiments – Klima / economic – wirtschaftlich / sense – Vernunft)

* A: **Is it true that Britain enjoys a rebate on its contributions to the EU budget?**
(enjoy – in den Genuss kommen / rebate – Nachlass / contribution – Beitrag)
B: **Yes, you're right. The rebate was negotiated by Margaret Thatcher. It continues to be a source of controversy, although the UK is a net contributor like Germany and Austria.**
(negotiate – aushandeln / source – Grund, Ursache / although – obwohl / UK – United Kingdom / net contributor – Nettozahler)

FINANCIAL MARKETS
Finanzmärkte

* **I don't think I have to tell you a lot about Frankfurt as a financial centre. It is well known internationally. But the importance of Munich, Düsseldorf and Hamburg should not be underestimated.**
(underestimate – unterschätzen)

* **True, the DAX is the most important share index in Germany. It is similar to the Dow Jones and includes 30 German blue chips.**
(true – stimmt / DAX – Deutscher Aktienindex / share index – Aktienindex / similar to – ähnlich / blue chip – Blue Chip; Spitzenwert; erstklassige Aktie)

* **A lot of German equities are traded in London, where the market is more liquid. On some days up to a third of the turnover in important German shares is done there.**
(equities – [Stamm-]Aktien / trade – handeln / market – Börse, Wertpapiermarkt / third – Drittel / turnover – Umsatz / do – tätigen)

* **Yes, insider trading is practised both in Germany and in Austria. This is a pity because it discourages some potential investors.**
(it is a pity – es ist schade / discourage – abhalten)

* **A: I assume that Vienna is the financial centre of Austria.**
(assume – annehmen)
B: Yes, all the big banks are based there and so is, of course, the Vienna Stock Exchange. We even have a Futures and Options Exchange.
(be based – [ihren] Sitz haben / stock exchange – Wertpapierbörse / futures and options exchange – Termin- und Optionenbörse)

* **Our banking system used to be pretty fragmented. We had too many banks with too many branches. But things have changed since we entered the EU.**
(used to be – war früher einmal / pretty – ziemlich / fragmented – zersplittert / branch – Filiale / change – sich ändern / enter – eintreten; sich anschließen)

* **The Vienna Stock Exchange is tiny by international standards, although it has expanded dramatically in the past few years.**
(tiny – winzig / by – gemessen an)

* **A: Austrian companies are fairly small and tend to rely on bank finance.**
(company – Gesellschaft, Unternehmen / fairly – ziemlich / tend – tendieren; dazu neigen / rely on – sich stützen auf)
B: No IPOs?
(IPO – Initial Public Offering | Erstemission)
A: Yes, of course, some of the bigger companies have gone public and have tapped the stock exchange.
(of course – natürlich / go public – an die Börse gehen / tap the stock exchange – Geld an der Börse auftreiben)
B: And what about private equity?
(private equity – Private Equity; Beteiligungsfinanzierung [für nicht börsennotierte Unternehmen])
A: Plays a much lesser role than in the UK and the States, or in Germany for that matter.
(lesser – geringer)

* A: **Private equity seems to have made great strides in Germany in recent years.**
(seem – scheinen / strides – Schritte nach vorne; Fortschritt / in recent years – in den letzten Jahren)
B: **Yes, and this in spite of one of our politicians describing PE firms as locusts.**
(in spite of – trotz / describe – beschreiben / locust – Heuschrecke)

SUSTAINABLE MANAGEMENT

Nachhaltiges Management

ENVIRONMENTAL ASPECTS AND REGULATIONS

Umweltaspekte und -vorschriften

* A: **What are environmental regulations like in your country?**
  (Wie sind die Umweltvorschriften in Ihrem Land?)
  B: **Well, actually I think they are a lot tougher than here in Britain.**
  (actually – eigentlich / a lot – viel / tough – streng)

* **We'll simply have to resign ourselves to tougher environmental standards.**
  (simple – einfach / resign oneself to – sich abfinden mit / standard – Norm, Grenzwert)

* **We decided to add a specialist on environmental law to our legal department. You simply need somebody to monitor the new developments in this field.**
  (decide – sich entschließen / add – zusätzlich einstellen / environmental law – Umweltrecht / legal department – Rechtsabteilung / need – brauchen / monitor – überwachen, verfolgen / development – Entwicklung / field – Gebiet)

* **It cost us €1.2 million to meet the stricter emission standards. But we developed most of the equipment in-house and this has given us a lead in filter technology.**
  (meet standard – Norm erfüllen; Grenzwert einhalten / develop – entwickeln / equipment – Geräte, Ausrüstung / in-house – firmenintern; in der eigenen Firma / lead – Vorsprung)

* **The new legislation has forced us to install filters in all our production facilities. It has cost us a bomb.**
(legislation – Gesetzgebung / force – zwingen / production facility – Produktionsstätte / bomb – Menge Geld)

* **I think you need somebody working closely with the design and manufacturing departments to look after the environmental aspects of the operation.**
(work closely with – eng zusammenarbeiten mit / design department – Konstruktionsabteilung / manufacturing department – Produktionsabteilung / look after – sich kümmern um / operation – Betrieb, Projekt)

* **We are considering transferring our manufacturing activities to Taiwan, where there are fewer environmental regulations.**
(consider – denken an; erwägen / transfer – verlegen / manufacture – fertigen, produzieren)

* **Doing business is no fun anymore. You need a permit for this and a permit for that. Government and citizens' groups are constantly breathing down your neck.**
(business – Geschäfte / no fun anymore – kein Spaß mehr / permit – Genehmigung / government – Regierung / citizens' group – Bürgerinitiative / breathe down sbdy.'s neck – jmdm. auf die Zehen steigen)

* **As far as I know, the new law will require an environmental impact assessment for all major projects.**
(require – verlangen, fordern / environmental impact assessment – Umweltverträglichkeitsprüfung / major – größer)

* **You know what the real problem is? The lack of uniformity in environmental legislation. Some countries have outlawed metal containers, which are perfectly legal in most others.**
(lack – Fehlen, Mangel / uniformity – Einheitlichkeit / outlaw – verbieten / container – Gefäß, Behälter, Verpackung)

* **We commissioned one of these new environmental consulting firms to carry out an environmental audit. It was a real eye-opener.**
(commission – beauftragen / consulting firm – Beratungsfirma / carry out – erstellen, durchführen / environmental audit – Umwelt-Audit, Umweltbilanz; erweiterte Wirtschaftlichkeitsrechnung)

* **A: What is your company doing for the environment?**
B: Not much, I'm afraid. Our management haven't really woken up to the fact that doing nothing may help reduce costs in the short term but is probably bad business in the long run.
(I'm afraid – leider / wake up to sthg. – etwas kapieren / in the short term – auf kurze Sicht / probably – wahrscheinlich / in the long run – auf lange Sicht)

WASTE

Abfall

* **We are quite proud of the fact that we now recycle close to 50 per cent of the solid waste generated in our plants.**
(quite – ziemlich / proud – stolz / recycle – wiederverwerten / close to – knapp / solid waste – feste Abfallstoffe / be generated – anfallen / plant – Werk, Anlage)

* **It's a shame that so much of our waste ends up in an incinerator. A lot of it could be recycled, I'm sure.**
(shame – Schande / end up – schließlich kommen / incinerator – [Müll-] Verbrennungsanlage / a lot of – eine Menge; viel)

* **We are very careful with our liquid waste. Two years ago leakage from a storage tank contaminated the ground water and we ended up paying a heavy fine.**
(careful – vorsichtig / liquid waste – flüssige Abfallstoffe / leakage – ausgelaufene Flüssigkeit / storage tank – Lagerbehälter / contaminate – verseuchen / end up doing sthg. – schließlich etwas machen / heavy fine – hohe Strafe; hohe Strafgebühr)

* A: **We have come to the conclusion that installing filters and scrubbers at the end of each pipe or smokestack is the wrong approach.**
(conclusion – Schluss, Schlussfolgerung / scrubber – Nassabscheider / pipe – Röhre, Leitung / smokestack – Fabriksschlot / approach – Methode, Vorgangsweise, Ansatz)
B: **Yes, redesigning the whole production process is a much better idea. This will not only cut emissions but also save raw materials and labour.**
(redesign – neu gestalten; neu konstruieren / cut – senken / save – einsparen / labour – Arbeitskräfte)

* **One of our engineers came up with the idea of capturing the waste heat from our kilns for heating purposes. Clever! Cut our fuel bill by more than 40 per cent and paid for itself within three years.**
(come up with idea – Idee haben / capture – auffangen, nutzen / waste heat – Abwärme / kiln – Brennofen / for heating purposes – für Heizzwecke / clever – brillant, schlau / cut – senken / fuel bill – Brennmaterialrechnung, -kosten / it pays for itself – es amortisiert sich)

* **Just imagine, Greenpeace came along and plugged up a pipe discharging toxic effluents into a small river. It was all on TV and knocked our image sideways.**
(Stellen Sie sich das nur vor, … / plug up – zustopfen / pipe – Rohr / discharge – einleiten / toxic effluents – giftige Abwässer / river – Fluss / knock sideways – ramponieren; Schlag versetzen)

* **We had to act really fast. The local authorities threatened to withdraw our business licence. They said we had to stop discharging untreated effluents into the local river.**
(local authorities – Lokalbehörde / threaten – drohen / withdraw – entziehen, widerrufen / business licence – Konzession; gewerberechtliche Genehmigung / discharge – einleiten / untreated effluents – unbehandelte Abwässer; unbehandelter Flüssigabfall)

* **Unfortunately the new waste water treatment facility was very expensive.**
(Leider war die neue Kläranlage sehr teuer.)

* **We are lucky. We have got a small landfill of our own where we can dump most of our solid waste. The small amount of hazardous waste we produce goes to a special reprocessing facility.**
(be lucky – Glück haben / landfill – Deponie / of one's own – eigen / dump – deponieren, ablagern / hazardous waste – gefährliche Abfallstoffe; Gefahrenmüll / reprocessing facility – Wiederaufbereitungsanlage)

* **We used to export most of our toxic waste, but under the new regulations this is no longer possible.**
(we used to export – früher einmal exportierten wir / toxic waste – Giftmüll / under – aufgrund)

* **We are looking into the possibility of using a deposit scheme for our containers. I think it would be good for our image.**
(look into sthg. – etwas [über]prüfen / possibility – Möglichkeit / deposit scheme – Pfandsystem / container – Behälter, Verpackung, Gefäß)

PRODUCTS

Produkte

* **Last year we introduced a line of phosphate-free detergents. They were a huge success. They attracted a lot of new customers and we can sell them at premium prices.**
(introduce – einführen / line – Produktlinie / detergent – Waschmittel / success – Erfolg / attract – anziehen / a lot of – eine Menge / premium price – hoher Preis; Hochpreis)

* **We stopped selling CFC aerosol cans two years ago.**
(CFC – chlorofluorcarbon | FCKW, Fluorchlorkohlenwasserstoff / aerosol can – Sprühdose)

* **To begin with, we developed a quiet electric lawnmower for the German market. It was awarded the Blue Angel eco-label.**
(to begin with – als Erstes / develop – entwickeln / quiet – leise, Flüster- / lawnmower – Rasenmäher / be awarded sthg. – etwas verliehen bekommen / eco-label – Umweltgütesiegel; ökologisch orientierte Warenauszeichnung)

* **Tell me more about your eco-labelling schemes.**
(scheme – Programm)

* **You won't believe it, but we are thinking of diversifying and buying into a health-food chain.**
(won't – will not / believe – glauben / buy into – Beteiligung erwerben an / health-food chain – Biokette)

* **My company has started importing green products from Austria. They are selling very well, at least that's what our sales people say.**
(sell – sich verkaufen / at least – zumindest / sales people – Mitarbeiter in der Verkaufsabteilung)

* **We buy some of the food for our works canteen from an organic farmer. Actually, it's a worker co-operative.**
(food – Lebensmittel / organic farmer – Biobauer / worker co-operative – Betrieb in Arbeiterselbstverwaltung; Produktivgenossenschaft)

* A: **R&D has developed a biodegradable plastic film.**
(R&D – Research and Development [department] | Forschung[s-] und Entwicklung[-sabteilung] / biodegradable – biologisch abbaubar / plastic film – Kunststofffolie)
B: **Great! I suggest we take out a patent and sell it to a packaging firm.**
(suggest – vorschlagen / take out a patent – ein Patent erwerben / packaging firm – Verpackungsfirma)

* **We are doing quite a lot to make our product range more environment-friendly. For one thing, we have switched to water-based paints.**
(quite – ziemlich / a lot – viel / product range – Produktpalette / for one thing – zum einen / switch to – umsteigen auf / water-based – auf Wasserbasis / paint – Farbe, Lack)

TRANSPORT, ENERGY AND EMISSIONS

Transport, Energie und Emissionen

* **We bought a couple of the new fuel-efficient lorries last year.**
(a couple of – ein paar / fuel-efficient – treibstoffsparend / lorry – Lastwagen)

* **Eventually we decided to fit all our delivery vans with catalytic converters. The clincher was that there is a tax incentive and it didn't cost us much.**
(eventually – letzten Endes / decide – beschließen / fit – ausrüsten / delivery van – Lieferwagen / catalytic converter – Katalysator / clincher – der entscheidende Punkt / tax incentive – steuerlicher Anreiz)

* **All our company cars run on unleaded petrol.**
(Alle unsere Firmenautos fahren mit bleifreiem Benzin.)

* **The ban on night-time lorries hasn't made life for our logistics people any easier.**
(ban on night-time lorries – Nachtfahrverbot für LKWs / not any easier – auch nicht gerade leichter)

* **Unfortunately, the piggyback service offered by our railway company is not particularly fast and efficient.**
(unfortunately – leider / piggyback service – Huckepackverkehr; rollende Landstraße / offer – anbieten / particular – besonders / fast – schnell)

* **If rail transport is to become competitive with road transport, they will have to invest a lot in new tracks, terminals and rolling stock.**
(rail – Eisenbahn / competitive – konkurrenzfähig / road – Straße / tracks – Gleisanlagen / rolling stock – rollendes Material)

* **I think in the long run we'll have to switch to rail transport, at least for our heavy equipment.**
(in the long run – langfristig gesehen / switch to – umsteigen auf / at least – zumindest / heavy – schwer / equipment – Ausrüstung, Geräte)

* **If they really decide to put this tax on road transport, JIT will become a less attractive proposition.**
(put tax on sthg. – etwas mit einer Steuer belegen / JIT – just in time | Lagerbestandsminimierungsstrategie / proposition – Sache, Angelegenheit)

* **Next time we replace our lorries, we must pay more attention to their CO_2 emissions.**
(next time – nächstes Mal / replace – ersetzen / lorry – Lastwagen / attention – Aufmerksamkeit)

* **I think we should take a look at carbon trading. It might be the cheaper alternative.**
(carbon trading – CO_2-Emissions-Handel)

SOCIAL ASPECTS

Soziale Aspekte

* A: **Honestly, we are not happy about the way workers in our supply chain are treated. But often we don't even know who our ultimate suppliers are.**
(honestly – ehrlich / way – Art und Weise / supply chain – Lieferkette / treat – behandeln / not even – nicht einmal / ultimate supplier – Letztlieferant)
B: **You're right. Our supply chain is just too long and too complicated.**
(just – einfach)

* **We should not have closed down the factory. Hurt our image. The damage was greater than the cost savings from shifting production abroad.**
(close down – schließen / factory – Fabrik / hurt – schaden / damage – Schaden / savings – Ersparnisse / shift abroad – ins Ausland verlagern)

* A: **Should we start a cooperation project with Fairtrade or at least put a few Fairtrade products on our shelves?**
(at least – zumindest / shelf – Regal)
B: **Well, that's not a bad idea. After all, brand awareness for the logo has gone up sharply in the past few years.**
(brand awareness – Bekanntheitsgrad einer Marke)
A: **Yes, if we can believe the latest survey, it is around 85 per cent. Wish one of our own brands was that well known.**
(believe – glauben / survey – Umfrage, Erhebung)

* A: **What is all this talk about Fairtrade? What does it mean anyway?**
(anyway – eigentlich)

B: **Well, the basic idea is quite simple: the organisation behind the logo makes sure that the small farmers in the scheme get a fair price. But that's not all: marketing feedback and market access are at least as important.**
(quite – ziemlich / make sure – sicherstellen / scheme – Programm, Projekt / access – Zutritt)

A: **What do you mean by *fair price*?**

B: **Well, it's a guaranteed minimum price that covers the cost of production and leaves a margin for a halfway decent living standard.**
(cover – abdecken / leave – übrig lassen / margin – Überschuss / halfway – halbwegs / decent – angemessen)

A: **And what about the farmers? Do they have to do anything for this privilege?**

B: **Certainly! For one thing, they have to comply with minimum environmental standards. No child labour and no discrimination, of course.**
(for one thing – erstens / comply with – einhalten / environmental standard – Umweltstandard / child labour – Kinderarbeit)

* A: **You know the latest? Two NGOs are organising a campaign against us.**
(Weißt Du schon das Neueste? … / NGO – non-governmental organisation | Nichtregierungsorganisation)

B: **And why is that?**

A: **They say we are sourcing most of our products from sweatshops in China. So they are soliciting signatures online for a petition against our procurement practices.**
(source – beziehen / sweatshop – Ausbeuterbetrieb / solicit – erbitten, sammeln / signature – Unterschrift / procurement – Beschaffung)

B: **So, it's all over the Internet. And I bet the bloggers have already started to add their bit.**
(bet – wetten / add their bit – das Ihre beitragen)

* **A: Our trade association has sent us a letter suggesting that we should sign the code of conduct they have drawn up.**
(trade association – Fachverband / suggest – vorschlagen / sign – unterschreiben / code of conduct – Verhaltenskodex / draw up – erstellen)
B: Have you had time to read it yet?
(yet – schon)
A: Yes, I had a short look at it. Sounds quite reasonable.
(sound – klingen / reasonable – vernünftig)
B: Maybe, but I am sure it would increase our costs.
(increase – erhöhen)

* **A: Here is the latest report on inventory shrinkage.**
(report – Bericht / inventory shrinkage – Lagerschwund)
B: Inventory shrinkage? My foot! Why don't we call it by its proper name *employee theft*?
(my foot – so ein Quatsch / call – nennen / proper – richtig, eigentlich / employee theft – Mitarbeiterdiebstahl)
A: Well, whatever you call it, the figure has gone up to 2.5 per cent of total sales and we must do something about it.
(figure – Zahl / total sales – Gesamtumsatz)

* **A: If we don't bribe the procurement officer or promise him some kickback, we won't stand a chance to win the tender.**
(bribe – bestechen / procurement officer – Beschaffungsmanager / promise – versprechen / kickback – Schmiergeld / stand a chance – eine Chance haben / tender – Ausschreibung)
B: But you know that's forbidden by our laws and the laws here in the host country.
(law – Gesetz / host country – Gastgeberland)
A: True! But everybody else is doing it.

* **A: Do we really need an ethics committee?**
(need – brauchen)
B: We don't have a choice. The accounting scandal last year was just too big.
(choice – Wahl / accounting scandal – Bilanzskandal / just – einfach)

* A: **The consulting agency has recommended that we appoint a chief CSR officer at the corporate level.**
(consult – beraten / recommend – empfehlen / appoint – ernennen / CSR – Corporate Social Responsibility | gesellschaftliche Verantwortung von Unternehmen / officer – Beauftragter, Referent / corporate level – Konzernebene)
B: **I don't think that our CEO is going to like this.**
(CEO – Chief Executive Officer | Generaldirektor, Vorstandsvorsitzender)
A: **Maybe, but somebody has to look after these things nowadays. Some of our competitors have already made the move.**
(look after – sich kümmern um / competitor – Konkurrent / move – Schritt)

* **We must be more careful. Just look what happened to one of our competitors in India. Had to close down two plants because they refused to allow their workers to join a trade union.**
(be careful – aufpassen / happen – passieren, geschehen / close down – schließen / plant – Werk / refuse – sich weigern / join – beitreten / trade union – Gewerkschaft)

* A: **The unions have just started a new campaign. They are calling on people to boycott goods made with child labour.**
(union – Gewerkschaft / call on sbdy. – jmdn. auffordern / child labour – Kinderarbeit)
B: **That's silly. By themselves, boycotts are counter-productive. There must be some form of help to the children and their families. After all, not buying the goods made by children means that they lose their jobs and the income that goes with them.**
(silly – unsinnig / by themselves – für sich genommen / after all – schließlich)

* A: **Look here what it says in the paper. The support for a bill protecting whistleblowers is growing.**
(paper – Zeitung / support – Unterstützung / bill – Gesetzesvorlage / whistleblower – Skandalaufdecker / grow – zunehmen)
B: **That's high time. In most companies it is still too dangerous for employees to call attention to a wrong.**
(dangerous – gefährlich / employee – Mitarbeiter / call attention to a wrong – Aufmerksamkeit auf ein Unrecht lenken)

* **Sexual harassment is difficult to define and prove.**
(harassment – Belästigung / prove – beweisen)

* **Ring up the HR-Department and tell them that they must change the wording in our vacancy ads. It must be quite clear that all those interested are welcome to apply, regardless of age, gender, marital status etc. We don't want to violate any equal opportunity laws and pay a heavy fine.**
(ring up – anrufen / HR – Human Resources / wording – Formulierung, Text / vacancy ad – Stellenanzeige / apply – sich bewerben / regardless – unabhängig / age – Alter / gender – Geschlecht / marital status – Familienstand / violate – verletzen / equal opportunity law – Gleichbehandlungsgesetz / heavy fine – hohe Strafe)

* **One reason why people are not satisfied with the present social and economic policies is the gap between executive compensation and ordinary pay.**
(reason – Grund / satisfied – zufrieden / present – gegenwärtig / economic – Wirtschafts- / gap – Lücke / executive compensation – Managervergütung / ordinary pay – Bezahlung für die normalen Beschäftigten)

PROMOTIONAL AND STRATEGIC ASPECTS

Kommunikationspolitische und strategische Aspekte

* **Our new advertising manager revamped our promotional activities to increase their appeal to the green consumer.**
(advertising manager – Werbeleiter / revamp – völlig neu gestalten / promotional activities – kommunikationspolitische Aktivitäten / increase – erhöhen / appeal – Attraktivität)

* **One of his ideas was that we should sponsor an environmental exhibition next year.**
(exhibition – Ausstellung)

* **We got the World Wide Fund for Nature to endorse some of our products.**
(get sbdy. to do sthg. – jmdn. dazu bringen, etwas zu tun / endorse – unterstützen)

* **The consultant suggested that we redesign our packaging to enhance its appeal to the environmentally sensitive consumer segment.**
(consultant – Konsulent, Berater / suggest – vorschlagen / redesign – neu gestalten / packaging – Verpackung, Aufmachung / enhance – erhöhen, verstärken / sensitive – bewusst, sensibel)

* A: **We publish an annual report on our environmental activities as part of our Social Audit.**
(publish – veröffentlichen / annual report – Jahresbericht / social audit – Sozialbilanz)
B: **What do you put in there?**
A: **Well, for instance we show the percentage of paper which is recycled, the value of services supplied to firms producing pollution-control equipment, the percentage of employees coming to work by bus, the percentage coming in car pools, and things like that.**
(for instance – zum Beispiel / percentage – Prozentsatz / value – Wert / service – Dienstleistung / supply – erbringen / pollution-control equipment – Umweltschutztechnologie, -geräte / employee – Arbeitnehmer / car pool – Fahrgemeinschaft)

* **We called in a specialist consultant to help us sort out our environmental problems. A lot of what he recommended was just PR, but he did have some useful ideas as well.**
(call in – beiziehen / sort out – lösen, regeln / recommend – empfehlen / just – nur, lediglich / PR – public relations / useful – sinnvoll, nützlich / as well – auch)

* A: **There is a business case for CSR, after all. Just look at our main competitors. Since they started pretending that they care for the environment and the poor – and I know that they are only pretending – they have attracted new customers and have had better recruitment results.**
(business case – wirtschaftliche Gründe / CSR – Corporate Social Responsibility | gesellschaftliche Verantwortung von Unternehmen / after all – schließlich / main competitor – Hauptkonkurrent / pretend – vorgeben / care for – sich kümmern um / recruitment – Personalbeschaffung)

B: **Surprise, surprise. So you have finally come round.**
(surprise – Überraschung / come round – einsehen)

A: **Yes, CSR really seems to be a win-win proposition.**
(seem – scheinen / proposition – Konzept)

B: **That's what I have been saying for years. You see, I have asked Accounts to cost the waste programme we talked about last month. It would pay for itself within two years. Less waste and more money!**
(Accounts – Buchhaltungsabteilung / cost – kalkulieren / waste – Abfall / pay for itself – sich amortisieren)

* A: **Strange, I met a guy at the trade association conference. He said that his company did not want to make a hue and cry about their social activities.**
(strange – seltsam, komisch / meet – treffen / trade association – Fachverband / make a hue and cry – viel Aufhebens machen)

B: **Most companies would do the opposite: do little and talk a lot about it.**
(opposite – Gegenteil / little – wenig)

* **Check the figures for donations to charitable organisations in the draft sustainability report. They seem too low, definitely lower than last year.**
(figures – Zahlen / donation – Spende, Schenkung / charitable – gemeinnützig, karitativ / draft – Entwurf / sustainability – Nachhaltigkeit)

* **We shouldn't overdo it. Many people are smart enough to see through the spin.**
(overdo – übertreiben / see through – durchschauen / spin – Spin, PR-Gewäsch)

* **What is a bit surprising in the history of sustainable management is that public sector organisations like universities lag behind the corporate sector.**
(surprising – überraschend / sustainable – nachhaltig / lag behind – nachhinken / corporate sector – Wirtschaft, Unternehmenssektor)

INDEX

Index

REGISTER

DIE AUTOREN

Univ.-Prof. Mag. Dr. Wolfgang Obenaus

Jahrgang 1953; Mag. rer. soc. oec. (Wirtschaftsuniversität Wien, 1976); Universitätsassistent am Institut für Englische Sprache / Wirtschaftsuniversität Wien (seit 1976); Forschungsstipendium / Georgetown University und Export-Import Bank in Washington, D.C. (1978); Dr. rer. soc. oec. (Wirtschaftsuniversität Wien / Wirtschaftsenglisch 1979); Lehrbeauftragter für Wirtschaftsenglisch an der Wirtschaftsuniversität Wien seit 1980; Forschungsstipendium / Georgetown University und Overseas Private Investment Corporation in Washington, D.C. (1982); 1990 Habilitation (»Die amerikanische Terminologie des Wechselkursrisikos und der Kurstechniken«); Forschungsstipendium / Harvard University in Cambridge, Mass. (Sommer 1990); seit März 1991 Universitätsprofessor für das Fach »Englische Wirtschaftssprache« an der Wirtschaftsuniversität Wien; Vortragender und Trainer auf dem Gebiet des Wirtschaftsenglischen im Rahmen von Managementseminaren für Praktiker; Veröffentlichungen und Übersetzungen auf dem Gebiet des Wirtschaftsenglischen, unter anderem Wolfgang Obenaus, Josef Weidacher: Englische Wirtschaftssprache, Übungen zur Grammatik, Wien 3. Aufl. 1992; Wolfgang Obenaus, Josef Weidacher: NEW Handbook of Business English. Keywords in Context, Wien 2006; Wolfgang Obenaus: Handbuch der amerikanischen Terminologie des Wechselkursrisikos und der Kurssicherungstechniken, Wien 1990.

a.o. Univ.-Prof. Dr. Josef Weidacher, M. A.

Jahrgang 1935; Stipendium / University of Minnesota (1959); Master of Arts (University of Minnesota 1961); Lehramt für Anglistik, Germanistik, Philosophie (Universität Wien, 1961); Ergänzungsprüfung aus Wirtschaftsenglisch (1963); Lehrtätigkeiten an Handelsschulen und -akademien (1961 bis 1968; Bundeslehrer / Lektor für Wirtschaftsenglisch (Hochschule für Welthandel / Wirtschaftsuniversität Wien seit 1968); Dr. phil. (Universität Wien / Wirtschaftslinguistik 1971); Seminarleiter an der Diplomatischen Akademie Wien (1979 bis 1984); Verleihung des Berufstitels »Außerordentlicher Universitätsprofessor« (1990); Veröffentlichungen, Übersetzungen und Vorträge auf dem Gebiet des

Wirtschaftsenglischen, unter anderem Wolfgang Obenaus, Josef Weidacher: Englische Wirtschaftssprache, Übungen zur Grammatik, Wien, 3. Auflage 1992. Wolfgang Obenaus, Josef Weidacher: NEW Handbook of Business English. Keywords in Context, Wien 2006.